The Gun Digest Book Of
MODERN GUN VALUES
2nd Edition

By Jack Lewis
Edited By Harold A. Murtz

Follett Publishing Company / Chicago

T-1196

OUR COVER

This edition's cover was taken at the Marksman Police and Shooters Supply Co., Glenview, Illinois, a new firm doing a brisk business in buying and selling used firearms of all types. Pictured are John P. Morgan, Jr. (left) and Jim Arcus. **Photo by John Hanusin.**

Production Editor
BOB SPRINGER

Art Director
SONYA KAISER

Production Coordinator
BETTY BURRIS

Associate Publisher
SHELDON L. FACTOR

Produced by

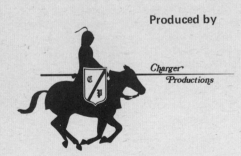

Charger
Productions

THE AUTHOR

After three years of research, searching, bugging his friends in the industry, contacting dealers, collectors and other experts in the firearms field, Jack Lewis has to have a reputation for tenacity that has resulted in this volume. He also admits that he has learned a lot more about used gun values than he ever expected to know.

But he is hardly a neophyte in the field. He has been the editor of GUN WORLD Magazine, as well as its publisher, for more than seventeen years, capping a many-faceted career. Over the years he has been a ranch hand, farm worker, horse wrangler, structural steel worker, laborer, private detective, motion picture stuntman, newspaper reporter, and screen and television writer. He is the author of a number of adventure and Western novels, as well as a humorous series dealing with Marine Corps combat correspondents and photographers.

A veteran of World War II and Korean actions, he is a lieutenant-colonel in the Marine Corps Reserve and was called to active duty in 1970 to pursue a special study in Vietnam. During 1976, he served six months on active duty, handling much of the Marine Corps' Bicentennial publicity. He also was included in the Bicentennial edition of Who's Who. In addition to publications in the firearms field, he is publisher of HORSE and HORSEMAN and BOW & ARROW magazines.

THOSE WHO HELPED

In alphabetical order, my thanks to the following: Bob Behn of Marlin; Eric Brooker of High Standard; Bill Brophy of Marlin for his devoted help on the L.C. Smith segment; Dan Byrne; Bob Cherry for his commemorative expertise; Dave Davis of Colt; Pete Dickey of Garcia; Dick Dietz of Remington; Bob Elz of the Elz Fargo Gunshop; John Falk of Winchester; John Goodwin, then of Ithaca; John B. Hansen for his general knowledge; Earl Harrington of Savage for devoted researching of obsolete Fox models; Gil Hebard for his expertise on Hammerli handguns; Hermann Koelling of Stoeger Industries; Bob Magee of Interarms for research on European models; Alan Mossberg of Mossberg; John Remling, a Webley collector of note, for his time-consuming efforts on those guns; Jack Sharry of Harrington & Richardson; Conrad Sundeen of Sundeen Guns for his contributions on English shotguns; Ralph Walker of Walker Arms for his expert aid in many areas; H.P. White Laboratories and J.B. Wood; and Joseph J. Schroeder, for his assistance in revising the handgun section.

Valuable assistance was offered by Walt Little of Bain and Davis Custom Guns; John Mladgen of Pachmayr Gun Works; Roger Green of Frontier Gun Shop; and Dan Cotterman, who sleuthed at length through personal interviews, many anonymous phone calls to used gun dealers, and sneak shopping to get the low-down update on used rifle prices.

This list would hardly be complete without thanks to Dean A. Grennell and Bob Springer of my own staff. Grennell suffered at my elbow, checking copy against photos, as well as contributing his knowledge to the handgun section. Springer oversaw production of the entire project and verged on an ulcer all the way.

And finally my deepest thanks to Harold A. Murtz of DBI, Books Inc., the publishers of this tome, for his philosophical acceptance of my own bad temper, his sufferance of late night phone calls and contributory arguments about dates, models and general content.

Capistrano Beach, California   Jack Lewis

CONTENTS

SHOTGUNS: The nuts and bolts of buying a used shotgun 168

COMMEMORATIVES: What is a commemorative and what gives it value? 265

FOREIGN FIREARMS MANUFACTURERS 286

AMERICAN ARMSMAKERS

A.I.G. Corp., 7 Grasso Ave., North Haven, CT 06473
A-J Ordnance, Inc., 1066 E. Edna Pl., Covina, CA 91722 (Thomas auto pistol)
AMT (Arcadia Machine & Tool), 11666 McBean Dr., El Monte, CA 91732
American Arms, 915 N.W. 72nd St., Miami, FL 33150
ArmaLite, 118 E. 16th St., Costa Mesa, CA 92627
Artistic Arms, Inc., Box 23, Hoagland, IN 46745 (Sharps-Borchardt)
Auto-Ordnance Corp., Box ZG, West Hurley, NY 12491
Bauer Firearms, 34750 Klein Ave., Fraser, MI 48026
Brown Precision Co., 5869 Indian Ave., San Jose, CA 95123 (High Country rifle)
Champlin Firearms, Inc., Box 3191, Enid, OK 73701
Charter Arms Corp., 430 Sniffens Ln., Stratford, CT 06497
Colt, 150 Huyshope Ave., Hartford, CT 06102
Commando Arms, Inc., Box 10214, Knoxville, TN 37919
Crown City Arms, P.O. Box 1126, Cortland, NY 13045 (45 auto handgun)
Cumberland Arms, Rt. 1, Shafer Rd., Blanton Chapel, Manchester, TN 37355
Day Arms Corp., 2412 S.W. Loop 410, San Antonio, TX 78227
Detonics 45 Associates, 2500 Seattle Tower, Seattle, WA 98101 (auto pistol)
DuBiel Arms Co., 1724 Baker Rd., Denison, TX 75090
EMF Co., Inc., Box 1248, Studio City, CA 91604 (T.D.A. rev.)
FTL Marketing Corp., 11100 Cumpston St., No. Hollywood, CA 91601
Falling Block Works, P.O. Box 22, Troy, MI 48084
Firearms Imp. & Exp. Co., 2470 N.W. 21st St., Miami, FL 33142 (FIE)
Freedom Arms Co., P.O. Box 158, Freedom, WY 83120 (Casull handgun)
Freshour Mfg. Co., 1914 - 15th Ave. N., Texas City, TX 77590 (Ranger rifle)
Harrington & Richardson, Industrial Rowe, Gardner, MA 01440
High Standard Sporting Firearms, 31 Prestige Park Circle, East Hartford, CT 06108
Hyper-Single Precision SS Rifles, 520 E. Beaver, Jenks, OK 74037
Ithaca Gun Co., Ithaca, NY 14850
Iver Johnson Arms Inc., P.O. Box 251, Middlesex, NJ 08846
J & R Carbine, (see: PJK Inc.)
Paul Jaeger, Inc., 211 Leedom St., Jenkintown, PA 19046
Ljutic Ind., Inc., P.O. Box 2117, Yakima, WA 98902 (Mono-Gun)
Marlin Firearms Co., 100 Kenna Dr. New Haven, CT 06473

Bob Meece Co., Inc., 1602 Stemmons, Suite C, Carrollton, TX 75006 (Snake Charmer)
Merrill Co. Inc., Box 187, Rockwell City, IA 50579
O.F. Mossberg & Sons, Inc., 7 Grasso St., No. Haven, CT 06473
Mowrey Gun Works, Box 28, Iowa Park, TX 76367
Navy Arms Co., 689 Bergen Blvd., Ridgefield, NJ 07657
Numrich Arms Corp., W. Hurley, NY 12491
Plainfield Machine Co., Inc., Box 447, Dunellen, NJ 08812
Plainfield Inc., 292 Vail Ave., Piscataway, NJ 08854
R G Industries, 2485 N.W. 20th SE, Miami, FL 33142
Raven Arms, 1300 Bixby Dr., Industry, CA 91745
Remington Arms Co., Bridgeport, CT 06602
Riedl Rifles, 15124 Weststate St., Westminster, CA 92683 (S.S.)
Ruger (see Sturm, Ruger & Co.)
Savage Arms Corp., Westfield, MA 01085
Sears, Roebuck & Co., 825 S. St. Louis, Chicago, IL 60607
Semmerling Corp., P.O. Box 400, Newton, MA 02160
Seventrees Ltd., 315 W. 39th St., New York, NY 10018
Shiloh Products, 37 Potter St., Farmingdale, NY 11735 (Sharps)
Smith & Wesson, Inc., 2100 Roosevelt Ave., Springfield, MA 01101
Sporting Arms, Inc., 9643 Alpaca St., So. El Monte, CA 91733 (M-1 carbine)
Springfield Armory, 111 E. Exchange St., Geneseo, IL 61254
Sterling Arms Corp., 4436 Prospect St., Gasport, NY 14067
Sturm, Ruger & Co., Southport, CT 06490
Thompson-Center Arms, Box 2405, Rochester, NH 03867
Triple-S Development Co., Inc., 1450 E. 289th St., Wickliffe, OH 44092 (Wickliffe S.S. rifle)
United Sporting Arms, Inc., 35 Gilpin Ave., Hauppauge, L.I., NY 11787
United States Arms Corp., Doctors Path and Middle Road, Riverhead, NY 11901 (Abilene SA rev.)
Universal Firearms, 3740 E. 10th Ct., Hialeah, FL 33013
Unordco, P.O. Box 15723, Nashville, TN 37215
Ward's, 619 W. Chicago, Chicago, IL 60607 (Western Field brand)
Weatherby's, 2781 E. Firestone Blvd., South Gate, CA 90280
Dan Wesson Arms, 293 S. Main St., Monson, MA 01057
Wichita Eng. & Supply, Inc., P.O. Box 11371, Wichita, KS 67202
Wildey Firearms Co., Inc., P.O. Box 284, Cold Spring, NY 10516
Wilkinson Arms, 803 N. Glendora Ave., Covina, CA 91724 (Diane 25 ACP auto pistol)
Winchester Repeating Arms Co., New Haven, CT 06504
Winslow Arms Co., Inc., P.O. Box 783, Camden, SC 29020

FIREARMS IMPORTERS

American International, 103 Social Hall Ave., Salt Lake City, UT 84111
Armoury Inc., Rte. 202, New Preston, CT 06777
Armsport, Inc., 2811 N.W. 75th Ave., Miami, FL 33122
Beretta Arms Co., Inc., P.O. Box 697, Ridgefield, CT 06877
Browning, Rt. 4, Box 624-B, Arnold, MO 63010
Centennial Arms Corp., 3318 W. Devon, Chicago (Lincolnwood), IL 60645
Century Arms Co., 3-5 Federal St., St. Albans, VT 05478
Champlin Firearms, Inc., Box 3191, Enid, OK 73701 (Gebruder Merkel)
Commercial Trading Imports, Inc., Marketing Serv. of Control Data, 8100 34th Ave. S., Bloomington, MN 55440 (Russian shotguns)
Connecticut Valley Arms Co., Saybrook Rd., Haddam, CT 06438 (CVA)
Continental Arms Corp., 697 Fifth Ave., New York, NY 10022
Walter Craig, Inc., Box 927-A, Selma, AL 36701
Creighton & Warren, P.O. Box 15723, Nashville, TN 37215 (Krieghoff combination guns)
Morton Cundy & Son, Ltd., P.O. Box 315, Lakeside, MT 59922
Davidson Firearms Co., 2703 High Pt. Rd., Greensboro, NC 27403 (shotguns)
Davis Gun Shop, 7213 Lee Highway, Falls Church, VA 22046 (Fanzoj, Ferlach; Spanish guns)
Diana Co., 842 Vallejo St., San Francisco, CA 94133 (Benelli, Breda shotguns)
Dixie Gun Works, Inc., Hwy. 51, South, Union City, TN 38261 ("Kentucky" rifles)
Eastern Sports International, Inc., Savage Rd., Milford, NH 03055 (Rottweil; Geco)
Excam Inc., 4480 E. 11 Ave., P.O. Box 3483, Hialeah, FL 33013
F.E.T.E. Corp., 2867 W. 7th St., Los Angeles, CA 90005 (A. Zoli guns)
Ferlach (Austria) of North America, P.O. Box 430435, S. Miami, FL 33143
Firearms Center Inc. (FCI), 308 Leisure Lane, Victoria, TX 77901
Firearms Imp. & Exp. Co., 2470 N.W. 21st St., Miami, FL 33142
Flaig's Lodge, Millvale, PA 15209
Freeland's Scope Stands, Inc., 3737 14th Ave., Rock Island, IL 61201
J.L. Galef & Son, Inc., 85 Chambers, New York, NY 10007
Golden Eagle Firearms, 5803 Sovereign, Suite 206, Houston, TX 77036
Hawes National Corp., 15424 Cabrito Rd., Van Nuys, CA 91406
Healthways, Box 45055, Los Angeles, CA 90061
Gil Hebard Guns, Box 1, Knoxville, IL 61448 (Hammerli)
Heckler & Koch, Inc., 933 N. Kenmore St., Suite 218, Arlington, VA 22201
A.D. Heller, Inc., Box 56, 2322 Grand Ave., Baldwin, NY 11510
Herter's, Waseca, MN 56093
IGI Domino, 200 Madison Ave., New York, NY 10016 (AYA)
Interarmco, see: Interarms (Walther)
Interarms Ltd., 10 Prince St., Alexandria, VA 22313 (Mauser, Valmet M-62/S)
International Distr., Inc., 7290 S.W. 42nd St., Miami, FL 33155 (Taurus rev.)

Ithaca Gun Co., Terrace Hill, Ithaca, NY 14850 (Perazzi)
Paul Jaeger Inc., 211 Leedom St., Jenkintown, PA 19046
Jana Intl. Co., Box 1107, Denver, CO 80201 (Parker-Hale)
J.J. Jenkins, 375 Pine Ave., No. 25, Goleta, CA 93017
Kassnar Imports, 5480 Linglestown Rd., Harrisburg, PA 17110
Kerr's Sport Shop, Inc., 9584 Wilshire Blvd., Beverly Hills, CA 90212
Kimel Industries, P.O. Box 355, Matthews, NC 28105
Kleinguenther's, P.O. Box 1261, Seguin, TX 78155
Knight & Knight, 5930 S.W. 48 St., Miami, FL 33155 (made-to-order only)
L.A. Distributors, 4 Centre Market Pl., New York, NY 10013
L.E.S., 3640 Dempster, Skokie, IL 60076 (Steyr, Mannlicher-Schönauer)
S.E. Laszlo, 200 Tillary St., Brooklyn, NY 11201
Liberty Arms Organization, Box 306, Montrose, CA 91020
McKeown's Guns, R.R. 1, Pekin, IL 61554
Mandall Shtg. Suppl. Corp., 3616 N. Scottsdale Rd., Scottsdale, AZ 85252
Markwell Arms Co., 2414 W. Devon, Chicago, IL 60645
Mars Equipment Corp., 3318 W. Devon, Chicago, IL 60645
Wm. Larkin Moore, 2890 Marlics St., Agoura, CA 91301 (AYA, Garbi)
Navy Arms Co., 689 Bergen Blvd., Ridgefield, NJ 07657
Harry Owen, P.O. Box 774, Sunnyvale, CA 94088
P.M. Air Services, Ltd., P.O. Box 1573, Costa Mesa, CA 92626
Pachmayr Gun Works, 1220 S. Grand Ave., Los Angeles, CA 90015
Pacific Intl. Merch. Corp., 2215 "J" St., Sacramento, CA 95816
Rob. Painter, 2901 Oakhurst Ave., Austin, TX 78703 (Chapuis)
Ed Paul Sptg. Goods, 172 Flatbush Ave., Brooklyn, NY 11217 (Premier)
Precise, 3 Chestnut, Suffern, NY 10901
Premier Shotguns, 172 Flatbush Ave., Brooklyn, NY 11217
Leonard Puccinelli Co., P.O. Box 668, San Anselmo, CA 94960 (I.A.B., Rizzini of Italy)
RG Industries, Inc. 2485 N.W. 20th St., Miami, FL 33142 (Erma)
Richland Arms Co., 321 W. Adrian St., Blissfield, MI 49228
SKB Sports Inc., 190 Shepard, Wheeling, IL 60090
Sanderson's, 724 W. Edgewater, Portage, WI 53901
Savage Arms Corp., Westfield, MA 01085 (Anschutz)
Security Arms Co., see: Heckler & Koch
Service Armament, 689 Bergen Blvd., Ridgefield, NJ 07657 (Greener Harpoon Gun)
Sherwood Dist., Inc., 18714 Parthenia St., Northridge, CA 91324
Simmons Spec., Inc., 700 Rogers Rd., Olathe, KS 66061
Sloan's Sprtg. Goods, Inc., 10 South St., Ridgefield, CT 06877
Steyr-Daimler-Puch of America, Inc., 3560-64 Roger B. Chaffee Blvd., Grand Rapids, MI 49508
Stoeger Arms Co., 55 Ruta Ct., S. Hackensack, NJ 07606
Tradewinds, Inc., P.O. Box 1191, Tacoma, WA 98401
Ultra-Hi Products Co., 150 Florence Ave., Hawthorne, NJ 07506 (ML)
Valor Imp. Corp., 5555 N.W. 36th Ave., Miami, FL 33142
Ventura Imports, P.O. Box 2782, Seal Beach, CA 90740 (European shotguns)
Weatherby's, 2781 Firestone Blvd., South Gate, CA 90280 (Sauer)

Introduction

IN THIS BOOK, we endeavor to suggest realistic selling prices for used guns. This is not quite so simple and clear-cut an operation as one might suppose. In fact, there are a lot of complexities. Let us examine a few of these.

First, these are retail prices throughout!

By way of preparatory groundwork, we conducted a series of surveys involving typical gundealers in various parts of the country, intent upon finding out how much variation could be expected in the price of this or that gun, depending upon the given region. We made up a list, covering four each of rifles, shotguns and handguns, all of a make sufficiently common to be well-known to the dealers being surveyed. In several instances, we were able to get the lists priced by more than one dealer in the same city.

Somewhat against casual expectations, there proved to be but little difference in the value put upon the same gun, regardless if the dealer did business in New England, the Deep South, the Midwestern Plains or the West Coast. Surprisingly enough, some of the sharpest discrepancies were noted between dealers in the same city.

In submitting the list of guns for pricing, we had specified that their hypothetical condition be assumed "NRA Very Good," and asked for the price that would be put on the gun when set out on the display racks for resale. Some of the prices were surprisingly uniform. As an example, a Colt .45 ACP auto pistol, commercial, Model 1911A1, MK IV, carrying a suggested retail price of $253.95, when new, was quoted from a low of $175 to a high of $200.

Shotguns seemed to show the largest spread in quoted prices, followed by high-powered rifles and both reflected the degree and type of hunting interest of the particular region rather closely. As another example, a Remington Model 870 pump shotgun, in 12 gauge, with twenty-eight-inch, full-choked barrel, retailing for $212.95 new, was quoted at $170 and $180 by two dealers within easy driving distance of Wisconsin's Horicon Marsh, where waterfowl are abundant in season, and at $100 to $110 by dealers in areas such as Southern Texas and Western Arizona. In much the same manner, guns of the general category commonly referred to as "deer rifles" tended to be valued more highly in those areas where the interest in deer hunting is keenest.

Of much greater significance than geographical location is that of the point in time. Twenty years ago, some of the guns on our survey list could have been purchased — with a bit of careful shopping — at prices ranging from one-quarter to one-half their current market value. As to what the state of the market may be twenty years hence, it would be most difficult to say with any pretense of certainty. One of my authors recalls selling a commercial Colt .45 ACP, in good condition, for $40 in 1955 and considering it to have been a good price for that time. Since a comparable gun seemed to be worth about $140 in 1975, three and one-half times as much, would it be safe to extrapolate a figure of $490 for a similar gun in 1995? Probably not, because history is not overly prone to follow straightline trends over the long haul.

First off, we had to make a decision: After all, entire books have been written on a single type of gun and there are editorial limitations.

After a good deal of soul-searching, haggling, et al., it was decided that — generally speaking — any firearm that is more than half a century old and discontinued is more likely to be considered a collector item rather than a practical firearm. As a result, we went back to 1925, actually the beginning of 1925, extending our time frame through 1974. That's fifty years of used guns.

Then came the question of how far afield we should go.

It was decided that the war surplus should not be included. To start with, there is little of it available these days that is any good; the really good pieces now seem to be in the hands of military collectors. Besides, unless customized, they are likely to be of little interest to the sporting arms group. Also excluded are the long-discontinued foreign arms, primarily handguns, for which it is virtually impossible to get parts.

It also should be pointed out that much of the material in this volume — particularly the years during which some models were made — has been difficult information to come by. Some American companies have changed hands several times, with such info not being passed on to new owners. In the case of many European models, the records were lost or destroyed during World War II. Collectors and authorities on specific models have been of great help here, but there may well be minor errors in production dates.

Another editorial decision had to do with organization. It finally was decided that, when a manufacturer made three models or fewer, those guns would be listed alphabetically under Miscellaneous in the proper section.

There is a matched pair of Latin phrases and they are quoteworthy in this connection: *Caveat emptor,* (let the buyer beware) and *caveat vendor,* (let the seller beware), to which we might add *caveat lector,* let the reader beware depending upon whether he or she is buying or selling.

There is a further source of much confusion in the matter of guns thought to be rare and therefore valuable. We refer to the house-brands. It once was and perhaps still may be common practice for hardware jobbers to commission gunmakers to produce a quantity of guns — shotguns, to give the most common example — under the jobber's specified brand name. To cite a hypothetical example, by way of illustration, let's assume that, in the Spring of 1936, the hardware-jobbing firm of Hobson & Choice ordered two hundred pump-action 12-gauge shotguns from the Waterfall Gun Works, of West Chokecherry, Connecticut, to be stamped on the action or barrel with the brand-name, "Regia."

The guns may have retailed at around $32.50 in 1936 and perhaps they did not move too briskly, so that H&C didn't bother to reorder when the last one was carted out onto the shipping dock. In fact, they may have bid it good riddance. However the decades ooze onward and, in 1979, an heir to an estate finds himself in possession of a 12-gauge Regia pump shotgun. Having some reasonable familiarity with firearms, he has never heard of a Regia and he wonders if he has lucked onto a rare and valuable collector's item, worth a few thousand dollars.

Alas for the new owner's high hopes, the answer in such an example is that its value is about that of any functional pump shotgun in the market of 1979 or whenever. In fact, its value may tend to be slightly less than average, due to the fact that few if any would-be buyers ever heard of a Regia shotgun. In 1936, standard patterns of a Remington

Model 31 or Winchester Model 12 sold for less than a ten-spot more than our imaginary Regia's $32.50. If Model 12s and 31s of that vintage haven't been maltreated or injudiciously modified, they can be sold at somewhere around the $250-$400 brackets, while our hypothetical Regia owner would be lucky to liquidate his inherited prize for much over $75.

Collectors are a little unpredictable, to put it mildly. These are days when a shrewd seller can get a C-note for a comic book that cost a dime per copy off the newstands in 1953, provided it happens to be the correct and desirable rarity. With such in mind, it would be rash to say future gun collectors will not focus their attention upon such specialized areas as those old hardware jobbers' house-brand guns. To the present, however, there has not been any heavy ground-swell of interest in that direction.

Getting back to the buyer's need to watch out for his/her interests in any given transaction, it is well to attain as much familiarity and expertise as possible in examining and evaluating a prospective purchase before laying out one's good, green banknotes. In general terms, the prices quoted in this book represent retail figures for a used gun in good to very-good condition. It is up to the buyer to make certain that the prospective purchase qualifies for that description.

The value of any particular make and model of gun can be reduced rather sharply, if it happens to be chambered for a cartridge or shotshell that is obsolescent or at the outer edges of the public favor. Sometimes, one sees a Remington Model 31 or Winchester Model 12 shotgun on the table at a gunshow, tagged at a figure that seems surprisingly low. The reason becomes apparent when you pick it up and note it's chambered for 16-gauge, instead of the more popular 12 or 20-gauge. Not that the 16-gauge isn't capable of excellent shooting, as its more devout devotees will point out at great length, but it is a size not overly beloved by the average shotgunner. This reduces the average value of such guns by a substantial percentage.

Modifications and the presence of factory options often affect values significantly. A solid or ventilated rib usually adds to the value of a shotgun, particularly if it's factory equipment. Muzzle devices such as variable chokes often reduce the value in comparison to the same gun, as-issued. Rechambering a rifle for a wildcat — that is, non-standard — cartridge can cut the value almost to zilch, so far as the average gun dealer is concerned.

Despite notable gains in the popularity of reloading and benchrest shooting, if the average, would-be gunbuyer cannot find factory ammunition in plentiful supply on his dealer's shelves, he is not too apt to be willing to pay much money for the gun in question. This is a fact of life that should be weighed thoughtfully before making any drastic modifications that will set a gun sharply apart from standard configurations.

It sometimes happens that the gun manufacturer, all unwittingly, contributes to the value fluctuation of prior production by introducing a change in current production.

The Winchester Model 70 rifle is one of the more noteworthy examples of this. In 1964, Winchester did a fairly drastic revamp of the Model 70, switching to stamped checkering on the pistol grip and forend and providing a generous free-floating clearance between the barrel and the forend. For the next six years or so, the buying public made it redundantly plain that they were not too impressed by the changes. In fact, it reached the point where pre-'64 Model 70s were changing hands briskly for prices well in excess of then-current retail prices of new guns.

Finally, around 1970, Winchester gave in and did a further revamp to return their Model 70 to something more nearly resembling its earlier form. "Winchester the way you want it," was the ad slogan they used and personnel of the New Haven firm were heard to mutter they hoped to hear the last of the "pre-'64" phrase, of which they'd become extremely unfond.

Buyers of guns can be categorized into two fairly distinct breeds. On the one hand, we have the shooter, interested primarily in the gun for its basic, utilitarian function. On the other, we have the collector, eternally in quest for the rarities and esoterica of the gunmaker's craft. The shooter tends to regard a gun simply as a tool for setting off ammunition and for directing its projectiles to the point of aim. To a collector, rare guns are *objets d'art* and valued accordingly.

Hence, you may see rare and exotic variants of the .45 ACP Government Model autoloading pistol on display at gunshows, with price tags up in the rarified levels above the $4000 mark. This is not to say that such a gun is twenty-eight times as accurate and reliable as its common counterpart, going for $175 at another table a little farther up the aisle; far from it. The costly rarity might not even group as closely. Its exalted value lies in its scarcity and in the hot yen that some other collector may have for getting it to fill a gap in his display cabinet.

This book has been produced with the shooter in mind, rather than the collector, and the prices quoted herein have been derived accordingly. If one has reasonable cause to believe some particular gun has value as a collectors' item, well in excess of its nominal or intrinsic quoted price, there are procedures that tend to minimize lost opportunities for profit. For example, contemporary modifications, such as sending it out to be re-blued, can and usually do neutralize any value it might have for collectors. Even if the present finish is in a sorry state, if it's the original finish, a surprisingly large amount of the value may remain intact.

The author and publishers of this book are not prepared to offer counsel as to the value of any given gun and, most emphatically, inquiries of such nature are not solicited. It is virtually impossible to offer any realistic value quotation without seeing the specific gun.

It should be noted that the listing of prices does not constitute an offer to buy or sell the various guns for the prices quoted. So please do not send checks, orders or inquiries as to the availability of the guns to the publisher nor to the author.

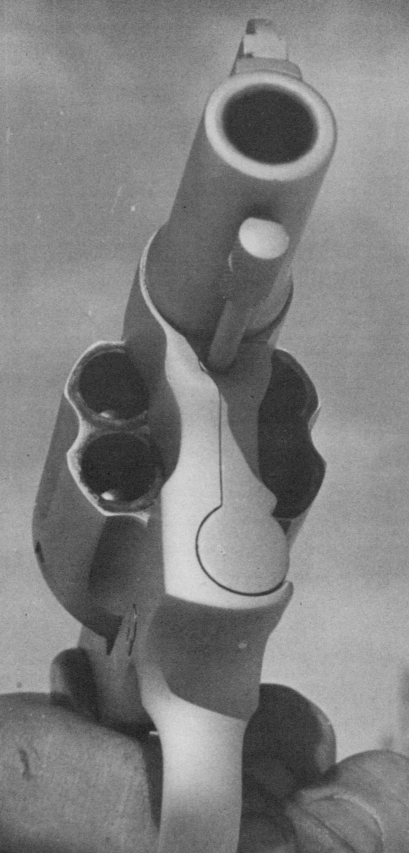

HANDGUNS

Timely Thoughts On Buying —
Or Selling — A Used Handgun

THERE ARE SOME basic guidelines to consider in buying — or selling — a used handgun. In the first category, the question would be the purpose; for what kind of shooting do you intend to use the handgun? Considerations, whether for a home defense gun, plinking, serious target work or big-game hunting are obvious.

Generally speaking, if you are buying a used handgun, the asking price will usually be about seventy-five percent of the new, retail price, depending upon condition and age. The latter are two important determining factors that dictate today's price. That same gun is worth considerably more in new condition now than it was ten years ago; and in many instances, the price has doubled. Simply stated, if you are buying a handgun that sold for $40 a decade ago, but is retailed at $80 today, you can probably plan on paying a minimum of $60 for it in used condition, even if it is one of the original versions, so long as it is in good shape.

There are exceptions, of course. An example is the Smith and Wesson Model 29 .44 Magnum. Whether by design or otherwise, this gun is in continuing short supply and has been since it was introduced. While the manufacturer's current retail price is around $310, these guns are selling for twice that much, used or new. It boils down to a matter of supply and demand and, I suspect, the popularity of this model has something to do with status symbolism as well.

At present, High Standard is introducing a .44 magnum revolver built along the same lines as the Model 29. This may induce Smith and Wesson to increase production of the Model 29 — to get more of them on the market — or the fact that a similar handgun is available may ultimately bring the retail price down to what Smith and Wesson suggests, but don't hold your breath!

The pre-WWII Colt Woodsman is another example of the premium gun. The author recalls pining wistfully over advertisements of the late Thirties, when the asking retail price for a new one was about $30. According to a 1945 catalog, the price had climbed to $34.50, for either the 4½ or 6½-inch barreled model, but hardly any were for sale. A used 6½-incher turned up in a gun store in Mountain Home, Idaho, late in 1945, tagged at $55.

Some years later, the Woodsman sold for about $60, with the thought that another could be bought when Colt got back into full production. But when the post-war version of the Woodsman appeared on dealer's shelves, it had been redesigned; it didn't look quite the same. In 1959, one of the 4½-inch pre-war models turned up at a gun show and I forked over the asking price of $95. Another nine years came and went before I encountered a second

specimen. Oddly enough, the asking price was $35 and that included a spare magazine!

In 1975, a friend of mine tried an early Woodsman and became so infatuated with it that he was willing to pay $180 for the 6½-inch target model. At the same time, the 4½-inch sport style was going for $220 while the pre-war Match Target model was going for up to $240.

Desirability of a used handgun seems to be a mixture of rarity, plus quality. With few exceptions, junk tends to stay junk, never commanding more than junk prices. Guns of good or excellent quality and workmanship gain in value with a degree of rapidity that verges on the amazing, even if they were made in considerable quantities.

The Model 1917 revolvers made by Colt and Smith and Wesson during World War I to supplement supplies of the then-new Model 1911 Government automatic, were selling for around $20 in 1960, rising to $30 by 1965. Currently, they are in the $100 to $150 bracket, with few available at that price!

I know one shooter who bought a used S&W Model 1950 target pistol in 1957. It was chambered for the .44 Special, had a four-inch barrel, and he paid $75 for it.

As with the pre-WWII Woodsman, the short-barreled version of this particular gun is less common; there aren't too many of the 6½-inch Model 1950s around, and the shorter ones are even more scarce. The owner of that four-inch model has suggested that he might consider $550 a fair price, but he's not overly interested in selling it!

At the time of its introduction in 1873, the Colt Single Action Army revolver retailed for about $16 and, at the outbreak of World War II, the price had advanced to $38.50. Not long ago, one specimen, authenticated as having belonged to Wyatt Earp, changed hands for $20,000! This is an extreme case, to be sure, and the personality involved has much to do with the value, but the spread from original to ultimate value is obvious.

One factor that will have a drastic and unpredictable effect upon the value of handguns is that of legislative restrictions on their use and ownership. There is no reliable method of predicting future value fluctuations caused by legislation.

A top consideration in shopping for a used handgun is whether the model still is being manufactured and if parts are available. Immediately following World War II, when handguns were still in short supply, a lot of imports came out of Spain. In fact, Eibar was then considered the gun-making capital of post-war Europe.

But there were problems. While there were major manufacturers with plenty of quality control in Eibar, some

Spanish exporters were contracting with independent gunsmiths and the same problem developed that existed at one time with handmade Swiss watches: each gunsmith was doing most of his work by hand with no standardization for interchangeable parts. As a result, there were no factory spare parts available and, if you wanted or needed the gun repaired, that meant your gunsmith had to spend some expensive hours making a part by hand.

In varying degrees, the same situation was true for guns coming out of Latin America, Italy and other European nations. Some of those guns are still around today, and even though they may be highly desirable pieces, remember that the cost of gunsmithing has increased considerably, and that means more expensive replacement parts.

As an example, shortly after World War II, I walked into a gun shop and bought a .32 automatic of Czechoslovakian make. It was a real bargain, I thought, at $25. I went away relatively happy, in spite of the fact that the barrel was pitted and would have to be replaced soon. However, as Czechoslovakia had disappeared behind the Iron Curtain — so had her gunworks.

I took the handgun to a reliable gunsmith to ask about the cost of having a new barrel made and he told me that I had a choice of throwing the automatic away and calling my initial investment the price of education, or paying $75 to have a new barrel made from the ground up.

It sounds silly, but I field stripped the gun and threw the parts, one by one, into a fast-running creek. My twenty-twenty hindsight tells me I should have peddled the gun to get back at least part of that twenty-five bucks.

In selecting a second-hand handgun, a simple test of condition and quality is to pick it up and shake it. If there is a definite rattle, it probably has some badly worn or poorly-fitted parts.

If purchasing a revolver, the shake-well-before-buying test can also prove effective. If the cylinder is loose, moving fore and aft in the frame under finger pressure, any one of three things can be wrong with the gun — all of them calling for repairs.

The star at the rear center of the cylinder may be badly worn. If so, this calls for a new cylinder on some models. It also can mean the revolver's bolt is badly worn, or that the hand, which rotates the cylinder to lock it in place and properly align the chamber with the barrel, is worn out.

One should determine whether the cylinder rolls under finger pressure; it is supposed to move a fraction, of course, but excessive looseness can be dangerous to a shooter if not remedied before firing. Chances are that the gun is out of time, the chambers failing to line up properly with the barrel.

If this should be the case, the least that can happen will be for the bullet, upon being fired, to be sheared on one side by its uneven contact with the rear of the barrel, causing the bullet to become slightly lopsided in shape. Poor accuracy is the obvious result of this problem.

While evidence of this problem usually is not obvious in the gun shop — the handgun having been cleaned and oiled before being placed on display — such looseness and the resulting lead throwing, will usually show shavings from the slug adhering to the end of the barrel just forward of the cylinder, at the chamber openings themselves or at the underside of the topstrap.

There are many good second-hand guns for sale to be sure, but the gun shop salesman can seldom take the time to lug every gun in the store to a range and personally determine whether it needs repair.

Whether automatic or revolver, the bore should be checked, using a light-reflecting surface under good illumination — a bore light is also recommended — if the design is not such that one can get a straight-through squint at it. Look for signs of pitting and corrosion, bulges or dents, caused by firing with an obstruction in the bore and for signs of excessive wear or maltreatment.

Examine the firing pin to make sure the tip hasn't been broken off. In center-fire guns, the end of the firing pin should be a smooth, hemispherical shape. If it has a chipped or flattened area or a sharp point, it could pierce the cartridge primer; this can cause leakage of high-pressure powder gases with possible damage to the gun, the shooter and bystanders.

Check for loose or missing screws, as well as for badly burred slots that indicate some kitchen mechanic went at it with a dime store screwdriver. Depending upon the design of the gun, and with the owner's consent, trying the trigger action by dry-firing is a good idea. At the risk of being tedious, the precautions for making certain the chamber is empty and the muzzle pointed in a safe direction, are important.

Once you have made your selection, examined it to your satisfaction, paid for it and found that the gun performs to your hopes and expectations, it is common sense not to degrade the value of this investment. This involves cleaning, lubrication and application of rust-preventing agents. A blued finish is by no means rustproof. Perspiration has an acid content and wiping down the metal parts with a flannel cloth moistened with silicone or other anti-rust preparation will prevent damage to the blued steel parts after handling.

This maintenance is less costly and more convenient than sending the gun out to be reblued since, in most cases, rebluing reduces value.

ASTRA Model 800: automatic; also called Condor; 9mm Luger; tubular-type design; 5-5/16" barrel; 8¼" overall length; 8-rd. magazine; fixed sights; blued finish; grooved plastic grips. Based on Model 400 design. Introduced in 1958; dropped, 1968. Few imported; produced primarily for European police, military use. Used value, $400 to $500.

ASTRA Model 900: Automatic; 7.63mm; 5½" barrel; 11½" overall length; 10-rd. fixed magazine; adjustable rear sight, fixed front; small ring hammer on early models, larger hammer on later; grooved walnut grips; lanyard ring. Based upon design of "broomhandle" Mauser, but has barrel, barrel extension as two parts rather than one as in German Mauser, different lockwork, etc. Introduced in 1928, dropped, 1940. Originally priced at $37; has collector value. Used value, $400 to $500.

ASTRA Model 200: vest pocket automatic; advertised as the Firecat; .25 ACP only; 2¼" barrel, 4-3/8" overall length; 6-rd. magazine; fixed sights; blued finish; plastic grips. Introduced in 1920; still in production; U.S. importation dropped in 1968. Used value, $80 to $110.

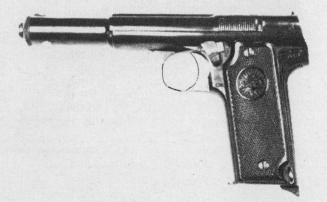

ASTRA Model 400: automatic; 9mm Bergmann-Bayard; 6" barrel, 10" overall length; 9-rd. magazine; fixed sights; blowback action; will also chamber and fire 9mm Luger and .38 ACP; blued finish; hard rubber or walnut grips. Introduced in 1921; dropped, 1946. Used value, $100 to $125.

ASTRA Model 600: military, police automatic; 9mm Luger; 5¼" barrel, 8" overall length; 8 rds.; fixed sights; blued finish, hard rubber or walnut grips. Introduced in 1942; dropped, 1946. Used value, $87.50 to $100.

ASTRA 4000: advertised as Falcon; automatic; .22 LR, .32 auto, .380 auto; 3-2/3'' barrel; 6½'' overall length; 10-rd. magazine in .22, 8 rds. in .32, 7 rds. in .380; thumb safety; exposed hammer; fixed sights; checkered black plastic grips; blued. Introduced in 1956; U.S. importation dropped, 1968. Used value, $135 to $150.

ASTRA Model 3000: pocket automatic; .32 auto, .380 auto; 4'' barrel; 5-3/8'' overall length; 7-rd. magazine in .32, 6-rd. in .380; fixed sights, blued finish, hard rubber grips. Introduced in 1922 in .380; dropped, 1958. Used value, $125 to $150.

ASTRA Cub: pocket automatic; .22 short, .25 auto; 2¼''

barrel; 4-7/16'' overall length; 6-rd. magazine; fixed sights; blued or chrome finish; plastic grips. Introduced in 1957; still in production, but U.S. importation dropped, 1968. Used value, $100 to $125.

ASTRA Constable: automatic; .22 LR, .32 ACP, .380 ACP; 3½'' barrel; 10-rd. magazine in .22 LR, 8-rd. in .32 ACP, 7 rds. in .380 ACP; adjustable rear sight, fixed front; moulded plastic grips; double action; nonglare rib on slide; quick, no-tool takedown feature; blued or chrome finish except .32, which is no longer available. Current importer is Interarms. Introduced in 1969; still in production. Used values, blued finish, $100 to $125; chrome, $110 to $135.

ASTRA 357: revolver; .357 magnum; 3'', 4'', 6'', 8½'' barrels; 6-rd. swing-out cylinder; integral rib, ejector rod; click-adjustable rear sight, ramp front; target hammer; checkered walnut grips; blued. Imported by Interarms. Introduced in 1972; still in production. Used value, $125 to $135.

Note: Astra also produced a number of .32 pocket automatics loosely resembling the Colt 1908, .32. Values $60 to $80; and S&W type revolvers, values $50 to $75.

BAYARD

Model 1930

Model 1908

BAYARD Model 1908: pocket automatic; .25 auto, .32 auto, .380 auto; 2¼" barrel; 4-7/8" overall length; 6-rd. magazine; fixed sights, blued finish; hard rubber grips. Introduced in 1908; dropped, 1939. Used value, $80 to $100.

BAYARD Model 1923: larger model pocket auto; .32 auto, .380 auto, 3-5/16" barrel; 4-5/16" overall length; 6-rd. magazine; fixed sights; blued finish, checkered grips of hard rubber. Introduced in 1923; dropped, 1930. Used value, $100 to $125.

BAYARD Model 1923: small model pocket auto; .25 auto only; 2-1/8" barrel; 4-5/16" overall length; fixed sights, blued finish; checkered grips of hard rubber. Scaled-down model of large Model 1923. Introduced in 1923; dropped, 1940. Used value, $80 to $100.

BAYARD Model 1930: pocket auto; .25 auto; has same general specifications as small Model 1923 auto pistol with improvements in finish, internal mechanism. Introduced in 1930; dropped, 1940. Used value, $100 to $125.

BERETTA

BERETTA 1919: pocket-type automatic; .25 auto only; 3½" barrel; 5¾" overall length; 8-rd. magazine; fixed sights; plastic grips; blued. Introduced in 1919, with several modifications (later version pictured); dropped, 1945. Used values: pre-WWII commercial model, $85 to $100. WWII model, $70 to $90.

BERETTA Cougar also Model 1934 or 934: pocket-type automatic; .380 auto, .32 auto; 3-3/8" barrel, 5-7/8" overall length; 7-rd. magazine; fixed sights; plastic grips; thumb safety; blued or chrome finish. Official Italian service sidearm in WWII; wartime version lacks quality of commercial model. Introduced in 1934; not legally importable; still in production. Used values: WWII model, $75 to $100; commercial model, blued, $90 to $110; chrome finished, $100 to $125.

BERETTA Model 70 Puma: pocket-type automatic; .32 auto only; 4'' barrel; 6'' overall length; 8-rd. magazine; fixed sights; plastic grips; crossbolt safety; blued, chrome-finish. Introduced in 1934; dropped, 1968. Used values: blued, $75 to $80; chrome finish, $80 to $85.

BERETTA 25: pocket-type automatic; .25 auto only; 2½'' barrel; 4½'' overall length; 8-rd. magazine; fixed sights; plastic grips; blued. Introduced in 1948; not importable, dropped, 1968. Used value, $75 to $85.

BERETTA Model 949 Olympionico: target automatic; .22 short only; 8¾'' barrel; 12½'' overall length; 5-rd. magazine; target sights; adjustable barrel weight; muzzle brake; hand-checkered walnut thumbrest grips; blued. Introduced in 1949; dropped, 1968. Used value $200 to $225.

BERETTA Model 950B Minx M2: automatic; .22 short only; 2-3/8'' barrel; 4¾'' overall length; 6-rd. magazine; rear sight milled in slide; fixed front; black plastic grips; blued. Introduced in 1950. Used value, $85 to $90.

Minx M4 has the same specifications as Model M2, except for 4'' barrel. Introduced in 1956. Used value, $85 to $90. Neither model importable since 1968.

BERETTA Model 950B Jetfire: automatic; .25 auto; 2-3/8'' barrel; 4¾'' overall length; 7-rd. magazine; has the same general specifications as Minx M2. Introduced in 1950; not importable since 1968. Used value, $90 to $110.

BERETTA Model 71 and Model 72 Jaguar Plinker: automatic; .22 LR only; 3½'' (Mod. 71), or 6'' (Mod. 72) barrels; 8-rd. magazine; rear sight milled in slide, fixed front; checkered plastic grips; blued. Introduced in 1956; dropped, 1968. Used value, $100 to $125.

Jaguar Model 101 has the same general specifications as Jaguar Plinker, except for 6'' barrel only; overall length, 8¾''; adjustable rear sight; wrap-around checkered plastic grips; lever thumb safety. Introduced in 1969; still in production. Used value, $100 to $125.

BERETTA Model 951: automatic; 9mm Luger; 4½'' barrel; 8'' overall length; advertised originally as Brigadier model; 8-rd. magazine; external hammer; cross-bolt safety; slide stays open after last shot; fixed sights; moulded grooved plastic grips; blued. Introduced in 1951; still in production. Used value, $170 to $200.

BERETTA Model 70S: automatic; .380 auto; 3-5/8'' barrel; 6½'' overall length; 7-rd. magazine; external hammer; fixed sights; checkered plastic wrap-around grips; blued. Introduced in 1971; still in production. Used value, $92.50 to $100.

BERETTA Model 70T: automatic; .32 auto; 6'' barrel; 8½'' overall length; 9-rd. magazine; adjustable rear sight, fixed front; external hammer; slide stays open after last shot; checkered plastic wrap-around grips. Introduced in 1969; dropped, 1975. Used value, $80 to $85.

BERETTA Model 90: double-action automatic; .32 auto; 3-5/8'' barrel; 6¾'' overall length; 8-rd. magazine; fixed sights, matted rib on slide; chamber-loaded indicator; external hammer; stainless steel barrel; moulded plastic wrap-around grips; blued. Introduced in 1969; still in production. Used value, $150 to $160.

BERETTA Model 76: automatic; .22 LR only; 6'' barrel; 9½'' overall length; 10-rd. magazine; adjustable rear sight, interchangeable blade front; non-glare, ribbed slide; heavy barrel; external hammer; checkered plastic wrap-around grips; blued. Introduced in 1971; still in production. Used value, $135 to $160.

BERNARDELLI

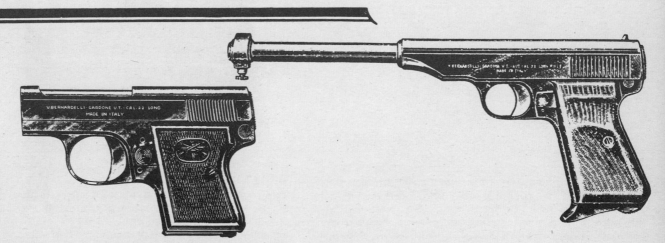

BERNARDELLI Vest Pocket Model: automatic; .22 LR, .25 auto; 2-1/8'' barrel; 4-1/8'' overall length; 6-rd. magazine in .22, 5-rd. in .25; 8-rd. extension magazine also available in .25; no sights, but sighting groove milled in slide; plastic grips; blued. Introduced in 1948; U.S. importation dropped, 1968. Used value, $100 to $125.

BERNARDELLI Standard: automatic; .22 LR only, 6'' 8'', 10'' barrels; with 10'' barrel, 13'' overall length; 10-rd. magazine; target sights; adjustable sight ramp; walnut target grips; blued. Introduced in 1949; still in production. Used value, $125 to $135.

BERNARDELLI Model 80: automatic; .22 LR, .32 auto, .380 auto; 3½" barrel; 6-5/16" overall length; 10-rd. magazine in .22, 8 rds. in .32, 7 rds. in .380; fixed or click-adjustable rear sight, post front; manual, magazine safeties; checkered plastic or checkered walnut thumbrest grips; blued. Imported by Interarms. Introduced in 1959; still in production. Used values: .32 cal., $65 to $70; .22 or .380, $70 to $80.

Model 90 is same as Model 80 except 6" barrel. Used value, $90 to $100.

BERNARDELLI Match 22: automatic .22 LR only; 5¾" barrel; 9" overall length; 10-rd. magazine; manual, magazine safeties; external hammer; adjustable rear sight, post front; hand-checkered thumbrest walnut grips; blued. Introduced in 1971; replaced by Model 100. Used value, $90 to $110.

BERNARDELLI Model 100: Heavy barrel version of Mod. 80 in .22 LR only; walnut grips; fully adjustable target sights. Used value, $135 to $150.

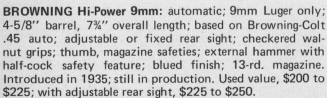

Browning

BROWNING Hi-Power 9mm: automatic; 9mm Luger only; 4-5/8" barrel, 7¾" overall length; based on Browning-Colt .45 auto; adjustable or fixed rear sight; checkered walnut grips; thumb, magazine safeties; external hammer with half-cock safety feature; blued finish; 13-rd. magazine. Introduced in 1935; still in production. Used value, $200 to $225; with adjustable rear sight, $225 to $250.

Hi-Power Renaissance model has the same specifications as standard model, except for chrome-plated finish, full engraving, polyester pearl grips. Introduced in 1954; still in production. Used value, $600 to $630.

BROWNING 380: automatic; .380, .32 ACP, 3-7/16" barrel, 6" overall length; 9-rd. magazine; pre-'68 models, fixed sights, now adjustable; hard rubber grips; blued finish. Introduced 1910, and a longer barreled version in 1922, redesigned in 1968; still in production. Used value, $100 to $125 except WWII manufacture, $75 to $90. Current models have 4½" barrel, are 7" overall.

The 380 Renaissance model has the same specifications as the standard Browning 380, except for chrome-plated finish, full engraving, polyester pearl grips. Introduced in 1954, still in production. Used value, $350 to $375.

BROWNING Model 1906 .25 Automatic: .25 ACP only; 2'' barrel; 4½'' overall length; 6-rd. magazine; fixed sights; blued or nickel finish; hard rubber grips. Almost identical to Colt Vest Pocket .25 auto. Introduced in 1906; dropped, 1940. Used value, $90 to $120.

BROWNING 25 "Baby": automatic; .25 ACP only; 2-1/8'' barrel; 4'' overall length; 6-rd. magazine; fixed sights, hard rubber grips; blued finish. Introduced in 1940; dropped, not importable, 1968. Used value, $100 to $125.

Browning 25 Lightweight has the same general specifications as the standard model, except that it is chrome plated, has polyester pearl grips, alloy frame. Introduced in 1954; dropped, 1968. Used value, $120 to $150.

Browning 25 Renaissance Model has the same specifications as the standard Browning 25, except for chrome-plated finish, polyester pearl grips, full engraving. Introduced in 1954; dropped, 1968. Used value, $380 to $400.

BROWNING Renaissance Set: includes Renaissance versions of Hi-Power 9mm, 380 Automatic, 25 Automatic in a specially fitted walnut case. Oddly, value depends to a degree upon condition of the case. Introduced in 1954; dropped, 1968. Used value $1350 to $1420.

BROWNING Nomad: automatic; .22 LR only; 4½'', 6¾'' barrels; overall length, 8-15/16'' with 4½'' barrel; 10-rd. magazine; screw adjustable rear sight, removable blade front; brown plastic grips; blued finish. Introduced in 1962; dropped, 1973. Used value, $100 to $125.

BROWNING Challenger: automatic; .22 LR only; 4½'', 6¾'' barrels; overall length, 11-7/16'' with 6¾'' barrel; 10-rd. magazine; screw-adjustable rear sight, removable blade front; hand-checkered walnut grips, blued finish. Introduced in 1962; dropped, 1974. Used value, $115 to $120. Reintroduced as Challenger II in 1977.

Challenger Gold Model has the same general specifications as standard Browning Challenger, except for gold wire inlays in metal; figured, hand-carved, checkered walnut grips. Introduced in 1971; dropped, 1974. Used value, $265 to $275.

Challenger Renaissance Model has the same exact specifications as standard Challenger, except for chrome-plated finish, full engraving, top-grade, hand-carved, figured walnut grips. Introduced in 1971; dropped, 1974. Used value, $310 to $325.

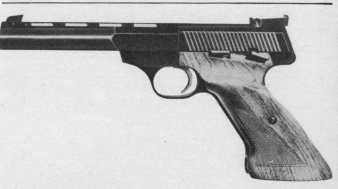

BROWNING Medalist: automatic; .22 LR only; 6¾'' barrel; 11-1/8'' overall length; 10-rd. magazine; vent rib; full wrap-around grips of select walnut; checkered with thumb rest; matching walnut forend; left-hand model available; screw adjustable rear sight, removable blade front; dry-firing mechanism; blued finish. Introduced in 1962; dropped, 1974. Used value, $200 to $210.

International Medalist has same general specifications as standard Medalist, but is sans forend; 5.9'' barrel, overall length, 10-15/16''; meets qualifications for International Shooting Union regulations. Introduced in 1964; dropped, 1974. Used value, $175 to $185.

Medalist Gold Model has the same specifications as standard Browning Medalist, except for gold wire inlays; better wood in grip. Introduced in 1963; dropped, 1974. Used value, $350 to $362.50.

Medalist Renaissance Model has the same specifications as standard Medalist, except for finely figured, hand-carved grips, chrome plating, full engraving. Introduced in 1964; dropped, 1974. Used value, $400 to $415.

CHARTER ARMS Undercover: double-action revolver; swing-out 5-rd. cylinder; .38 Special; 2", 3" barrels; with 2" barrel, 6¼" overall length; walnut standard or bulldog grips; fixed rear sight, serrated ramp front; blued or nickel finish. Introduced in 1965; still in production. Used values, blued, with regular grips, $113.50 to $117.50; bulldog grips, $117.50 to $122.50; nickel finish, $120 to $125.

CHARTER ARMS Undercoverette: double-action revolver; has same general specifications as Undercover, but with 6-rd. .32 S&W long chambering, 2" barrel only; designed for policewomen or ladies' purse; blued only. Introduced in 1969; still in production. Used value, $77.50 to $80.

CHARTER ARMS Pathfinder: double-action revolver; has the same general specifications as Undercover model, except in .22 LR only, 3" barrel only, adjustable rear sight, ramp front; blued finish only. Introduced in 1971; still in production. Used value, $88.50 to $92.50.

Dual Pathfinder has the same general specifications as standard Pathfinder model, except an extra cylinder is chambered for .22 WRM cartridge; hand-checkered walnut grips. Introduced in 1971; dropped, 1971. Used value, $90 to $97.50.

CHARTER ARMS Bulldog: double-action revolver; .44 Special only; 5-rd. swing-out cylinder; 3" barrel only; chrome-moly steel frame; wide trigger, hammer; square notch fixed rear sight, Patridge-type front; checkered walnut grips; blued only. Introduced in 1973; still in production. Used value, $115 to $120.

COLT

COLT New Service: double-action revolver; large frame, swing-out 6-rd. cylinder; .38 Special, .357 magnum, .38-40, .38-44, .44 Russian, .44 Special, .44-40, .45 Long Colt, .45 ACP, .450 Ely, .455 Ely, .476 Ely; 4″, 4½″, 5″, 5½″, 6″, 7½″ barrels. Special run in .45 Auto during WWI was designated as Model 1917 Revolver under government contract. Fixed open notch rear sight milled in top strap, fixed front; hand-checkered walnut grips; lanyard loop on most variations; blued, nickel finish. Introduced in 1897; dropped, 1943. Used values, 1917 military model, $120 to $125; .357 magnum, which was introduced in 1936, $230 to $235; other models, $210 to $220.

New Service Target Model has the same general specifications as standard New Service model, except for rear sight adjustable for windage, front adjustable for elevation; top strap is flat; action is hand finished; 5″, 6″, 7½″ barrels; .44 Special, .44 Russian, .45 Long Colt, .45 ACP, .450 Ely, .455 Ely, .476 Ely; blued finish, hand-checkered walnut grips. Introduced in 1900; dropped, 1940. Used value, $360 to $375.

COLT Model 1873: also known as Frontier, Peacemaker, Single-Action Army; single-action revolver; originally made in black powder calibers; .22 LR, long, short; .22 WRF, .32 Colt, .32-20, .32 S&W, .32 rimfire, .38 Colt, .38 S&W, .38 Special, .38-40, .357 magnum, .41 Colt, .44 rimfire, .44 Russian, .44-40, .44 Special, .45 Colt, .45 ACP, .450 Boxer, .450 Eley, .455 Eley, .476 Eley; currently made in .357 magnum, .45 Long Colt only; barrels, 3″, 4″ sans ejector, dropped; 4¾″, 5½″, 7½″ with ejector; overall length, 10¼″ with 4¾″ barrel; one-piece uncheckered walnut grip or checkered black rubber; standard model has fixed sights; target model has target sights, flat top strap; blued finish, case-hardened frame or nickel-plated. Those with serial numbers after 165,000 fire smokeless powder; black powder only should be used in lower numbered guns. Change was made in 1896, when spring catch was substituted for cylinder pin screw. Introduced in 1873; dropped, 1942. New production began in 1955 with serial number 1001SA. Used values for pre-WWII models, .22 Target Model, sans ejector, $1750 to $1820; other calibers, $780 to $825; Storekeeper Model, sans ejector, $725 to $750; .45 Artillery Model with 5½″ barrel, $650 to $680; .45 Cavalry Model, 7½″ barrel, $660 to $700; .44-40 Frontier Model, $500 to $520; standard model, $380 to $395. Post-1955 model, $165 to $195.

Colt .45 Buntline Special is same as post-1955 standard Model 1873, except for 12″ barrel; .45 Long Colt only; designed after guns made as presentation pieces by author Ned Buntline. Introduced in 1957; dropped, 1975. Used value, $350 to $400.

New Frontier Single-Action Army has the same specifications as Model 1873, except for flat-top frame, smooth walnut grips, 5½″, 7½″ barrel; .357 magnum, .45 Long Colt; adjustable target-type rear sight, ramp front. Introduced in 1961; still in production. Used value, $250 to $300.

New Frontier Buntline Special has the same specifications as New Frontier Single-Action Army model, except for 12″ barrel. Introduced in 1962; dropped, 1966. Used value, $300 to $325.

COLT Pocket Positive: double-action revolver, based upon New Pocket model; dropped in 1905; .32 Short Colt, .32 Long Colt, .32 Colt New Police (interchangeable with .32 S&W long, S&W short cartridges); 2½″, 3½″, 6″ barrels; overall length, 7½″ with 3½″ barrel; 6-rd. cylinder; rear sight groove milled in top strap, rounded front sight; positive lock feature; hard rubber grips; blued or nickel finish. Introduced in 1905; dropped, 1940. Used value, $125 to $150.

COLT Police Positive: double-action revolver; 6-shot swing-out cylinder; replaced New Police model; dropped in 1905; .22 LR, .22 WRF, .32 Short Colt, .32 Long Colt, .32 Colt New Police, .38 S&W; 2½", 4", 5", 6" barrels; overall length, 8½" with 4" barrel; fixed sights; checkered walnut, plastic, hard rubber grips; top of frame matted to reduce glare. Introduced in 1905; dropped, 1947. Used value, $100 to $125.

Police Positive Target model has same general specifications as standard Police Positive. Chambered for .32 Short Colt, .32 Long Colt, .32 New Police, .32 S&W short, .32 S&W long; .22 LR. Introduced in 1910; in 1932, cylinder was modified by countersinking heads for safety with high-velocity .22 ammo; those with noncountersunk chambers should be fired only with standard velocity .22 LR ammo. Has 6" barrel, overall length, 10½"; rear sight adjustable for windage, front for elevation; checkered walnut grips; blued; backstrap, hammer spur, trigger checkered. Introduced in 1905; dropped, 1940. Used value, $225 to $250.

Police Positive Special has generally the same specifications as standard Police Positive, except that frame is lengthened to accommodate a longer cylinder, permitting chambering of .38 Special, .32-20; also made in .32 and .38 Colt New Police; 4", 5", 6" barrels; with 4" barrel, overall length, 8¾"; blued or nickel. Introduced in 1907; dropped, 1973. Used values, blued, $130 to $135; nickel finish, $140 to $150.

COLT Officer's Model Target: double-action revolver; second issue replaced first issue, discontinued in 1908; .22 LR, .32 Police Positive, .38 special; 6" barrel in .22 LR and .32 PP, 4", 4½", 5", 6", 7½", in .38 Special; overall length, 11¼" with 6" barrel; hand-finished action; 6-rd. cylinder; hand-checkered walnut grips; adjustable rear target sight, blade front; blued finish. The .38 Special was introduced in 1908, .22 LR in 1930, .32 PP in 1932; .32 PP dropped in 1942; model dropped, 1949. Used values, .22 LR, $195 to $205; .32 PP, $180 to $192.50; .38 Special, $220 to $230.

Officers' Model Special is basically the same as second issue Officer's Model Target gun, but with heavier barrel, ramp front sight, Coltmaster adjustable rear sight, redesigned hammer; checkered plastic stocks; 6" barrel, .22 LR, .38 Special; blued finish. Introduced in 1949; dropped, 1953.

Used value, $155 to $160.

Officers' Model Match has the same general specifications as Officers' Model Special, which it replaced. Exceptions are target grips of checkered walnut, tapered heavy barrel, wide hammer spur. Introduced in 1953; dropped, 1970. Used value, $160 to $168.

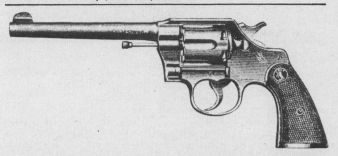

COLT Army Special: double-action revolver, .41 caliber frame; .32-20, .38 Special, .41 Colt; 6-rd. cylinder; barrel lengths, 4", 4½", 5", 6"; overall length, 9¼" with 4" barrel; hard rubber grips; fixed sights; blued or nickel finish. Not safe for modern .38 Special high velocity loads in guns chambered for that caliber. Introduced in 1908; dropped, 1928. Used value, $180 to $190.

COLT Model 1917 Army: double-action, swing-out 6-rd. cylinder; based upon New Service revolver to fire .45 ACP cartridge with steel half-moon clips; later, shoulder permitted firing ammo sans clip; .45 Auto Rim cartridge can be fired in conventional manner; 5½" barrel, 10.8" overall length; smooth walnut grips; fixed sights; dull finish. Should be checked for damage by corrosive primers before purchase. Introduced in 1917; dropped, 1925. Used value, $125 to $135.

COLT Camp Perry Model (First Issue): target single-shot; built on frame for Colt Officers' Model; .22 LR only, with countersunk chamber for high velocity ammo after 1930; 10" barrel, 13¾" overall length; checkered walnut grips; hand-finished action; adjustable target sights; trigger, backstrap, hammer spur checkered; blued finish, with top, back of frame stippled to reduce glare. Resembles Colt revolvers, but chamber, barrel are single unit, pivoting to side for loading and extraction when latch is released. Introduced in 1926; dropped, 1934. Used value, $415 to $425.

Camp Perry Model (Second Issue) has the same general specifications as first issue, except for 8" barrel, 12" overall length; shorter hammer fall. As only 440 were produced, it has some collector value over original version. Introduced in 1934; dropped, 1941. Used value, $500 to $520.

COLT Detective Special: swing-out cylinder; double-action revolver; 6-rd. capacity; .32 New Police, .38 New Police, .38 Special; 2'' barrel, 6¾'' overall length. Other specifications are identical to those of Police Positive Special, with rounded butt introduced in 1933. Introduced in 1926; dropped, 1972. Used values, .32 variations, $115 to $120; .38 Special, $135 to $145.

Detective Special (1972) is revamp of original with heavier barrel; integral protective shroud enclosing ejector rod; frame, side-plate, cylinder, barrel, internal parts are of high-tensile alloy steel; .38 Special only; walnut bulldog-type grips; rear sight is fixed; notch milled in top strap, serrated ramp front; checkered hammer spur; blued, nickel finish. Introduced in 1972; still in production. Used values, blued, $125 to $130; nickel finish, $135 to $140.

COLT Bankers Special: double-action revolver; swing-out 6-rd. cylinder essentially the same as pre-1972 Detective Special, but with shorter cylinder of Police Positive rather than that of Police Positive Special; .22 LR, with countersunk chambers after 1932, .38 New Police, .38 S&W; 2'' barrel, 6½'' overall length; a few produced with Fitzgerald cutaway trigger guard; checkered hammer spur, trigger; blued or nickel finish. Low production run on .22 gives it collector value. Introduced in 1926; dropped, 1940. Used values, .22, blued, $525 to $550; nickel finish, $560 to $575; .38 blued, $250 to $265; nickel, $270 to $300.

COLT Official Police: double-action revolver; .22 LR, .32-20, .38 Special, .41 Long Colt; 2'', 6'' heavy barrels in .38 Special only; 4'', 6'', in .22 LR only; 4'', 5'', 6'', in other calibers; checkered walnut grips, plastic grips on post-WWII models. Version made to military specs in WWII was called Commando model, had sand-blasted blue finish. Introduced in 1928 as replacement for Army Special; dropped, 1969. Used values, standard model, $145 to $155; military model, $100 to $112.

COLT Shooting Master: double-action revolver; swing-out 6-rd. cylinder; deluxe target version of New Service; .38 Special, .357 magnum, .45 ACP/Auto Rim; .45 Long Colt; 6'' barrel, 11¼'' overall length; checkered walnut grips, rounded butt; rear sight adjustable for windage, front for elevation; blued. Introduced in 1932; dropped, 1941. Used value, $430 to $450.

COLT Cobra: double-action revolver; 6-rd. swing-out cylinder; .32 New Police, .38 New Police, .38 Special; based upon design of pre-1972 Detective Special, except that frame, side plate are of Coltalloy, high-tensile aluminum alloy; 2'', 3'', 4'', 5'' barrels; Coltwood plastic grips; square butt was on early issues, replaced by round butt; optional hammer shroud; blue finish, matted on top, rear of frame. Old model shown. Introduced in 1951; dropped, 1972; 3'', 4'', 5'' barrel styles were special order. Used value, $140 to $150.

Cobra 1973 Model, like original version, has frame, side plate of alloy, steel cylinder, barrel; integral protective shroud enclosing ejector rod; other specifications are identical to 1972 Detective Special, with exception of heavier Cobra barrel, blued, nickel finish. Introduced in 1973; still in production. Used values, blued, $115 to $120; nickel finish, $125 to $130.

COLT Three-Fifty-Seven: double-action revolver; 6-rd. swing-out cylinder; .357 magnum only; 4'', 6'' barrels; 9¼'' overall length with 4'' barrel; available as service revolver or in target version; latter has wide hammer spur, target grips; checkered walnut grips; Accro rear sight, ramp front; blued finish. Introduced in 1953; dropped, 1961. Used values, standard model, $165 to $175; target model, $175 to $180.

COLT Agent: double-action revolver; 6-rd. swing-out cylinder; .38 Special only; 2" barrel, 6¾" overall length; minor variation of Cobra Model with shorter, stub grip for maximum concealment; Coltalloy frame, side plate; steel cylinder, barrel; no housing around ejector rod; square butt; blued finish. Old model shown. Introduced in 1955; dropped, 1972. Used value, $135 to $140.

Agent 1973 Model closely resembles 1973 Cobra Model, except for grip design, which extends just below bottom of frame; 2" barrel, overall length, 6-5/8"; checkered walnut grips; .38 Special only; blued finish. Introduced in 1973; still in production. Used value, $130 to $145.

COLT Frontier Scout: single-action revolver; scaled-down version of Model 1873 Army; .22 LR, long, short; interchangeable cylinder for .22 WRF magnum; 4½" barrel, 9-15/16" overall length; originally introduced with alloy frame; steel frame, blue finish introduced in 1959; fixed sights; plastic or wooden grips. Introduced in 1958; dropped, 1971. Used values, alloy frame, $65 to $70; blue finish, plastic grips, $75 to $80; nickel finish, wood grips, $95 to $100; interchangeable magnum cylinder, add $10 to $12.50.

Scout Buntline has same specifications as Frontier Scout with steel frame, wood grips, except for 9½" barrel. Introduced in 1959; dropped, 1971. Used value, $100 to $110.

COLT Diamondback: double-action revolver; swing-out 6-rd cylinder; scaled-down version of Python; .38 Special; .22 LR; 2½", 4" barrel; available in nickel, .22 with 4" only; vent rib barrel; target-type rear sight adjustable for windage, elevation; ramp front; full checkered walnut grips; integral rounded rib beneath barrel shrouds ejector rod; broad checkered hammer spur. Introduced in 1966; still in production. Used values, .38 nickel-plated with 4" barrel, $160 to $170; other models, $150 to $160.

COLT Python: double-action revolver, 6-rd. swing-out cylinder; .357 magnum only, but will handle .38 Special; made first appearance in 6" barrel, later with 2½", 4"; checkered walnut grips contoured for support for middle finger of shooting hand; vent rib barrel; ramp front sight, rear adjustable for windage, elevation; full-length ejector rod shroud; wide-spur hammer, grooved trigger; blued, nickel finish. Introduced in 1955; still in production. Used values, blued, $195 to $205; nickel finish, $225 to $240.

COLT Metropolitan MKIII: double-action revolver; swing-out 6-rd. cylinder; designed for urban law enforcement; 4" barrel, .38 Special only; fixed sights; choice of service, target grips of checkered walnut; blued finish, standard; nickel, optional. Introduced in 1969; dropped, 1972. Used values, blued, $95 to $105; nickel finish, $110 to $120.

COLT Official Police MKIII: double-action revolver; an old name, but a renewed design, incorporating coil mainsprings in place of leaf springs; .38 Special only; 4" barrel, 9-3/8" overall length; square-butt, checkered walnut grips; fixed rear sight notch milled in top strap, fixed ramp front; grooved front surface on trigger, checkered hammer spur. Introduced in 1969; dropped, 1975. Used value, $105 to $112.50.

COLT Lawman MKIII: similar to Official Police MKIII, but beefed up to handle .357 Magnum; will also chamber .38 Special; 2", 4" barrels; with 4" barrel, overall length, 9-3/8"; choice of square, round-butt walnut grips; fixed sights; blued, nickel finish. Introduced in 1969; still in production. Used values, blued, $110 to $115; nickel, $120 to $125.

COLT Trooper MKIII: double-action revolver; .357 magnum only; chambers .38 Special as well; 4", 6" barrels; with 4" barrel, overall length, 9½"; rear sight adjustable for windage/elevation, ramp front; shrouded ejector rod; check-

ered walnut target grips; target hammer, wide target trigger; blued, nickel finish. Introduced in 1969; still in production. Used values, blued, $145 to $152.50; nickel, $155 to $162.50.

COLT Trooper: double-action revolver; swing-out 6-rd. cylinder; has the same specifications as Officer's Match model, except for 4" barrel; .38 Special, .357 Magnum; ramp front sight; choice of standard hammer, service grips, wide hammer spur, target grips. Introduced in 1953; dropped, 1969. Used values, standard service model, $152.50 to $157.50; target model, $160 to $167.50.

COLT New Frontier .22: single-action revolver; scaled-down version of New Frontier .45; 6-rd. capacity; furnished with dual cylinders for .22 LR, .22 WMRF ammo; 4-3/8", 6", 7½" barrels; with 6" barrel, overall length, 11½"; target-type rear sight adjustable for windage, elevation, ramp front; checkered black plastic grips; flat top strap; color case-hardened frame, rest blued. Introduced in 1973; dropped, 1975. Used values, 7½" barrel, $100 to $110; others, $90 to $100.

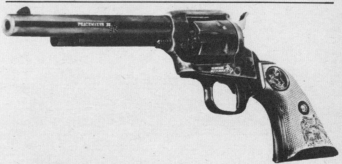

COLT Peacemaker .22: single-action revolver; scaled-down version of century-old Model 1873; 6-rd. capacity; furnished with dual cylinders for .22 LR, .22 WMRF ammo; rear sight notch milled into rounded top strap, fixed blade front; color case-hardened frame, rest blued; black plastic grips; 4-3/8", 6", 7½" barrels; overall length with 6" barrel, 11¼". Introduced in 1973; dropped, 1975. Used values, 7½" barrel, $100 to $110; others, $85 to $100.

Model 1911

COLT Pocket Model 25: advertised as vest pocket model; hammerless automatic; .25 ACP only; 2" barrel, 4½" overall length; 6-rd. magazine; hard rubber or checkered walnut grips; fixed sights, milled in top of slide; incorporates straight-line striker, rather than pivoting hammer, firing pin; slide-locking safety, grip safety; magazine disconnector added in 1917 at serial No. 141,000; blued, with case-hardened safety lever, grip safety, trigger, or nickel finished. Introduced in 1908; dropped, 1941. Used values, blued, $100 to $150; nickel finish, $175 to $200.

COLT Model 1911: automatic, also known as Government Model; .45 ACP only; 5" barrel, 8½" overall length; 7-rd. magazine; checkered walnut grips; fixed sights; military versions have Parkerized or other nonglare finish; commercial versions have blued finish with letter "C" preceding serial number. Introduced in 1911; produced from 1923 on as Model 1911A1. Used value, $175 to $200.

Model 1911A1 has the same specifications as Model 1911, except for a longer grip safety spur, checkered, arched mainspring housing; plastic grips. During WWI and WWII, other firms produced the Government model under Colt license; included were Remington UMC, Remington-Rand, Ithaca Gun Co., North American Arms of Canada (rare), Singer Sewing Machine (rare), Union Switch & Signal Co. and Springfield Armory. These government models bear imprint of licensee on slide. Model was redesigned and redesignated as Government Model MKIV Series 70 in 1970, approximately 850 1911A1 guns were equipped with split-collet barrel bushing — this adds to their collector value. Introduced in 1923. Used values, military model, $160 to $170; commercial model, $200 to $225; nickel finish, $225 to $250.

1911 Commerical Model

Model 1911A1

COLT Pocket Model 32 (Second Issue): replaced first issue, dropped, 1911. Automatic; .32 ACP only; 4" barrel, 7" overall length; 8-rd. magazine; fixed sights; concealed hammer beneath slide; slide lock, grip safeties; blued finish; hard rubber grips. Introduced in 1911; dropped, 1926. Used value, $100 to $135.

Model 32 (Third Issue) has same specifications as second issue, except for 3¾" barrel; overall length, 6¾"; machine-checkered walnut grips. On all guns above serial No. 468097, safety disconnector prevents firing cartridge in

chamber if magazine is removed. Introduced in 1926; dropped, 1945. Used value, $100 to $125.

COLT Pocket Model 380 (Second Issue): replaced first issue, dropped 1911; automatic; .380 ACP only; 4" barrel, 7" overall length; has the same general specifications as Model 32 (Second Issue), except for chambering, 7-rd. magazine capacity. Introduced in 1911; dropped, 1926. Used value, $125 to $150.

Model 380 (Third Issue) has same specifications as second issue Model 380, except for 3¾" barrel; overall length, 6¾"; machine-checkered walnut grips. Safety disconnector installed on guns with serial numbers above 92,894. Introduced in 1926; dropped, 1945. Used value, $125 to $150.

Woodsman 1st Issue

Woodsman 3rd Issue

COLT Woodsman (First Issue): target automatic; .22 LR standard velocity; 6½" barrel, 10½" overall length; 10-rd. magazine; prior to 1927, designated as .22 Target Model. Designation, "The Woodsman," added after serial No. 34,000; adjustable sights, checkered walnut grips. Introduced in 1915; dropped, 1932. Used value, $175 to $185.

Woodsman Second Issue has basically the same specifications as first issue, except for substitution of heat-treated mainspring housing for use with high velocity cartridges, heavier barrel. Introduced in 1932; dropped, 1948. Used value, $200 to $225.

Woodsman Third Issue has the same basic specifications as earlier Woodsman issues, except for longer grip, larger thumb safety, slide stop, magazine disconnector, thumb rest, plastic or walnut grips, magazine catch on left side; click adjustable rear sight, ramp front. Introduced in 1948; dropped, 1977. Used value, $110 to $120.

COLT Super 38: identical to Government Model or 1911A1 automatic, except for capacity of magazine, caliber; .38 Colt Super; 9-rd. magazine; fixed sights. Introduced in 1928; still in production as Government Model MKIV/Series 70. Used value, $200 to $225. From 1935 to 1941 a few "Super Match" Super .38s were made with adjustable target sights. Used value, $375 to $400.

COLT National Match: target automatic; .45 ACP; has same specifications as Government Model .45 automatic, except for adjustable rear sight, ramp front; match-grade barrel, hand-honed action. Also available with fixed sights. Introduced in 1932; still in production. Used values, fixed sights, $225 to $240; target sights, $295 to $320.

Woodsman Targetsman

COLT Woodsman Sport Model (First Issue): has the same general specifications as second issue Woodsman Target model, except for adjustable rear sight, adjustable or fixed front; 4½" barrel, 8½" overall length; fires standard or high velocity .22 LR ammo. Introduced in 1933; dropped, 1948.

Used value, $210 to $225.

Woodsman Sport Model (Second Issue) has the same specifications as the third-issue Woodsman Target model, except for 4½" barrel, overall length of 9"; plastic grips. Introduced in 1948; dropped, 1976. Used value, $110 to $135.

Woodsman Targetsman has generally the same specifications as third-issue Woodsman Target model, except for no automatic slide stop, less expensive adjustable rear sight. Introduced in 1969; dropped, 1976. Used value, $100 to $125.

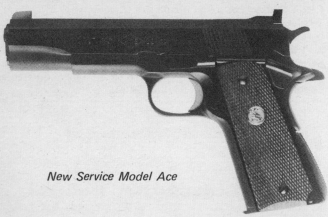

New Service Model Ace

COLT Ace: automatic; built on same frame as Government Model .45 automatic; .22 LR only, standard or high velocity; 4¾" barrel, 8¼" overall length; adjustable rear sight, fixed front; target barrel, hand-honed action. Introduced in 1930; dropped, 1947. Used value, $320 to $335.

Service Model Ace has specifications identical to those of National Match Model 45 automatic, except for magazine capacity, caliber; .22 LR, standard or high velocity; 10-rd. magazine; specially designed chamber increases recoil four-fold to approximate that of .45 auto. Introduced in 1935; dropped, 1945; reintroduced, 1978. Collector interest affects value. Used value, $425 to $450.

Match Target 1st Issue

COLT Match Target (First Issue): target automatic; .22 LR only; 6½" flat-sided barrel, 11" overall length; adjustable rear sight, blade front; checkered walnut one-piece extension grips; blued; same basic design as earlier Woodsman models. Introduced in 1938; dropped, 1942. Used value, $135 to $150.

Match Target (Second Issue) has the same general specifications as third-issue Target Woodsman. Flat-sided 6" heavy barrel, 10½" overall length; .22 LR, standard or high velocity ammo; checkered walnut or plastic grips; click adjustable rear sight, ramp front; blued. Introduced in 1948; dropped, 1976. Used value, $125 to $150.

Match Target 4½ has the same specifications as second-issue Match Target, except for 4½" barrel; measures 9" overall. Introduced in 1950; dropped, 1976. Used value, $125 to $150.

COLT Challenger Huntsman: automatic; .22 LR only; has same basic specifications of third-issue Target Woodsman, with fewer features; slide does not stay open after last shot; fixed sights; 4½", 5" barrels; overall length, 9" with 4½" barrel; checkered plastic grips; blued finish. Challenger introduced in 1950; dropped, 1955. Used value, $65 to $70.

Huntsman has exactly the same specifications as Challenger model, with name change for marketing purposes. Introduced in 1955; dropped, 1976. Used value, $70 to $75.

COLT Commander: lightweight automatic; .45 ACP; .38 Super auto; 9mm Luger; 4¼" barrel, 8" overall length; 7-rd. magazine for .45, 9 rds. for other calibers; basic design of Government Model auto, but is of lightweight alloy, reducing weight; early versions had plastic checkered grips, present production have checkered walnut; fixed sights; rounded hammer spur; blued, nickel finish. Introduced in 1950; still in production. Used values, blued, $135 to $150; nickel, $145 to $175.

COLT Junior: pocket model automatic; .22 short, .25 ACP; 2¼" barrel; overall length, 4-3/8"; 6-rd. magazine; exposed hammer with round spur; checkered walnut stocks; fixed sights; blued. Initially produced in Spain by Astra, with early versions having Spanish markings as well as Colt identity; parts were assembled in U.S., sans Spanish identification after GCA '68 import ban. Introduced in 1958; dropped, 1973. Used values; Spanish versions, $95 to $105; U.S.-made versions, $115 to $120.

Gold Cup 45, except it is chambered only for .38 Special mid-range ammo. Introduced in 1960; dropped, 1974. Used value, $275 to $300.

COLT Gold Cup 45: National Match grade automatic; .45 ACP only; same general specifications as Government Model .45 auto; has match grade barrel, bushing; long, wide trigger; adjustable trigger stop; flat mainspring housing; adjustable rear sight, target front; hand-fitted slide; wider ejection port; checkered walnut grips. Introduced in 1957; still in production. Used value, $225 to $250.

Gold Cup 38 Special has same general specifications as

COLT MK IV/Series '70 45 Govt. Model: .45 ACP, 9mm Luger, .38 Super; is identical to .38 Super and previous .45 Government Model, except for improved collet-type barrel bushing and reverse taper barrel to improve accuracy. Introduced in 1970, still in production. Used value, $135 to $150.

SERIAL NUMBERS OF COLT SINGLE ACTION ARMY AND BISLEY MODEL REVOLVERS

BY YEAR OF PRODUCTION

YEAR	STARTING NUMBER	YEAR	STARTING NUMBER	YEAR	STARTING NUMBER
1873	1	1902	220,001	1931	354,101
1874	201	1903	238,001	1932	354,501
1875	15,001	1904	250,001	1933	354,801
1876	22,001	1905	261,001	1934	355,001
1877	33,001	1906	273,001	1935	355,201
1878	41,001	1907	288,001	1936	355,301
1879	49,001	1908	304,001	1937	355,401
1880	53,001	1909	308,001	1938	356,101
1881	62,001	1910	312,001	1939	356,601
1882	73,001	1911	316,001	1940	357,001*
1883	85,001	1912	321,001	*Pre-war production ends at about No. 357,869.	
1884	102,001	1913	325,001		
1885	114,001	1914	328,001		
1886	117,001	1915	329,501	1956	0001SA
1887	119,001	1916	332,001	1957	8800SA
1888	125,001	1917	335,001	1958	18500SA
1889	128,001	1918	337,001	1959	23400SA
1890	130,001	1919	337,201	1960	28500SA
1891	136,001	1920	338,001	1961	33600SA
1892	144,001	1921	341,001	1962	35650SA
1893	149,001	1922	343,001	1963	37300SA
1894	154,001	1923	344,501	1964	38500SA
1895	159,001	1924	346,401	1965	40000SA
1896	163,001	1925	347,301	1966	41500SA
1897	168,001	1926	348,201	1967	43800SA
1898	175,001	1927	349,801	1968	46300SA
1899	182,001	1928	351,301	1969	49000SA
1900	192,001	1929	352,401	1970	52600SA
1901	203,001	1930	353,801	1971	59000SA

Hämmerli

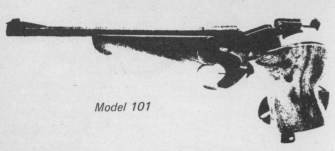

Model 101

HAMMERLI Model 100 Free Pistol: single-shot, slow-fire target model; .22 LR only; 11½" barrel; adjustable set trigger; micrometer rear sight, interchangeable post or bead front; European walnut grips, forearm; blued. Introduced in 1947; redesignated as Model 101 in 1960; dropped, 1962. Used value, $400 to $425.

HAMMERLI Model 110 Free Pistol: single-shot, slow-fire target model. Has exactly the same specifications as Model 100, except for highly polished, blued barrel. Introduced in 1957; redesignated as Model 102 in 1960; dropped, 1962. Used value, $440 to $460.

Model 103 Showing Custom Variations

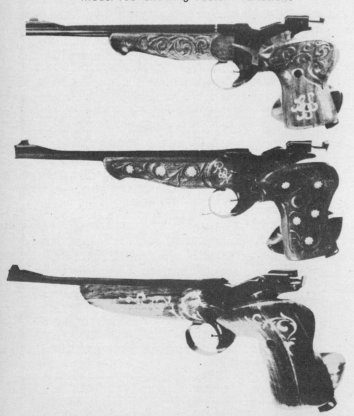

HAMMERLI Model 103 Free Pistol: single-shot, slow-fire target model. Has the same specifications as Model 102,

except for deluxe carving of wood. Introduced in 1960; dropped, 1963. Used values, $525 to $550; with inlaid ivory carvings, $565 to $575.

Model 200 Olympia

HAMMERLI WALTHER Model 200 Olympia: automatic; also advertised as Quickfire model; .22 LR, short; 7½" barrel; 8-rd. magazine; muzzle brake; adjustable barrel weights; walnut thumbrest grip; micrometer rear sight; ramp front; blued. Based on 1936 Olympia with some parts interchangeable. Introduced in 1950. In 1957, muzzle brake was redesigned. Cartridges are not interchangeable. Dropped, 1963. Used value, $210 to $230.

Model 201 has the same specifications as Model 200, except for standard adjustable sights and adjustable custom grip. Introduced in 1950; dropped, 1957. Used value, $225 to $240.

Model 202 has the same specifications as Model 201, except for 9½" barrel. Introduced in 1957; dropped, 1959. Used value, $225 to $250.

Model 203, called the American Model, has the same general specifications as Model 201, except for micrometer rear sight, slide stop. Introduced in 1957; dropped, 1959. Used value, $240 to $250.

Model 204 is the same as the Model 203, except it is equipped with the standard thumbrest grips. Introduced in 1947; dropped, 1963. Used value, $195 to $210.

Model 205 has the same specifications as Model 204, except for hand-checkered French walnut grip; detachable muzzle brake. Introduced in 1960; dropped, 1964. Used value, $250 to $270.

HAMMERLI International Model 206: automatic; rapid-fire target model; .22 LR and short; 7-1/16" barrel; 8-rd. magazine; muzzle brake; slide stop; checkered walnut thumbrest grips; adjustable trigger, blued. Cartridges not interchangeable. Introduced in 1964; dropped, 1967. Used value, $210 to $225.

Model 207

International Model 207 has exactly the same specifications as Model 206, except for uncheckered walnut grips, with adjustable grip plates. Introduced in 1964; dropped, 1969. Used value, $230 to $245.

Hammerli Model 208 has the same specifications as Model 207, except that barrel is shortened to 6", no muzzle brake, adjustable trigger pull; .22 LR only. Introduced in 1968; still in production. Used value, $400 to $450.

HAMMERLI International Model 211: automatic; .22 LR only; 5-9/10" barrel, 10" overall length; micrometer bridged rear sight, post ramp front; externally adjustable trigger with backlash stop; hand-checkered European walnut thumbrest grips; blued. Introduced in 1973; still in production. Used value, $450 to $500.

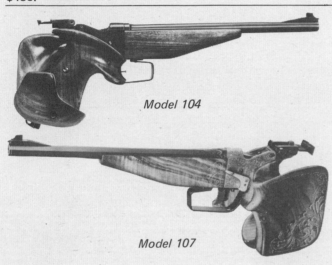

Model 104

Model 107

Model 120 Standard

HAMMERLI Match Pistol Model 104: single-shot free pistol; .22 LR only; 11½" barrel; micrometer rear sight; post front; uncheckered selected walnut grips with trigger-finger ramp, adjustable hand plate, custom finish; blued. Introduced in 1963; dropped, 1965. Used value, $230 to $240.

Match Pistol Model 105 has exactly the same specifications as Model 104, except for octagonal barrel, highly polished metal, French walnut grip plates. Introduced in 1963; dropped, 1965. Used value, $285 to $300.

Model 106 has the same general specifications as Model 104, but with matte blue finish on barrel to reduce glare; other minor changes. Replaced Model 106. Introduced in 1966; dropped, 1972. Used value, $290 to $300.

Model 107 has the same specifications as Model 105, which it replaced. Has matte blue finish on barrel to reduce glare, other minor improvements. Introduced in 1966; dropped, 1972. Used value, $380 to $400.

HAMMERLI International Model 210: automatic; .22 short only; has the same general design as Model 207, but with lightweight bolt to reduce the recoil movement; six gas-escape ports in rear of barrel; barrel vents, adjustable muzzle brake to reduce muzzle jump, adjustable grip plates. Introduced in 1967; dropped, 1970. Used value, $240 to $250.

Model 209 has exactly the same specifications as Model 210, except for nonadjustable grips. Introduced in 1967; dropped, 1970. Used value, $220 to $225.

HAMMERLI Model 120: single-shot free pistol; .22 LR only; 10" barrel; 14¾" overall length; internally adjustable trigger for two-stage, single-stage pull; micrometer rear sight; post front; hand-checkered walnut target grips; blued. Introduced in 1972; still in production. Redesignated as Model 120-1 in 1973. Used value, $160 to $170.

Model 120-2 has the same general specifications as Model 120-1, except for special contoured walnut hand rest. Both sights can be moved forward or rearward; blued. Introduced in 1973; still in production. Used value, $175 to $185.

Model 120 heavy barrel model was designed for sale in Great Britain to conform with existing laws governing sporting handgun specs. It has the same specifications as Model 120-1, except for 5¾" barrel. Introduced in 1973; still in production. Used values, with standard grips, $170 to $180; with adjustable grips, $195 to $210.

HAMMERLI Model 150: single-shot free pistol; .22 LR only; 11-3/8" barrel; 15-3/8" overall length; moveable front sight on collar, micrometer rear; Martini-type action; straight-line firing pin, no hammer; adjustable set trigger; uncheckered adjustable palm-shelf grip. Introduced in 1973; still in production. Used value, $425 to $450.

Harrington & Richardson

HARRINGTON & RICHARDSON American: double-action solid-frame revolver; .32 S&W Long, .38 S&W; 2½", 4½", 6" barrels; 6-rd. cylinder in .32, 5-rd. in .38; fixed sights, hard rubber grips; blued, nickel finish. Introduced in 1883; dropped during WWII. Used value, $35 to $45.

HARRINGTON & RICHARDSON Automatic Ejecting Model: double-action hinged-frame revolver; .32 S&W Long, .38 S&W; 3¼", 4", 5", 6" barrels; 6-rd. cylinder in .32, 5-rd. in .38; fixed sights; hard rubber grips; blued, nickel finish. Introduced in 1891; dropped, 1941. Used value, $45 to $50.

HARRINGTON & RICHARDSON Young America: double-action solid-frame revolver; .22 LR, .32 S&W Short; 2" 4½", 6" barrels; 7-rd. cylinder in .22, 5-rd, in .32; fixed sights, hard rubber grips; blued, nickel finish. Introduced in 1885; dropped during WWII. Used value, $35 to $45.

HARRINGTON & RICHARDSON Premier Model: double-action hinged-frame revolver; .22 LR, .32 S&W Short; 2", 3", 4", 5", 6" barrels; 7-rd. cylinder in .22, 5-rd. in .32; fixed sights; hard rubber grips; blued, nickel finish. Introduced in 1895; dropped, 1941. Used value, $40 to $50.

HARRINGTON & RICHARDSON Vest Pocket Model: double-action solid-frame revolver; .22 long, .32 S&W Short; 1-1/8" barrel; spurless hammer; 7-rd. cylinder in .22, 5-rd. in .32; no sights except for milled slot in top frame; hard rubber grips; blued, nickel finish. Introduced in 1891; dropped during WWII. Used value, $35 to $45.

HARRINGTON & RICHARDSON Model 40 Hammerless: double-action small hinged-frame revolver; .22 LR, .32 S&W Short; 2", 3", 4", 5", 6" barrels; 7-rd. cylinder in 22, 5-rd. in .32; fixed sights; hard rubber stocks; blued, nickel finish. Also listed during late production as Model 45. Introduced in 1899; dropped, 1941. Used value, $50 to $60.

HARRINGTON & RICHARDSON Model 50 Hammerless: double-action large hinged-frame revolver; .32 S&W Long, .38 S&W; 3¼", 4", 5", 6" barrels; 6-rd. cylinder in .32, 5-rd. in .38; fixed sights; hard rubber grips; blued, nickel finish. Also listed in later production as Model 55. Introduced in 1899; dropped, 1941. Used value, $60 to $65.

HARRINGTON & RICHARDSON Trapper Model: double-action solid-frame revolver; .22 LR only; 6" octagonal barrel; 7-rd. cylinder; fixed sights; checkered walnut stocks; blued. Introduced in 1924; dropped during WWII. Used value, $45 to $55.

HARRINGTON & RICHARDSON Model 4: double-action solid-frame revolver; .32 S&W Long, .38 S&W; 2½", 4½", 6" barrels; 6-rd. cylinder for .32, 5-rd. for .38; fixed sights, hard rubber grips; blued, nickel finish. Introduced in 1905; dropped, 1941. Used value, $35 to $45.

HARRINGTON & RICHARDSON .22 Special: double-action heavy hinged-frame revolver; .22 LR, .22 WRF; 6" barrel, 9-rd. cylinder; fixed rear sight; gold-plated front; checkered walnut grips; blued. Originally introduced as Model 944; later version with recessed cylinder for high speed ammo was listed as Model 945. Introduced in 1925; dropped, 1941. Used value, $60 to $70.

HARRINGTON & RICHARDSON Model 5: double-action solid-frame revolver; .32 S&W Short only; 2½", 4½", 6" barrels; 5-rd. cylinder; fixed sights; hard rubber grips; blued nickel finish. Introduced in 1905; dropped, 1939. Used value, $35 to $45.

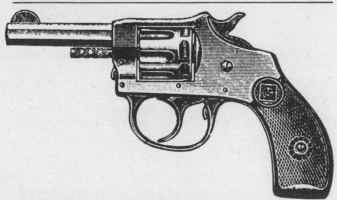

HARRINGTON & RICHARDSON Model 766: double-action target revolver; hinged frame; .22 LR, .22 WRF; 6" barrel; 7-rd. cylinder; fixed sights; checkered walnut grips; blued. Introduced in 1926; dropped, 1936. Used value, $60 to $70.

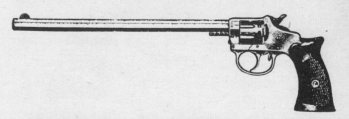

HARRINGTON & RICHARDSON Model 6: double-action solid-frame revolver; .22 LR only; 2½", 4½", 6" barrels; 7-rd. cylinder; fixed sights; hard rubber grips; blued, nickel finish. Introduced in 1906; dropped, 1941. Used value, $35 to $45.

HARRINGTON & RICHARDSON Hunter Model: double-action solid-frame revolver; .22 LR only; 10" octagon barrel; 9-rd. cylinder; fixed sights; checkered walnut grips; blued. Introduced in 1926; dropped, 1941. Used value, $60 to $70.

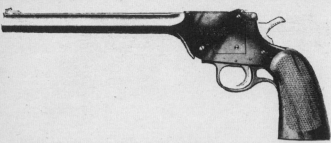

HARRINGTON & RICHARDSON USRA Model: single-shot hinged-frame target pistol; .22 LR only; 7", 8", 10" barrels; adjustable target sights; checkered walnut grips; blued. Introduced in 1928; dropped, 1943. Used value, $195 to $210.

HARRINGTON & RICHARDSON Model 922: double-action solid-frame revolver; .22 LR only; 4", 6", 10" barrels; 9-rd. cylinder; fixed sights; checkered walnut or Tenite grips; blued or chrome finish. Introduced in 1929. Early production had octagon 10" barrel, later dropped. Still in production in 4", 6" lengths. Used value, $45 to $50.

Model 922 Bantamweight has the same specifications as standard model, except for 2½" barrel, rounded butt. Introduced in 1951; still in production. Used value, $45 to $50.

HARRINGTON & RICHARDSON Expert: has the same general specifications as the .22 Special Model 945, except for being produced with 10" barrel. Listed as Model 955. Introduced in 1929; dropped, 1941. Used value, $60 to $70.

HARRINGTON & RICHARDSON No. 199: advertised as Sportsman Model; single-action hinged-frame revolver; .22 LR only; 6" barrel, 11" overall length; 9-rd. cylinder; adjustable target sights; checkered walnut grips; blued. Introduced in 1933; dropped, 1951. Used value, $72.50 to $77.50.

HARRINGTON & RICHARDSON No. 999: double-action hinged-frame revolver; .22 LR, .22 WRF. Has the same general specifications as No. 199. Current style is in .22 LR only, has vent-rib barrel, redesigned hammer. Introduced in 1936; still in production. Used value, $70 to $75.

HARRINGTON & RICHARDSON New Defender: also listed as Model 299; double-action hinged-frame revolver; .22 LR only; 2" barrel; 6¼" overall length; has the same basic specifications, except for barrel length, as Model 999; adjustable sights; checkered walnut grips, round butt; blued. Introduced in 1936; dropped, 1941. Used value, $92.50 to $100.

HARRINGTON & RICHARDSON Bobby Model: also listed as Model 15; double-action hinged-frame revolver; .32 S&W Long, .38 S&W; 4" barrel; 9" overall length; 6-rd. cylinder in .32, 5-rd. in .38; fixed sights; checkered walnut grips; blued. Designed for use by London police during WWII. Introduced in 1941; dropped, 1943. Used value, $70 to $75.

HARRINGTON & RICHARDSON Guardsman: double-action solid-frame revolver; .32 S&W Long only; 2½", 4" barrels; 6-rd. cylinder; fixed sights; checkered Tenite grips; blued, chrome finish. Introduced in 1946; dropped, 1957. Used values, blued, $37.50 to $42.50; chrome finish, $45 to $50.

HARRINGTON & RICHARDSON Model 929: advertised as Sidekick Model; double-action revolver; solid-frame; swing-out cylinder; .22 LR, short; 2½", 4", 6" barrels; 9-rd. cylinder; fixed sights; checkered plastic grips; blued. Introduced in 1956; still in production. Used value, $45 to $50.

HARRINGTON & RICHARDSON Model 939: advertised as Ultra Sidekick Model; double-action revolver; solid-frame; swing-out 9-rd. cylinder; 6" barrel, with vent rib; adjustable rear sight, ramp front; checkered walnut grips; blued. Introduced in 1958; still in production. Used value, $55 to $65.

HARRINGTON & RICHARDSON Model 949: advertised as Forty-Niner Model; double-action revolver; solid-frame; side-loading, ejection; 9-rd. cylinder; .22 LR, long, short; 5½" barrel; adjustable rear sight, blade front; one-piece plain walnut grip; blued, nickel finish. Introduced in 1960; still in production. Used value, $45 to $55.

Model 622

HARRINGTON & RICHARDSON Model 622: double-action revolver; solid-frame; .22 LR, long, short; 2½", 4", 6" barrels; 6-rd. cylinder; fixed sights; checkered plastic grips; blued. Introduced in 1957, 6" barrel dropped. Others still in production. Used value, $35 to $40.

Model 623 has exactly the same specifications as Model 622, except for chrome finish. Introduced in 1957; dropped, 1963. Used value, $40 to $45.

Model 900

HARRINGTON & RICHARDSON Model 900: double-action revolver; solid-frame; snap-out, 9-rd. cylinder; .22 LR, long, short; 2½", 4", 6" barrels; fixed sights; high impact plastic grips; blued. Introduced in 1962; dropped, 1973. Used value, $40 to $50.

Model 901 has the same specifications as Model 900, except for chrome finish, white plastic grips. Introduced in 1962; dropped, 1963. Used value, $45 to $55.

Model 732

HARRINGTON & RICHARDSON Model 732: double-action revolver; solid-frame; 6-rd. swing-out cylinder; .32 S&W, .32 S&W Long; 2½", 4" barrels; rear sight adjustable for windage on 4" model, fixed on shorter barrel; ramp front; plastic checkered grips; blued. Introduced in 1958; still in production. Used value, $35 to $40.

Model 733 has the same specifications as Model 732, except for nickel finish. Used value, $40 to $45.

HARRINGTON & RICHARDSON Model 925: advertised as the Defender Model; originally introduced as Model 25. Double-action revolver; hinged-frame; .38 S&W only; 5-rd. cylinder; 2½" barrel; adjustable rear sight, fixed front; one-piece smooth plastic grip; blued. Introduced in 1964; still in production. Used value, $55 to $65.

HIGH STANDARD

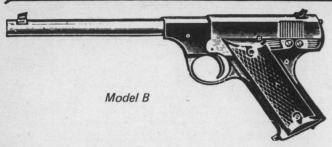

Model B

HI-STANDARD Model B: automatic; hammerless; .22 LR only; 4¾", 6¾" barrels; 10¾" overall length, with 6¾" barrel; 10-rd. magazine; fixed sights; checkered hard rubber grips, blued. Introduced in 1932; dropped, 1942. Used value, $100 to $125.

Model S-B has the same specifications as Model B, except with 5¾" barrel only; smoothbore for .22 shot cartridge. Introduced in 1939; dropped, 1940. Used value, $200 to $250.

Model H-B has the same general specifications as the Model B, except there is no thumb safety; has visible hammer. Introduced in 1940; dropped, 1942. Used value, $150 to $175.

HI-STANDARD Model C: automatic; hammerless; .22 short only. Other specifications are identical to those of Model B Hi-Standard auto. Introduced in 1936; dropped, 1942. Used value, $90 to $100.

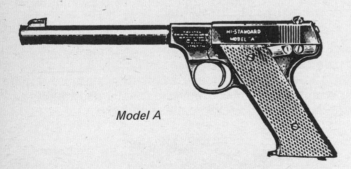

Model A

HI-STANDARD Model A: automatic; hammerless; .22 LR only; 4½", 6¾" barrel; 11½" overall length, with 6¾" barrel; adjustable target-type sights; checkered walnut grips; blued. Actually an updated version of Model B. Introduced in 1938; dropped, 1942. Used value, $100 to $110.

Model H-A has the same specifications as the Model A, but has visible hammer, sans thumb safety. Introduced in 1940; dropped, 1942. Used value, $110 to $125.

HI-STANDARD Model D: automatic; hammerless; .22 LR only; has the same specifications as Model A, except with heavy barrel. Introduced in 1938; dropped, 1942. Used value, $110 to $115.

Model H-D has the same specifications as Model D, except for visible hammer, sans thumb safety. Introduced in 1940; dropped in 1942. Used value, $125 to $150.

Model H-DM has the same general specifications as Model H-D, but with thumb safety added. Introduced in 1946; dropped, 1951. Used value, $115 to $130.

Model E

HI-STANDARD Model E: automatic; hammerless; .22 LR only; has same general specifications as Model A, except for thumb rest grips, heavy barrel. Introduced in 1937; dropped, 1942. Used value, $135 to $145.

Model H-E has the same specifications as Model E, except for visible hammer, sans thumb safety. Introduced in 1940; dropped, 1942. Used value, $160 to $180.

HI-STANDARD Model G-380: automatic; takedown; .380 Auto only; 5" barrel; visible hammer; thumb safety; fixed sights; checkered plastic grips; blued. Introduced in 1947; dropped, 1950. Used value, $140 to $160.

Model G-B

HI-STANDARD Model G-B: automatic; hammerless; takedown; .22 LR only; interchangeable barrels of 4½", 6¾"; with 6¾" barrel, overall length, 10¾"; fixed sights; checkered plastic grips; blued. Introduced in 1949; dropped, 1951. Used values, with two barrels. $105 to $107.50; one barrel, $87.50 to $90.

Model G-D has same general specifications as Model G-B, including interchangeable barrels; except for target sights, checkered walnut grips. Introduced in 1949; dropped, 1951. Used values, with two barrels, $125 to $130; one barrel, $110 to $115.

Model G-E has same general specifications as Model G-D,

except for thumb-rest walnut grips, heavy barrels. Introduced in 1949; dropped, 1951. Used values, with both barrels, $160 to $165; one barrel, $140 to $150.

First Model Olympic

Supermatic Citation

HI-STANDARD Olympic (First Model): automatic hammerless; .22 short; light alloy slide; other specifications are same as Model G-E, including interchangeable barrels. Introduced in 1950; dropped, 1951. Used values, with both barrels, $225 to $235; one barrel, $205 to $225.

Olympic (Second Model) is hammerless, takedown automatic; .22 short only; interchangeable 4½", 6¾" barrels; with 6¾" barrel, 11½" overall length; 10-rd. magazine; target sights; adjustable barrel weights; alloy slide; checkered plastic thumb-rest grips; blued. Introduced in 1951; dropped, 1958. Used values, with both barrels, $125 to $140; one barrel, $110 to $115.

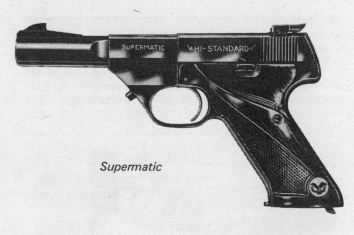

Supermatic

Supermatic Tournament

HI-STANDARD Supermatic: automatic; hammerless; takedown; .22 LR only; 4½", 6¾" interchangeable barrels; 10-rd. magazine; late models have recoil stabilizer on longer barrel; 11½" overall length, with 6¾" barrel; 2, 3-oz. adjustable barrel weights; target sights; checkered plastic thumbrest grips; blued. Introduced in 1951; dropped, 1958. Used values, with both barrels, $120 to $130; one barrel, $110 to $120.

Supermatic Tournament model is .22 LR only, with same specifications of standard Supermatic, except for interchangeable 5½" bull barrel, and 6¾" barrel; barrels drilled, notched for stabilizer, weights; click adjustable rear sight, undercut ramp front; checkered walnut grips; blued finish. Introduced in 1958; dropped, 1963. Used values, both barrels, $120 to $130; one barrel, $110 to $120.

Supermatic Citation has the same general specifications as Tournament model, except for choice of 5½" bull barrel, 6¾", 8", 10" tapered barrels, with stabilizer, 2 removable weights; adjustable trigger pull; click adjustable rear sight; ramp front; checkered laminated wood grips; bull barrel model has checkered walnut grips with thumb rest. Introduced in 1958; dropped, 1966. Used values, tapered barrel, $120 to $125; bull barrel, $120 to $130.

Supermatic Standard Citation is a simplified version of original Citation, but with 5½" bull barrel only; 10" overall length; over-travel trigger adjustment; rebounding firing pin; click adjustable square notch rear sight, undercut ramp front; checkered walnut grips with or without thumb rest, right or left-hand. Dropped, 1977. Used value, $120 to $130.

Supermatic Citation Military model has same specs as Standard Citation model, except for military-style grip, positive magazine latch, stippled front, backstraps; 5½" bull barrel or 7¾" fluted barrel. Still in production. Used value, $120 to $130.

Supermatic Trophy has the same specifications as original Citation model, except for choice of 5½" bull barrel, 7¼" fluted style; extra magazine; high-lustre blue finish. Introduced in 1963; dropped, 1966. Used value, $135 to $140.

Supermatic Trophy Military model has same general specifications as standard Trophy model, except that grip duplicates feel of Government Model .45; trigger adjustable for pull, over-travel; stippled front, backstrap; checkered walnut grips with or without thumb rest; right or left-hand; frame-mounted click adjustable rear sight; undercut ramp front. Still in production. Used value, $140 to $145.

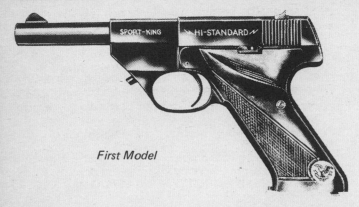

First Model

HI-STANDARD Sport-King (First Model): automatic; hammerless; .22 LR only; 4½", 6¾" interchangeable barrels; with 6¾" barrel, 11½" overall length; 10-rd. magazine; fixed sights; checkered thumb-rest plastic grips; blued. Introduced in 1951; dropped, 1958. Used values, with both barrels, $90 to $95; one barrel, $70 to $80.

Lightweight Sport-King has the same specifications as the standard Sport-King model, except frame is of forged aluminum alloy. Introduced in 1954; dropped, 1965. Used values, both barrels, $90 to $95; one barrel, $70 to $80.

Sport-King (Second Model) is all-steel, .22 LR; minor interior design changes from first model Sport-King, interchangeable barrel retained. Introduced in 1958; still in production. Used values, both barrels, $70 to $75; one barrel, $60 to $66.

HI-STANDARD Dura-Matic: automatic; hammerless takedown; .22 LR only; 4½", 6½" interchangeable barrels; with 6½" barrel, overall length, 10-7/8"; usually sold with one barrel only; fixed sights; checkered plastic grips; blued. Introduced in 1955; dropped, 1969. Used value, $60 to $70.

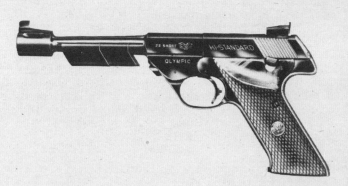

HI-STANDARD Flight-King (First Model): automatic; hammerless; .22 short only; other specifications are identical to those of Sport-King model, except for aluminum alloy frame, slide. Introduced in 1953; dropped, 1958. Used values, with both barrels, $90 to $100; one barrel, $75 to $80.

Flight-King (Second Model) has the same general specifications as first-model Flight-King, except for all-steel construction; .22 LR only. Introduced in 1958; dropped, 1966. Used values, with both barrels, $75 to $80; one barrel, $65 to $70.

HI-STANDARD Olympic ISU: target automatic; hammerless; .22 short only; 6¾" barrel; (5½" bull, 8" tapered; dropped, 1964) 10-rd. magazine; detachable weights, integral stabilizer; trigger adjustable for pull, over-travel; click adjustable square notch rear sight; undercut ramp front; checkered walnut grips with or without thumb rest; left, right-hand; blued finish. Meets International Shooting Union regulations. Introduced in 1958; dropped, 1977. Used value, $155 to $160.

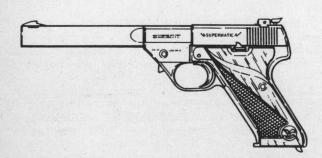

HI-STANDARD Field-King: automatic; hammerless .22 LR only; has the same general specifications as Sport-King model, but with target sights, heavier 6¾" barrel; late model with recoil stabilizer. Introduced in 1951; dropped, 1958. Used value, $85 to $95.

HI-STANDARD Plinker: automatic; hammerless; .22 LR only; interchangeable 4½", 6½" barrels; 9" overall length with 4½" barrel; 10-rd. magazine; grooved trigger; checkered plastic target grips; fixed square notch rear sight; ramp front; blued. Introduced in 1972; dropped, 1975. Used value, $50 to $60.

HI-STANDARD Sharpshooter: automatic; hammerless; .22 LR only; 5½" barrel; 9-rd. magazine; push-button take-down feature; scored trigger; adjustable square notch rear sight, ramp front; slide lock; checkered laminated plastic grips; blued. Introduced in 1972; still in production. Used value, $90 to $95.

HI-STANDARD Victor: automatic; hammerless; .22 LR only; 4½", 5½" barrels; 8¾" overall length with shorter barrel; vent or solid aluminum rib; 10-rd. magazine; interchangeable barrel feature; rib-mounted click-adjustable rear sight, undercut ramp front; checkered walnut grips with thumb rest; blued. Introduced in 1973; still in production. Used values, solid rib, $155 to $160; vent rib, $162.50 to $167.50.

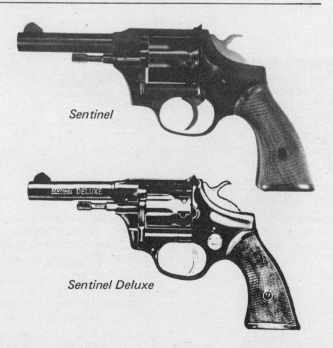

Sentinel

Sentinel Deluxe

HI-STANDARD Sentinel: double-action revolver; solid aluminum alloy frame; 9-rd. swing-out cylinder; .22 LR only; 3", 4", 6" barrels; with 4" barrel, overall length, 9"; fixed sights; checkered plastic grips; blued, nickel finish. Introduced in 1955; dropped, 1974. Used values, blued, $55 to $57.50; nickel, $57.50 to $60.

Sentinel Deluxe has the same specifications as the standard Sentinel; exceptions are movable rear sight, two-piece square-butt checkered walnut grips, wide trigger; 4", 6" barrels only. Introduced in 1957; dropped, 1974. Used value, $60 to $65.

Sentinel Snub model has same specifications as Sentinel Deluxe, except for checkered bird's-head-type grips, 2-3/8" barrel. Introduced in 1957; dropped, 1974. Used value, $60 to $67.50.

Sentinel Imperial has the same general specifications as standard Sentinel model, except for ramp front sight, two-piece checkered walnut grips, onyx-black or nickel finish. Introduced in 1962; dropped, 1965. Used values, black finish, $55 to $60; nickel finish, $60 to $65.

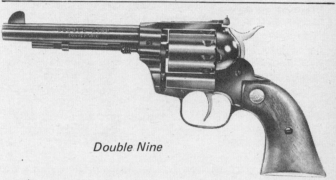

Double Nine

HI-STANDARD Double-Nine: double-action revolver; Western-styled version of Sentinel; .22 short or LR; 5½" barrel; 11" overall length; 9-rd. swing-out cylinder; dummy ejection rod housing; spring-loaded ejection; rebounding hammer; movable notch rear sight, blade front; plastic ivory-like, grips; blued, nickel finish. Introduced in 1959; dropped, 1971. Used values, blued, $55 to $57.50; nickel, $50 to $65.

Double-Nine Convertible model has the same general specifications as original Double-Nine, except primary cylinder is chambered for .22 LR, long, short; extra cylinder fires .22 Win. rimfire magnum; smooth frontier-type walnut grips; movable notched rear sight, blade front; blued, nickel finish. Introduced in 1972; still in production. Used values, blued, $78 to $82.50; nickel, $90 to 95.

HIGH STANDARD Kit Gun: double action; .22 LR, long, short; 4" barrel; 9" overall length; 9-rd. swing-out cylinder; micro-adjustable rear sight, target ramp front; checkered walnut grips; blued. Introduced in 1970; dropped, 1973. Used value, $42.50 to $46.50.

HANDGUNS

HI-STANDARD Natchez: double-action revolver; same general specifications as Double-Nine, except for 4½" barrel; 10" overall length; ivory-like plastic bird's-head grips; blued. Introduced in 1961; dropped, 1966. Used value, $57.50 to $62.50.

HI-STANDARD Posse: double-action revolver; same general design as Double-Nine, except for 3½" barrel; 9" overall length; uncheckered walnut grips; brass grip frame, trigger guard; blued. Introduced in 1961; dropped, 1966. Used value, $57.50 to $62.50.

HI-STANDARD Longhorn: double-action revolver; same general specifications as Double-Nine; original version has 4½" barrel, pearl-like plastic grips; model with 5½" barrel has plastic staghorn grips; later model has walnut grips, 9½" barrel; aluminum alloy frame; blued finish. Long barreled model introduced in 1970; dropped, 1971. Other models introduced in 1961; dropped, 1966. Used values, 9½" barrel, walnut grips, $75 to $80; other models, $60 to $65.

Longhorn Convertible has the same general specifications as standard Longhorn, but with 9½" barrel only; smooth walnut grips; dual cylinder to fire .22 Win. rimfire magnum cartridge. Introduced in 1971; still in production. Used value, $90 to $95.

HI-STANDARD Derringer: double-action; hammerless; over/under 2" barrels; 5" overall length; 2-shot; .22 LR, long, short; .22 rimfire magnum; plastic grips; fixed sights; standard model has blue, nickel finish. Presentation model is gold plated, introduced in 1965; dropped, 1966. Presentation model has some collector value. Standard model, introduced in 1963, .22 long rifle version dropped in 1977, .22 magnum still in production. Used values, standard model, $60 to $65; presentation model, $125 to $135; matched pair, presentation model, consecutive serial numbers, $300 to $350.

HI-STANDARD Durango: double-action revolver; has the same general specifications as the Double-Nine model; .22 LR, long, short; 4½", 5½" barrels; 10" overall length with shorter barrel; brass-finished trigger guard, backstrap; uncheckered walnut grips; blued only in shorter barrel length; blued, nickel in 5½" barrel. Introduced in 1972; dropped, 1975. Used values, blued, $45 to $47.50; nickel, $47.50 to $50.

Produced in a limited edition of 1000 guns, High Standard issued this highly engraved version of their Supermatic Military Trophy in 1972 at a price of $550 each. Called the Benner Commemorative, it honors M/Sgt. Huelet L. "Joe" Benner's Olympic victory in 1952.

IVER JOHNSON

IVER JOHNSON Safety Hammer Model: double-action revolver; hinged frame; .22 LR, .32 S&W long, .32 S&W; 2", 3", 3¼", 4", 5", 6" barrels; in .22 LR, 7-rd. cylinder; in .32 S&W long, 6 rds., 5-rd. capacity in others; fixed sights; hard rubber grips with round butt, square butt with rubber or walnut; heavier frame for .32 S&W long, .38 S&W; blued, nickel finish. Introduced in 1892; dropped, 1950. Used value, $45 to $47.50.

IVER JOHNSON Safety Hammerless Model: double-action revolver; hinged frame; basic design comparable to Safety Hammer model; .22 LR, .32 S&W Long, .32 S&W, .38 S&W; 2", 3", 3¼", 4", 5", 6" barrels; in .22 LR, 7-rd. cylinder; in .32 S&W long, 6 rds., 5-rd. capacity in others; fixed sights, hard rubber grips with round butt, square butt with rubber or walnut; heavier frame for .32 S&W Long, .38 S&W; blued, nickel finish. Introduced in 1895; dropped, 1950. Used value, $50 to $52.50.

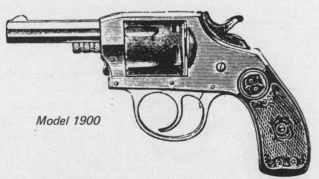

Model 1900

IVER JOHNSON Model 1900: double-action revolver; solid frame; .22 rimfire, .32 S&W Long, .32 S&W, .38 S&W; 2½", 4½", 6" barrels; 7-rd. cylinder in .22, 6 rds. in .32 S&W, 5 rds. in .32 S&W long; fixed sights; hard rubber grips; blued, nickel finish. Introduced in 1900; dropped, 1947. Used value, $37.50 to $40.

Model 1900 Target utilizes same frame as standard model; .22 LR only; 6", 9" barrels; 7-rd. cylinder; fixed sights; checkered walnut grips; blued finish. Introduced in 1925; dropped, 1942. Used value, $60 to $62.50.

IVER JOHNSON 22 Supershot: double-action revolver; hinged frame; .22 LR only; 6" barrel; 7-rd. cylinder; fixed sights; checkered walnut grips; blued finish. Introduced in 1929; dropped, 1949. Used value, $47.50 to $50.

Supershot 9-shot has hinged frame, .22 LR only, 9-rd. cylinder; pre-WWII model has adjustable finger rest. Other specifications are same as standard model. Introduced in 1929; dropped, 1949. Used value, $60 to $62.50.

IVER JOHNSON Target 9-Shot: double-action revolver; solid frame; .22 LR only; 6", 10" barrels; 10¾" overall length with 6" barrel; 9-rd. cylinder; fixed sights; checkered diamond panel walnut grips; blued finish. Introduced in 1929; dropped, 1946. Used value, $47.50 to $50.

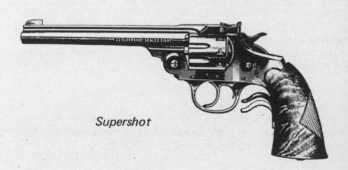

Sealed 8 Target

Supershot

IVER JOHNSON Sealed Eight Supershot: double-action revolver; hinged frame; .22 LR only; 6" barrel; 8-rd. cylinder counterbored for high velocity ammo; 10¾" overall length; pre-WWII version has adjustable finger rest; adjustable target sights; checkered diamond panel walnut grips; blued finish. Introduced in 1931; dropped, 1957. Used value, $77.50 to $80.

Sealed Eight Target has solid frame; 6", 10" barrels; fixed sights. Other specifications are same as Sealed Eight Supershot. Introduced in 1931; dropped, 1957. Used value, $57.50 to $60.

Sealed Eight Protector has hinged frame; 2½" barrel; 7¼" overall length; fixed sights, checkered walnut grips; blued finish. Introduced in 1933; dropped, 1949. Used value, $60 to $62.50.

IVER JOHNSON Champion: single-action target revolver; hinged frame; .22 LR only; 6″ barrel; 10¾″ overall length; 8-rd. cylinder; countersunk chambers for high velocity ammo; adjustable finger rest; adjustable target-type sights; checkered walnut grips; blued finish. Introduced in 1938; dropped, 1948. Used value, $72.50 to $75.

IVER JOHNSON Trigger-Cocking Model: single-action target revolver; hinged frame; .22 LR only; 6″ barrel; 10¾″ overall length; 8-rd. cylinder, with countersunk chambers; adjustable target sights, grips; blued finish; checkered walnut grips. First pull on the trigger cocks the hammer; second releases hammer. Introduced in 1940; dropped, 1947. Some collector value. Used value, $80 to $85.

IVER JOHNSON Supershot Model 844: double-action revolver; hinged frame; .22 LR only; 4½″, 6″ barrels; 9¼″ overall length, with 4½″ barrel; 8-rd. cylinder; adjustable sights; one-piece checkered walnut grip; blued finish. Introduced in 1955; dropped, 1956. Used value, $62.50 to $65.

IVER JOHNSON Armsworth Model 855: single-action revolver; hinged frame; .22 LR only; 6″ barrel; 10¾″ overall length; adjustable finger rest; adjustable sights; one-piece checkered walnut grip; blued finish. Introduced in 1955; dropped, 1957. Used value, $72.50 to $75.

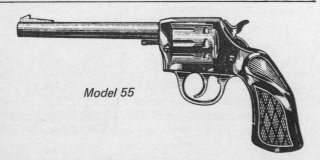

Model 55

IVER JOHNSON Model 55: double-action target revolver; solid frame; .22 LR, long, short; 4½″, 6″ barrels; 10¾″ overall length, with 6″ barrel; 8-rd. cylinder; fixed sights; checkered walnut grips; blued finish. Introduced in 1955; dropped 1961. Used value, $30 to $32.50.

Model 55A has the same specifications as Model 55, ex-

cept for incorporation of a loading gate. Introduced in 1962; still in production. Used value, $35 to $38.

Model 57

IVER JOHNSON Model 57: double-action target revolver; solid frame; .22 LR, long, short; 4″, 5″ barrels; 8-rd. cylinder; 10¾″ overall length with 6″ barrel; adjustable sights, checkered plastic grip, with thumb channel; blued finish. Introduced in 1956; dropped, 1961. Used value, $35 to $37.50.

Model 57A has the same specifications as Model 57, except for addition of loading gate. Introduced in 1962; still in production. Used value, $40 to $42.50.

Model 66 Trailsman

IVER JOHNSON Model 66 Trailsman: double-action revolver; hinged frame; .22 LR, long, short; 6″ barrel; 11″ overall length; 8-rd. cylinder; rebounding hammer; adjustable sights checkered plastic grips with thumb channel; blued finish. Introduced in 1958; still in production. Used value, $40 to $42.50.

Trailsman 66 Snubby model has same general specifications as standard Model 66, except for 2¾″ barrel; 7″ overall length; smooth, rounded plastic grips; also available in .32 S&W, .38 S&W with 5-rd. cylinder; Introduced in 1961; dropped, 1972. Used value, $42.50 to $45.

IVER JOHNSON Model 50A Sidewinder: frontier-style double action revolver; solid frame; .22 LR, long short; 6″ barrel; 11¼″ overall length; 8-rd cylinder; fixed sights; plastic staghorn grips; blued finish. Introduced in 1961; still in production in varying configurations as Models 524, 624, 724, 824, some with adjustable sights. Used value, $35 to $42.50.

Model 55S-A

Model 67S

IVER JOHNSON Model 55S Cadet: double-action revolver; solid frame; .22 LR, long, short, .32 S&W, .38 S&W; 2½" barrel; 7" overall length; .22 has 8-rd. cylinder, others, 5-rd. capacity; fixed sights; plastic grips; blued finish. Introduced in 1955; dropped, 1961. Used value, $30 to $35.

Model 55S-A has the same specifications as Model 55S, except for addition of a loading gate. Introduced in 1962; still in production. Used value, $35 to $45.

IVER JOHNSON Model 67 Viking: double-action revolver; hinged frame; .22 LR, long, short; 4½", 6" barrels; 11" overall length, with 6" barrel; 8-rd. cylinder; adjustable sights; plastic grips with thumb channel. Introduced in 1964; dropped, 1974. Used value, $45 to $50.

Model 67S Viking Snubby has the same general specifications as standard Model 67, except for 2¾" barrel, 7" overall length; small plastic grips; also available in .32 S&W, .38 S&W, with 5-rd. cylinder. Introduced in 1964; dropped, 1974. Used value, $45 to $50.

LLAMA

thumbrest plastic grips; adjustable target sights; grip safety; blued. Imported by Stoeger. Introduced in 1951; still in production. Used value, $85 to $90.

LLAMA Model IIIA: automatic; .380 auto only; 3-11/16" barrel; 6½" overall length; 7-rd. magazine; checkered thumbrest plastic grips; adjustable target sights; vent rib; grip safety; blued. Early versions were sans vent rib, had lanyard ring, no thumbrest on grips. Imported by Stoeger. Introduced in 1951; still in production. Used value, $85 to $92.50.

LLAMA Model XA: automatic; .32 auto only; 3-11/16" barrel; 6½" overall length; 8-rd. magazine; checkered

LLAMA Model XV: automatic; .22 LR only; 3-11/16" barrel; 6½" overall length; 8-rd. magazine; checkered thumbrest plastic grips; adjustable target sights; vent rib; grip safety; blued. Imported by Stoeger. Introduced in 1951; still in production. Used value, $80 to $85.

LLAMA Model VIII: automatic; .38 Super only; 5" barrel; 8½" overall length; 9-rd. magazine; hand-checkered walnut grips; fixed sights; vent rib; grip safety; blued. Imported by Stoeger. Introduced in 1952; still in production. Used value, $120 to $125.

LLAMA Model XI: automatic; 9mm Parabellum; 5" barrel; 8½" overall length; 8-rd. magazine; checkered thumbrest plastic grips; adjustable rear sight, fixed front; vent rib; grip safety; blued. Imported by Stoeger Arms. Introduced in 1954 by Stoeger; still in production. Used value, $115 to $120.

LLAMA Martial: double-action revolver; .22 LR, .22 magnum, .38 Special; 4" barrel in .38 only, 6" in .22; 11¼" overall length with 6" barrel; hand-checkered walnut grips; target sights; blued. Imported by Stoeger. Introduced in 1969; still in production. Used value, $95 to $100.

LLAMA Model IXA: automatic; .45 auto only; 5" barrel; 8½" overall length; 7-rd. magazine; hand-checkered walnut grips; vent rib; fixed sights; grip safety; blued. Introduced in 1952; still in production. Used value, $120 to $125.

LLAMA Comanche: double-action revolver; has the same specifications as Martial model, except that it chambers .357 magnum cartridge. Introduced in 1975; still in production. Used value, $115 to $120.

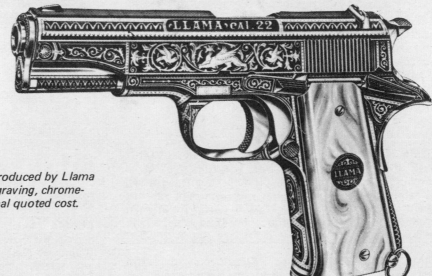

Virtually all of today's models being produced by Llama can be special ordered with factory engraving, chrome-plating and gold inlay work at additional quoted cost.

MAB

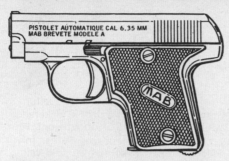

MAB Model A: automatic; .25 auto; 2½" barrel; 4½" overall length; based on Browning design; 6-rd. magazine; no rear sight, fixed front; checkered plastic or hard rubber grips; blued. Introduced in 1921; production suspended in 1942. Production resumed in 1945 for importation into U.S. as WAC Model A or Le Defendeur; importation dropped in 1968. Manufactured by Manufacture d'armes de Bayonne, France. Used value, $65 to $75.

MAB Model B: automatic; .25 auto; 2" barrel; 4½" overall length; 6-rd. magazine; no rear sight; fixed front; hard rubber grips; blued. Introduced in 1932; dropped in 1967. Never imported into U.S. Used value, $65 to $75.

MAB Model C: automatic; .32, .380 auto; 3¾" barrel; 6" overall length; 7-rd. magazine in .32, 6 rds. in .380; push-button magazine release behind trigger; fixed sights; checkered black hard rubber grips; blued. Introduced in 1933; made under German supervision during WWII. Importation dropped, 1968. Used value, $60 to $70.

MAB Model D: automatic; .32, .380 auto; 3½" barrel; 7" overall length; 9-rd. magazine in .32, 8 rds. in

.380; push-button magazine release; fixed sights; checkered black hard rubber grips; blued. Introduced in 1933; made under German supervision in WWII. Imported to U.S. as WAC Model D or MAB Le Gendarme. Importation dropped, 1968. Used value, $75 to $90.

MAB Model E: automatic; .25 auto; 3¼" barrel; 6.1" overall length; 10-rd. magazine; fixed sights; plastic grips; blued. Introduced in 1949; imported into U.S. as WAC Model E. Importation dropped, 1968. Used value, $70 to $85.

MAB Model R: automatic; .22 LR, 4½" or 7" barrel; external hammer; 10-rd. magazine. Introduced in 1950; never imported into U.S. Still in production. Used value, $90 to $100.

MAB Model P-15: 9mm Parabellum; 4½" barrel; 8" overall length; 15-rd. magazine; fixed sights; checkered plastic grips; blued; still in production. Used value, $125 to $150.

MAB Model F: automatic; .22 LR; 3¾", 6", 7¼" barrels; 10¾" overall length; 10-rd. magazine; windage adjustable rear sight, ramp front; plastic thumbrest grips; blued. Introduced in 1950; variation imported into U.S. as Le Chasseur model. Importation dropped, 1968. Used value, $60 to $75.

MAUSER

2½" barrel; 4½" overall length; 6-rd. magazine; checkered hard rubber grips; blued. Introduced in 1922; dropped, 1938. Used value, $130 to $150.

MAUSER Model 1910 Pocket Pistol: automatic; .25 auto, 3-3/16" barrel; 5-3/8" overall length; 9-rd. magazine; fixed sights; checkered hard rubber or walnut grips; blued. Introduced in 1910; dropped, 1939. Used value, $100 to $132.50.

Model 1914 Pocket Pistol in .32 auto has same general design as .25, but has 3½" barrel, 5-7/8" overall length, 8-rd. magazine. Introduced in 1914; dropped 1939. Used value, $100 to $135.

Second Model WTP is smaller, lighter in weight. Introduced in 1938; dropped during WWII. Used value, $150 to $160.

MAUSER Bolo Model 96: automatic; 7.63mm Mauser; locked-bolt design; 4" barrel; 10¾" overall length; 10-rd. box magazine; adjustable rear sight, fixed front; serrated walnut grips. Based upon original Model 96 design, but barrel reduced in length in accordance with Versailles Treaty. Introduced in 1922 for export; dropped, 1930. Used value, $300 to $350.

MAUSER Model 1930: 7.63mm Mauser, 5¼" barrel, serrated walnut grips; introduced in 1930, dropped, ca. 1939. Used value, $400 to $450.

MAUSER Model HSc: double-action automatic; .32 auto, .380 auto; 3-3/8" barrel; 6.05" overall length; 7-rd. magazine; fixed sights; checkered walnut grips; blued, nickel finish. Introduced in 1939; still in production. Imported by Interarms. Used values, blued, $145 to $155; nickel, $150 to $160.

MAUSER Parabellum: automatic; .30 Luger, 9mm Parabellum; 4" barrel in 9mm, 4", 6" in .30; with 4" barrel, overall length, 8.7"; fixed sights; manual, grip safeties; checkered walnut grips; blued. American eagle over chamber; follows Swiss Luger style. Currently imported by Interarms. Introduced in 1966; still in production. Used value, $220 to $225.

Parabellum P-08 has the same general specifications as 1906 model, except for redesigned takedown lever; curved front strap, improved safety, trigger; Mauser banner on toggle. Introduced in 1908; resurrected in 1975; still in production. Imported by Interarms. Used value, $310 to $320.

MAUSER WTP (First Model): automatic; advertised as Westentaschen-Pistole or vest-pocket pistol; .25 auto only;

Pre-WWII MAUSER Lugers: 9mm (rarely 7.65mm) marked "Mauser," "S/42," or "byf" on toggle. Prices often reflect collector interest. Used values, $200 up.

RUGER

RUGER Standard Model: automatic; .22 LR only; 4¾", 6" barrels; with 4¾" barrel, 8¾" overall length; 9-rd. magazine; checkered hard rubber grips, walnut optional; square-notch rear sight adjustable for windage only, fixed wide blade front; blued. Introduced in 1949; still in production. Until 1951, featured red eagle insignia in grips; changed to black upon death of Alex Sturm. This type has considerable collector value. Used values: red eagle model, $200 to $250; current model, $58.50 to $60.

RUGER Mark I: automatic, target model; .22 LR only; 5¼" bull barrel, 6-7/8" tapered; with 6-7/8" barrel, 10-1/8" overall length; 9-rd. magazine; adjustable micrometer rear sight, fixed 1/8" blade front; checkered hard rubber grips, walnut optional; blued. Basically the same design as Standard model. Introduced in 1951; still in production. Early issue had red eagle in grips; changed to black late in 1951. Former has collector value. Used values: red eagle model, $200 to $250; current model, $72.50 to $80.

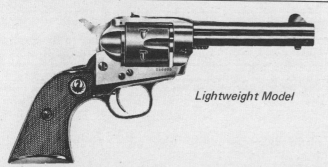

Lightweight Model

RUGER Single Six: single-action revolver; .22 LR, .22 rimfire magnum; 4-5/8", 5½", 6½", 9½" barrels; with 4-5/8"

barrel, overall length, 10"; 6-rd. cylinder; checkered hard rubber grips on early production, uncheckered walnut on later versions; rear sight adjustable for windage only; blued. Introduced in 1953; dropped, 1972. Used value, $70 to $75.

Lightweight Single Six has same specifications as standard model, except cylinder, cylinder frame, grip frame are of alloy, 4-5/8" barrel only. Aluminum cylinder has Moultin Hard Coat finish. Some guns have blued steel cylinder. Introduced in 1956; dropped, 1958. Used value, $125 to $150.

Single Six Convertible has the same general specifications as standard model, except for interchangeable cylinders, one handling .22 LR, long, short, the other .22 rimfire magnum cartridges; 5½", 6½" barrels only. Introduced in 1962; dropped, 1972. Used value, $80 to $85.

Super Single Six Convertible has same general specifications as standard model, except for interchangeable .22 LR, .22 rimfire magnum cylinders; ramp front sight, click adjustable rear sight with protective ribs. Introduced in 1964; dropped, 1972. Used value, $85 to $90.

New Model Super Single Six is improved version of original model, with new Ruger interlocked mechanism, independent firing pin, music wire springs throughout, hardened chrome-moly steel frame, other improvements; .22 LR, long, short; .22 rimfire magnum in extra cylinder; fully adjustable rear sight, ramp patridge front; 4-5/8", 5½", 6½", 9½" barrels. Introduced in 1973; still in production. Used values, 9½" barrel, $85 to $90; other lengths, $77.50 to $80.

New Model Blackhawk

RUGER .357 Magnum Blackhawk: single-action revolver; .357 magnum; 4-5/8", 6½", 10" barrels; with 6½" barrel, 12" overall length; 6-rd. cylinder; checkered hard rubber or uncheckered walnut grips; click adjustable rear sight, ramp front; blued. Introduced in 1955; dropped, 1972. Used value, $115 to $120.

Ruger New Model Blackhawk has same general outward specs as original .357 model, but is chambered for .357 magnum, .41 magnum; 6-rd. cylinder; new Ruger interlocked mechanism; transfer bar ignition; hardened chrome-moly steel frame; wide trigger, music wire springs, independent firing pin; blued. Introduced in 1973; still in production. Used value, $95 to $100.

Ruger .357/9mm has the same specifications as .357 magnum, except furnished with interchangeable cylinders for 9mm Parabellum, .357 magnum cartridges. Introduced in 1967; still in production. Used value, $115 to $120.

RUGER 44 Magnum Blackhawk: single-action revolver; .44 magnum; 6½", 7½", 10" barrels; 12-1/8" overall length; 6-rd. cylinder; adjustable rear sight, ramp front; uncheckered walnut grips; blued. Introduced in 1956; dropped, 1963. Used value, $200 to $225.

Super Bearcat

RUGER Bearcat: single-action revolver; .22 LR, long, short; 4" barrel, 8-7/8" overall length; 6-rd. nonfluted cylinder; fixed sights; uncheckered walnut grips; blued. Introduced in 1958; dropped, 1971. Used value, $125 to $150.

Super Bearcat is improved version of original, but with same general specifications. All-steel construction; music Introduced in 1971; dropped, 1975. Used value, $110 to $135.

Super Blackhawk

RUGER Super Blackhawk: single-action revolver; .44 magnum; 7½" barrel, 13-3/8" overall length; 6-rd. unfluted cylinder; steel, brass grip frame; uncheckered walnut grips; click adjustable rear sight, ramp front; square-back trigger guard; blued. Introduced in 1959; dropped, 1972. Used value, $160 to $175.

New Model Super Blackhawk has the same exterior specifications as original, but fires .44 Special as well as .44 magnum cartridge. Has new interlocked mechanism, steel grip frame, wide trigger, wide hammer spur, nonfluted cylinder. Introduced in 1973; still in production. Used value, $140 to $150.

RUGER Hawkeye: single-shot, single-action pistol; standard frame with cylinder replaced with rotating breech block; 8½" barrel; 14½" overall length; chambered for short-lived .256 magnum cartridge; uncheckered walnut grips; click adjustable rear sight, ramp front; barrel drilled, tapped for scope mounts; blued. Introduced in 1963; dropped, 1964. Used value, $350 to $450.

RUGER 41 Magnum Blackhawk: single-action revolver; .41 magnum; 4-5/8", 6½" barrels; with 6½" barrel, 12" overall length. Has same general specifications as Ruger Blackhawk .357 magnum, except for chambering, smaller frame. Introduced in 1965; dropped, 1972. Used value, $120 to $130.

RUGER 30 Carbine Blackhawk: single-action revolver; has the same general specifications as other pre-1972 Blackhawk models, except for chambering for .30 military carbine cartridge; 7½" barrel only, has fluted cylinder; round-back trigger guard. Introduced in 1967; still in production. Used value, $105 to $115.

RUGER .45 Colt: single-action revolver; .45 Long Colt only; 4-5/8", 7½" barrels; with 7½" barrel, 13-1/8" overall; adjustable micro click rear sight, 1/8" ramp front; uncheckered walnut grips; Ruger interlocked mechanism; similar in design to Super Blackhawk. Introduced in 1971; still in production. Used value, $110 to $125.

Ruger .45 Colt/.45 ACP convertible has the same specifications as .45 Colt, but is furnished with interchangeable .45 ACP cylinder. Introduced in 1971; still in production. Used value, $120 to $130.

RUGER Police Service-Six Model 107: double-action revolver; .357 magnum; 2¾", 4", 6" barrels; 6" barrel dropped in 1973; with 4" barrel, 9¼" overall length; 6-rd. cylinder; solid frame with barrel, sighting rib, ejector rod housing in single integral part; semitarget-type checkered walnut grips; early model had choice of fixed or adjustable rear sight; blued. Introduced in 1972; still in production. Used value, $100 to $110.

RUGER Police Service-Six Model 108: double-action revolver; .38 Special. Has exactly the same specifications as Model 107, except for chambering. Introduced in 1972; still in production. Used value, $95 to $105.

RUGER Security Six Model 117: double-action revolver; .357 magnum; 2¾", 4", 6" barrels; with 4" barrel, 9¼" overall length; 6-rd. cylinder; externally has same general appearance as Model 107. Has hand-checkered semitarget walnut grips, adjustable rear sight, patridge-type front on ramp; music wire coiled springs throughout. Introduced in 1974; still in production. Used value, $110 to $120.

RUGER Security Six Model 717: double-action revolver; .357 magnum. Has exactly the same specifications as Model 117, except that all metal parts except sights are of stainless steel. Sights are black alloy for visibility. Introduced in 1974; still in production. Used value, $130 to $140.

RUGER Speed Six Model 207: double-action revolver; .357 magnum; 2¾", 4" barrel; 9¼" overall length; square-notch fixed rear sight, patridge-type front; all-steel construction; music wire coil springs throughout; round-butt, diamond-pattern checkered walnut grips; blued. Also available without hammer spur. Introduced in 1974; still in production. Used value, $105 to $115.

Model 208

RUGER Speed Six Model 208: double-action revolver; .38 Special. Has exactly the same specifications as Model 207, except for chambering. Introduced in 1974; still in production. Used value, $90 to $100.

SAUER Model 1913: pocket automatic; .32 auto; 3" barrel; 5-7/8" overall length; 7-rd. magazine; fixed sights; checkered hard rubber black grips; blued finish. Introduced in 1913; dropped, 1930. Used value, $90 to $95.

SAUER Pocket 25: automatic; same general design as Model 1913, but smaller in size; .25 auto; 2½" barrel; 4¼" overall length; improved grip, safety features. Introduced about 1920; dropped, 1930. Used value, $140 to $145.

SAUER Model 1930 (Behorden Modell): improved version of the Model 1913; .32 auto; black plastic grips; blued finish. Introduced, 1930; dropped, 1938. Used value, $110 to $125.

SAUER WTM: automatic; .25 auto; 4-1/8" overall length; top ejection; 6-rd. magazine; fixed sights; checkered hard rubber grips; fluted slide; blued. Introduced about 1924; dropped about 1927. Used value, $130 to $135.

SAUER Model 28: automatic; .25 auto; 3-15/16" overall length; slanted serrations on slide; top ejection; same general design as WTM, but smaller in size; checkered black rubber grips with Sauer imprint; blued. Introduced about 1928; dropped, about 1938. Used value, $135 to $140.

SAUER Model 38(H): double-action automatic; .32 auto; 3¼" barrel; 6¼" overall length; 7-rds., fixed sights; black plastic grips; blued. Introduced in 1938; dropped, 1944. Used value, $100 to $125. Note: .22 and .380 very rare, very valuable.

SMITH & WESSON

SMITH & WESSON Safety Hammerless: produced for over 54 years; discontinued at the start of WWII; also called the New Departure; was the last of S&W's top-break designs. Having no exposed hammer, it was a true pocket gun and would not snag on the draw; could be fired without removing from the pocket. Capacity, 5 rds.; chambered for .32 S&W and .38 S&W; 17 oz., with overall length of 6¼"; antisnag type sights with fixed blade front and U-notch rear; checkered Circassian walnut or hard rubber grips with S&W monogram; blued or nickel finish; featured grip safety and the action provided a distinct pause prior to let-off, giving the effect of single-action pull. Used value, $200 to $250.

SMITH & WESSON Model 10 Military & Police: the back-bone of S&W's line; basic frame is termed S&W's K-frame, the derivative source of the K-38, et al. It is, quite possibly, the most popular, widely accepted police duty revolver ever made. Introduced about 1902. Has been made with square-butt checkered walnut stocks and in round-butt pattern with choice of hard rubber or checkered walnut, in barrel lengths from 2" to 6½", as well as Airweight version.

Currently made in .38 Special, capacity, 6 rds.; with 6" barrel, overall length is 11-1/8" in square butt, about ¼" less for round butt type; weight is 31 oz; sights, 1/10" service type front and square notch rear, nonadjustable; finishes, blued or nickel. Currently available in standard or heavy-barrel version, nickel or blue finish. Used value, blue, $90 to $100; nickel, $100 to $115. A version of the

Military & Police was offered in .32 WCF (also called .32-20), from the introduction of the design to the beginning of WWII; current used value, $130 to $135.

SMITH & WESSON Military & Police Target Model: from the early Twenties to 1941, S&W introduced various versions of their M&P, refined for target work; modifications included rear sights adjustable for windage and elevation; with few, if any, exceptions, barrel lengths were 6". Calibers, .38 Special, .32 S&W Long, .22 LR; a few were made up on a custom basis in .32 WCF. All had 6-shot cylinders, with overall lengths of 11-1/8"; weights spanned from 32 oz. for the .38 to 35 oz. for the .22 versions. Pre-WWII target models are identifiable by the absence of a rib on the barrel. Stocks, checkered walnut, but not of the later magna pattern. Used value, $200 to $220 for the .32 S&W Long and .22 LR; $157.50 to $170 for the .38 Special; up to $300 for the .32 WCF from original factory production.

SMITH & WESSON Model 30 Hand Ejector: early swing-out cylinder design. Chambered for .32 S&W Long; will accept the .32 S&W and the .32 S&W Long wadcutter load; capacity, 6 rds. Currently made with 2", 3" and 4" barrels; 6" was available at one time; checkered walnut with medallion; formerly hard rubber; fixed sights, with 1/10" serrated ramp front and square notch rear; overall length, 8" with 4" barrel; weight, 18 oz; finish, blue or nickel. Introduced in 1903; still in production. Used value, $85 to $95.

SMITH & WESSON .22/32 Target: a forerunner of the Model 35; made for the .22 LR, capacity 6 rds.; chambers were countersunk at the heads around 1935, for the high-velocity cartridges introduced at that time; furnished only

in blued finish; 6" barrel, with overall length of 10½"; won the "Any Revolver" event of the U.S.R.A. matches several times; sights, 1/10" or 1/8" Patridge front, square notch rear sight adjustable for windage and elevation; stocks, special, oversize, square-butt pattern in checkered Circassian walnut, with S&W monogram. Introduced in 1911; superseded by the Model 35 in 1953. Retail price, new, just before WWII, $35. Used value, $175 to $190.

SMITH & WESSON Model 33 Regulation Police: similar to Model 31, except for its caliber; chambered for the .38 S&W, it will accept the .38 Colt New Police; capacity, 5 rds.; 4" barrel; overall length, 8½"; weight, 18 oz; fixed sights, with 1/10" serrated ramp front and square notch rear; stocks, checkered walnut, with medallion; blue, nickel finish. Introduced in 1917; dropped, 1974. Used value, $90 to $100.

SMITH & WESSON Military Model of 1917: entry of the U.S. into WWI found facilities unable to produce sufficient quantities of the recently adopted Government Model auto pistol, so approximately 175,000 Smith & Wesson revolvers were manufactured, being chambered to fire the .45 ACP cartridge by means of the two 3-rd. steel clips; also fires the .45 Auto Rim round, introduced after the war without clips. The wartime units had a duller blued finish and smooth walnut grips, with 5½" barrel; overall length, 10¼"; weight, 36¼ oz., with lanyard ring in the butt. A commercial version remained in production after the end of WWI to the start of WWII, distinguished by a bright blue finish and checkered walnut stocks. Used value, $170 to $185, for military; $225 to $235, for commercial.

SMITH & WESSON Regulation Police, Target Model: target version of the Model 31; 6" barrel and adjustable target sights; made only in .32 S&W Long (accepting .32 S&W and .32 Colt New Police); length, 10¼"; weight, 20 oz; checkered walnut stocks and blued finish; capacity, 6 rds. Introduced, 1917; dropped, 1941. Used value, $150 to $165.

SMITH & WESSON Model 31 Regulation Police: similar to the Model 33, except for caliber; chambered for the .32 S&W Long, it will accept the .32 S&W, .32 Colt New Police; capacity, 6 rds.; barrel lengths, 2", 3", 3¼", 4", 4¼" and 6"; currently, 2", 3" and 4", only. With 4" barrel, 8½" in length, weight, 18¾ oz.; fixed sights, with 1/10" serrated ramp front and square notch rear; stocks, checkered walnut, with medallion; finish, blue, nickel. Introduced in 1917; still in production. Used value, $90 to $100.

SMITH & WESSON Straightline Single-shot Target: chambered for the .22 LR cartridge, the S&W Straightline was made from 1925 through 1936; had a 10" barrel and was 11-5/16" in overall length, weighing 34¼ oz.; was made only in blued finish, with target sights; stocks were of walnut, usually not checkered. As with many long-discontinued pistols, the current market value is weighted by the interest of dedicated collectors, rather than shooters, most of whom would be disappointed by the accuracy potential of typical examples. Used value, $400 to $425, if complete with original metal case and accessories; $300 to $350 without.

SMITH & WESSON Model 1926 .44 Military: modified version of S&W's earlier New Century hand-ejector, minus the triple-lock feature, but retaining the heavy shroud around the ejector rod; primarily produced in .44 Special, sometimes encountered in .45 Long Colt, .455 Webley or .455 Eley; barrel lengths, 4″, 5″ and 6½″; overall length, 11¾″ with 6½″ barrel; weight, 39½ oz. with 6½″ barrel; capacity, 6 rds.; sights, 1/10″ service-type front and fixed square notch rear; stocks, checkered walnut, square or magna-type, with S&W medallion; finish, blued or nickel. Discontinued at the start of WWII; replaced after the war by the 1950 model. Used value, $250 to $260 in blue; $265 to $275, nickel.

SMITH & WESSON Model 1926 Target: a target version of the 1926 Model; rear sight adjustable for windage and elevation; produced from 1926 to the beginning of WWII; replaced after the war by the 1950 Target Model 24. Used value, $350 to $365.

SMITH & WESSON Model 20 .38/44 Heavy Duty: six-shot, .38 Special revolver, built on the S&W .44 frame, often termed their N-frame, hence the .38/44 designation; designed to handle high-velocity .38 Special ammunition; barrel lengths, 4″, 5″ and 6½″; with 5″ barrel, overall length, 10-3/8″ and weight, 40 oz.; fixed sights, with 1/10″ service-

type (semi-circle) front and square notch rear; stocks, checkered walnut, magna-type with S&W medallion; finish, blued or nickel. Introduced in 1930; discontinued, 1967. Used value, $235 to $250.

SMITH & WESSON .38/44 Outdoorsman Model 23: introduced in 1930 as a companion to the Model 20; reintroduced about 1950 with ribbed barrel and magna-type stocks; was made only in blue, with 6½″ barrel; plain Patridge 1/8″ front sight, S&W micrometer click rear adjustable for windage and elevation; capacity, 6 rds. of .38 Special; overall length, 11¾″; weight, 41¾ oz. Discontinued, 1967. Used value, $275 to $290.

SMITH & WESSON Model 27 .357 Magnum: introduced with the .357 magnum cartridge in 1935; essentially the same as the .38 Special, except case is lengthened by 0.135″, loaded to substantially higher pressures in order to obtain higher velocities (The case was lengthened to prevent its use in guns chambered for the .38 Special round); Pre-WWII Model 27s offered in barrel lengths of 3½″, 5″, 6″, 6½″, 8-3/8″ and 8¾″; could be custom-ordered with barrels of any length up to 8¾″; weights were 41 oz. for 3½″, 42½ oz. for 5″, 44 oz. for 6″, 44½ oz. for 6½″ and 47 oz. for 8-3/8″; overall length, 11-3/8″ for 6″ barrel; could be ordered with any of S&W's standard target sights; the 3½″ version usually was furnished with a Baughman quick-draw sight on a plain King ramp; finely checkered top strap matched barrel rib, with vertically grooved front and rear grip straps and grooved trigger; capacity, 6 rds. of .357 mag; also could fire .38 Special; S&W bright blue or nickel finishes; checkered Circassian walnut stocks, with S&W medallion in choice of square or magna type. Retail price at beginning of WWII, $60. Post-WWII production was similar, with the hammer redesigned to incorporate a wider spur and inclusion of the present pattern of S&W click micrometer rear sight; blue or nickel finish. Still in production. Model 27 was the first center-fire revolver with recessed cylinders; the .357 required registration with registration no. stamped in yoke of frame; about 6000 made before registration stopped. The papers, themselves, have some collector value without the gun!

Used value, up to $650 for pre-WWII model with registration papers furnished at that time; $200 to $225 for post-war versions.

SMITH & WESSON .22/32 Kit Gun: a compact, outdoorsman's revolver, based on the .22/32 Target, modified by a round-butt stock pattern and 4" barrel; made with 1/10" Patridge or pocket revolver front sight, with rear sight adjustable for elevation and windage; checkered Circassian walnut or hard rubber stocks; blued or nickel finishes; barrel length, 4"; overall length, 8" with round butt (small or special oversized target square-butt stocks were offered on special order); weight, 21 oz.; capacity, 6 rds.; chambered only for the .22 LR. Introduced in 1935; replaced, 1953, by the Model 34. Used value, $150 to $175.

SMITH & WESSON Model 32 Terrier: essentially a 2" version of the Model 30 Hand Ejector; stocks, round-butt pattern in checkered walnut with medallion; blued finish standard, nickel at extra cost; length, 6¼"; weight, 17 oz; capacity, 5 rds. of .38 S&W (or .38 Colt New Police); fixed sights, with 1/10" serrated ramp front and square notch rear. Introduced in 1936, discontinued, 1974. Used value, $125 to $135.

SMITH & WESSON Model 17 K-22 Masterpiece: redesigned version of Model 16. Introduced around 1947; still in production. Postwar production added the refinement of a broad barrel rib, intended to compensate for weight variations between the three available calibers: .38 Special, .32

S&W Long and .22 LR. Likewise added were the redesigned hammer, with its broad spur and thumb-tip relief notch, an adjustable anti-backlash stop for the trigger and the magna-type grips developed in the mid-Thirties to help cushion the recoil of the .357 Magnum. 6" barrel is standard, with 8-3/8" available. Capacity, 6 rds.; overall length, 11-1/8" with 6" barrel; loaded weight, 38½ oz. for 6", 42½ oz. for 8-3/8". Blue finish only. Currently offered in .22 LR only. Used value, 6" barrel, $115 to $125; 8-3/8" barrel, $120 to $130.

SMITH & WESSON Victory Model: WWII version of the Model 10; usually in 4" barrel length, Parkerized with sand-blasted or brushed finish, smooth (non-magna) walnut stocks and lanyard ring in square butt; usually in .38 Special, though a version termed the .38-200 was made for the British forces. The Victory Model is inferior in external fit, finish to commercial production, though collectors may be willing to pay prices slightly higher than those listed for the standard Model 10 revolver. Used value, $110 to $120.

SMITH & WESSON Model 16 K-32 Masterpiece: Originating as a target version of the hand-ejector in .32 S&W Long, about 1935 and dropped at the beginning of WWII, the Model 16 appeared in its present form in the late Forties, designated the K-32 as a companion to the K-22 and K-38. A double-action revolver, holding 6 rds. of .32 S&W Long, it was made only with 6" barrel and blued finish. Walnut, magna-pattern stocks with medallions were standard, factory target stocks in exotic woods available as options. Other options included target hammer, target trigger, red insert front sight, white outline rear sight and choice of Patridge or Baughman front sights. Dropped in 1973. Used values: .32 hand-ejector model, $425 to $475; post-war version, $225 to $235.

SMITH & WESSON Model 14 K-38 Masterpiece: double-action revolver; .38 Special only; 6", 8-3/8" barrels; with 6" barrel, 11-1/8" overall length; 6-rd. swing-out cylinder; built on S&W K frame; micrometer rear sight; 1/8" Patridge-type front; hand-checkered service-type walnut grips; blued. Introduced in 1947; still in production. Used value, 6" barrel, $130 to $140; 8-3/8" barrel, $135 to $155.

Model 14 Masterpiece Single Action has the same general specifications as standard Model 14, except for being single

HANDGUNS

action only; has target hammer, target trigger. Used value, 6" barrel, $120 to $125; 8-3/8" barrel, $135 to $160.

SMITH & WESSON Model 48 K-22 Masterpiece WMRF: a modification of the K-22 Model 17; chambered to accept the .22 WMRF cartridge; available with 4" barrel, without being distinctly designated as a Combat Masterpiece, and in the 6" and 8-3/8" lengths, as well; weight, with the 6" barrel, 39 oz.; auxiliary cylinder was offered to permit the use of this model with the .22 LR cartridge. The quoted price of this accessory was $35.50, as of 1969. Used value, with 6" barrel, $150 to $170; $160 to $180 for 8-3/8" barrel; add $40, if equipped with .22 LR as well as .22 WMRF cylinder.

SMITH & WESSON Model 21 1950 .44 Military: post-WWII version of the S&W Model 1926 with minor design refinements; made in 5½" barrel; chambered for the .44 Special (also handles the .44 Russian); length, 10¾"; weight, 36¼ oz.; fixed sights; finish, blued or nickel; stocks, checkered walnut, magna-type, with S&W medallion. Discontinued, 1967. Used value, $200 to $220.

SMITH & WESSON Model 22 1950 Army: post-WWII version of the Model '17, with minor design refinements; remained in production until 1967; has the usual semi-circu-

lar front sight and U-shaped notch rear sight milled in the top of the receiver strap, the same as the M'17. A target version was made, having adjustable rear sight. Used value, $150 to $185.

SMITH & WESSON 1950/1955 Model 25 .45 Target: introduced in 1950 as a companion to the 1950 Model 24 .44 Target; identical except being chambered for .45 ACP/Auto Rim. The 1950 .45 Target was redesigned in 1955 to become the 1955 .45 Target, superseding the 1950 version. Modifications consisted of a heavier barrel with broad rib, similar to that of the K-38, S&W target stocks in place of the magna-type, a target hammer and broad, target-type trigger. Standard barrel length, 6½"; no factory production of 4" has been reported, although some owners have had them cut down to 4" length; capacity, 6 rds.; overall length, 11-7/8"; weight, 45 oz.; sights, 1/8" plain Patridge front, S&W micrometer click rear, adjustable for windage and elevation; finish, blue; stocks, checkered walnut, pattern as noted, with S&W medallion. Continues in production, though in limited quantities. Used value, over that of new guns. The .45 Long Colt made on Special order only.

SMITH & WESSON Model 24 1950 .44 Target: introduced in 1950 as a refined version of the 1926 Target Model; customarily produced with 6½" barrel and Patridge-type front sight having vertical rear blade surface, with S&W micrometer click rear sight adjustable for windage and elevation; limited quantity was produced in a 4" barreled version, with Baughman quick-draw front sight on serrated ramp, with the same type of rear sight. As with most S&W target models, blued finish was standard, although a few specimens may have been custom-ordered in nickel. Chambered for the .44 Special (also handles the shorter .44 Russian cartridge); capacity, 6 rds.; with 4" barrel, overall length is 9¼" and weight is 40 oz. Discontinued about 1966. Used value, $250 to $275 for the 6½" barrel; $500 to $550 for the 4" barrel.

SMITH & WESSON Model 15 .38 Combat Masterpiece: it took some years after WWII to reestablish commercial production and begin catching up with civilian demands at S&W. By the early Fifties, the situation was bright enough to warrant introducing a 4" version of the K-38, which was designated the .38 Combat Masterpiece. Its only nominal companion was the .22 Combat Masterpiece and no attempt was made to match loaded weights, as in the K-series; the .38 weighing 34 oz. empty, compared to 36½ oz. for the .22 version. Barrel ribs were more narrow than the K-series and front sights were of the Baughman, quick-draw ramp pattern, replacing the vertical surface of the K-series Patridge type; overall length, 9-1/8"; finish, blue or nickel; capacity, 6 rds.; chambered for .38 Special. Used value, $90 to $115; $105 to $125, nickel.

SMITH & WESSON Model 18 .22 Combat Masterpiece: companion to the .38 Combat Masterpiece Model 15, with Baughman 1/8" quick-draw front sight on plain ramp and S&W micrometer click rear sight adjustable for windage and elevation; chambered for .22 LR, handling .22 long and .22 short, as well; capacity, 6 rds.; length of barrel, 4"; overall length, 9-1/8"; loaded weight, 36½ oz.; stocks, checkered walnut, magna-type, with S&W medallion; finish, blue only; available options include broad-spur target hammer, wide target trigger, hand-filling target stocks, red front sight insert and white outlined rear sight notch. Still in production. Used value, $125 to $140.

SMITH & WESSON Model 12 Military & Police Airweight: similar to the Model 10, except for the incorporation of an aluminum alloy frame; made only in .38 Special, with capacity of 6 rds.; barrel lengths, 2" and 4"; stocks, checkered walnut magna-type, round or square butt; weight, 18 oz.; with 2" barrel and round butt; overall length 6-7/8" (2", round butt); sights, fixed 1/8" serrated ramp front, square notch rear. Introduced about 1952; still produced. Used value, $100 to $110, blue; $105 to $120, nickel.

SMITH & WESSON Model 34 1953 .22/32 Kit Gun: updated version of the earlier .22/32 Kit Gun, the 1953 version — still in production — features a ribbed varrel, micro-

meter rear sight adjustable for elevation and windage, magna-type stocks; flattened cylinder latch employed on many of S&W's later small pocket designs. Available barrel lengths, 2" and 4"; overall length, 8" with 4" barrel and round butt; weight, 22½ oz. in 4" barrel; stocks, checkered walnut, round or square butt; sights, 1/10" serrated ramp front, square notch rear adjustable for windage and elevation. Used value, up to $90 for blue; $97.50 for nickel. (Refer to entry for Model 43).

SMITH & WESSON Model 36 Chiefs Special: double action revolver; descended from Model 32 Terrier Model, with longer cylinder. Round butt pattern of grips is most common; although square butt design was available. Barrel lengths, 2", 3"; with 3" barrel, 7½" overall length; fixed square-notch rear sight, 1/10" serrated ramp front; 5-rd. cylinder; .38 Special only; blued or nickel. Introduced in 1952; still in production. Used values; blued, $95 to $110; nickel, $100 to $115.

Model 37

SMITH & WESSON Model 37 Chiefs Special Airweight: lightweight version of the Model 36, incorporating aluminum alloy frame, reducing weight to 14 oz.; general specs are the same as for Model 36; finish, blue, nickel. Used values, blue, $95 to $110; nickel, $110 to $115.

Model 43
(page 56)

HANDGUNS

SMITH & WESSON Airweight Kit Gun Model 43: identical to Model 34, except for aluminum alloy frame; made only in 3½" barrel; weight, 14¼ oz.; square-butt stocks of checkered walnut; overall length, 8". Discontinued about 1974; blue or nickel finish. Used value, respectively, $150 to $165 and $160 to $175.

SMITH & WESSON Model 40 Centennial: swing-out version of earlier, top-break Safety Hammerless; has hammerless design, with grip safety. In .38 Special only, with capacity of 5 rds.; barrel length 2", with overall length of 6½"; weight, 19 oz.; fixed sights with 1/10" serrated ramp front and square notch rear. Introduced in 1953; dropped, 1974. Airweight (Model 42), blue, $175 to $200; nickel, $190 to $210.

SMITH & WESSON Model 35 1953 .22/32: a redesign of the .22/32, which had been developed on the .32 Hand Ejector. Departing from the .22/32 Target Model, it added the post-war magna stocks, a rib atop the barrel, and modern S&W front sight and micrometer rear sight. Chambered for the .22 LR, capacity, 6 rds.; barrel length, 6", with 10½" overall length; weight 25 oz., finished only in blue. Introduced in 1953; dropped, 1974. Used value, $175 to $200.

SMITH & WESSON Model 28 Highway Patrolman: introduced in 1954 as a functional version of the Model 27

minus the cost-raising frills such as the checkered top strap; made only in 4" and 6" barrel lengths; overall length, 11¼" with 6" barrel; weight, 41¾ oz. with 4" barrel; 44 oz. with 6" barrel; sights, 1/8" Baughman quick-draw front on plain ramp, S&W micrometer click rear, adjustable for elevation and windage; stocks, checkered walnut, magna-type, with S&W medallion; target stocks at extra cost; finish, blued, with sandblast stippling of barrel rib and frame edging. Still in production. Used value, $130 to $150.

SMITH & WESSON Model 38 Bodyguard Airweight: features a shrouded hammer that can be cocked manually for single-action firing; .38 Special only; capacity, 5 rds.; length of barrel 2"; overall length, 6-3/8"; weight, 14½ oz.; fixed sights, with 1/10" serrated ramp front and square notch rear. Introduced in 1955; still in production. Used values, blue, $135 to $150; nickel, $150 to $165.

SMITH & WESSON Model 29 .44 Magnum: introduced in 1956; still in rather limited production; nominal retail price of the Model 29 is listed at $310 for most versions, $319.50 for the 8-3/8" barrel. Supply has lagged so far behind demand that Model 29s have been reported selling for up to twice the suggested retail, with used guns in good condition selling for nearly as much. As with the Model 27, the Model 29 was developed to take a new cartridge developed by lengthening the .44 Special case by 0.125" — this being intended to prevent use of .44 mag ammo in guns chambered for the .44 Special. The .44 mag is loaded to pressures approximately twice that of the .44 Special. The six-shot cylinder also will handle .44 Special or .44 Russian. Barrel lengths, 4", 5", 6½", 8-3/8"; length, 11-7/8" with 6½" barrel; weights, 43 oz. with 4", 47 oz. with 6½" and 51½ oz. with 8-3/8" barrel; sights, 1/8" red ramp front, S&W micrometer click rear, adjustable for elevation and windage; stocks, target type of goncalo alves, with S&W medallion. Broad, grooved target trigger, wide-spur target hammer. Finish, bright blue or nickel. Used value, up to $400 for 4" or 6½" barrel; up to $550 for 8-3/8" barrel. In this instance, largely a matter of supply and demand.

alloy, increasing the weight to 20½ oz. Finished in blue, nickel. Introduced about 1959; still in production. Used values, blue, $125 to $140; nickel, $140 to $150.

SMITH & WESSON Model 19 Combat Magnum: introduced about 1956; built on the lighter S&W K-frame, as used on the K-38, et al., rather than on the heavier N-frame, used for the Model 27 and 28; its six-shot cylinder is chambered for the .357 magnum cartridge; capable of firing .38 Special ammo; finish, S&W bright blue or nickel; stocks, checkered goncalo alves with S&W medallion; sights, 1/8" Baughman quick-draw front plain ramp, S&W micrometer click rear, adjustable for windage and elevation; available with 2½", 4" or 6" barrel; with 4" barrel, length is 9½" and weight is 35 oz. Used value, $165 to $185.

SMITH & WESSON Model 53 .22 Magnum: starting in the late Fifties, there was considerable interest in converting K-22s to center-fire wildcat (i.e., nonstandard cartridge) configurations, usually being chambered for a shortened version of the .22 Hornet, known as the .22 Harvey K-Chuck. With the intent of capitalizing on this interest, S&W introduced the .22 Remington CFM or center-fire magnum cartridge — also termed the .22 Jet — and the Model 53, chambered for it. The .22 magnum was a necked-down .357 case, designed to use a bullet of .222-.223" diameter. The Model 53 was supplied with six chamber bushings, adapting it for firing .22 rimfire ammo, by means of repositioning the striker on the hammer. Alternatively, a standard .22 LR cylinder was offered as a factory-fitted accessory, at about $35.30, for interchanging with the .22 Jet cylinder. Capacity, 6 rds.; barrel, 4", 6" and 8-3/8"; with 6" barrel, length was 11¼" and weight, 40 oz.; finish, blued only; stocks, checkered walnut with S&W medallion; sights, 1/8" Baughman ramp front, S&W micrometer click rear, adjustable for elevation and windage; Model 53 was dropped from production in 1974, having been introduced about 1960. Used value, $300 to $325; if complete with chamber inserts and/or fitted .22 LR cylinder; $40 to $50 higher with 8-3/8" barrel.

SMITH & WESSON Model 58 .41 Magnum: also known as the .41 Military & Police, this is a fixed-sight version of the Model 57; available only in 4" barrel, in blue or nickel; capacity, 6 rds.; overall length, 9¼"; weight, 41 oz.; sights, 1/8" serrated ramp front, square notch rear; stocks, checkered walnut, with S&W medallion, in magna pattern. Used values, blue, $165 to $185; nickel, $175 to $200.

SMITH & WESSON Model 49 Bodyguard: identical to the Model 38; except for all-steel frame, rather than aluminum

SMITH & WESSON Model 51 1960 .22/32 Kit Gun M.R.F.: identical to the Model 43, except that it is chambered for the .22 Winchester magnum rimfire cartridge and weighs 24 oz.; has an all-steel frame, 3½" barrel. Introduced in 1960; dropped, 1974. Retail, new, was $105.50 in blue, $113.50 in nickel. Used value, $185 to $200, blue; $210 to $225, nickel.

HANDGUNS

SMITH & WESSON .22 Auto Target Model 41: introduced about 1957; still in production; chambered for the .22 LR, the Model 41 is also available in .22 short for international competition; capacity, either caliber, 10 rds. in magazine; barrel lengths, 5" or 7-3/8". With 7-3/8" barrel, overall length is 12", weight is 43½ oz. Sights, 1/8" undercut Patridge type in front, S&W micrometer click rear, adjustable for windage and elevation; stocks, checkered walnut with modified thumb rest, usable by right- or left-handed shooters; finish, S&W bright blue, only; trigger, 3/8" wide, grooved, with adjustable stop; detachable muzzle brake supplied with 7-3/8" barrel only. Used value, $175 to $200.

The Model 41 was also made in a heavy-barrel variant, with or without an extendible front sight and in a less elaborate version, called the Model 46, with moulded nylon stocks. Values are approximately the same as quoted here.

SMITH & WESSON Model 60 Stainless Chiefs Special: identical to Model 36 Chiefs Special, except that all metal parts are of corrosion-resistant steel alloys. Introduced in 1965, still in production. Used value, $135 to $150.

SMITH & WESSON Model 61 Escort: automatic; hammerless; .22 LR only; 2.175" barrel; 4-13/16" overall length; 5-rd. magazine; thumb safety on left side of grip; fixed sights; cocking indicator; checkered plastic grips; blued or nickel finish. Introduced in 1970; dropped, 1973. Used values, blued, $75 to $80; nickel finish, $90 to $95.

SMITH & WESSON Model 57 .41 Magnum: introduced as a deluxe companion to the Model 58, both being chambered for a new cartridge developed especially for them at that time, carrying a bullet of .410" diameter. The old .41 Long Colt cartridge cannot be fired in guns chambered for the .41 magnum, nor can any other standard cartridge. Ammo is loaded by Rem-Peters and by Win-Western, with 210-grain lead or 210-grain JSP bullets, respectively to medium and high velocities. Capacity, 6 rds.; barrel lengths, 4", 6" and 8-3/8"; finish, bright blue or nickel; with 6" barrel, length is 11-3/8" and weight is 48 oz. Sights, 1/8" red ramp front, S&W micrometer click rear, adjustable for elevation and windage, with white outline notch; stocks, special over-size target-type of goncalo alves, with S&W medallion; wide, grooved target trigger and broad-spur target hammer. Introduced in 1964; still in production; blued, nickel. Used values, 4" and 6" barrels, $250 to $275; 8-3/8" barrel, $275 to $300.

.32 Auto

SMITH & WESSON .32 Auto: successor to S&W's original auto pistol, which was chambered for the caliber .35 S&W

Auto cartridge, this gun was chambered for the common .32 Auto or 7.65mm cartridge, having a magazine capacity of 8 rds., barrel length of 4" and weight of about 28 oz., measuring 7" overall; stocks, walnut, not checkered; finish, blued or nickel. Features included an unusual grip-safety, just below the trigger guard. Introduced in 1924; discontinued, 1937. Used value, $500 to $600.

aluminum alloy type, currently commanding premium prices, as noted here. Used value, blued, $125 to $150; nickel, $140 to $160. Steel-frame model, to $550.

SMITH & WESSON Model 39 9mm Auto: introduced in 1954; still in production; furnished with two 8-rd. magazines; barrel length, 4"; length overall 7-7/16"; weight, 26½ oz., without magazine; sights, 1/8" serrated ramp front, rear sight adjustable only for windage, with square notch; stocks, checkered walnut, with S&W medallion; finish, S&W bright blue or nickel. During the first dozen years of its production, a limited number of Model 39s were made with steel frames, rather than the standard

SMITH & WESSON Model 52 .38 Target Auto: introduced in 1961; still in production; designed to fire a mid-range loading of the .38 Special cartridge, requiring a wadcutter bullet seated flush with the case mouth; action is straight blowback, thus not suited for firing of high-velocity .38 Special ammo; magazine holds 5 rds.; barrel, 5", length overall, 8-5/8"; weight, 41 oz.; sights, Patridge-type front on ramp, S&W micrometer click rear, adjustable for elevation and windage; stocks, checkered walnut, with S&W medallion; available only in blue. Used value, $205 to $215.

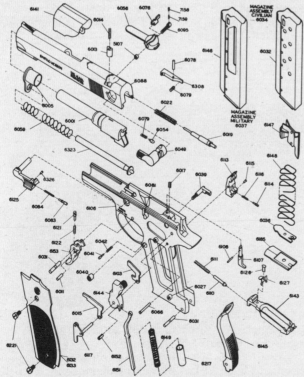

Model 39 Exploded View

SMITH & WESSON Model 59 9mm Auto: introduced in the early Seventies; similar to the Model 39, except for incorporation of a staggered-column magazine holding 14 rds.; weight, 27½ oz., without magazine; stocks, checkered, high-impact moulded nylon. Like the Model 39, the 59 offers the option of carrying a round in the chamber, with hammer down, available for firing via a double-action pull of the trigger. Other specs are the same as for the Model 39. Blue or nickel finish. Used value, $185 to $200 for blue finish; $200 to $225, nickel.

STAR

STAR Model A: automatic; 7.63mm Mauser, 9mm Bergmann (9mm Largo), .45 auto; modified version of Colt Model 1911 .45 auto, appearing almost identical to Browning patent; 5" barrel; 8½" overall length; 8-rd. magazine; checkered walnut grips; fixed sights; blued. The first locked breech pistol manufactured commercially by Bonifacio Echeverria, S.A., in Eibar, Spain. Currently designated as Model AS, in .38 Super auto only. Not currently imported. Introduced in 1922; still in production. Used value, $125 to $150.

STAR Model B: automatic; 9mm Parabellum; 9-rd. magazine; has the same design, other specifications as Model A. Early versions, had choice of barrel lengths: 4-3/16", 4-1/8" or 6-5/16". Introduced in early Twenties, dropped in WWII. Used value, $100 to $110.

STAR Model CO: automatic, pocket model; .25 auto only; 2¾" barrel; 4½" overall length; fixed sights; 6-rd. magazine; checkered plastic grips; blued. Introduced in 1934; dropped, 1957. Used value, $80 to $85. Engraved at added cost.

STAR Model H: pocket automatic; .32 auto; 7-rd. magazine. Identical in design to Model CO, except for caliber, magazine capcity. Introduced in 1934; dropped, 1941. Used value, $75 to $80.

STAR Model I: automatic, police model; .32 auto; 4¾" barrel; 7½" overall length; 9-rd. magazine; fixed sights, checkered plastic grips; blued. Not imported into U.S. Introduced in 1934; dropped, 1945. Used value, $85 to $90.

Model IN has the same general specifications as Model I, except chambered for .380 auto only; 8-rd. magazine. Introduced in 1934; still in production, but importation prohibited by Firearms Act of 1968. Used value, $85 to $90.

STAR Model M: automatic; .380 auto, 9mm Luger, 9mm Bergmann, .45 auto; 5" barrel, 8½" overall length; 7-rd. magazine for .45 Auto, 8 rds. for all other calibers; modification of Model 1911 Colt automatic model; fixed sights; checkered walnut grips; blued. Not imported into U.S. Introduced in 1935; still in production and marketed abroad. Used value, $105 to $110.

STAR Model S: automatic; .380 auto only; 4" barrel, 6½" overall length; 7-rd. magazine; fixed sights; checkered plastic grips, blued. Scaled-down modification of Colt 1911 automatic. Introduced in 1941; still in production, but importation into U.S. banned in 1968. Used value, $105 to $110.

Model SI has the same general specifications as Model S, except for chambering in .32 auto only, 7-rd. magazine. Introduced in 1941; still in production, but importation banned in 1968. Used value, $105 to $110.

Super S has the same general specifications as standard Model S, but with improved luminous sights for aiming in darkness, magazine safety, disarming bolt, indicator to show number of unfired cartridges. Introduced in 1942; dropped, 1954. Used value, $115 to $122.50.

Super SI has the same specifications as Super S, except for being chambered in .32 auto only. Introduced in 1942; dropped, 1954. Used value, $115 to $122.50.

STAR Super Star Model: 9mm parabellum, .38 Super auto, .380 auto; has the same general specifications as the Model M, except for addition of disarming bolt, improved luminous sights, magazine safety, indicator for number of unfired cartridges. Introduced in 1942; dropped, 1954. Not imported. Used value, $120 to $125.

Super Star Target Model has the same general specifications as Super Star model, except for substitution of adjustable target-type rear sight. Introduced in 1942; dropped, 1954. Used value, $120 to $125.

Model F Target

STAR Model F: automatic; .22 LR only; 4½" barrel, 7¼" overall length; 10-rd. magazine; fixed sights; checkered thumbrest plastic grips; blued. Introduced in 1942; dropped, 1969. Used value, $80 to $87.50.

Model F Sport model has the same general specifications as standard Model F, but with substitution of 6" barrel, adjustable target-type rear sight. Introduced in 1942;

dropped, 1969. Used value, $85 to $90.

Model F Target model has the same general specifications as standard Model F, except for substitution of adjustable target sights, 7" barrel, weights. Introduced in 1942; dropped, 1969. Used value, $85 to $90.

Model FRS is improved version of Model F, replacing the original version, but with same general specifications; 6" barrel; alloy frame. Available in blued, chrome finish, with checkered walnut grips. Introduced in 1969; still in production. No longer imported. Used values, blued, $90 to $92.50; chrome, $100 to $105.

Model FM has the same general specifications as the Model FRS, except for 4¼" barrel. Introduced in 1969; still in production. No longer imported. Used values, blued, $90 to $92.50; chrome, $100 to $105.

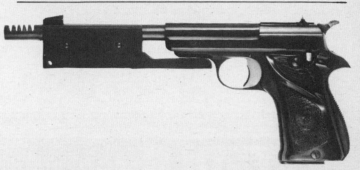

STAR Olympia Model: automatic; designed for International rapid-fire target competition; .22 short only; 7" barrel; 11-1/16" overall length; 9-rd. magazine; alloy slide; muzzle brake; adjustable barrel weights; adjustable rear target sight; checkered plastic grips. Introduced in 1950; still in production. Not currently imported. Used value, $130 to $137.50.

STAR Model HK: automatic; .32 auto, .380 auto; 2¾" barrel; 5-9/16" overall length; 6-rd. magazine in .380, 7 rds. in .32; fixed sights, plastic grips; blued. Introduced in 1955; still in production. Never imported into U.S. Used value, $80 to $85.

STAR Model DK: automatic; .380 auto; overall length, 5-11/16" has aluminum alloy frame. Designation originally used for long discontinued .22 pistol. New .380 version introduced in 1958; never imported into United States. Used value, $60 to $65.

STAR Model BKS: automatic; advertised as Star Starlight Model; 9mm Parabellum only; 4½" barrel; 8-rd. magazine; fixed sights; magazine, manual safeties; checkered plastic grips; blued, chrome finish. Introduced in 1970; still in production as BKM with duraluminum frame. Model BM, with steel frame. Imported by Interarms. Used values, blued, $120 to $125; chrome finish, $127.50 to $132.50.

STAR Super SM: automatic; .380 auto; 4" barrel; 6-5/8" overall length; 10-rd. magazine; thumb safety; loaded chamber indicator; adjustable rear sight, blade front; checkered plastic grips; blued, chrome finish. Introduced in 1970; still in production. No longer imported. Used values, blued, $107 to $112; chrome finish, $115 to $120.

STERLINGARMS

STERLING Model 283: also designated as the Target 300; automatic; .22 LR only; 4½" 6", 8" barrels; overall length, 9" with 4½" barrel; 10-rd. magazine; micrometer rear sight, blade front; checkered plastic grips; external hammer; adjustable trigger; all steel construction; blued finish. Introduced in 1970; dropped, 1972. Used value, $65 to $75.

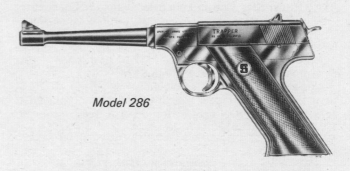

Model 286

Model 284

STERLING Model 284: also designated as Target 300L; automatic; .22 LR only; 4½", 6" tapered barrel; overall length, 9" with 4½" barrel; 10-rd. magazine; micrometer rear sight, blade front; checkered plastic grips; external spur hammer; adjustable trigger; all-steel construction; blued finish. Introduced in 1970; dropped, 1972. Used value, $77.50 to $85.

STERLING Model 286: advertised as the Trapper Model; automatic; .22 LR only; 4½", 6" tapered barrel; overall length, 9" with 4½" barrel; 10-rd. magazine, fixed rear sight, serrated ramp front; checkered plastic grips; external hammer; target-type trigger; all-steel construction; blued finish. Introduced in 1970; dropped, 1972. Used value, $50 to $60.

STERLING Model 295: advertised as Husky Model; automatic; .22 LR only; 4½" heavy barrel; overall length, 9"; 10-rd. magazine; fixed rear sight, serrated ramp front; checkered plastic grips; external hammer; target-type trigger; all-steel construction; blued finish. Introduced in 1970; dropped, 1972. Used value, $78.50 to $82.50.

plastic. Introduced in 1972; still in production. Used values, blued, $50 to $55; nickel, $60 to $65.

STERLING Model 300: automatic; blow-back action; .25 auto; 2½" barrel; overall length, 4½"; 6-rd. magazine; no sights; black, white plastic grips; blue, satin nickel finish; all-steel construction. Introduced in 1971; still in production. Used values, blued, $52.50 to $56.50; nickel, $60 to $65.

STERLING Model 400: automatic; blow-back double-action; .380 ACP; 3½" barrel; overall length, 6½"; micrometer rear sight, fixed ramp front; checkered rosewood grips; blue, satin nickel finish; thumb-roll safety; all-steel construction. Introduced in 1973; still in production as Model 400 MKII. Used values, blued, $95 to $100; nickel, $105 to $108.

STERLING Model 302: automatic; blow-back action; .22 LR; other specifications are generally the same as those of the Model 300, except that grips are available only in black

STERLING Model 402: automatic; blow-back double-action; .22 LR only; other specifications are generally the same as those of the Model 400. Introduced in 1973; dropped, 1974. Used values, blued $95 to $100; nickel, $105 to $108.

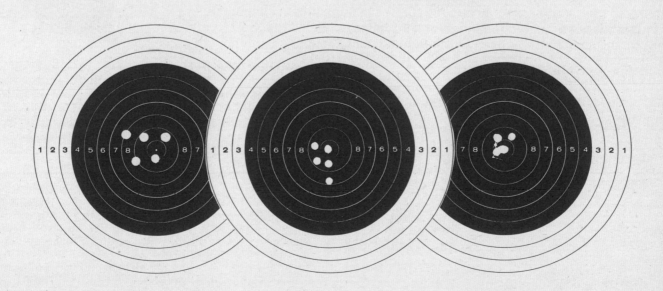

WALTHER

WALTHER Model 8: automatic; .25 Auto only; 2-7/8" barrel; 5-1/8" overall length; 8-rd. magazine; fixed sights; checkered plastic grips; blued. Manufactured by Waffenfabrik Walther, Zella-Mehlis, Germany. Introduced in 1920; dropped, 1945. Used value, $140 to $150.

Model 8 Lightweight has exactly the same specifications as the standard Model 8, except for use of aluminum alloy in slide, elements of frame. Introduced in 1927; dropped, 1945. Used value, $165 to $175.

WALTHER Model 9: automatic; vest pocket type; .25 Auto only; 2" barrel, 3-15/16" overall length; 6-rd. magazine; checkered plastic grips, fixed sights; blued. Introduced in 1921; dropped, 1945. Used value, $140 to $150.

WALTHER Model PP: automatic; designed as Law-enforcement Model; .22 LR, .25 Auto, .32 Auto, .380 Auto; 3.7/8" barrel, 6-5/16" overall length; 8-rd. magazine; fixed sights, checkered plastic grips, blued. WWII production has less value because of poorer workmanship. Introduced in 1929; dropped, 1945. Used values, wartime models, $180 to $185; .32, .380 calibers, $210 to $220; .22 caliber, $200 to $250; .25 caliber, $450 to $500.

Model PP Lightweight has the same specifications as standard model, except for use of aluminum alloy in construction. Introduced in 1929; dropped, 1945. Used values, .32, .380 calibers, $310 to $315; .22 caliber, $380 to $400; .25 caliber, $500 to $550.

Post-WWII Model PP is being manufactured currently by Carl Walther Waffenfabrik, Ulm/Donau, West Germany. It has the same specifications as the prewar model except not made in .25. Still in production. Imported by Interarms. Used value, $140 to $145.

Model PP Mark II is being made in France by Manufacture De Machines D Haut-Rhin and has the same specifications as the pre-WWII model. Introduced in 1953; still in production. Used value, $130 to $135.

WALTHER Model PPK: automatic; designated as the detective pistol; .22 LR, .25 Auto, .32 Auto, .380 Auto; 3¼" barrel, 5-7/8" overall length; 7-rd. magazine; checkered plastic grips; fixed sights; blued finish. WWII production has less value due to poorer workmanship. Introduced in 1931; still in production. Used values, wartime models, $205 to $220; .32, .380 calibers, $230 to $245; .22 caliber, $250 to $300; .25 caliber, $450 to $500.

Model PPK Lightweight has the same specifications as standard model, except for incorporation of aluminum alloys. Introduced in 1933; dropped, 1945. Used values, .32, .380, $325 to $345; .22, .25, $440 to $455.

Post-WW II PPK model is being manufactured in West Germany by Carl Walther Waffenfabrik. It has the same general specifications as the prewar model, with construction either of steel or aluminum alloy. Still in production, although U.S. importation was dropped in 1968. Used value, $250 to $265.

Model PPK Mark II is produced in France by Manufacture De Machines Du Haut-Rhin. It has the same specifications as pre-WWII model. Introduced in 1953; still in production. Used value, $225 to $240.

Model PPK Mark II Lightweight has the same specifications as the standard model, except that the receiver is of Dural and chambering is .22 LR, .32 auto only. Introduced in 1953; still in production. Used value, $225 to $235.

WALTHER Target Model: automatic; hammerless; .22 LR only; 6", 9" barrels; adjustable trigger; spring-driven firing pin; 10-rd. magazine capacity; safety on rear left side of frame; fixed front sight; rear adjustable for windage; hard rubber grips; Introduced in 1932; dropped during WWII. Used value, $115 to $125.

WALTHER Self-Loading Model: automatic; sport design; .22 LR only; 6", 9" barrels; with 6" barrel, 9-7/8" overall length; checkered one-piece walnut or plastic grip; adjustable target sights; blued. Introduced in 1932; dropped during WWII. Used value, $275 to $285.

WALTHER Olympia Sport Model: automatic; .22 LR only; 7-3/8" barrel; 10-11/16" overall length; checkered plastic grips; adjustable target sights; blued. Available with set of four detachable weights. Introduced in 1936; dropped during WWII. Used value, $300 to $315.

Olympia Hunting Model has the same specifications as Sport Model, except for 4" barrel. Introduced in 1936; dropped during WWII. Used value, $295 to $315.

Olympia Rapid Fire Model is automatic design; .22 short only; 7-7/16" barrel; 10-11/16" overall length; detachable muzzle weight; checkered plastic grips; adjustable target sights; blued finish. Introduced in 1936; dropped during

WWII. Used value, $410 to $425.

Olympia Funkampf Model is automatic design; .22 LR only; 9-5/8" barrel; 13" overall length; set of four detachable weights; checkered plastic grips; adjustable target sights; blued. Introduced in 1937; dropped during WWII. Used value, $525 to $535.

WALTHER Model HP: automatic; 9mm Luger; 5" barrel; 8-3/8" overall length; 10-rd. magazine; checkered walnut or plastic grips; fixed sights; blued. Introduced as commercial handgun in 1939; dropped during WWII. Used value, $410 to $425.

WALTHER P-38 Military Model: 9mm Luger; same specifications as the Model HP, but adopted as official German military sidearm in 1938 and produced throughout World War II by Walther, Mauser and others. Quality, in most cases, is substandard to that of HP due to wartime production requirements. Introduced in 1938; dropped, 1945. Used value, $175 to $200.

Post-war Model P-38 is manufactured currently by Carl Walther Waffenfabrik in Western Germany. It has the same general specifications as the WWII military model, except for improved workmanship and use of alloys in construction. Still in production. Imported by Interarms. Used value, $200 to $225.

Webley

WEBLEY Mark III Police Model: revolver; double action; hinged frame; .38 S&W only; 6-rd. cylinder; 3", 4" barrels; with 4" barrel, overall length, 9½"; fixed sights; checkered Vulcanite or walnut grips; blued finish. Introduced in 1897; dropped, 1945. Used value, $70 to $75.

WEBLEY Police & Civilian Pocket Model: revolver; double action; hinged frame; .32 S&W only; 3½" barrel; 6¼" overall length; 8-rd. cylinder; checkered plastic grips; fixed sights; blued finish. Introduced in 1906; dropped, 1940. Used value, $50 to $55.

WEBLEY Model 1906: automatic; .380 auto, .32 auto; 3½" barrel; 6¼" overall length; 7-rd. magazine in .380, 8 rds. in .32; exposed hammer; checkered hard rubber grips; checkered walnut grips on special order; blued; popular in Commonwealth for police use; law enforcement version has rear sight; those for civilian consumption have sight groove full length of slide. Introduced in 1905; dropped, 1940. Used value, $100 to $110.

WEBLEY Model 1909: automatic; hammerless; .25 auto only; 2-1/8" barrel; 4¼" overall length; 6-rd. magazine; front, rear sights mounted on slide; ejection port at top of slide; checkered black composition grips. Introduced in 1909; dropped, 1940. Used value, $175 to $180.

Model 1909 Improved is in 9mm Browning Long only; limited production, some for the government of the Union of South Africa. It differs from the original in several features: grip frame is angled more than on other Webley autos; magazine release button is behind trigger guard; no grip safety; lanyard ring mounted at bottom of backstrap; safety lever on left side of slide; checkered black plastic grips. Introduced in 1909; dropped, 1930. Has considerable collector value. Used value, $300 to $320.

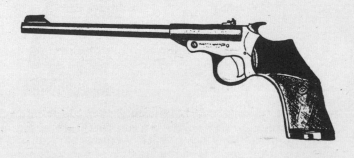

WEBLEY Model 1906: automatic; .25 auto only; 2-1/8" barrel; overall length, 4¼"; 6-rd. magazine; checkered hard rubber grips; resembles Model 1913 in appearance, but had no sights, no sight groove on slide. Introduced in 1906; dropped, 1940. Used value, $125 to $135.

WEBLEY Model 1909: single-shot; tip-up action; .22, .32 S&W, .38 S&W; 9-7/8" barrel; blade front sight; plastic thumbrest target grips; late versions had ballast chamber in butt to permit weight adjustment; rebounding hammer; matte-finish barrel; blued. Introduced in 1909; dropped, 1965. Used value, $100 to $115.

WEBLEY Model 1913: automatic; .455 only; commercial version of model adopted by Royal Navy in 1913; overall length, 8½"; 7-rd. magazine; grip safety; movable rear sight; fixed blade front; checkered black composition grips; checkered walnut grips on special order. Introduced in 1911; dropped, 1931. Has some collector value. Used value, $200 to $225.

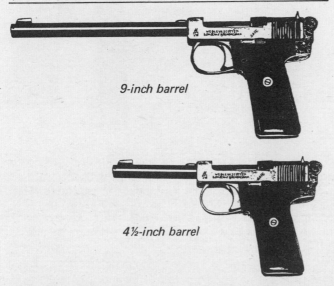

9-inch barrel

4½-inch barrel

WEBLEY Model 1911: single-shot; .22 rimfire only; has appearance of automatic as it is built on Model 1906 frame; 4½" and 9" barrels; originally introduced as police training arm; some were available with removable wooden stock. Introduced in 1911; dropped, 1927. Only a few hundred produced, affording it collector interest. Used value, $150 to $165.

WEBLEY Mark IV Police Model: revolver; double action; hinged frame; .38 S&W only; 6-rd. cylinder; 3", 4", 5", 6"

barrels; with 5" barrel, overall length, 9-1/8"; fixed or target sights; checkered plastic grips; lanyard ring; blued finish. Introduced in 1929; dropped, 1968. Used value, $60 to $65.

Mark IV War Model has the same general specifications as the Police Model. Built during WWII, it usually has poor fitting, blued-over unpolished surfaces. To protect the corporate reputation, most were stamped, "War Finish." Used value, $50 to $55.

WEBLEY Mark IV Target Model: revolver; double action; .22 LR only; built in small quantities on the Mark IV .38 frame; fitted with adjustable rear sight. Introduced in 1931; dropped, 1968. Virtually a custom-produced handgun. Used value, $100 to $110.

WEBLEY Mark IV .32 Police: revolver; double action; .32 S&W; has the same specifications as .38 S&W Mark IV Police version, except is chambered for smaller caliber. Introduced in 1968; dropped, 1968. Used value, $70 to $80.

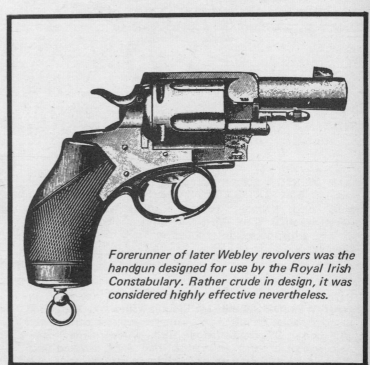

Forerunner of later Webley revolvers was the handgun designed for use by the Royal Irish Constabulary. Rather crude in design, it was considered highly effective nevertheless.

spur hammer; recessed barrel nut; blued, nickel, matte nickel finish. Introduced in 1971; dropped, 1975. Replaced by Model 14-2. Used values, blued, $110 to $120; nickel, $125 to $130; matte nickel, $135 to $140.

DAN WESSON Model 11: double-action revolver; .357 magnum only; 2½", 4", 6" interchangeable barrels; with 4" barrel, 9¼" overall length; 6-rd. cylinder; interchangeable grips; adjustable dovetail rear sight, serrated ramp front. Marketed with tools for changing barrels, grips; recessed barrel nut, blued. Introduced in 1970; dropped, 1974. Used value, $100 to $110.

DAN WESSON Model 15: double-action revolver; .357 magnum only; 2¼", 3¾", 5¾" interchangeable barrels; has same general specifications as Model 14, except for rear sight adjustable for windage, elevation. Introduced in 1971; dropped, 1975. Replaced by Model 15-2. Used values, blued, $140 to $150; nickel, $150 to $160; matte nickel, $165 to $175.

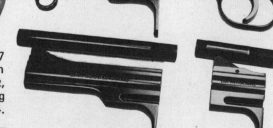

DAN WESSON Model 12: double-action revolver; .357 magnum only; 2¼", 3¾", 5¾" interchangeable barrels; with grips; 6-rd. cylinder; adjustable target-type rear sight, serrated ramp front. Marketed with tools for changing barrels, grips; blued. Introduced in 1970; dropped, 1974. Used value, $135 to $150.

DAN WESSON Model 14: double-action revolver; .357 magnum only; 2¼", 3¾", 5¾" interchangeable barrels; with 3¾" barrel, 9" overall length; 6-rd. cylinder; interchangeable walnut grips; fixed dovetail rear sight, serrated ramp front; wide trigger with adjustable overtravel stop; wide

Novelty of the Dan Wesson handgun lies in the fact that the barrels are easily and quickly interchangeable.

MISCELLANEOUS GUNS

AMERICAN 25: .25 auto, 8-rd. magazine; 4.4" overall length, 2.1" barrel; fixed sights; walnut grips; blued ordnance steel or stainless steel; manufactured by American Firearms Manufacturing Co., Inc. Introduced in 1966; dropped, 1974. Used values, blued steel model, $52.50 to $55; stainless steel model, $65 to $67.50.

AMERICAN FIREARMS Derringer: 2-shot; .38 Special, .22 LR, .22 WRM; 3" barrel; fixed open sights; checkered plastic grips; entirely of stainless steel; spur trigger, half-cock safety. Introduced in 1972; dropped, 1974. Used value, $47.50 to $50.

AUTO MAG: automatic; .357 Auto Mag., .44 Auto Mag.; 6½" barrel; 11½" overall length; 7-rd. magazine; short recoil, rotary bolt system; stainless steel construction; checkered plastic grips. fully adjustable rear sight, ramp front. Introduced in 1970; still in production. Used value, $360 to $375.

BAUER 25: automatic; .25 auto; 2-1/8" barrel; 4" overall length; 6-rd. magazine; stainless steel construction; fixed sights; plastic pearl or checkered walnut grips; manual, magazine safeties. Introduced in 1973; still in production. Used value, $70 to $75.

BUDISCHOWSKY TP-70: double-action automatic; .22 LR, .25 auto; 2-7/16" barrel; 4-2/3" overall length; 6-rd. magazine; fixed sights; all stainless steel construction; manual, magazine safeties. Introduced in 1973; still in production. Used value, $110 to $120.

CATTLEMAN Buckhorn Magnum: 6-rd. cylinder; single-action revolver, .357, .38 Special, .44 magnum, .44 Long Colt; 6½", 7½" barrels; smooth walnut grips; adjustable

rear sight, ramp front; single-action; case-hardened frame, blued barrel, brass backstrap, trigger guard; imported by LA Distributors (now Iver Johnson). Used value, .44 magnum, $90 to $97.50; other calibers, $75 to $80.

Cattleman Buntline Buckhorn Magnum is same as standard Buckhorn Magnum, except for 18" barrel. Used value, .44 magnum, $160 to $170; other calibers, $147.50 to $157.50.

Cattleman Magnum differs from standard Buckhorn Magnum only in that barrel lengths range from 4¾" to 7½"; not available in .38 Special; fixed sights. Used value, .44 magnum, $77.50 to $82.50; other calibers, $72.50 to $75.

CATTLEMAN Trailblazer: single-action revolver; 6-rd. cylinder; .22 long, LR; .22 magnum; comes with interchangeable magnum cylinder; 5½", 6½" barrel; smooth walnut grips; adjustable rear sight, ramp front; case-hardened frame, backstrap, trigger guard. Scaled-down version of Buckhorn model. Used value, $65 to $67.50.

CLERKE First Model: double-action revolver; .32 S&W, .22 LR, long, short; 2¼" barrel, 6¼" overall length; fixed sights; 5-rd. swing-out cylinder in .32, 6 rds. in .22; checkered plastic grips; blued, nickel finish. Introduced in 1973; dropped, 1974. Used value, $10 to $12.

ERMA Automatic: .22 LR target pistol, 10-rd. magazine, interchangeable 8-3/16", 11¾" barrels; adjustable target sights; checkered plastic grips; blued finish. Used value, $72.50 to $75.

ERMA KGP 68: auto pistol; .32 auto (KGP32), 6-rd. magazine; .380 auto (KGP38), 5-rd. magazine; 3½" barrel, overall length, 6¾"; adjustable blade front sight, fixed rear; checkered walnut grips; side-lock manual safety. Imported by Excam. Used value, $75 to $80.

ERMA KGP 69: auto pistol; .22 LR, 8-rd. magazine; 4" barrel, overall length, 7-5/16"; checkered walnut grips; adjustable blade front sight, fixed rear; slide stays open after last shot; imported from Germany by Excam as the KGP22. Used value, $72.50 to $75.

GARCIA Regent: revolver, .22 LR only; 3", 4", 6" barrels; 8-rd. swing-out cylinder; fixed rear sight, ramp front; checkered plastic grips; blued. Introduced in 1972; dropped, 1977. Used value, $35 to $40.

HARTFORD Target Automatic: in .22 LR only; 6¾" barrel; 10¾" overall length; 10-rd. magazine; checkered black rubber grips; target sights; blued finish. Bears close resemblance to early High Standard automatic models. Introduced in 1929; dropped, 1930. Has more collector than shooter value. Used value, $175 to $200.

HARTFORD Repeating Pistol: has the same general outward design characteristics as target auto; .22 LR only; hand-operated repeater, with slide being moved rearward by hand to eject cartridge case, forward to chamber new round. Introduced in 1929; dropped, 1930. Used value, $150 to $175.

HARTFORD Target Single-Shot: same general outward appearance as Hartford target auto, but with 5¾" barrel; 10¾" overall length; .22 LR only; black rubber or walnut grips, target sights, color case-hardened frame, blued barrel. Introduced in 1929; dropped, 1930. Used value, $150 to $175.

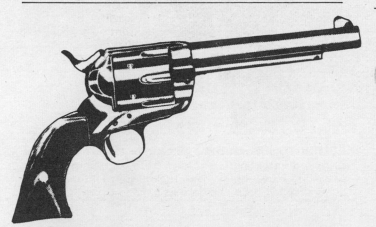

HAWES Western Marshal: single-action revolver; 6-rd. cylinder; .357 magnum, .44 magnum, .45 Long Colt, .22 magnum, .22 LR; 6" barrel for center-fire calibers; 5" barrel for .22 magnum, .22 LR; rosewood grips on center-fire models, plastic moulded stag, rimfire; interchangeable cylinders within calibers for all models — .357 magnum/9mm, .44 magnum/.44/40, .45 Long Colt/.45 ACP, .22 LR/.22 magnum. Used values with single cylinders, .357 magnum, .44 magnum, .45 Long Colt, $75 to $77.50; above, with interchangeable cylinders, $87.50 to $90; .22 magnum or .22 LR with single cylinders, $47.50 to $50; with interchangeable cylinders, $55 to $60. Still in production.

HAWES Chief Marshal: single-action; 6-rd. cylinder; .357 magnum, .44 magnum, .45 Long Colt; 6" barrel; extra-large smooth rosewood grips; adjustable rear sight, ramp target front; heavy frame; imported from West Germany by Hawes Firearms Co. Used value, $80 to $82.50.

Heckler & Koch HK-4

HECKLER & KOCH HK-4: auto double-action pistol; .380 auto; 8-rd. magazine; 3½" barrel, 6" overall length; checkered black plastic grips; rear sight adjustable for windage, front, fixed. Early version was available with interchangeable barrels, magazines for four calibers. Imported from Germany originally by Harrington & Richardson, currently by Heckler & Koch, Inc. Used value, single caliber, $90 to $100; with four barrels as set, $140 to $155.

HECKLER & KOCH P9S: 9mm Parabellum; 9-rd. magazine; 4" barrel, 5.4" overall length; fixed sights, checkered plastic grips; double-action; loaded/cocked indicators; hammer cocking lever; originally imported from Germany by Gold Rush Gun Shop, currently by Heckler & Koch, Inc. Used value, $175 to $200.

MKE Model TPK: double-action auto pistol; .32 auto, 8-rd. magazine .380, 7-rd. magazine; 4" barrel, 6½" overall length; adjustable notch rear sight, fixed front; checkered plastic grips; exposed hammer; safety blocks firing pin, drops hammer; chamber loaded indicator pin. Copy of Walther PP. Imported from Turkey by Firearms Center, Inc. Used value, $75 to $85.

MOSSBERG Brownie: double-action, pocket pistol; four 2½" barrels; revolving firing pin; .22 LR, long, short; break-open action; steel extractor. Introduced in 1919; dropped, 1932. Has some collector interest. Used value, $65 to $75.

ORTGIES Pocket Pistol: automatic; blowback action; .32 auto; 3¼" barrel; 6½" overall length; 8-rd. magazine; constructed without screws, uses pins and spring-loaded catches; grip safety protrudes only when firing pin is cocked; fixed sights, unchecked walnut grips; blued. Introduced about 1919; dropped, 1926. Used value, $65 to $70.

Ortgies .380 auto has same specifications as the .32, except for additional thumb-operated safety catch; 7-rd. magazine. Introduced in 1922; dropped, 1926. Used value, $80 to $90.

Ortgies .25 auto is scaled-down version of .32 auto; 6-rd. magazine; 2¾" barrel, 5-3/16" overall length. Introduced in 1920; dropped, 1926. Used value, $65 to $70.

REMINGTON Model 95: superposed double-barrel derringer; single-action; .41 short rimfire; 3" barrels, 4-7/8" overall length. Introduced in 1866; dropped, 1935. Prior to 1888, the model was stamped E. Remington & Sons; from 1888 to 1910, the derringers were marked Remington Arms Co.; from 1910 to 1935, guns were marked Remington Arms-U.M.C. Co. The early styles have a two-armed extractor, long hammer spur. In later models, a few have no extractor; majority have sliding extractor, short hammer spur.

Available with all-blued finish; full nickel plate, blued barrels, nickel-plated frame; factory engraving; choice of checkered hard rubber, walnut, mother-of-pearl, ivory grips; fixed rear groove sight, front blade cast on top barrel. Value of gun on modern market is primarily as collector item. Used value, plain model, $250 to $265; all nickel, $275 to $290; engraved model with mother-of-pearl or ivory grips, $395 to $425.

REMINGTON Model 51: automatic pistol; .32 auto, .380 auto; 7-rd. magazine; 3½" barrel, 3-5/8" overall length; fixed sights, blued finish; hard rubber grips. Introduced in 1918; dropped, 1934. Used value, $125 to $150.

REMINGTON Model XP-100: single-shot pistol; bolt-action; .221 Remington Fireball only; 6½" barrel, 15¾" overall length; vent rib; blade front sight, adjustable rear; receiver drilled, tapped for scope mounts; one-piece brown nylon stock; blued finish. Introduced in 1963; still in production. Used value, $100 to $110.

SAVAGE Model 1917: automatic pistol; .32 auto, 10-rd. magazine; .380 auto, 9-rd. magazine; 3¾" barrel in .32, 4½" barrel in .380; spurred hammer; blued finish, fixed sights, hard rubber grips. Introduced in 1920 to replace Model 1915; dropped, 1928. Used value, $125 to $135.

SAVAGE Model 101: single-action single-shot; .22 LR, long, short; 5½" barrel integral with chamber; overall length, 9"; fake cylinder swings out for loading, ejection; manual ejection with spring-rod ejector; compressed, plastic-impregnated wood grips; adjustable slotted rear sight, blade front; blued. Introduced in 1968; dropped 1969. Used value, $20 to $27.50.

SHERIDAN Knockabout: single-shot pistol; tip-up action; .22 short, long, 5" barrel, 8¾" overall length; checkered plastic grips; blued finish; fixed sights. Introduced in 1953; dropped, 1960. Used value, $60 to $70.

SIG 210: auto pistol; .22 LR; 7.65mm, 9mm Parabellum; 8-rd. magazine; 4¾" barrel, 8½" overall length; fixed notch rear sight, blade front; checkered plastic or grooved walnut grips; thumb safety, external hammer; originally imported from Switzerland by Gold Rush Gun Shop. Still in production; not imported. Used value, $200 to $250.

STEYR Model SP: automatic; double-action pocket pistol; .32 auto; 7-rd. detachable magazine; revolver-type trigger; movable rear sight, fixed front; checkered black plastic grips; blued finish. Introduced in 1957; still in production, but not imported since 1968 Gun Control Act. Used value, $125 to $150.

STOEGER Luger: automatic; .22 LR only; 11-rd. magazine; 4½", 5½" barrel; based upon original Luger design, but made in U.S. by Stoeger Arms; checkered or smooth wooden grips; blued. Introduced in 1970; still in production. Used value, $75 to $80.

STEVENS No. 35: single-shot target pistol; .22 LR only; 6", 8", 12¼" barrels; tip-up action; walnut grips; target sights; blued. Also produced to handle .410 shotshell. Introduced in 1907; dropped, 1939. Has mostly collector value. Used value, $150 to $160.

THOMPSON/CENTER Contender: introduced in 1967; still in production. Single-shot, break-open pistol with exposed hammer, the action being opened by pressing rearward and upward on the tang of the trigger guard. Barrels are interchangeable, permitting the firing of different calibers from the same receiver. A circular insert in the face of the hammer is pivoted one-half turn to switch between the center-fire and rimfire firing pins. Barrels have been factory chambered and custom rechambered for a variety of different cartridges, many of them nonstandard, or "wildcat" numbers. A detachable choke tube was developed originally for a barrel chambered for the .45 Long Colt which, with choke installed, could fire 3" .410 shotshells effectively. Production of this barrel was discontinued at the suggestion of BATF; the .45 LC/.410 barrels have changed hands at prices of $150 or more, due to their scarcity. Currently, two types of choked barrels are made: an external model and an internal choke, the latter being furnished on the vent-ribbed barrel; both being made in .357 magnum and .44 magnum permitting the firing of solid-bullet loads when the choke is removed or T/C's "HotShot" capsules with choke in place.

Rimfire calibers are .22 LR (also handling .22 BB caps, CB caps, short, long or shot loads), .22 WMRF, 5mm Rem.; center-fire calibers are .22 Hornet, .22 K-Hornet, .22 Rem. Jet, .218 Bee, .221 Rem. Fire Ball, .222 Rem., .256 Win. magnum, .25-35 WCF, .30 M-1 Carbine, .30-30 WCF, .38 Super Auto, .38 Special, .357 magnum, .357/44 Bain & Davis, 9mm Parabellum (Luger), .45 ACP, .45 Long Colt, .44 magnum. The .357, .44 and .45 LC can be had with choke or without; unfluted "bull barrels" are offered in .30

Herrett and .357 Herrett, these being two wildcat cartridges based upon the .30-30 case; standard barrel lengths, 8¾" and 10", although a few have been made in 6" length; standard forends snap on, but a special screw-held forend is supplied with the bull barrels; two designs of grips have been furnished, the early type having a decorative metal butt cap and the current one having a black plastic butt cap; decorative game scene etching is standard on both sides of all receivers; later models have adjustable trigger-stop in rear of trigger guard; standard sights consist of an undercut Patridge front sight on a ramp, with square-notch rear sight adjustable for windage or elevation; scope mounts available from T/C and other suppliers to fit the holes drilled and tapped for rear sight; weight, with 10" barrel, about 43 oz.; finish, blued; stocks, checkered walnut forend and handgrip, with thumb rest grips that must be ordered for right-hand or left-hand use, no extra charge for left-hand grips. Most early models embody a receiver design which makes it necessary to reset the action by pulling the trigger guard tang rearward before the hammer can be cocked. Used values, $110 to $115 for standard gun, complete with one barrel; $115 to $120 for gun with ventilated rib/internal choke or full bull barrel less sights; $120 to $125 for gun with bull barrel and iron sights; $40 to $42.50 for standard barrel alone; up to $46.50 for ventilated rib/internal choke or bull barrel less sights; $45 to $50 for bull barrel alone, fitted with iron sights. Scarce, discontinued barrels in exotic chamberings, may command higher figures.

WHITNEY Wolverine: autoloader; .22 LR only; 4-4/8" barrel; 9" overall length; aluminum alloy frame; rear sight movable for windage only; 1/8" Patridge-type front; top of slide serrated to reduce reflection; checkered plastic grips; blued or nickel finish. Introduced in 1956; dropped, 1963. Has some collector interest. Used values, blued finish, $70 to $80; nickel, $90 to $100.

HANDGUN NOTES

RIFLES

Here Are The Pitfalls To Avoid In Buying — Or Selling — A Used Rifle!

AS A GENERAL RULE, a rifle holds its highest value at that moment when its first owner plunks down his long green and the dealer wraps it up and fills out the required paper work. At that time, its condition is comparable to what coin collectors term "uncirculated" and as it is owned and used, its mint-new brightness deteriorates to some inevitable extent, according to Dean A. Grennell, who has thirty-odd years' experience in gun dealings.

Which is to say that the condition of a rifle weighs heavily in influencing its value when its resale comes under discussion. In addition, the status of the would-be buyer plays its part in establishing a realistic and agreeable level of value. The average shooter will be inclined to pay somewhat more than you can expect to obtain from a typical gun dealer for the simple and obvious reason that he's accustomed to the retail level of prices rather than wholesale costs. This comment presupposes that you are selling, rather than buying. By turnabout reasoning, you may be able to buy a given rifle for less money from a private owner than you'd have to pay for the same gun at a retail store.

There are advantages and disadvantages in conducting transactions with dealers or private owners, whether buying or selling. A private party may pay more, but you're faced with the challenge of finding him, dickering with him and collecting the cash. Your would-be buyer may want to give you a few dollars down and the rest in easy installments.

The dealer, though inclined to pay less in the long run, usually will count the agreed-upon sum of cash out of the till and hand it to you. So straightforward an approach has undeniable appeal. Alternatively, the dealer may have some other gun in stock that catches your eye and tickles your fancy, and you may consummate the deal with a comparatively small amount of cash changing hands.

There are several promising approaches to follow when you're on the prowl for a rifle. The obvious first step is to decide, within suitably broad or narrow limits, just what type of rifle you want or need. Having established that, try to form an accurate evaluation of typical current and local values, so you won't snap up the first one you see at a price of $225, only to find you could have bought the same thing for $180 had you kept looking a while longer.

Having saved up most or all of the needed cash, you can commence reading the appropriate section of the classified advertisements of the local newspaper each day, calling or contacting those whose ads sound interesting. At the same time, maintain a routine patrol of your local gun dealers, reviewing their ever-changing stocks with polite interest. If there are gun shows being held within reasonable traveling distances, program a few visits to those as well.

Gun shows are interesting and educational, though they do not tend to be rich veins of super bargains. Most of those who have guns on display have a fairly shrewd idea of the value of their wares and the prices are pegged accordingly. Usually, the price tags reflect some amount of margin for haggling.

The last hour or two before the show closes finds conditions most favorable for the would-be buyer. The displayers are contemplating the chore of packing their wares for the homeward trip. Perhaps they've not moved the volume they'd hoped to sell. Maybe they've spotted a gun they fancy at a nearby table, but need to raise cash in order to buy it. Considerations such as these can make them more amenable to offers well below their tagged prices.

Garage sales, auctions and swap meets turn up occasional treasures at modest prices but you can get most royally stung if you neglect elementary precautions. If you do not examine the proffered rifle with the keenest, most cynical eye, you can end up with a nonworking or unsafe piece of costly trash.

There is a timeworn cliche: Hotter than a two-dollar pistol. Trite, but highly relevant. Does the would-be seller have clear and unencumbered title to his wares, or is the serial number going to get you some earnest conversation with the police when you decide to trade it in at a legitimate gun dealer's shop? Swap meets, flea markets and similar dubious phenomena are notorious for flimflams of this nature and it doesn't help much if all you can tell the police department's investigator is that the guy you bought it from had long hair, a beard, wore dark glasses and sniffled constantly.

It's reasonable to ask the seller for identification, if you're in doubt. Check his driver's license, jotting down the particulars and perhaps his auto license number as well. If he balks at this, walk away, making note of the car license as a sensible precaution. Gun thieves are none too popular with shooters and your local police department may be interested.

When the shoe is on the other foot, much the same applies. If you know the buyer personally, that's one thing. If not, obtain reliable identification and keep a record of it. Exchange informal documents: a bill of sale and receipt to the buyer and a receipt for the gun to the seller, giving the make, model, caliber and serial number of the rifle, as well as the date and time of the transaction. If the gun is used in a crime, ditched and recovered by the police, such a receipt can be worth its weight in just about any valued commodity.

Rifles span a broad gamut as to value and utility. There are examples of primary interest to the shooter, others with interest to the collector and a middle ground of specimens with combined appeal in both areas.

In theory, if you buy a rifle and take good care of it, it is reasonable to anticipate that the day will come when it can be sold for your original purchase price, perhaps for a higher figure. In certain examples, this effect is much more radical and impressive than in others.

If the rifle has an inherent excellence of design, material and workmanship, its value will decline little, if at all, and the passing years will augment the investment at a rate to make a stockbroker's eyes glaze over. In our inflationary economy this trend is reflected strongly in the rising value of high-quality firearms, rifles included.

The secret lies in the ability to spot and extrapolate potential trends, getting in on the ground floor and riding with the tide. If one has this Nostradamic ability to outstanding extents, he is wasting his efforts in trading in firearms and should have been packing his portfolio with Xerox and Polaroid common stock when both issues were well down into the calculated-risk category.

If we may dwell upon intangibles for just a bit, it boils down to a question of class. This is an ephemeral quality, but one that cannot be disregarded. It cannot be equated on a one-for-one basis to the number of man-hours expended in the creation of any given rifle, although that is a potential factor. What really counts lies in what the men did for all those hours.

As an example, let us consider the matter of checkering. Good checkering enhances value, but smooth wood is much preferred over bad checkering.

Let us take an example and term it hypothetical. Turn back the clocks and calendars to some point in the mid-Sixties. A shooter/shopper strolls idly into the emporium of a midwestern gun dealer, spots an interesting specimen and requests a closer examination. A clerk picks it up and hands it to him. The shopper's first move is to crank open the bolt and check the breech for emptiness. Routine? Yes, certainly, but a routine not to be neglected.

The rifle started its career as a high-number Springfield and has the desirable milled trigger guard, but embarrassing things have befallen it. Some well-meaning former owner has treated it to a sporter-type stock and has essayed to checker said stock, with much more enthusiasm than skill, alas. It appears the intrepid soul may have borrowed his spouse's nail file to use as a checkering tool. The pistol grip and forend are desecrated with random grooves at a pitch of about six lines to the inch, no line approaching straightness.

The usual price tag is not looped into the trigger guard. The shopper asks the obvious question. The clerk bustles off to confer with the owner of the shop and returns with the requested data.

"Forty dollars with the scope, twenty-five without."

The scope is one of the early K8 Weavers from the era when making adjustments moved the crosshairs bodily, rather than the image, leaving the reticle centered permanently. The crosshairs now intersect in the upper left quadrant of the scope's image but, for all that, the receiver has been drilled and tapped for Weaver blocks and the bolt handle has been modified to clear the eyepiece of the K8. He communes with his wallet and reaches a decision.

"For you, I have good news," he confides, "I will haul it away to spare you further embarrassment of this sort."

Fifteen years come and go. The antique K8 Weaver has been transferred to a Winchester Model 43 in .218 Bee. The odious but blessedly shallow checkering was obliterated from the pistol grip and forend with a few hours of deftly wielded sandpaper, followed by several lovingly rubbed coats of boiled linseed. The resulting unassuming but functional Springfield turned out to be a heartwarming super-grouper. At a point just a tad short of 1979's vernal equinox, the basic rifle, sans any scope, could be liquidated for right around six hundred percent of its original purchase price.

Nestling in the rack next to the salvaged Springfield stands a Model 70 Winchester, purchased in 1966 when it labored under the handicap of being Winchester's discontinued model. Yes, indeed, a pre-'64 Model 70 in .300 Winchester magnum, acquired for a trifling $49, due to its disreputable status at the time.

Along the way, it has dotted off groups under one-half-inch from a distance of two hundred yards.

Next down the line stands a massive mauler of a bench-rest rifle, tipping the beam at well over sixteen pounds; a tack-driving rascal, chambered for the .22-250 cartridge. Like the resurrected Springfield, it's been around since the early Sixties. Once, in a weak moment, it was taken in to a midwestern gun shop with intent to sell it or barter it for some fancied gewgaw of the moment. Learning that the caliber was .22-250, the dealer professed zilch interest in it at any price. For those were the days before Remington legitimatized the .22-250 round and, for that state of affairs, the ongoing owner of record is appropriately grateful.

Military arms, such as the old Springfield, have innate potential desirability to the extent that they are high in quality. Once a drug upon the market, all the good ones have found loving homes, long since and saleable specimens have appreciated in value to a rather extravagant extent. Examples such as the Carcano never will make it because they lacked class and that touch of style.

Commercial rifles, lovingly made and capable of outstanding performance, such as the pre-'64 Model 70 Winchester, are coveted and cherished. It is conceivable that this may come to be true, even if they suffer the handicap of stamped checkering. Anything is possible.

The ammo a gun is designed to consume helps to dictate its intrinsic value. You may see prestige make/model shotguns at gun shows, going for a song for the simple reason that they are incapable of consuming anything other than 16-gauge shells. The .22-250 cartridge is one of the great numbers of all time. In 1979, everyone — well, practically everyone — agrees upon that, but it was not always thus. The .22 Savage Hi-Power was a nifty little load in its day, but the sunset of that day was long ago.

There are collectors who will shell out fancy prices for a coveted rarity. But they are scarce and far between. If the rarity in question can handle cartridges still in abundant supply, and handle it with *savoir faire,* aplomb and fly-scalping accuracy, then you have a rifle of wide potential appeal, warranting the investment of whatever it takes to acquire clear title. In time, its value will come around to substantiating your judgment.

If the rifle in question has little more than the ability to set off a cartridge, containing its pressures without overly endangering the soul who tugged its trigger, delivering the projectile out the muzzle in some morning-glory configuration of direction toward the target, meanwhile retaining esthetic aspects mindful of an unmade bed, with a stock of the finest sycamore that ever flourished along the banks of the Wabash, stained to resemble the color of walnut from a distance of sixty feet in wan light, with stamped simulated fleur-de-lis that almost match from one side to the other, on both pistol grip and forend, perhaps dipped into black paint for the first couple inches to suggest an ebony forend cap — well, in that case, buy it if you want a shooter of sorts, but don't count on doubling your investment over the course of the first year.

Anschutz

Model 64S

ANSCHUTZ Model 64: bolt-action, single-shot match rifle; .22 LR only; 26" barrel; walnut-finished hardwood stock; cheekpiece; hand-checkered pistol grip, beavertail forearm; adjustable butt plate; no sights; scope blocks, receiver grooved for Anschutz sights; adjustable single-stage trigger; sliding side safety; forward sling swivel for competition sling. Marketed in U.S. as Savage/Anschutz Model 64. Introduced in 1967; still in production. Used value, $152.50 to $159.50.

Model 64L has the same specifications as Model 64, except for left-hand action. Still in production. Used value, $169 to $175.50.

Model 64S has the same specifications as standard Model 64, except for addition of Anschutz No. 6723 match sight set. Still in production. Used value, $206 to $208.

Model 64SL has the same specifications as Model 64S except for left-hand action. Still in production. Used value, $214.50 to $224.50.

ANSCHUTZ Model 1407: bolt-action, single-shot match rifle; action based upon that of Savage/Anschutz Model 54; .22 LR only; 26" barrel; length, weight conform to ISU competition requirements, also suitable for NRA matches; French walnut prone-style stock; Monte Carlo, cast-off cheekpiece; hand-checkered pistol grip, forearm; swivel rail, adjustable swivel; adjustable rubber butt plate; no sights; receiver grooved for Anschutz sights; scope blocks; single-stage trigger; wing safety. Marketed in U.S. by Savage. Introduced in 1967; still in production. Used value, right-hand model, $325 to $331.50; left-hand stock, $344.50 to $354.

ANSCHUTZ Model 1411: bolt-action, single-shot match rifle; built on same action as Savage/Anschutz Model 54; .22 LR only; has same basic specifications as Model 1407, except for longer overall length of 46"; 27½" barrel. Introduced in 1967; still in production. Used value, $370.50 to $377; left-hand stock, $390 to $399.50.

ANSCHUTZ Model 1413: bolt-action, single-shot match rifle; has the same specifications as Model 1411, except for International-type French walnut stock; adjustable aluminum hook butt plate; adjustable cheekpiece. Introduced in 1967; still in production. Used value, $572 to $578.50; left-hand stock, $598 to $624.50.

Browning

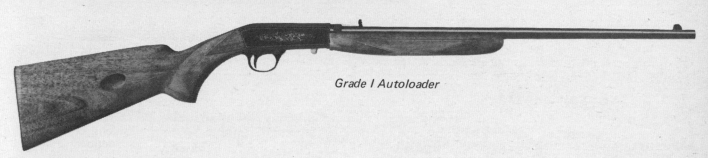

Grade I Autoloader

BROWNING Grade I Autoloader .22: same action as discontinued Remington Model 241A; takedown; .22 LR, .22 short, not interchangeable; 19¼" barrel for LR, 22¼" for short cartridge; butt stock tube magazine, holding 11 LR, 16 short cartridges; select American walnut stock; hand-checkered pistol grip, semi-beavertail forearm; open rear sight, bead front; engraved receiver, grooved for tip-off scope mount; cross-bolt safety. Introduced in 1958. Manufactured in Belgium until 1972; production transferred to Miroku in Japan; still in production. Used value, $115 to $125.

Grade II has identical specifications to Grade I, except for gold-plated trigger; .22 LR only; 11-rd. capacity; satin chrome-plated receiver, small game animal scenes engraved on receiver. Still in production. Used value, $190 to $199.50.

Grade III has same specifications as Grade I, except for gold-plated trigger, extra-fancy walnut stock, forearm; skip checkering on pistol grip, forearm; satin chrome-plated receiver; hand-carved, engraved scrolls, leaves, dog/game bird scenes; .22 LR only. Still in production. Used value, $362.50 to $375.

Safari Grade Heavy Barrel

Olympian Grade

BROWNING High-Power Safari Grade: standard Mauser-type bolt-action; .270 Win., .30/06, 7mm Rem. magnum, .300 Win. magnum; .308 Norma magnum, .338 Win. magnum, .375 Holland & Holland magnum, .458 Win. magnum; 24" barrel in magnum calibers, 22" in others; 4-rd. magazine capacity for magnum cartridges, 6 rds. for others; European walnut stock; hand-checkered pistol grip, forearm; Monte Carlo cheekpiece; recoil pad on magnum models; folding leaf rear sight, hooded ramp front; quick-detachable sling swivels. Introduced in 1960; dropped, 1974. Used value, $480 to $495.

Safari grade short action has the same specifications as standard grade Safari except for short action; .222 Rem., .222 Rem. magnum; 22" lightweight, 24" heavy barrel. Dropped, 1974. Used value, $442.50 to $465.

Safari grade medium action model has same specifications as standard model except for action length; .22-250, .243 Win., .284 Win., .308 Win.; 22" lightweight barrel standard, but available in .22-250, .243 with heavy barrel. Dropped, 1974. Used value, $465 to $477.50.

Medallion grade has the same specifications as standard Safari grade with exception of scroll-engraved receiver, barrel; engraved ram's head on floor plate; select European walnut stock has rosewood grip cap, forearm tip. Dropped 1974. Used value, $765 to $787.50.

Olympian grade High-Power has the same specifications as Safari, except for engraving on barrel; chrome-plated floor plate, trigger guard, receiver, all engraved with game scenes; figured European walnut stock; rosewood forearm tip, grip cap; grip cap is inlaid with 18-karat gold medallion. Discontinued, 1974. Used value, $1335 to $1390.

Model T-2

BROWNING Model T-1 T-Bolt: straight-pull bolt-action; .22 LR only; 24" barrel; 5-rd. clip magazine; uncheckered walnut pistol-grip stock; peep rear sight, ramped blade front; in either left or right-hand model. Introduced in 1965;

dropped, 1973. Used value, $62 to $65.

Model T-2 has same specifications as Model T-1, except for figured, hand-checkered walnut stock. Dropped, 1973. Used value, $90 to $95.

Grade II BAR

Grade IV BAR

BROWNING BAR: not to be confused with military Browning selective fire rifle; semiautomatic; .243 Win., .308 Win., .270 Win., .30/06, 7mm Rem. magnum, .300 Win. magnum, .338 Win. magnum; 22" barrel; 4-rd. detachable box magazine for standard calibers, 3-rd. for magnums; adjustable folding leaf rear sight, gold bead hooded ramp front; receiver tapped for scope mounts; checkered walnut

pistol-grip stock, forearm. Grades I, II introduced in 1967; Grades II, III, V still in production. Grades vary according to amount of checkering, carving, engraving, inlay work. Used values, standard calibers Grade I, $370 to $390; II, $415 to $440; III, $485 to $515; IV, $750 to $805; V, $830 to $860; magnum calibers, Grade I, $400 to $420; II, $435 to $460; III, $545 to $600; IV, $775 to $835; V, $920 to $1060.

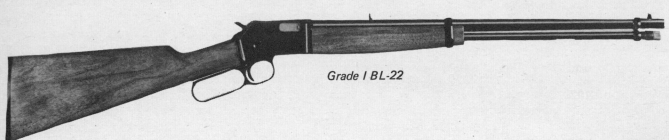

Grade I BL-22

BROWNING BL-22 Grade I: lever-action; .22 LR, long, short; 20" barrel; tube magazine holds 22 rds. in .22 short, 17 rds. in long, 15 LR; folding leaf rear sight, bead post front; two-piece uncheckered walnut stock, forearm; barrel band; half-cock safety; receiver grooved for tip-off mounts.

Grade II has engraved receiver, checkered grip, forearm. Produced by Miroku Firearms, Tokyo, Japan, to Browning specifications. Introduced in 1970; still in production. Used values, $95 to $105 for Grade I; $110 to $115 for Grade II.

BROWNING BLR: lever-action; .308 Win., .243 Win.; 20" | barrel; 4-rd. detachable magazine; square-notch adjustable rear sight, gold bead hooded ramp front; receiver tapped for scope mount; recoil pad; straight-grip stock, forearm, checkered, oil finished; wide, grooved trigger. Introduced 1971; made to Browning specifications by Miroku Firearms, Tokyo, Japan, since May '74; still in production. Used value, $205 to $225.

BROWNING Model 78: single-shot; falling block action; .22-250, 6mm Rem., .25/06, .30/06; 26" round or tapered barrel; no sights; drilled, tapped for scope mount; rubber recoil pad; select walnut stock, hand checkered, hand rubbed; exposed hammer; automatic ejector, half-cock safety. Produced to Browning specifications by Miroku Firearms, Tokyo, Japan. Introduced in 1973; still in production. Used value, $225 to $245.

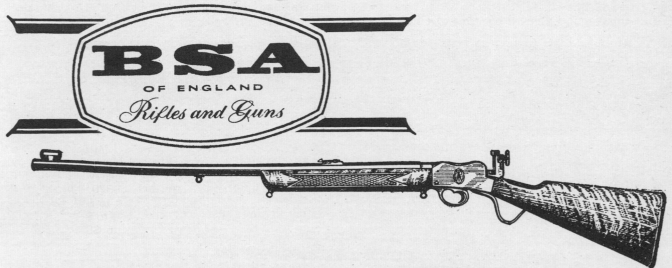

BSA No. 12: single-shot Martini-action target rifle; .22 LR only; 29" barrel; straight-grip walnut stock; hand-checkered forearm; Parker-Hale No. 7 rear sight, hooded front. Introduced in 1912; dropped, 1929. Used value, $176 to $181.50.

BSA No. 13: same general specifications as No. 12, but lighter in weight, 25" barrel; .22 LR only. Introduced, 1913; dropped, 1929. Used value, $192.50 to $200.

No. 13 Sporter has same specs as standard No. 13, except for Parker-Hale Sportarget rear sight, bead front. Available also in .22 Hornet. Dropped, 1932. Used values, .22 LR, $187 to $198; .22 Hornet, $214.50 to $230.

BSA Model 15: single-shot Martini-action target rifle; .22 LR only; same general specifications as No. 12; 29" barrel; uncheckered walnut target stock; cheekpiece, pistol grip, long semi-beavertail forearm; BSA No. 30 rear sight, No. 20 front. Introduced in 1915; dropped, 1932. Used value, $187 to $198.

BSA Centurion: has the same basic specifications as Model 15, but was outfitted with Centurion match barrel; maker guaranteed 1.5" groups at 100 yards. Dropped, 1932. Used value, $214.50 to $230.

BSA-Parker Model 12/15: single-shot Martini-action target rifle; allegedly combined best features of No. 12 and Model 15; .22 LR only; 29" barrel; walnut target stock with high comb, cheekpiece, beavertail forearm; forward sling swivel; Parker-Hale PH-7A rear sight, PH-22 front. Introduced in 1938; dropped at beginning of WWII. Used value, $181.50 to $192.50.

RIFLES

BSA Model 12/15: has the same specifications as BSA Parker Model 12/15, but this was designation given rifle when reintroduced following WWII. Dropped, 1950. Used value, $187 to $200.

BSA Heavy Model 12/15 has same specifications as standard Model 12/15, except for extra-heavy competition barrel. Used value, $210 to $225.

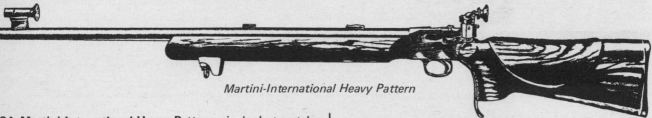

Martini-International Heavy Pattern

BSA Martini-International Heavy Pattern: single-shot match rifle, Martini-type action; .22 LR only; 29" heavy barrel; uncheckered two-piece target stock; full cheekpiece, pistol grip, broad beavertail forearm; hand stop; swivels; right or left-hand styles. Introduced in 1950; dropped, 1953. Used value $220 to $230.

Martini-International Light Pattern has same general specifications, except for lightweight 26" barrel. Used value, $220 to $230.

Martini-International Mark II has same specifications as 1950 model, with choice of light, heavy barrel. Improvements to original include redesigned stock, forearm, trigger mechanism, ejection system. Introduced in 1953; dropped, 1959. Used value, $240 to $250.

Martini-International Mark III has same specifications as Mark II heavy barrel model, plus redesigned stock, forearm, free-floating barrel, longer frame with alloy strut to attach forearm. Introduced in 1959; dropped, 1967. Used value, $275 to $285.

BSA Imperial: bolt-action; .270 Winchester, .308 Winchester, .30/06 in lightweight model; .22 Hornet, .222 Remington, .243 Winchester, .257 Roberts, 7x57mm, 300 Savage and .30/06 in standard weight; 22" barrel; recoil reducer cut into muzzle; fully adjustable trigger; European walnut cheekpiece stock; hand-checkered pistol grip, schnabel forearm; black butt plate, pistol grip cap with white spacers; drilled, tapped for scope mounts. Introduced in 1959; dropped, 1964. Used value, $180 to $195.

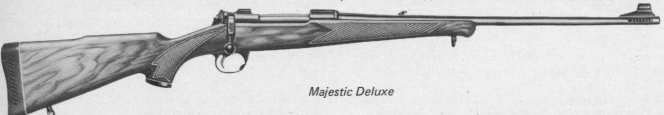

Majestic Deluxe

BSA Majestic Deluxe: Mauser-type bolt-action; .22 Hornet, .222 Rem., .243 Win., .308 Win., .30/06, 7x57mm; 22" barrel; 4-rd. magazine; European walnut stock; checkered pistol grip, forearm; cheekpiece, schnabel forearm; folding leaf rear sight, hooded ramp front; sling swivels. Introduced in 1959; dropped, 1965. Used value, $190 to $200.

Majestic Deluxe Featherweight has the same general specifications as standard Majestic Deluxe, except for recoil pad, lightweight barrel, recoil reducer; .243 Win., .270 Win., .308 Win., .30/06, .458 Win. magnum. Used value, .458 Win. magnum, $220 to $235; other calibers, $190 to $200.

Monarch Deluxe

BSA Monarch Deluxe: Mauser-type bolt-action; .222 Rem., .243 Win., .270 Win., 7mm Rem. magnum, .308 Win., .30/06; 22" barrel. Has same general specifications as Majestic Deluxe standard model, except for redesigned stock, with hardwood forearm tip, grip cap. Introduced in 1965; dropped, 1977. Used value, $165 to $175.

Monarch Deluxe Varmint model has same specifications as standard Monarch Deluxe except for 24" heavy barrel; .222 Rem., .243 Win. Used value, $170 to $180.

COLT

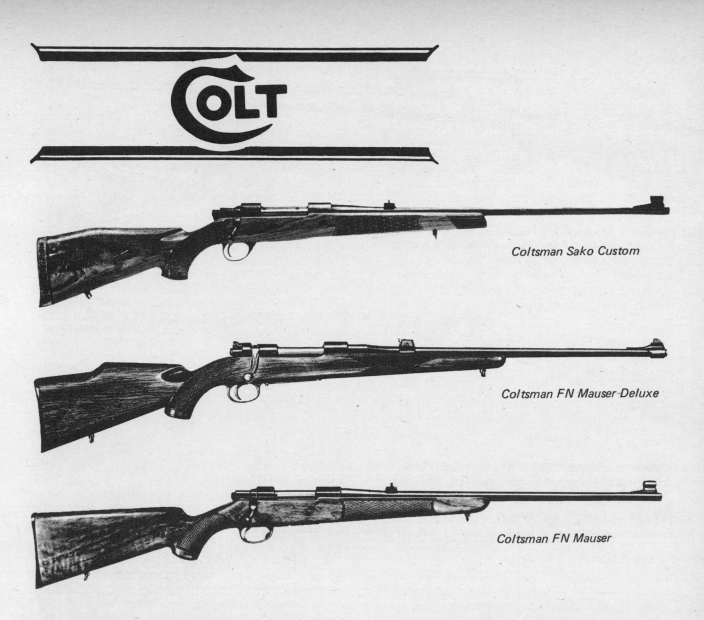

Coltsman Sako Custom

Coltsman FN Mauser Deluxe

Coltsman FN Mauser

COLT Standard Coltsman: bolt-action; FN Mauser action; .30/06, 300 Holland & Holland magnum; 22″ barrel; hand-checkered pistol-grip walnut stock; 5-rd. box magazine; no rear sight, ramp front; quick-detachable sling swivels. Introduced in 1957; replaced in 1962 by Sako action model; dropped, 1965. Used value, $227.50 to $240.50.

Coltsman Deluxe model has the same specifications as standard model, except for better checkering, wood. Adjustable rear sight, ramp front. Introduced in 1957; dropped in 1962. Used value, $253.50 to $273.50.

Coltsman Custom model has same specifications as standard model, except for fancy walnut stock, Monte Carlo comb, cheekpiece, engraved floor plate. Introduced in 1957; replaced in 1962 by Sako action; dropped, 1965. Used value, $288.50 to $312.50.

Coltsman Sako short-action Standard model is bolt-action; made from 1957 to 1961 in .243 Winchester, .308 Winchester; from 1962 to 1966, in .222, .222 magnum only; other specifications are virtually the same as those of the FN Mauser model. Used value, $227.50 to $240.50.

Coltsman Sako short-action Deluxe model has same general specifications as FN Mauser version except made in .243, .308 Winchester calibers only from 1957 to 1961. Dropped in this grade in 1961. Action had integral scope blocks. Used value, $253.50 to $273.50.

Coltsman Sako short-action Custom model has same

general specifications as FN Mauser version except for action; made in .243, .308 Winchester calibers only from 1957 to 1961; in .222, .222 magnum from 1962 to 1966; dropped, 1966. Used value, $292.50 to $312.50.

Coltsman medium-action Sako Standard model has hinged floor plate, hand-checkered walnut stock, standard sling swivels; bead front sight on hooded ramp, folding leaf rear; sliding safety; in .243 Winchester, .308 Winchester. Introduced in 1962; dropped, 1966. Used value, $227.50 to $235.

Coltsman Custom medium-action Sako has same specifications, calibers as Standard, except for fancy Monte Carlo stock, recoil pad, dark wood forearm tip, pistol-grip cap, skip-line checkering. Introduced in 1962; dropped, 1966. Used value, $292.50 to $312.50.

Coltsman Standard long-action Sako model is chambered for .264 Winchester, .270 Winchester, .30/06, .300 Holland & Holland, .375 Holland & Holland. With exception of action, calibers, other specifications are same as those of Standard Sako medium-action version. Introduced in 1962; dropped, 1966. Used value, $227.50 to $240.50.

Coltsman Custom long-action Sako is the same as Standard version, except for fancy Monte Carlo stock, recoil pad, dark wood forearm tip and pistol-grip cap, skip-line checkering. Introduced in 1962; dropped, 1966. Used value, $292.50 to $312.50.

COLT Colteer 1-22: single-shot bolt-action; .22 LR, long short; 20", 22" barrels; open rear sight, ramp front; un-checkered walnut pistol-grip Monte Carlo stock. Introduced in 1957; dropped 1967. Used value, $27.50 to $35.50.

COLT Colteer: autoloader; .22 LR only; 19-3/8" barrel; 15-rd. tube magazine; open rear sight, hooded ramp front; uncheckered straight Western-style carbine stock; barrel band; alloy receiver. Introduced in 1964; dropped, 1975. Used value, $60.50 to $66.

COLT Stagecoach: autoloader; .22 LR only; has the same general specifications as Colteer model, except for saddle ring, 16½" barrel, 13 rd. magazine, engraved receiver. Introduced in 1965; dropped, 1975. Used value, $71.50 to $82.50.

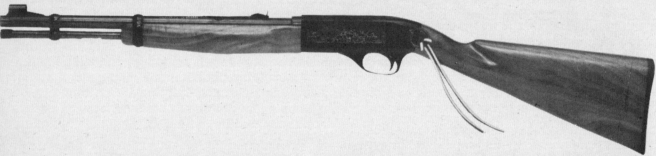

Colt Sauer Standard Model

COLT Sauer Sporter: bolt-action; standard model uses long action made in Germany by Sauer and Sohn; .25/06, .270 Win., .30/06, 7mm Rem. magnum, .300 Weatherby magnum, .300 Win. magnum; 24" barrel; 3-rd. detachable box magazine; no sights; hand-checkered American walnut pistol-grip stock; rosewood pistol grip, forearm caps; recoil pad; quick-detachable sling swivels. Introduced in 1971; still in production. Used value, $400 to $420.

Colt-Sauer short action has the same general specifications as standard long action model, except chambering for .22-250, .243 Win., .308 Win. Introduced in 1974; still in production. Used value, $415 to $440.

Colt-Sauer Grand African has the same general specifications, except for .458 Win. chambering only; bubinga wood stock; finer checkering, adjustable sliding rear sight, ivory bead front. Still in production. Used value, $515 to $550.

Harrington & Richardson

HARRINGTON & RICHARDSON Model 165: called the Leatherneck Model, it was a variation of Model 65 military autoloader used to train Marines in basic marksmanship during WWII. Blow-back autoloader; .22 LR only; 23" barrel; 10-rd. detachable box magazine; uncheckered hardwood pistol-grip stock; Redfield No. 70 rear peep sight, blade front on ramp; sling swivels, web sling. Introduced in 1945; dropped, 1961. Used value, $85 to $95.

HARRINGTON & RICHARDSON Model 265: called the Reg'lar Model in advertising; bolt-action repeater; .22 LR only; 22" barrel; 10-shot detachable box magazine; uncheckered hardwood pistol-grip stock; Lyman No. 55 rear peep sight, blade front on ramp. Introduced in 1946; dropped, 1949. Used value, $38.50 to $42.

HARRINGTON & RICHARDSON Model 365: called the Ace in advertising; bolt-action single-shot; .22 LR only; 22" barrel; uncheckered hardwood pistol-grip stock; Lyman No. 55 rear peep sight, blade front on ramp. Introduced in 1946; dropped, 1947. Used value, $22 to $25.50.

HARRINGTON & RICHARDSON Model 465: advertised as Targeteer Special; bolt-action repeater; .22 LR only; 25" barrel; 10-shot detachable box magazine; uncheckered walnut pistol-grip stock; Lyman No. 57 rear peep sight, blade front on ramp; sling swivels, web sling. Introduced in 1946; dropped, 1947. Used value, $66 to $74.50.

Targeteer Jr. has the same basic specifications as Model 465, except for 20" barrel; shorter youth stock; 5-rd. detachable box magazine; Redfield No. 70 rear peep sight, Lyman No. 17A front. Introduced in 1948; dropped, 1951. Used value, $64.50 to $71.50.

HARRINGTON & RICHARDSON Model 450: bolt-action repeater; .22 LR only; 26" barrel; 5-shot detachable box magazine; uncheckered walnut target stock with full pistol grip, thick forearm; scope bases; no sights; sling swivels, sling. Introduced in 1948; dropped, 1961. Used value, $88 to $101.50.

HARRINGTON & RICHARDSON Model 451: advertised as Medalist Model; has the same specifications as Model 450, except for addition of Lyman 524F extension rear sight, Lyman No. 77 front sight. Introduced in 1948; dropped, 1961. Used value, $115.50 to $121.

HARRINGTON & RICHARDSON Model 250: advertised as the Sportster Model; bolt-action repeater; .22 LR only; 23" barrel; 5-rd. detachable box magazine; uncheckered hardwood pistol-grip stock; open rear sight, blade front on ramp. Introduced in 1948; dropped, 1961. Used value, $43.50 to $45.

HARRINGTON & RICHARDSON Model 251: has the same specifications as Model 250, except for addition of Lyman No. 55H rear sight. Introduced in 1948; dropped, 1961. Used value, $46.50 to $49.50.

HARRINGTON & RICHARDSON Model 765: bolt-action, single-shot; .22 LR, long, short; 24" barrel; uncheckered hardwood pistol-grip stock; open rear sight, hooded bead front. Introduced in 1948; dropped, 1954. Used value, $22.50 to $24.50.

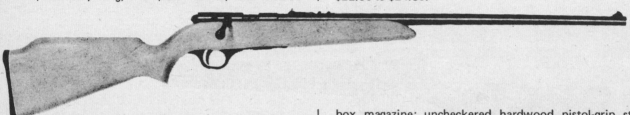

HARRINGTON & RICHARDSON Model 865: bolt-action repeater; .22 LR, long, short; 24" barrel; 5-rd. detachable box magazine; uncheckered hardwood pistol-grip stock; open rear sight, bead front. Introduced in 1949; still in production. Used value, $38.50 to $41.50.

HARRINGTON & RICHARDSON Model 150: autoloader; .22 LR only; 22" barrel; 5-rd. detachable box magazine; uncheckered pistol-grip stock; open rear sight, blade front on ramp. Introduced in 1949; dropped, 1953. Used value, $55 to $58.50.

HARRINGTON & RICHARDSON Model 151: has the same specifications as Model 150, except for substitution of Redfield No. 70 peep rear sight. Introduced in 1949; dropped, 1953. Used value, $58.50 to $60.50.

HARRINGTON & RICHARDSON Model 852: bolt-action repeater; .22 LR, long, short; 24" barrel; tube magazine with capacity of 15 LR, 17 long, 21 short cartridges; uncheckered pistol-grip hardwood stock; open rear sight, bead front. Introduced in 1952; dropped, 1953. Used value, $41.50 to $44.50.

HARRINGTON & RICHARDSON Model 422: slide-action repeater; .22 LR, long, short; 24" barrel; tube magazine, capacity of 15 LR, 17 long, 21 short cartridges; uncheckered walnut pistol-grip stock, grooved slide handle; open rear sight, ramp front. Introduced in 1952; dropped, 1958. Used value, $61.50 to $64.50.

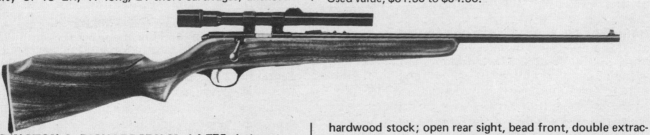

HARRINGTON & RICHARDSON Model 750: bolt-action single-shot; .22 LR, long, short; 24" barrel; uncheckered hardwood stock; open rear sight, bead front, double extractors; feed ramp. Introduced in 1954; still in production. Used value, $30 to $37.50.

HARRINGTON & RICHARDSON Model 800: autoloader; .22 LR only; 22″ barrel; 5, 10-rd. clip-type magazine; un-

checkered walnut pistol-grip stock; open rear sight, bead ramp front. Introduced in 1958; dropped, 1960. Used value, $49.50 to $55.

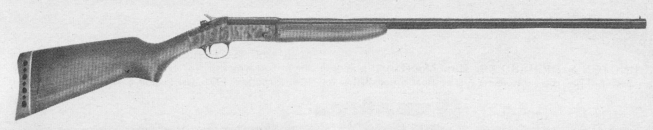

HARRINGTON & RICHARDSON Model 158 Topper 30: single-shot combo rifle; shotgun-type action; visible hammer; side lever; automatic ejector; 22″ interchangeable barrels, available in .22 Hornet, .30-30; unchecked walnut pistol-grip stock, forearm; recoil pad; Lyman folding adjustable open rear sight, ramp front. Introduced in 1963; still in production. Used value, $47.50 to $52.50.

Model 158 Topper Jet has the same general specifications as Model 158 Topper 30, except standard caliber is .22 Rem. Jet, interchangeable with 20-ga., .410-ga., .30-30 barrels. Introduced in 1963; dropped, 1967. Used values, standard .22 Rem. Jet, $46.50; additional .30-30 barrel, $20 to $24.50; 20-ga. barrel, $16.50 to $19.50; .410 barrel, $16.50 to $19.50.

HARRINGTON & RICHARDSON Model 755: advertised as the Sahara Model; single-shot .22 LR, long, short; 22″ barrel; blow-back action; automatic ejection; hardwood

Mannlicher-type stock; open rear sight, military front. Introduced in 1963; dropped, 1971. Used value, $38.50 to $41.50.

HARRINGTON & RICHARDSON Model 164: single-shot; has same specifications as Model 158, except for straight-

grip unchecked walnut stock, contoured forearm; gold-plated hammer, trigger. Introduced in 1964; dropped, 1967. Used value, $52 to $58.

HARRINGTON & RICHARDSON Model 760: single-shot; has the same specifications as Model 755, except for sub-

stitution of conventional hardwood sporter stock. Introduced in 1965; dropped, 1970. Used value, $33 to $36.50.

HARRINGTON & RICHARDSON Ultra Model 300: bolt-action, FN Mauser action; .22-250, .243 Win., .270 Win., .30/06, .308 Win., .300 Win. magnum, 7mm Rem. magnum; 22″ barrel; 3-rd. magazine for magnums, 5-rd. for others;

hand-checkered American walnut stock; cheekpiece, full pistol grip; pistol-grip cap, forearm tip of contrasting exotic wood; open rear sight, ramp front; rubber butt plate, sling swivels. Introduced in 1965; still in production. Used value, $215 to $230.

HARRINGTON & RICHARDSON Ultra Model 301: bolt-action carbine; has the same general specifications as Ultra Model 300, except for 18" barrel, Mannlicher-style stock; metal forearm tip. Not available in .22-250. Introduced in 1965; dropped, 1976. Used value, $240 to $265.

HARRINGTON & RICHARDSON Ultra Model 317: advertised as the Ultra Wildcat; .17 Rem., .222 Rem., .223 Rem., .17/223 handloads; 20" tapered barrel; same general specifications as Ultra Model 300, except for 6-rd. magazine, no sights; receiver dovetailed for integral scope mounts. Introduced in 1966; dropped, 1976. Used value, $230 to $239.

Ultra Model 317P has same specifications as Model 317, except for better grade of walnut, basket-weave checkering. Dropped, 1976. Used value, $297 to $313.50.

HARRINGTON & RICHARDSON Ultra Model 370: advertised as Ultra Medalist; built on Sako action; .22-250, .243 Win., 6mm Rem.; 24" heavy target/varmint barrel; uncheckered, oil-finished walnut stock; roll-over comb; no sights; tapped for open sights and/or scope mounts; adjustable trigger; recoil pad, sling swivels. Introduced in 1967; dropped, 1974. Used value, $203.50 to $214.50.

HARRINGTON & RICHARDSON Model 308: autoloader, gas operated; .264 Win., .308 Win.; 22" barrel; 3-rd. detachable box magazine; hand-checkered walnut stock; roll-over cheekpiece, full pistol grip, exotic wood pistol-grip cap, forearm tip; sling swivels; open adjustable rear sight, gold bead front. Introduced in 1967; dropped, 1973. Used value, $165 to $170.50.

HARRINGTON & RICHARDSON Ultra Model 360: has exactly the same specifications as Model 308, except chambered for .243 Win., .308 Win. Introduced in 1967; still in production. Used value, $187 to $195.50.

HARRINGTON & RICHARDSON Model 866: bolt-action repeater; has the same specifications as Model 865, except for substitution of Mannlicher-style walnut stock. Produced only in 1971. Used value, $52.50 to $55.

HIGH STANDARD

Sport King

HIGH STANDARD Sport King: autoloader; standard version was advertised as Field Model; .22 LR, long, short; 22¼" barrel; tube magazine has capacity of 15 LR, 17 long, 21 short cartridges; uncheckered pistol-grip stock; open rear sight, bead post front. Introduced in 1960; still in production. Used value, $54.50 to $57.50.

Sport King Special has the same specifications as the standard or Field Model, except for Monte Carlo stock, semi-beavertail forearm. Introduced in 1950; dropped,

1966. Used value, $57.50 to $61.50.

Sport King Deluxe has the same specifications as Special Model, except for impressed checkering on stock. Introduced in 1966; dropped, 1975. Used value, $63.50 to $67.50.

Sport King carbine has the same action as Sport King Special; 18¼" barrel; open rear sight, bead post front; straight grip stock; brass buttplate; sling swivels. Tube magazine holds 12 LR, 14 long, 17 short cartridges; receiver grooved for scope mounts; golden trigger guard, trigger, safety. Introduced in 1962; dropped, 1972. Used value, $44.50 to $46.50.

Hi-Power Deluxe

Hi-Power Field

HIGH STANDARD Hi-Power: bolt-action; standard model was advertised as Field Model; built on Mauser-type action; .270, .30/06; 22" barrel; 4-rd. magazine; uncheckered walnut field-style pistol-grip stock; sliding safety; quick-detachable sling swivels; folding leaf open rear sight, ramp front.

Introduced in 1962; dropped, 1966. Used value, $178.50 to $184.50.

Hi-Power Deluxe model has the same specifications as the standard version, except for impressed checkering on Monte Carlo stock, sling swivels. Introduced in 1962; dropped, 1966. Used value, $195.50 to $201.50.

Flite King Pump

HIGH STANDARD Flite King: pump action; hammerless; .22 LR, long, short; 24" barrel; tube magazine holds 17 LR, 19 long, 24 short cartridges; uncheckered hardwood Monte

Carlo pistol-grip stock, grooved semi-beavertail forearm; patridge-type rear sight, bead front. Introduced in 1962; still in production. Used value, $57.50 to $60.50.

HUSQVARNA

HUSQVARNA Hi-Power: Mauser-type bolt-action; .220 Swift, .270 Win., .30/06, 6.5x55, 8x57, 9.3x57; 23¾'' barrel; 5-rd. box magazine; hand-checkered pistol-grip beech stock; open rear sight, hooded ramp front; sling swivels. Introduced in 1946; dropped, 1959. Used value, $165 to $184.

HUSQVARNA Model 1950: Mauser-type bolt-action; has the same specifications as Hi-Power model, except chambered only in .220 Swift, .270 Win., .30/06. Introduced in 1950; dropped, 1952. Used value, $175 to $195.

Model 1951 Hi-Power

HUSQVARNA Model 1951 Hi-Power: has the same specifications as the Model 1950, except for a high-comb stock, low safety. Produced under model designation only in 1951. Used value, $190 to $201.50.

HUSQVARNA Series 1100: Mauser-type bolt-action sporter; .220 Swift, .30/06, 6.5x55, 8x57, 9.3x57; 23½'' barrel; other specifications generally the same as Model 1951 except for European walnut stock, jeweled bolt. Introduced in 1952; dropped, 1956. Used value, $241.50 to $253.

HUSQVARNA Series 1000: Mauser-type bolt-action; has the same general specifications as Model 1951, except for substitution of European walnut stock, with cheekpiece, Monte Carlo comb. Introduced in 1952; dropped, 1956. Used value, $230 to $247.50.

HUSQVARNA Series 3100: advertised as Crown Grade; Husqvarna improved Mauser action; .243 Win., .270 Win., 7mm Rem., .30/06, .308 Win.; 23¾'' barrel; 5-rd. box magazine; hand-checkered European walnut pistol-grip stock; cheekpiece; black forearm tip, pistol-grip cap; open rear sight, hooded ramp front; sling swivels. Introduced in 1954; dropped, 1976. Used value, $244.50 to $259.

HUSQVARNA Series 3000: Husqvarna improved Mauser action; has the same specifications as Series 3100, except for substitution of Monte Carlo-style stock. Introduced in 1954; dropped, 1976. Used value, $247 to $258.50.

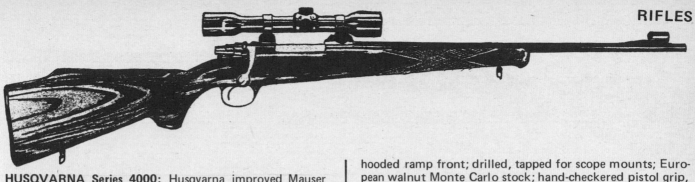

HUSQVARNA Series 4000: Husqvarna improved Mauser action; .243 Win., .270 Win., .30/06, .308 Win., 7mm Rem. magnum; 20½" barrel; 5-rd. box magazine; no rear sight, hooded ramp front; drilled, tapped for scope mounts; European walnut Monte Carlo stock; hand-checkered pistol grip, forearm; sling swivels. Introduced in 1954; dropped, 1976. Used value, $235 to $253.50.

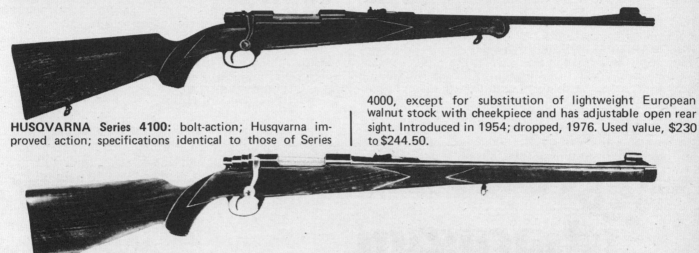

HUSQVARNA Series 4100: bolt-action; Husqvarna improved action; specifications identical to those of Series 4000, except for substitution of lightweight European walnut stock with cheekpiece and has adjustable open rear sight. Introduced in 1954; dropped, 1976. Used value, $230 to $244.50.

HUSQVARNA Model 456: full-stock bolt-action sporter; has the same general specifications as Series 4000, except for full-length sporter stock, open adjustable rear sight, metal forearm cap, slope-away cheekpiece. Introduced in 1959; dropped, 1970. Used value, $253 to $267.50.

HUSQVARNA Series 6000: advertised as Imperial Custom Grade; .243 Win., .270 Win., .30/06, .308 Win., 7mm Rem. magnum; other specifications the same as Series 3100, except for fancy walnut stock, adjustable trigger, three-leaf folding rear sight. Introduced in 1968; dropped, 1970. Used value, $293 to $310.50.

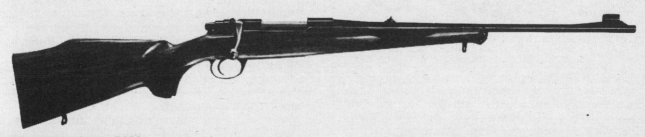

HUSQVARNA Series 7000: advertised as Imperial Monte Carlo Lightweight Model; .243 Win., .270 Win., .30/06, .308 Win.; other specifications are identical to those of Series 4000, except for fancy walnut stock, adjustable trigger, three-leaf folding rear sight. Introduced in 1968; dropped, 1970. Used value, $284 to $299.50.

HUSQVARNA Series P-3000: advertised as Presentation grade; .243 Win., .270 Win., .30/06, 7mm Rem. magnum; other specifications identical to those of Series 3000, except for engraved action, adjustable trigger, top grade walnut stock. Introduced in 1968; dropped, 1970. Used value, $505 to $525.

HUSQVARNA Model 8000: advertised as Imperial grade; improved Husqvarna bolt-action; .270 Win., .30/06, .300 Win. magnum, 7mm Rem. magnum; 23¾" barrel; jeweled bolt; hand-checkered deluxe French walnut stock; Monte Carlo cheekpiece, rosewood forearm tip, pistol-grip cap; adjustable trigger; 5-rd. box magazine, hinged engraved floor plate; no sights. Introduced in 1971; dropped, 1972. Used value, $322 to $333.50.

HUSQVARNA Model 9000: advertised as Crown grade; has the same specifications as Model 8000, except for folding leaf rear sight, hooded ramp front; Monte Carlo cheekpiece stock, no jeweling on bolt, no engraving on floor plate. Introduced in 1971; dropped, 1972. Used value $230 to $244.50.

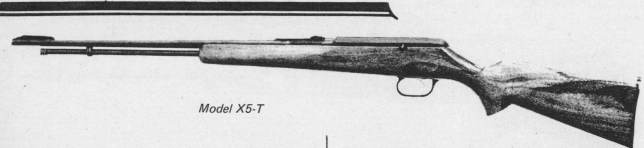

ithacagun

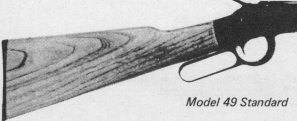

Model X5-T

ITHACA Model X5-C: takedown autoloader; .22 LR only; 22" barrel; 7-rd. clip-type magazine; uncheckered hardwood pistol-grip stock, grooved forearm; open rear sight, Raybar front. Introduced in 1958; dropped, 1964. Used value, $46 to $49.

Model X5-T has the same specifications as the Model X5-C, except for 16-rd. tube magazine; ungrooved forearm. Introduced in 1959; dropped, 1963. Used value, $49 to $52.

Model 49 Standard

ITHACA Model 49: advertised as Saddlegun; lever-action single-shot; .22 LR, long, short; 28" barrel; blank tube magazine for appearance only; straight uncheckered Western-style carbine stock; barrel band on forearm; open adjustable rear sight, bead post front. Introduced in 1961; still in production. Used value, $37.50 to $40.50.

Model 49 Youth Saddlegun has same specifications as the standard model, except for shorter stock. Introduced in 1961; still in production. Used value, $37.50 to $40.50.

Model 49 Magnum has same specifications as standard Model 49, except is chambered for .22 rimfire magnum cartridge. Introduced in 1962; still in production. Used value, $43 to $49.

Model 49 Deluxe has the same specifications as standard model, except for figured walnut stock, gold-plated hammer, trigger, sling swivels. Introduced in 1962; dropped, 1975. Used value, $52 to $57.50.

Model 49 Presentation has same specifications as standard Model 49, except for fancy figured walnut stock, gold nameplate inlay, gold trigger and hammer, engraved receiver; in .22 LR, .22 WMR only. Introduced in 1962; dropped, 1974. Used value, $115 to $144.50.

ITHACA Model 72: lever-action repeater; .22 LR, .22 rimfire magnum; 18½" barrel; uncheckered Western-style straight American walnut stock, barrel band on forearm; 15-rd. tube magazine; half-cock safety; step-adjustable open rear sight, hooded ramp front; receiver grooved for scope mounts. Introduced in 1972; still in production. Used value, .22 LR, $92 to $95; .22 WMR, $106 to $112.

Model LSA-55 Standard

ITHACA LSA-55: bolt-action repeater; .243 Win., .308 Win., .22-250, .222 Rem., 6mm Rem., .25/06, .270 Win., .30/06; 23" free-floating barrel; European walnut pistol-grip Monte Carlo stock. Early versions had impressed checkering on pistol grip, forearm; as of 1974, stocks are hand checkered. Removeable adjustable rear sight, hooded ramp front; 3-rd. detachable box magazine; adjustable trigger; receiver drilled, tapped for scope mounts. Introduced in 1972; still in production. Used values, $207 to $218.50; with heavy barrel, .222, .22-250 only, $270 to $279.

LSA-55 Deluxe has same specifications as standard model, except pre-'74 version had hand-checkered stock; also, roll-over cheekpiece, rosewood forearm tip, grip cap, white spacers; sling swivel, no heavy barrel. Used value, $244.50 to $250.

MANNLICHER

MANNLICHER-SCHOENAUER Model 1903: bolt-action carbine sporter; 6.5x53mm only; 17.7" barrel; full-length uncheckered European walnut Mannlicher-style stock; metal forearm cap; pistol grip; cartridge trap in butt plate; 5-rd. rotary magazine; double-set trigger; two-leaf rear sight, ramp front; flat bolt handle; sling swivels. Introduced in 1903; dropped, 1937. Used value, $390 to $422.50.

MANNLICHER-SCHOENAUER Model 1905: bolt-action carbine sporter; 9x56mm only; 19.7" barrel. Other specifications identical to those of Model 1903. Introduced in 1905; dropped, 1937. Used value, $455 to $471.50.

MANNLICHER-SCHOENAUER Model 1908: bolt-action carbine; 7x57mm and 8x56mm; all other specifications identical to those of Model 1905. Introduced in 1908; dropped, 1937. Used value, $461.50 to $474.50.

MANNLICHER-SCHOENAUER Model 1910: bolt-action sporting carbine; 9.5x57mm only; other specifications identical to those of Model 1908. Introduced in 1910; dropped, 1937. Used value, $422.50 to $439.50.

MANNLICHER-SCHOENAUER High Velocity: bolt-action sporting rifle; .30/06, 7x64 Brenneke, 8x60 magnum, 9.3x62, 10.75x66mm; 23.6'' barrel; hand-checkered traditional sporting stock of European walnut; cheekpiece, pistol grip; 5-rd. rotary magazine; British-type three-leaf open rear sight, ramp front; sling swivels. Introduced in 1922; dropped, 1937. Used value, $533 to $542.50.

MANNLICHER-SCHOENAUER Model 1924: bolt-action carbine; .30/06 only; aimed at American market; other specifications identical to those of Model 1908. Introduced in 1924; dropped, 1937. Used value, $572 to $601.50.

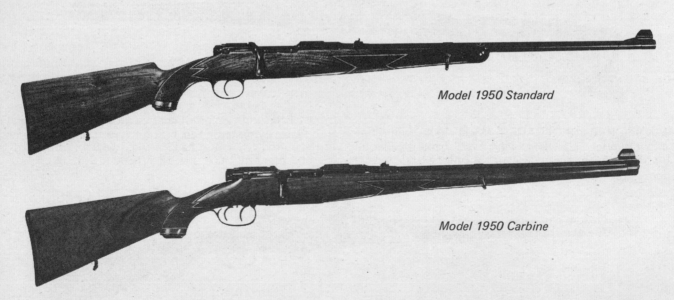

Model 1950 Standard

Model 1950 Carbine

MANNLICHER-SCHOENAUER Model 1950: bolt-action sporter; designed primarily for the U.S. market; .257 Roberts, .270 Win., .30/06; 24'' barrel; standard hand-checkered European walnut sporting stock; pistol grip, cheekpiece; ebony forend tip; 5-rd. rotary magazine; single or double-set trigger; flat bolt handle; folding leaf open rear sight, hooded ramp front; shotgun-type safety; sling swivels. Introduced in 1950; dropped, 1952. Used value, $543 to $552.50.

Model 1950 carbine has the same specifications as standard Model 1950 rifle, except for full-length Mannlicher-type stock, metal forearm cap; 20'' barrel. Introduced in 1950; dropped, 1952. Used value, $546 to $559.50.

Model 1950 6.5 carbine has same specifications as Model 1950 carbine, except for 18¼'' barrel chambered for 6.5x53mm only. Introduced in 1950; dropped, 1952. Used value, $513.50 to $533.50.

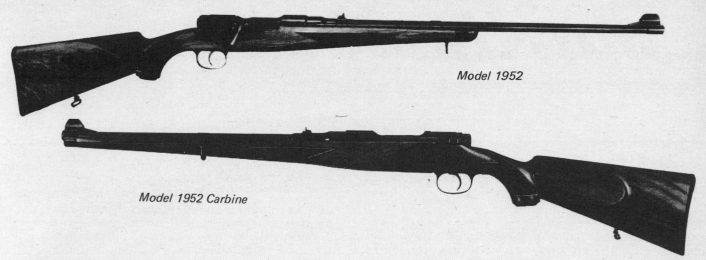

Model 1952

Model 1952 Carbine

MANNLICHER-SCHOENAUER Model 1952: bolt-action sporting rifle; .257 Roberts, .270 Win., .30/06, 9.3x62mm; improved version of Model 1950; has same specifications, except for swept-back bolt handle, improved stock design. Introduced in 1952; dropped, 1956. Used value, $390 to $410.50.

Model 1952 carbine has the same specifications as the Model 1950 carbine, except for full-length Mannlicher stock design, swept-back bolt handle; .257 Roberts, .270 Win., .30/06, 7mm Rem. mag. Introduced in 1952; dropped, 1956. Used value, $396.50 to $409.50.

Model 1952 6.5 carbine has the same specifications as Model 1950 6.5 carbine, except for swept-back bolt handle, improved stock design. Chambered for 6.5x53mm only. Introduced in 1952; dropped, 1956. Used value, $494 to $507.

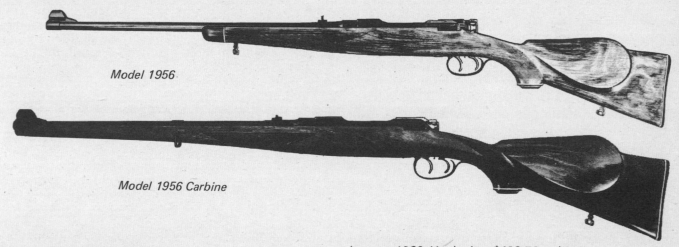

Model 1956

Model 1956 Carbine

MANNLICHER-SCHOENAUER Model 1956: bolt-action sporting rifle; .243 Win., .30/06; has the same general specifications as Model 1952 rifle, except for high-comb improved walnut stock, 22" barrel. Introduced in 1956; dropped, 1960. Used value, $409.50 to $419.

Model 1956 carbine has the same general specifications as Model 1952 carbine, except for redesigned high-comb walnut stock; .243 Win., .257 Roberts, .270 Win., .30/06; dropped, 1960. Used value, $416 to $429.

1961-MCA Carbine

MANNLICHER-SCHOENAUER Model 1961-MCA: bolt-action rifle; .243 Win., .270 Win., .30/06; has the same specifications as Model 1956 rifle, except for substitution of Monte Carlo-style walnut stock. Introduced in 1961; dropped, 1971. Used value, $517.50 to $532. Model 1961-MCA carbine has the same general specifications as Model 1956 carbine, except for substitution of walnut Monte Carlo stock; .243 Win., .270 Win., .30/06, .308 Win., 6.5x53mm. Introduced in 1961; dropped, 1971. Used value $592 to $611.50.

Marlin

MARLIN Model 94: lever-action, carbine repeater; solid frame or takedown; .25-20, .32-40, .44-40; 10-rd. tube magazine; 24" round, octagonal barrel; open rear sight, bead front; carbine barrel band; available with either straight-grip or pistol grip walnut stock; uncheckered. Prior to 1906, it was known as the Model 1894. Introduced in 1894; dropped, 1934. Used value, $345 to $356.50.

MARLIN Model 27-S: slide-action repeater; variation on Model 27, which was discontinued in 1916. Takedown; exposed hammer, 24" round barrel; in .25 Stevens rimfire, .25-20, .32-20; tube magazine holds 7 rds.; open rear sight, bead front; uncheckered straight walnut stock; grooved slide handle. Introduced in 1920; dropped, 1932. Used value, $140 to $149.50.

MARLIN Model 38: slide-action repeater; hammerless takedown; .22 long, .22 LR, .22 short; tube magazine holds 10 LR, 12 long, 15 short cartridges; 24" octagon barrel; open rear sight, bead front; uncheckered pistol-grip walnut stock, grooved slide handle. Introduced in 1920; dropped, 1930. Used value, $144 to $152.50.

MARLIN Model 50: autoloader; takedown; .22 LR only; 6-rd. detachable box magazine; 22" barrel; open rear sight adjustable for elevation, bead front; uncheckered pistol-grip walnut stock, grooved forearm. Introduced in 1931; dropped, 1934. Used value, $46 to $52.

Model 50E has same specs as Model 50, except for hooded front sight, peep rear. Used value, $49 to $52.

MARLIN Model 65: bolt-action single-shot; .22 LR, .22 long, .22 short; 24" barrel; open rear sight, bead front; uncheckered walnut pistol-grip stock, grooved forearm. Introduced in 1932; dropped, 1938. Used value, $34.50 to $39.50.

Model 65E is the same as Model 65, but is equipped with hooded front sight, peep rear. Used value, $37.50 to $40.50.

Model 89C

MARLIN Model 89C: same general specifications as Model 88-C, except with clip magazine. Early version had 7-rd. clip; 12-rd. clip in later versions. Introduced in 1950; dropped, 1961. Used value, $48.50 to $54.

Marlin Model 89DL has same specifications as Model 89-C, except for addition of sling swivels, receiver peep sight. Used value, $51.50 to $54.50.

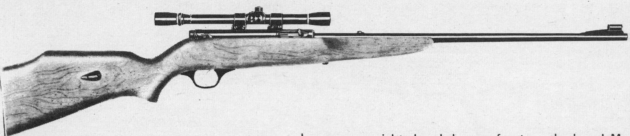

MARLIN Model 98: solid frame autoloader; .22 LR only; butt stock tube magazine has 15-rd. capacity; 22" barrel; open rear sight, hooded ramp front; uncheckered Monte Carlo stock, cheekpiece. Introduced in 1950; dropped, 1961. Used value, $48.50 to $52.

MARLIN Model 101: Improved version of Model 100; current version has improved bolt, redesigned stock, 22" barrel; semi-buckhorn folding sight adjustable for windage, elevation, hooded Wide-Scan front; black plastic trigger guard; T-shaped cocking piece; uncheckered walnut stock has beavertail forearm; receiver grooved for tip-off scope mount. Introduced in 1951; dropped, 1976. Used value, $34.50 to $37.50.

MARLIN MODEL 36: lever-action, carbine repeater; .32 Special, .30-30; 6-rd. tube magazine; 20" barrel; uncheckered walnut pistol-grip stock, semi-beavertail forearm; carbine barrel band; open rear sight, bead front. Introduced in 1936; dropped, 1948. Used value, $167 to $178.50.

Model 36A has same specs as Model 36 standard, except for shorter tube magazine holding 5 rds.; 24" barrel; hooded front sight. Used value, $167 to $178.

Model 36A-DL has same specs as Model 36A, except for sling swivels, hand-checkered walnut stock, forearm. Used value, $195.50 to $204.

Model 36 Sporting carbine has same general specs as Model 30A, except for a 20" barrel. Used value, $172.50 to $178.

Model 336C

MARLIN Model 336C: lever-action repeating carbine; updated version of Model 36 carbine; specs are virtually the same, except for round breech bolt; gold-plated trigger; offset hammer spur; semi-buckhorn adjustable folding rear sight; ramp front with Wide-Scan hood; receiver tapped for scope mounts; top of receiver sand-blasted to reduce glare.

Introduced in 1948; still in production, in .30-30, .35 Rem.; latter was introduced in 1953; .32 Win. Special discontinued, 1963. Used value in .32 Win. Special, $115 to $120.50; other calibers, $109.50 to $112.

Model 336A is same as 336C, except it has 24" round barrel; half-length magazine tube; 5-rd. capacity; blued forearm cap, sling swivels; available now only in .30-30; .35 Rem. discontinued in 1963. Introduced in 1950; still in production. Used value, $109.50 to $112.

Model 336A-DL has the same specifications as Model 336A, except for sling, swivels, hand-checkered stock, forearm. Dropped, 1963. Used value, $129.50 to $132.

Model 336 Sporting Carbine has same specifications as

Model 336A, except for 20" barrel. Dropped, 1963. Used value, $106.50 to $109.

Model 336 Zipper is same as Model 336 sporting carbine, but was chambered only in .219 Zipper. Introduced in 1955; dropped, 1961. Used value, $195.50 to $207.

Model 336T, called the Texan Model, has same specs as Model 336 carbine, except for straight-grip uncheckered walnut stock, squared lever. Introduced in 1953; still in production. Originally chambered in .30-30, .35 Rem.; was chambered in .44 magnum from 1963 to 1967. Produced currently only in .30-30. Used value, $109.50 to $112.

Model 336 Marauder is same as Model 336T, except with 16¾" barrel. Introduced in 1963; dropped, 1964. Used value, $115 to $120.50.

Model 81-DC

MARLIN Model 81: bolt-action, takedown repeater; .22 LR, .22 long, .22 short; tube magazine holds 18 LR, 20 long, 24 short cartridges; 24" barrel; open rear sight, bead front; uncheckered pistol-grip stock. Introduced in 1937; dropped, 1965. Used value, $43 to $46.

Model 81E differs from standard Model 81 only in that it has hooded front sight, peep rear. Used value, $46 to $52.

Model 81C is an improved version of standard Model 81; specifications differ only in that the stock has semi-

beavertail forearm. Introduced in 1940; dropped, 1970. Used value, $52 to $54.50.

Model 81-DC has same specs as Model 81-C, except for hooded front sight, peep rear, sling swivels. Introduced in 1940; dropped, 1965. Used value, $54.50 to $60.50.

Marlin-Glenfield Model 81G has the same specs as Model 81C, except the stock is of less expensive wood; has bead front sight. Introduced in 1960; dropped, 1965. Used value, $44 to $49.

MARLIN Model 39: lever-action takedown repeater; .22 LR, .22 long, .22 short; tube magazine holds 18 LR, 20 long, 25 short cartridges; 24" octagon barrel, open rear

sight, bead front; uncheckered pistol-grip walnut stock, forearm. Introduced in 1938; dropped, 1958. Used $207 to $224.50.

Model 39A Standard

Model 39A Mountie

Golden Model 39A, has gold-plated trigger, other refinements. Used value, $103.50 to $109.

Model 39A Mountie is virtually the same as the Model 39A, but with straight-grip stock, slim forearm; 20" barrel; tube magazine holds 15 LR, 16 long, 21 short cartridges. Introduced in 1953; dropped, 1960. Used value, $103.50 to $109.

MARLIN Model 39A: same general specs as Model 39, but with heavier stock, semi-beavertail forearm, round barrel. Introduced in 1939; still in production. Used value, $98 to $103.50.

MARLIN Model 80: bolt-action, takedown; .22 LR, .22 long, .22 short; 8-rd. detachable box magazine; 24" barrel; open rear sight, bead front; uncheckered walnut pistol-grip stock; black butt plate. Introduced in 1934; dropped, 1939. Used value, $43 to $46.

Model 80E has the same specifications as standard Model 80, except for peep rear sight, hooded front. Used value, $46 to $49.

Model 80-C replaced standard Model 80 in 1940; dropped in 1970. Has same general specs as Model 80, except that stock has semi-beavertail forearm. Used value, $46 to $49.

Model 80-DL, introduced in 1940, dropped, 1965, has same specifications as the Model 80-C, except for peep rear sight, hooded front; sling swivels. Used value, $49 to $54.50.

Model A-1

MARLIN Model A-1: autoloading, takedown; .22 LR only; 6-rd. detachable box magazine; 24" barrel; open rear sight, bead front; uncheckered walnut pistol-grip stock. Introduced in 1935; dropped, 1946. Used value, $43 to $49.

Model A1E has the same specifications as standard Model A-1, except for a hooded front sight, peep rear. Used value, $52 to $55.

Model A-1C was introduced in 1940; dropped, 1946; has same specifications as Model A-1, except that stock has semi-beavertail forearm. Used value, $55 to $58.

Model A-1DL has same specs as Model A-1C, except for sling swivels, hooded front sight, peep rear. Used value, $58 to $61.

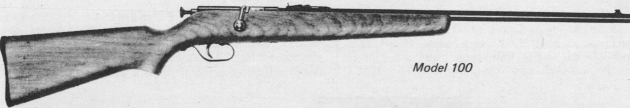

Model 100

MARLIN Model 100: bolt-action, takedown single-shot; .22 LR, .22 long, .22 short; 24" barrel; open rear sight adjustable for elevation, bead front; uncheckered walnut pistol-grip stock. Introduced in 1936; dropped, 1960. Used value, $29 to $32.

Model 100S was introduced in 1936; dropped, 1946. It is known as the Tom Mix Special, allegedly because Tom Mix used such a rifle in his vaudeville act in the Thirties. It

has the same specifications as standard Model 100 except for sling, peep rear sight, hooded front. Value is based largely upon rarity. Used value, $60.50 to $66.

Model 100SB is the same as Model 100, except it is smoothbore for use with .22 shot cartridge; has shotgun sight. Actually, this probably is the version used by Tom Mix in his act, as he used shot cartridges for breaking glass balls and other on-stage targets. Introduced in 1936; dropped, 1941. Used value, $26 to $32.

Model 88-C

MARLIN Model 88-C: takedown autoloader; .22 LR only; tube magazine in butt stock; 14-rd. capacity; open rear sight, hooded front; unchecked pistol-grip stock. Introduced in 1947; dropped, 1956. Used value, $49.50 to $52.

MARLIN Model 332: bolt-action, varmint rifle; .222 Rem. only; short Sako Mauser-type action; 24" barrel; 3-rd. clip-

Model 88-DL was introduced in 1953; dropped, 1956; same specs as Model 88-C, except for hand-checkered stock, sling swivels, receiver peep sight in rear. Used value, $54.50 to $60.

type magazine; checkered walnut stock; two-position peep sight in rear, hooded ramp front. Introduced in 1954; dropped, 1957. Used value, $207 to $210.

MARLIN Model 455: bolt-action; FN Mauser action; Sako trigger; .308, .30/06, .270 Win.; 5-rd. box magazine; 24" stainless steel barrel; checkered walnut Monte Carlo stock

with cheekpiece; Lyman No. 48 receiver sight, hooded ramp front. Introduced in 1957; dropped, 1959. Used value, $210 to $218.50.

MARLIN-Glenfield Model 30A: lever action carbine; .30-30 Winchester only; has the same specifications as the Marlin

336C, except for impressed checkering on pistol grip, forearm; stock of walnut-finished hardwood. Introduced in 1958, still in production. Used value, $103.50 to $109.

Model 57

MARLIN Model 57: lever-action; .22 LR, .22 long, .22 short; tube magazine holds 27 shorts, 21 longs, 19 LR; 22" barrel; unchecked Monte Carlo-type pistol-grip stock; open rear sight, hooded ramp front. Introduced in 1959;

dropped, 1965. Used value, $72 to $74.

Model 57M has the same specifications as standard Model 57, except for 24" barrel, 15-rd. magazine, chambered for .22 Win. rimfire magnum cartridge. Introduced in 1959; dropped, 1969. Used value, $87 to $90.

MARLIN Model 56: same as Model 57, except equipped

with clip-loading magazine; 8-rd. capacity. Introduced in 1955; dropped, 1964. Used value, $72 to $75.

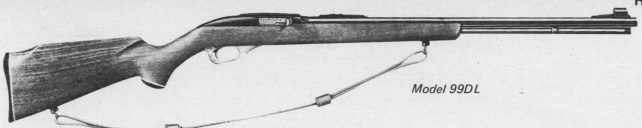

Model 99DL

MARLIN Model 99: autoloader; .22 LR only; 22" barrel; 18-rd. tube magazine; unchecked walnut pistol-grip stock; open rear sight, hooded ramp front. Introduced in 1959; dropped, 1961. Used value, $52 to $55.

Model 99C has same specs as standard Model 99, except for unchecked Monte Carlo stock; grooved receiver for tip-off scope mounts; gold-plated trigger. Later production features checkering on pistol-grip, forearm. Introduced in 1962; still in production. Used value, $52 to $57.50.

Model 99DL has same specs as standard Model 99, except for unchecked black walnut Monte Carlo stock; jeweled bolt; gold-plated trigger, sling, sling swivels. Intro- duced in 1960; dropped, 1965. Used value, $48.50 to $52.

Model 99M1 carbine, designed after U.S. 30M1 carbine, but otherwise using same action as Model 99C; 18" barrel; 9-rd. tube magazine; unchecked pistol grip carbine stock; hand guard with barrel band; open rear sight, military-type ramp front; sling swivels. Introduced in 1966; still in production. Used value, $52 to $57.50.

MARLIN Model 980: bolt-action repeater; .22 Win. rimfire magnum only; 8-rd. clip-type magazine; 24" barrel; open rear sight adjustable for elevation, hooded ramp front; un- checkered walnut Monte Carlo style stock with white spacers at pistol grip and butt plate; sling, sling swivels. Introduced in 1962; dropped, 1970. Used value, $75 to $77.50.

MARLIN 989: autoloader; .22 LR only; 7-rd clip magazine; 22" barrel; open adjustable rear sight; hooded ramp front; unchecked Monte Carlo-type pistol-grip stock of black walnut; black butt plate. Introduced in 1962; dropped, 1966. Used value, $37.50 to $40.

Model 989M2 carbine is the same as the Model 99M1, except for 7-rd. clip-type detachable magazine. Introduced in 1966; still in production. Used value, $43 to $49.

Model 989G Marlin-Glenfield is the same as the Model 989, except for plain stock, bead front sight. Introduced in 1962; discontinued, 1964. Used value, $34.50 to $38.

MARLIN Model 122: single-shot; bolt-action, junior target model with shortened unchecked stock; .22 LR, .22 long, .22 short; 22" barrel; open rear sight, hooded ramp front; walnut Monte Carlo pistol-grip stock; sling, sling swivels. Introduced in 1961; dropped, 1965. Used value, $42.50 to $46.

MARLIN Model 62: lever-action repeater; .256 magnum, .30 carbine; 23" barrel, 4-rd. clip magazine; open rear sight adjustable for elevation, hooded ramp front; swivels, sling; unchecked Monte Carlo-type pistol-grip stock. The .256 magnum was introduced in 1963; dropped, 1969. Used value, .256 magnum, $86 to $89; .30 carbine, $95 to $103.50.

MARLIN Model 444: lever-action repeater; action is strengthened version of Model 336; .444 Marlin cartridge only; 4-rd. tube magazine; 24" barrel; open rear sight adjustable for elevation, hooded ramp front; straight-grip Monte Carlo stock of uncheckered walnut; recoil pad; carbine forearm, barrel band; sling, sling swivels. Introduced in 1965; dropped, 1972. Used value, $138 to $149.50.

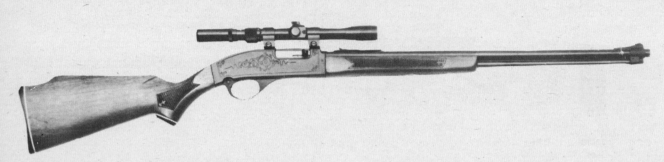

MARLIN Model 49DL: autoloader; .22 LR only; same specs as Model 99 standard model, except for capped pistol grip, checkered forearm and pistol grip, gold trigger; scroll-engraved receiver; grooved for tip-off scope mounts. Introduced in 1970; still in production. Used value, $55 to $57.50.

MARLIN Model 1894: .44 magnum only; 10-rd. tube magazine; 20" carbine barrel; uncheckered straight grip black walnut stock, forearm; gold-plated trigger; receiver tapped for scope mount; offset hammer spur; solid top receiver is sand-blasted to reduce glare; hooded ramp front sight, semi-buckhorn adjustable rear. Supposedly a recreation of the Model 94 of the last century, actually it is built on the Model 336 action. Introduced, 1971; still in production. Used value, $100.50 to $109.

MARLIN Model 1895: .45-70 only; 22" round barrel; 4-rd. tube magazine; uncheckered straight grip stock, forearm of black walnut; solid receiver tapped for scope mounts, receiver sights; offset hammer spur; adjustable semi-buck-horn folding rear sight, bead front. Meant to be a recreation of the original Model 1895, discontinued in 1915. Actually built on action of Marlin Model 444. Introduced in 1972; still in production. Used value, $149.50 to $155.

MAUSER

MAUSER Standard Model 98: introduced after World War I; commercial version of the German military 98k model; bolt-action repeater; 7mm Mauser, 7.9mm Mauser; 23½" barrel, 5-rd. box magazine; military-style uncheckered European walnut stock; straight military-type bolt handle; adjustable rear sight, blade front; sling swivels; Mauser trademark on receiver ring. Dropped, 1938. Used value, $130 to $260.

MAUSER Special British Model: bolt-action Type A standard Mauser Model 98 action; 7x57, 8x60, 9x57, 9.3x62mm, .30/06; 23½" barrel; 5-rd. box magazine; hand-checkered pistol-grip Circassian walnut sporting stock; buffalo horn grip cap, forearm tip; Express rear sight, hooded ramp front; military-type trigger; detachable sling swivels. Introduced before WWI, dropped, 1938. Used value, $260 to $390.

MAUSER Type A Short Model: has the same general specifications as standard Type A, except for short action, 21½" barrel; 6.5x54, 8x51mm, .250-3000. Introduced before WWI; dropped, 1938. Used value, $325 to $390.

Type A Magnum Model has the same general specifications as standard Type A model, except for heavier magnum action; 10.75x68mm, .280 Ross, .318 Westley Richards Express, .404 Nitro Express. Introduced before WWI; dropped, 1938. Used value, $390 to $520.

MAUSER Type B: bolt-action sporter; 7x57, 8x57, 8x60, 9x57, 9.3x62, 10.75x68mm, .30/06; 23½" barrel; 5-rd. box magazine; hand-checkered walnut pistol-grip stock; schnabel forearm tip; grip cap; double-set triggers; sling swivels; three-leaf rear sight, ramp front. Introduced before WWI; dropped, 1939. Used value, $535 to $550.

MAUSER Type M: bolt-action sporting carbine; 6.5x54, 7x57, 8x51, 8x60, 9x57mm, .30/06; 19¾" barrel; 5-shot box magazine; full-length Mannlicher-type walnut stock with steel forearm cap; hand-checkered pistol grip, forearm; pistol-grip cap; sling swivels; double-set triggers; flat bolt handle; three-leaf rear sight, ramp front. Introduced before WWI; dropped, 1939. Used value, $580 to $600.

RIFLES

MAUSER Type K: bolt-action sporter; has the same general specifications as Type B, except for short action, 21½" barrel; 6.5x54, 8x57mm, .30/06. Introduced before WWI; dropped, 1939. Used value, $325 to $455.

MAUSER Type S: bolt-action sporting carbine; 6.5x55 Swedish Mauser, 7x57, 8x60, 9x57mm; 19¾" barrel; 5-rd. box magazine; full-length Mannlicher-type walnut stock; hand-checkered pistol grip; pistol-grip cap; schnabel forearm tip; double-set trigger; flat bolt handle; three-leaf rear sight, ramp front. Introduced before WWI; dropped, 1939. Used value, $390 to $455.

MAUSER Model ES350: bolt-action repeater; .22 LR rifle only; 27½" barrel; target-style walnut stock; hand-checkered pistol grip, forearm; grip cap; open micrometer rear sight, ramp front. Introduced in 1925; dropped, 1935. Used value, $145 to $175.

MAUSER Model EL320: bolt-action, single-shot; .22 LR only, 23½" barrel; sporting-style European walnut stock; hand-checkered pistol grip; adjustable open rear sight, bead front; sling swivels. Introduced in 1927; dropped, 1935. Used value, $115 to $175.

Model MS420B

MAUSER Model MS420: bolt-action repeater; .22 LR only; 25½" barrel; 5-rd. detachable box magazine; European walnut sporting stock; hand-checkered pistol grip, grooved forearm, sling swivels; tangent curve open rear sight, ramp front. Introduced in 1925; dropped, 1935. Used value, $200 to $230.

Model MS420B has the same general specifications as MS420, except for better wood, 25¾" barrel. Introduced in 1935; dropped, 1939. Used value, $220 to $255.

Model MM410

MAUSER Model MM410: bolt-action repeater; .22 LR only; 23½" barrel; 5-rd. detachable box magazine; European walnut sporting stock; hand-checkered pistol grip; tangent curve open rear sight, ramp front; sling swivels. Introduced in 1926; dropped, 1935. Used value, $145 to $175.

Model MM410B has the same general specifications as MM410, except for lightweight sporting stock. Introduced in 1935; dropped, 1939. Used value, $145 to $200.

MAUSER Model DSM34: bolt-action single-shot; .22 LR only; 26" barrel; Model 98 Mauser military-type stock; no checkering; tangent curve open rear sight, barleycorn front; sling swivels. Introduced in 1934; dropped, 1939. Used value, $115 to $170.

MAUSER Model ES340: bolt-action single-shot target rifle; .22 LR only; 25½" barrel; European walnut sporting stock; hand-checkered pistol grip, grooved forearm; tangent curve rear sight, ramp front; sling swivels. Introduced in 1923; dropped, 1935. Used value, $175 to $230.

MAUSER Model KKW: bolt-action single-shot target rifle; .22 LR, 26" barrel; Model 98 Mauser military-type walnut stock; no checkering; tangent curve open rear sight, barleycorn front; sling swivels; improved model was used in training German troops in WWII. Target model introduced in 1935; dropped, 1939. Used value, $115 to $175.

MAUSER Model EX340B: bolt-action single-shot target rifle; replaced ES340; has same general specifications, except for 26¾" barrel, uncheckered pistol-grip stock. Introduced in 1935; dropped, 1939. Used value, $200 to $260.

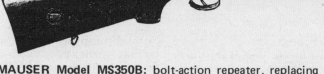

MAUSER Model MS350B: bolt-action repeater, replacing Model ES350; same general specifications; .22 LR only; 26¾" barrel; 5-rd. detachable box magazine; target stock of European walnut; hand-checkered pistol grip, forearm; barrel grooved for detachable rear sight/scope; micrometer open rear sight, ramp front; sling swivels. Introduced in 1935; dropped, 1939. Used value, $145 to $165.

MAUSER Model ES350B: bolt-action single-shot target rifle; has the same general specifications as Model MS350B, except is single-shot. Introduced in 1935; dropped, 1938. Used value, $260 to $280.

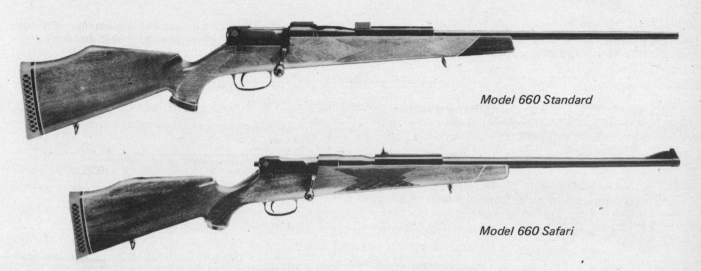

Model 660 Standard

Model 660 Safari

MAUSER Model 660: bolt-action; .243 Win., .25/06, .270 Win., .308 Win., .30/06, 7x57, 7mm Rem. magnum; 24" barrel; short action; adjustable single-stage trigger; push-button safety; no sights; drilled, tapped for scope mounts; detachable sling swivels; interchangeable barrels; hand-checkered European walnut stock; Monte Carlo roll; white line pistol-grip cap, recoil pad. Introduced in 1973; importation discontinued, 1975. Still in production. Used value, $355 to $395.

Model 660 Safari has the same basic specifications as standard 660, except chambered in .458 Win. magnum, .375 Holland & Holland magnum, .338 Win. magnum, 7mm Rem. magnum; 28" barrel, express rear sight, fixed ramp front. Importation discontinued, 1975. Still in production. Used value, $425 to $445.

MAUSER Model 10 Varminter: bolt-action; .22-250 only; 24" heavy barrel; no sights; drilled, tapped for scope mounts; externally adjustable trigger; hammer-forged barrel; hand-checkered European walnut Monte Carlo pistol-grip stock; 5-rd. box magazine. Introduced in 1973; importation discontinued, 1975. Still in production. Used value, $240 to $260.

MAUSER Model 3000: bolt-action; .243 Win., .270 Win., .308 Win., .30/06, .375 Holland & Holland magnum, 7mm Rem. magnum; 22" barrel in standard calibers, 26" in magnum; no sights; drilled, tapped for scope mounts; sliding safety; fully adjustable trigger; hand-checkered, European walnut, Monte Carlo stock; white line spacer on pistol-grip cap, recoil pad. Left-hand action at added cost. Introduced in 1973; dropped, 1975. Used values, standard calibers, $250 to $260; left-hand action, $285 to $300; magnums, $260 to $280; left-hand magnums, $310 to $330.

MOSSBERG Model K: takedown slide-action repeater; hammerless; .22 LR, long, short; tube magazine holds 14 LR, 16 long, 20 short cartridges; 22" barrel; uncheckered straight-grip walnut stock, grooved slide handle; open rear sight, bead front. Introduced in 1922; dropped, 1931. Used value, $55 to $57.50.

MOSSBERG Model M: has same specifications as Mossberg Model K, except for 24" octagonal barrel, pistol-grip stock. Introduced in 1928; dropped, 1931. Used value, $60.50 to $66.

MOSSBERG Model L: takedown, single-shot; .22 LR, long, short; Martini-design falling-block lever-action; 24" barrel; uncheckered walnut pistol-grip stock, forearm; open rear sight, bead front. Introduced in 1929; dropped, 1932. Used value, $167 to $175.50.

MOSSBERG Model B: single-shot, takedown; .22 LR, long, short; 22" barrel; uncheckered pistol-grip walnut stock. Introduced in 1930; dropped, 1932. Used value, $32 to $34.

MOSSBERG Model R: bolt-action repeater; takedown; .22 LR, long, short; 24" barrel, tube magazine; uncheckered pistol-grip stock; open rear sight, bead front. Introduced in 1930; dropped, 1932. Used value, $32 to $38.

MOSSBERG Model 10: bolt-action, takedown, single-shot; .22 LR, long, short; 22" barrel; uncheckered walnut pistol-grip stock, swivels, sling; open rear sight, bead front. Introduced in 1933; dropped, 1935. Used value, $29 to $34.

MOSSBERG Model 20: bolt-action, takedown, single-shot; .22 LR, long, short; 24" barrel; uncheckered pistol-grip stock, forearm with finger grooves; open rear sight, bead front. Introduced in 1933; dropped, 1935. Used value, $29 to $34.

MOSSBERG Model 30: bolt-action, takedown, single-shot; .22 LR, long, short; 24" barrel; uncheckered pistol-grip stock, grooved forearm; rear peep sight, hooded ramp bead front. Introduced in 1933; dropped, 1935. Used value, $29 to $34.

MOSSBERG Model 40: bolt-action, takedown repeater; has same general specifications as Model 30, except for tube magazine with capacity of 16 LR, 18 long, 22 short cartridges. Introduced in 1933; dropped, 1935. Used value, $32 to $38.

MOSSBERG Model 14: bolt-action, takedown, single-shot; .22 LR, long, short; 24" barrel; uncheckered pistol-grip stock, semi-beavertail forearm; rear peep sight, hooded ramp front; sling swivels. Introduced in 1934; dropped, 1935. Used value, $29 to $34.

MOSSBERG Model 34: bolt-action, takedown, single-shot; .22 LR, long, short; 24″ barrel; uncheckered pistol-grip stock with semi-beavertail forearm; rear peep sight, hooded ramp front. Introduced in 1934; dropped, 1935. Used value, $29 to $32.

MOSSBERG Model 44: bolt-action, takedown, repeater; .22 LR, long, short; 24″ barrel; tube magazine, holding 16 LR, 18 long, 22 short cartridges; uncheckered walnut pistol-grip stock, semi-beavertail forearm; rear peep sight, hooded ramp front; sling swivels. Introduced in 1934; dropped, 1935. Used value, $40 to $46.

MOSSBERG Model 25: bolt-action, takedown, single-shot; .22 LR, long, short; 24″ barrel; uncheckered pistol-grip stock, semi-beavertail forearm; rear peep sight, hooded ramp front; sling swivels. Introduced in 1935; dropped, 1936. Used value, $29 to $32.

Model 26A is the same as Model 25, except for minor improvements, including better wood and finish. Introduced in 1936; dropped, 1938. Used value, $32 to $35.

MOSSBERG Model 35: bolt-action, single-shot; target grade; .22 LR only; 26″ barrel, target stock with full pistol grip, beavertail forearm; micrometer rear peep sight; hooded ramp front; sling swivels. Introduced in 1935; dropped, 1937. Used value, $69 to $75.

Model 42C

MOSSBERG Model 42: bolt-action, takedown, repeater; .22 LR, long, short; 7-rd. detachable box magazine; 24″ barrel; uncheckered walnut pistol-grip stock; receiver peep sight, open rear sight, hooded ramp front; sling swivels. Introduced in 1935; dropped, 1937. Used value, $40 to $44.

Model 42A has same general specifications as Model 42, with only minor upgrading. Introduced in 1937 to replace dropped Model 42; dropped in 1938. Used value, $44 to $48.50.

Model L42A is the same as Model 42A, but with left-handed action. Introduced in 1938; dropped, 1941. Used value, $43 to $46.

Model 42B has same general specs as Model 42A, with minor design improvements and replaced the latter; had micrometer peep sight, with open rear, 5-rd. detachable box magazine. Introduced in 1938; dropped, 1941. Used value, $43 to $46.

Model 42C has same specs as Model 42B, except it is sans rear peep sight. Used value, $40 to $44.

Model 42M is updated version of Model 42, replacing discontinued models. Has 23″ barrel; .22 long, LR, short; 7-rd. detachable box magazine; two-piece Mannlicher-type stock with pistol-grip, cheekpiece; micrometer receiver peep sight, open rear sight, hooded ramp front; sling swivels. Introduced in 1940; dropped, 1950. Used value, $43 to $52.

Model 42MB has the same specifications as Model 42; made specifically for Great Britain, British proofmarks. Produced only during World War II. Some collector value. Used value, $46 to $57.50.

Model 45 Standard

MOSSBERG Model 45: bolt-action, takedown, repeater; .22 LR, long, short; tube magazine holds 15 LR, 18 long, 22 short cartridges; uncheckered pistol-grip stock; receiver peep sight, open rear, hooded ramp front; sling swivels. Introduced in 1935; dropped, 1937. Used value, $40 to $43.

Model 45C has same specifications as standard Model 45, except that it has no sights; designed for use only with scope sight. Used value, $34.50 to $40.

Model 45A is improved version of discontinued Model 45, with minor design variations. Introduced in 1937; dropped, 1938. Used value, $40 to $46.

Model 45AC is the same as the Model 45A, but without receiver peep sight. Used value, $40 to $46.

Model L45A is the same as the Model 45A, except for having a left-hand action. Introduced in 1937; dropped, 1938. Used value, $40 to $44.

Model 45B has same general specs as Model 45A, but with open rear sight. Introduced in 1938; dropped, 1940. Used value, $46 to $49.50.

Model 46

Model 46B

MOSSBERG Model 46: bolt-action, takedown repeater; .22 LR, long, short; 26" barrel; tube magazine holds 15 LR, 18 long, 22 short cartridges; uncheckered walnut pistol-grip stock with cheekpiece, beavertail forearm; micrometer rear peep sight; hooded ramp front; sling swivels. Introduced in 1935; dropped, 1937. Used value, $43 to $46.

Model 46C has same specs as standard Model 45, except for heavier barrel. Used value. $46 to $49.50.

Model 46A has virtually the same specifications as discontinued Model 46, but with minor design improvements, detachable sling swivels. Introduced in 1937; dropped, 1938. Used value, $46 to $52.

Model 46AC differs from Model 46A only in that it has open rear sight instead of micrometer peep sight. Used value, $43 to $49.

Model 46A-LS is the same as the Model 46A, except it is equipped with factory-supplied Lyman No. 57 receiver sight. Used value, $55 to $60.

Model L-46A-LS differs from Model 46A-LS only in fact that it has left-handed action. Used value, $52 to $58.50.

Model 46B is updated version of Model 46A, but with receiver peep and open rear sights. Introduced in 1938; dropped, 1940. Used value, $46 to $49.

Model 46BT differs from Model 46B only in the fact that it has a heavier barrel, target-styled stock. Introduced in 1938; dropped, 1939. Used value, $57.50 to $61.

Model 46M dates back to design of original Model 46, incorporating many of changes in discontinued models. Has 23" barrel; .22 LR, long, short; tube magazine holds 15 LR, 18 long, 22 short cartridges; two-piece Mannlicher-type stock with pistol grip, cheekpiece; micrometer receiver peep sight, open rear, hooded ramp front; sling swivels. Introduced in 1940; dropped, 1952. Used value, $52 to $55.

MOSSBERG Model 35A: bolt-action, single-shot; .22 LR only; 26" heavy barrel; uncheckered target stock with cheekpiece, full pistol grip; micrometer rear peep sight, hood front; sling swivels. Introduced in 1937; dropped, 1938. Used value, $43 to $49.

Model 35A-LS is the same as standard Model 35A, except for substitution of Lyman 17A front sight, Lyman No. 57 rear. Used value, $52 to $57.50.

Model 35B is not a variation of Model 35, as might plausibly be expected. Instead, it has the same specifications as the Model 44B, but is single-shot. Introduced in 1938; dropped, 1940. Used value, $57.50 to $63.50.

MOSSBERG Model 43: bolt-action repeater; .22 LR only; adjustable trigger, speed lock; 26" barrel, 7-rd. detachable box magazine; target stock with cheekpiece, full pistol grip; beavertail forearm; Lyman No. 57 rear sight, selective aperture front; adjustable front swivel. Introduced in 1937; dropped, 1938. Used value, $57.50 to $63.50.

Model L43 is the same as standard Model 43, except it was made with left-hand action. Used value, $57.50 to $60.50.

Model 43B is not styled after standard Model 43, but has same specifications as Model 44B, except for substitution of Lyman No. 57 receiver sight, Lyman No. 17A front. Introduced in 1938; dropped, 1939. Used value, $78 to $86.50.

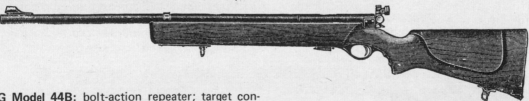

MOSSBERG Model 44B: bolt-action repeater; target configuration; bears little resemblance to standard Model 44; .22 LR only; 26" heavy barrel; 7-rd. detachable box magazine; walnut target stock with cheekpiece, full pistol grip; beavertail forearm; adjustable sling swivels; micrometer receiver peep sight; hooded front. Introduced in 1938; dropped, 1943. Used value, $72 to $75.

MOSSBERG Model 50: takedown autoloader; .22 LR only; 24" barrel, 15-rd. tube magazine in butt stock; uncheckered walnut pistol-grip stock; finger grooves in grip; open rear sight, hooded ramp front. Introduced in 1939; dropped, 1942. Used value, $52 to $55.

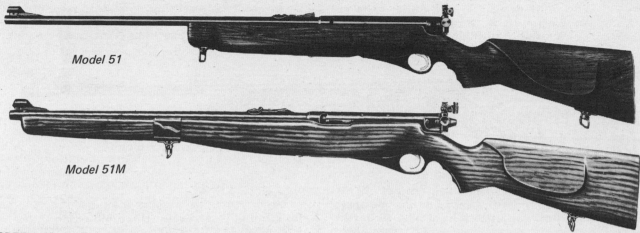

Model 51

Model 51M

MOSSBERG Model 51: has the same general specifications as Model 50, except for addition of receiver peep sight, sling swivels, cheekpiece stock, beavertail forearm. Made only in 1939. Used value, $54.50 to $61.

Model 51M has the same specifications as Model 51, except for substitution of two-piece Mannlicher-style stock, 20" barrel. Introduced in 1946; dropped, 1949. Used value, $57.50 to $63.50.

MOSSBERG Model 44US: bolt-action repeater; redesign of Model 44B, designed primarily for teaching marksmanship to Armed Forces during World War II; .22 LR only; 26"

heavy barrel; 7-rd. detachable box magazine; uncheckered walnut target stock; sling swivels; micrometer receiver peep sight, hooded front. Introduced in 1943; dropped, 1948. Used value, $63 to $66.

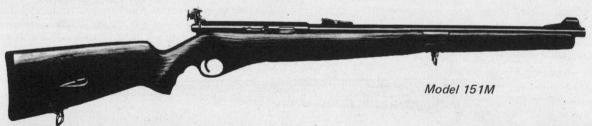

Model 151M

MOSSBERG Model 151M: takedown autoloader; has same general specifications of Model 51M, with minor mechanical improvements. The action is removable without tools. Introduced in 1946; dropped, 1958. Used value, $55 to $60.

Model 151K has same general specifications as Model 151M, except for 24" barrel; is without peep sight, sling swivels. Uncheckered stock has Monte Carlo comb, cheekpiece. Introduced in 1950; dropped, 1951. Used value, $52 to $57.50.

Model 152 Standard

MOSSBERG Model 152: autoloading carbine; .22 LR only; 18" barrel, 7-rd. detachable box magazine; Monte Carlo pistol-grip stock; hinged forearm swings down to act as forward handgrip; sling swivels are mounted on left side;

rear peep sight, military type ramp front. Introduced in 1948; dropped, 1957. Used value, $68 to $75.

Model 152K has same specifications as Model 152, except peep sight is replaced by open sight. Introduced in 1950; dropped, 1957. Used value, $70 to $72.50.

RIFLES

MOSSBERG Model 142: bolt-action carbine; .22 LR, long, short; 18" barrel, 7-rd. detachable box magazine; walnut Monte Carlo pistol-grip stock; as with Model 52, sling swivels mount on left side of stock, forearm hinges down to act as handgrip; rear peep sight, military style ramp front.

Introduced in 1949; dropped, 1957. Used value, $49 to $52.

Model 142K has same specifications as Model 142, except peep sight is replaced by open sight. Introduced in 1953; dropped, 1957. Used value, $46 to $49.50.

Model 144 Standard

MOSSBERG Model 144: bolt-action target model; .22 LR only; 26" heavy barrel; 7-rd. detachable box magazine; pistol-grip target stock; adjustable hand stop; beavertail forearm; sling swivels; micrometer receiver peep sight, hooded front. Introduced in 1949; dropped, 1954. Used

value, $72 to $77.50.

Model 144LS has the same specs as Model 144, except for substitution of Lyman No. 57MS receiver peep sight, Lyman No. 17A front. Introduced in 1954; still in production. Used value, $75 to $81.

MOSSBERG Model 146B: bolt-action, takedown repeater; .22 LR, long, short; 26" barrel; tube magazine holds 20 LR, 23 long, 30 short cartridges; uncheckered walnut pistol-grip

stock, Monte Carlo type with cheekpiece, schnabel forearm; micrometer peep sight; hooded front sight; sling swivels. Introduced in 1949; dropped, 1954. Used value, $52 to $55.

MOSSBERG Model 140K: bolt-action repeater; .22 LR, long, short; 7-rd. clip magazine; 24½" barrel; uncheckered walnut pistol-grip stock, Monte Carlo with cheekpiece; open rear sight, bead front; sling swivels. Introduced

in 1955; dropped, 1958. Used value, $46 to $50.50.

Model 140B is target/sporter version of Model 140K; only difference in specifications is substitution of peep rear sight, ramp front. Introduced in 1957; dropped, 1958. Used value, $46 to $49.

Model 346B

MOSSBERG Model 346K: hammerless bolt-action repeater; .22 LR, long, short; 24" barrel; tube magazine with capacity of 18 LR, 20 long, 25 short cartridges; uncheckered walnut stock with pistol grip, Monte Carlo comb, cheekpiece; open rear sight, bead front; quick-

detachable sling swivels. Introduced in 1958; dropped, 1971. Used value, $55 to $60.50.

Model 346B has same specifications as Model 346K, except for hooded ramp front sight, receiver peep with open rear. Introduced in 1958; dropped, 1967. Used value, $57.50 to $63.50.

Model 320 K

MOSSBERG Model 320K: single-shot, hammerless bolt-action; same specifications as Model 346K, except single-shot with drop-in loading platform; automatic safety. Introduced in 1958; dropped, 1960. Used value, $37.50 to $40.

Model 320B, designated by manufacturer as a Boy Scout target model, has the same specifications as the Model 340K, except it is single-shot with automatic safety. Introduced in 1960; dropped, 1971. Used value, $46 to $52.

Model 340B

MOSSBERG Model 340B: hammerless, bolt-action repeater; target/sporter model is the same as Model 346K, except for clip-type 7-rd. magazine; rear peep sight, hooded ramp front. Introduced in 1958; still in production. Used value, $54.50 to $57.50.

Model 340K is the same as Model 340B, except for open rear sight, bead front. Introduced in 1958; dropped, 1971.

Used value, $46 to $49.

340TR has same general specifications as Model 340K, except for smooth bore; rifled and choke adapters screw on muzzle for shooting bullets or shot. Smooth bore was designed for trap shooting with handtrap. Special device fitted barrel to allow shooter to spring trap. Introduced in 1960; dropped, 1962. Used values, $29 to $35; with Model 1A trap installed, $40 to $46.

Model 340M is the same as Model 340K, except for 18½" barrel, Mannlicher-style stock, sling, sling swivels. Introduced in 1970; dropped, 1971. Used value, $54.50 to $60.50.

Model 342

MOSSBERG Model 342: hammerless autoloading carbine; .22 LR, long, short; 18" tapered barrel; 7-rd. clip magazine; uncheckered walnut Monte Carlo pistol-grip stock; two-position forearm that folds down for rest or handgrip; peep rear sight, bead front; receiver grooved for scope mounts; thumb safety; sling swivels; web sling. Introduced in 1958, still in production. Used value, $48 to $52.

Model 342K is the same as Model 342, except with open rear sight. Used value, $46 to $49.

MOSSBERG Model 350K: autoloader; .22 LR, long, high-speed short; 23½" barrel; 7-rd. clip magazine; walnut Monte Carlo pistol-grip stock; open rear sight, bead front. Introduced in 1958; dropped, 1971. Used value, $52 to $55.

Model 352K

MOSSBERG Model 352: autoloading carbine; .22 LR, long, short; 18" barrel; uncheckered walnut Monte Carlo pistol-grip stock; two-position Tenite forearm extension folds down for rest or handgrip; peep rear sight, bead front; sling swivels, web sling. Introduced in 1958; dropped, 1971. Used value, $52 to $55.

Model 352K is the same as Model 352, except with open rear sight. Used value, $49 to $52.

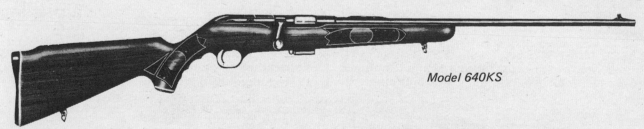

Model 640KS

MOSSBERG Model 640K: hammerless bolt-action; .22 rimfire magnum only; 24" barrel, 5-rd. detachable clip magazine; walnut Monte Carlo pistol-grip stock, with cheekpiece; open rear sight, bead front; sling swivels; impressed checkering on pistol grip, forearm. Introduced in 1959; still in production. Used value, $57.50 to $63.

Model 640KS is the same as Model 640K, but with select walnut stock, checkered pistol grip, forearm; gold-plated front sight, rear sight elevator and trigger. Dropped, 1974. Used value, $63 to $69.

MOSSBERG Model 620K: same as Model 640K, except is single-shot. Introduced in 1958; dropped, 1974. Used value, $29 to $32.

Model 351C

MOSSBERG Model 351K: autoloading sporter; .22 LR only; 24" barrel; 15-rd. tube magazine in butt stock; walnut Monte Carlo pistol-grip stock; open rear sight, bead front.

Introduced in 1960; dropped, 1971. Used value, $46 to $52.

Model 351C carbine is the same as Model 351K, except for 18½" barrel, straight Western-type carbine stock, with barrel band; sling swivels. Introduced in 1965; dropped, 1971. Used value, $52 to $55.

MOSSBERG Model 400 Palomino: lever action repeater; .22 LR, long, short; 24" barrel; tube magazine has capacity of 15 LR, 17 long, 20 short cartridges; open notch rear

sight adjustable for windage, elevation; bead front; blued finish; receiver grooved for scope. Introduced in 1959, dropped, 1963. Used value, $46 to $52.

MOSSBERG Model 402: hammerless lever-action; .22 LR, long, short; 24" barrel; tube magazine holds 13 LR, 15 long, 18 short cartridges; walnut Monte Carlo stock;

checkered pistol grip, beavertail forearm; barrel band; open rear sight; bead front; sling swivels. Introduced in 1961; dropped, 1971. Used value, $69 to $75.

MOSSBERG Model 430: autoloader; .22 LR only; 24" barrel, 18-rd. tube magazine; walnut Monte Carlo stock;

checkered pistol grip, forearm; open rear sight, bead front. Introduced in 1970; dropped, 1971. Used value, $60.50 to $63.50.

MOSSBERG Model 432: autoloading carbine; same as Model 430, except for uncheckered straight-grip carbine

stock, forearm; barrel band; sling swivels. 15-rd. tube magazine. Introduced in 1970; dropped, 1971. Used value, $54.50 to $57.50.

MOSSBERG Model 321K: bolt-action, single-shot; .22 LR, long, short; 24" barrel; hardwood stock with walnut finish; cheekpiece; checkered pistol grip, forearm; hammerless bolt-action with drop-in loading platform; automatic safety;

adjustable open rear sight, ramp front. Introduced in 1972; still in production. Used value, $48.50 to $52.50.

Model 321B is the same as Model 321K, except with S330 peep sight with ¼-minute click adjustments. Dropped, 1976. Used value, $51.50 to $55.50.

MOSSBERG Model 341: bolt-action; .22 LR, long, short; 24" barrel; 7-rd. clip magazine; walnut Monte Carlo stock with checkered pistol grip, forearm; plastic butt plate with

white line spacer; open rear sight adjustable for windage, elevation; bead post front; sliding side safety. Introduced in 1972; dropped, 1976. Used value, $54.50 to $57.50.

MOSSBERG Model 353: autoloader; updated version of Model 352K; specifications are primarily the same; pistol

grip, forearm are checkered; receiver is grooved for scope mount. Introduced in 1972; still in production. Used value, $60.50 to $66.

NOBLE

NOBLE Model 33: slide-action hammerless repeater; .22 LR, long, short; 24" barrel; tube magazine holds 15 LR, 17 long, 21 short cartridges; Tenite stock, grooved wood slide handle; open rear sight, bead front. Introduced in 1949; dropped, 1953. Used value, $40 to $43.

Model 33A has the same general specifications as the Model 33, except that the stock and slide handle are of hardwood. Introduced in 1953, as replacement for Model 33. Dropped, 1955. Used value, $40 to $49.

NOBLE Model 235: slide-action hammerless repeater; .22 LR, long, short; 24" barrel; tube magazine holds 15 LR, 17 long, 21 short cartridges; hardwood pistol-grip stock, grooved wood slide handle; open rear sight, ramp front. Introduced in 1951; dropped, 1973. Used value, $43 to $48.50.

NOBLE Model 10: bolt-action, single-shot; .22 LR, long, short; 24" barrel; uncheckered hardwood pistol-grip stock; open rear sight, bead front. Introduced in 1955; dropped, 1958. Used value, $20 to $23.

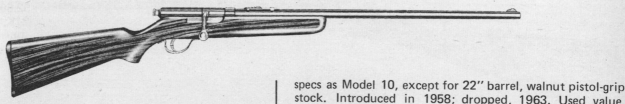

NOBLE Model 20: bolt-action, single-shot; same general specs as Model 10, except for 22" barrel, walnut pistol-grip stock. Introduced in 1958; dropped, 1963. Used value, $23.50 to $26.50.

NOBLE Model 222: bolt-action, single-shot; .22 LR, long, short. Barrel, receiver milled as integral unit; uncheckered hardwood pistol-grip stock; interchangeable peep and V-notch rear sight, ramp front; scope mounting base. Introduced in 1958; dropped, 1971. Used value, $28.50 to $32.

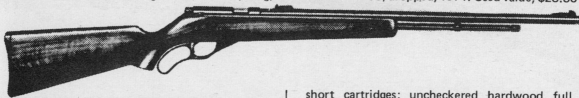

NOBLE Model 275: lever-action, hammerless; .22 LR, long, short; 24" barrel; tube magazine holds 15 LR, 17 long, 21 short cartridges; uncheckered hardwood full pistol-grip stock; open rear sight, ramp front. Introduced in 1958; dropped, 1971. Used value, $54.50 to $60.50.

Remington

Remington No. 4

REMINGTON No. 4: single-shot, rolling-block action; solid frame or takedown; .22 short, long, LR; 25-10 Stevens rimfire; .32 short, long rimfire; has 22½" octagonal barrel; 24" barrel available for .32 rimfire only; blade front sight, open rear; plain walnut stock, forearm. Introduced in 1890; dropped, 1933. (1890 to 1901 solid frame; 1901 to 1926 first takedown with lever on right side; 1926 to 1933 second takedown with large screw head.) Used value, $75 to $150.

Remington No. 4S

REMINGTON No. 4S: Also known as Model 22 military single-shot rifle; rolling-block action; in .22 short or .22 LR only; 26" barrel; blade front sight, military-type rear; military stock, including stacking swivel, sling; bayonet stud on barrel; bayonet, scabbard originally included. Prior to the time the Boy Scouts of America down-graded militarism for fear of being compared with the Hitler Youth Movement, this was called the Boy Scout rifle and was the official rifle of the BSA. Introduced in 1913; dropped, 1933. Used value, $149.50 to $161.

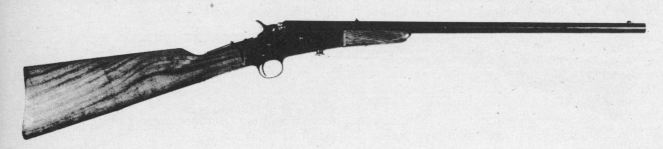

REMINGTON No. 6: single-shot, takedown; rolling block; .22 short, long, LR; .32 rimfire short, long; 20" barrel; plain straight stock, forearm; open front, rear sights; tang peep sight optional. Introduced in 1901; dropped, 1933. Used value, $92 to $103.50.

REMINGTON Model 8A: autoloading takedown; .25, .30, .32, .35 Rem. calibers; detachable box magazine with 5 rd. capacity; 22" barrel; plain walnut straight stock, forearm; bead front sight, open rear. Introduced in 1906; dropped, 1936. Used value, $150 to $200.

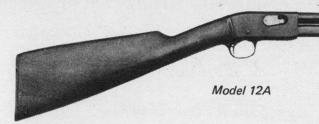

Model 12A

REMINGTON Model 12A: hammerless, takedown slide action; .22 short, long, LR; tube magazine holds 15 shorts, 12 longs, 10 LR; 22" barrel, bead front sight, open rear; uncheckered straight stock; grooved slide handle. Introduced in 1909; dropped, 1936. Used value, $103.50 to $112.

Model 12B differs from Model 12A in that it is chambered for .22 short only. Used value, $106.50 to $115.

Model 12C is the same as standard Model 12A, except for pistol-grip stock, octagonal barrel. Used value, $144 to $149.50.

Model 12CS is the same as Model 12C, except it is chambered for .22 WRF; magazine holds 12 rds. Used value, $109 to $120.50.

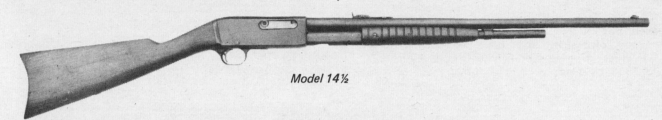

Model 14½

REMINGTON Model 14A: center-fire slide-action repeater; hammerless, takedown; .25, .30, .32 Rem. calibers; 5-rd. tube magazine; 22" barrel, bead front sight, open rear; uncheckered walnut straight stock, grooved slide handle. Introduced in 1912; dropped, 1935. Used value, $172.50 to $181.

Model 14R carbine; same as standard Model 14A, except

for 18" barrel, straight stock. Used value, $200 to $205.

Model 14½ rifle is same as Model 14A, except in .38/40, .44/40 calibers; 11-shot full-length tube magazine; 22½" barrel. Introduced in 1912; dropped, 1925. Used value, $184 to $195.50.

Model 14½ carbine is same as 14½ rifle, except for 9-rd. magazine, 18½" barrel. Used value, $224.50 to $236.

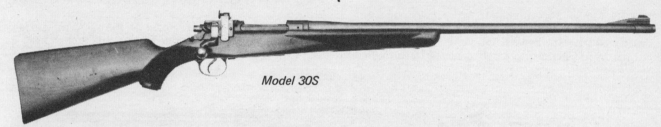

Model 30S

REMINGTON Model 30A: bolt-action center-fire; modified commercial version of 1917 Enfield action; early models had 24" barrel; military-type double-stage trigger, schnabel forearm tip; later versions have 22" barrel. In .25, .30, .32, .35 Rem., 7mm Mauser, .30/06; 5-rd. box magazine; checkered walnut stock, forearm on later versions, uncheckered on earlier with finger groove in forearm; pistol grip; bead front sight, open rear. Introduced in 1921; dropped, 1940. Used value, $172.50 to $190.

Model 30R carbine is same as Model 30A, except for 20" barrel, plain stock. Used value, $172.50 to $190.

Model 30S sporting model has same action as 30A; .257 Roberts, 7mm Mauser, .30/06; 5-shot box magazine, 24" barrel; bead front sight, No. 48 Lyman receiver sight; has long full forearm, high comb checkered stock. Introduced in 1930; dropped, 1940. Used value, $224.50 to $231.

REMINGTON Model 33: takedown bolt-action single-shot; .22 short, long, LR; 24" barrel; bead front sight, open rear; uncheckered pistol-grip stock, grooved forearm. Introduced in 1931; dropped, 1936. Used value, $43 to $49.

Model 33 NRA Junior target model is same as standard Model 33, except for 7/8" sling, swivels; Patridge front sight, Lyman peep style rear. Used value, $57.50 to $63.

RIFLES

REMINGTON Model 24A: takedown autoloader; .22 short only or .22 LR only; tube magazine in butt stock carries 10 LR or 15 short cartridges; 21" barrel; bead front sight, open rear; uncheckered walnut stock, forearm. Introduced, 1922; dropped, 1935. Used value, $115 to $126.50.

Remington Model 24A Speedmaster replaces standard Model 24A; introduced in 1935; dropped, 1951. Has same general configuration as original model, but with 24" barrel. Used value, $126.50 to $138.

Model 25A

REMINGTON Model 25A: slide-action repeater; hammerless, takedown; .25/20, .32/20; 10-rd. tube magazine; 24" barrel; blade front sight, open rear; uncheckered walnut pistol-grip stock, grooved slide handle. Introduced in 1923; dropped, 1936. Used value, $95 to $100.50.

Model 25R carbine is same as standard Model 25A, except for 18" barrel, 6-rd. magazine; straight stock. Used value, $115 to $126.50.

Model 34 Standard

REMINGTON Model 34: bolt-action, takedown repeater; .22 short, long, LR; tube magazine holds 15 LR, 17 longs or 22 shorts; 24" barrel; bead front sight, open rear; uncheckered hardwood pistol-grip stock, grooved forearm. In-

troduced in 1932; dropped, 1936. Used value, $52 to $57.50.

Model 34 NRA target model is the same as standard Model 34, except for Patridge front sight, Lyman peep in rear; swivels, 7/8" sling. Used value, $57.50 to $65.50.

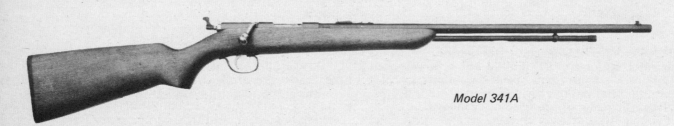

Model 341A

REMINGTON Model 341A: takedown bolt-action repeater; .22 short, long, LR; tube magazine holds 15 LR, 17 longs, 22 shorts; 27" barrel; bead front sight, open rear; uncheckered hardwood pistol-grip stock. Introduced in 1936; dropped, 1940. Used value, $52 to $57.50.

Model 341P, for target shooting, is same as standard

Model 341A, except for hooded front sight, peep rear. Used value, $57.50 to $63.50.

Model 341SB is same as Model 341A, except it is smoothbore for use with .22 shot cartridges. Used value, $43 to $49.

Model 41P

REMINGTON Model 41A Targetmaster: takedown bolt-action single-shot; .22 short, long, LR; 27" barrel; bead front sight; open rear; uncheckered pistol-grip stock. Intro-

duced in 1936; dropped, 1940. Used value, $43 to $49.

Model 41AS differs from 41A Targetmaster only in that

it is chambered only for .22 WRF cartridge. Used value, $34.50 to $40.50.

Model 41P is same as standard model 41A, except that it has hooded front sight, peep-type rear. Used value, $49 to

$54.50.

Model 41SB is same as standard 41A Targetmaster, except it is smoothbore only for .22 shot cartridges. Used value, $37.50 to $40.50.

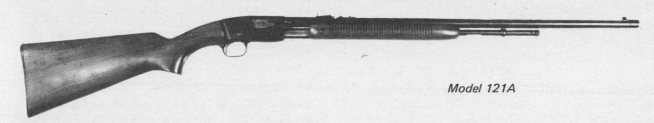

Model 121A

REMINGTON Model 121A Fieldmaster: slide-action takedown, hammerless repeater; .22 short, long, LR; tube magazine holds 20 shorts, 15 longs, 14 LR; 24" round barrel; unchecked pistol-grip stock, grooved semi-beavertail slide handle; ramp front sight, open rear. Introduced in 1936; dropped, 1954. Used value, $172.50 to $181.

Model 121S is same as Model 121A, except chambered for .22 WRF; magazine holds 12 rds. Used value, $115 to $126.50.

Model 121SB; same as Model 121A, except smoothbore for use of .22 shot cartridge. Used value, $103.50 to $109.

REMINGTON Model 81A Woods-Master: takedown autoloader; .30, .32, .35 Rem., .300 Savage; 5-shot nondetachable box magazine; 22" barrel; bead front sight, open rear;

unchecked walnut pistol-grip stock, forearm. Introduced in 1936; dropped, 1950. Used value, $201.50 to $213.

REMINGTON Model 141A Gamemaster: hammerless, takedown slide-action; .30, .32, .35 Rem.; 5-shot tube magazine; 24" barrel; bead front sight, open rear; unchecked

walnut pistol-grip stock, grooved slide handle. Introduced in 1936; dropped, 1950. Used value, $172.50 to $184.

Model 37 (1940)

REMINGTON Model 37 Rangemaster: produced in two variations; the first was produced from 1937 to 1940; the second from 1940 to 1954; 1937 model is .22 LR only; 5-shot box magazine; single-shot adapter supplied as standard; 22" heavy barrel; Remington peep rear sight, hooded front; scope bases; unchecked target stock, with sling, swivels. When introduced, barrel band held forward

section of stock to barrel; with modification of forearm, barrel band was eliminated in 1938. Used values, without sights, $195.50 to $207; with factory sights, $224 to $241.50.

Model 37 of 1940 has same basic configuration as original; changes include Miracle trigger mechanism; high comb stock, beavertail forearm. Used values, without sights, $230 to $247.50; with factory sights, $264.50 to $276.

Model 510A

REMINGTON Model 510A: takedown bolt-action single-shot; .22 short, long, LR; 25" barrel; bead front sight; open rear; uncheckered walnut pistol-grip stock. Introduced in 1939; dropped, 1962. Used value, $40 to $46.

Model 510P is same as standard Model 510, except for Patridge-design front sight on ramp, peep rear. Used value, $49 to $54.50.

Model 510SB is same as standard model, except for being smoothbore for .22 shot cartridge; shotgun bead front sight, no rear sight. Used value, $37.50 to $45.

Model 510X was introduced in 1964; dropped, 1966. Had aspirations to be a target rifle; differed from original model only in improved sights. Used value, $52 to $54.50.

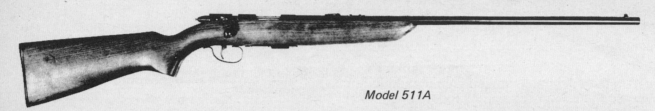

Model 511A

REMINGTON Model 511A: takedown bolt-action repeater; .22 short, long, LR; 6-rd. detachable box magazine; 25" barrel; bead front sight; open rear; uncheckered pistol-grip stock. Introduced in 1939; dropped, 1962. Used value, $57.50 to $63.50.

Model 511P is same as standard model, except for peep sight on rear of receiver; Patridge-type ramp blade front. Used value, $60 to $69.

Model 511X same as model 511A, except for clip-type magazine; improved sight. Introduced in 1953; dropped, 1966. Used value, $60 to $69.

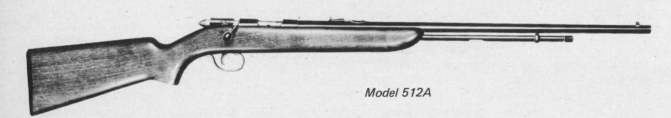

Model 512A

REMINGTON Model 512A: takedown bolt-action repeater; .22 short, long, LR; tube magazine holds 22 shorts, 17 longs, 15 LR; 25" barrel; bead front sight, open rear; uncheckered pistol-grip stock; semi-beavertail forearm. Introduced in 1940; dropped, 1962. Used value, $63 to $69.

Model 512P is same as standard 512A, except for blade front sight on ramp, peep rear. Used value, $66 to $75.

Model 512X; same as standard Model 512A, except for improved sight. Introduced in 1964; dropped, 1966. Used value, $63 to $72.

Model 513TR

REMINGTON Model 513TR Matchmaster: bolt-action target rifle; .22 LR only; 6-shot detachable box magazine; 27" barrel; uncheckered target stock; sling, swivels; globe front sight, Redfield No. 70 peep type rear. Introduced in 1941; dropped, 1969. Used value, $115 to $126.50.

Model 513S differs from 513TR Matchmaster in that it has checkered sporter-style stock; Patridge-type front sight, Marble open rear. Introduced in 1941; dropped, 1956. Used value, $109.50 to $115.

Model 550A

REMINGTON Model 550A: autoloader; features floating chamber for interchangeable use of .22 short, long, LR ammo; tube magazine holds 22 shorts, 17 longs, 15 LR; 24″ barrel; unchecked hardwood pistol-grip stock; bead front sight, open rear. Introduced in 1941; dropped, 1971. Used value, $66 to $78.

Model 550P is same as standard 550A, except for blade front sight on ramp, peep-type rear. Used value, $72 to $81.

Model 550-2G was originally listed as Gallery Special; same as standard model, except for fired shell deflector; screw eye for counter chain; 22″ barrel. Used value, $72 to $86.50.

Model 720A

REMINGTON Model 720A: bolt-action; .30/06, .270 Win., .257 Roberts; 5-rd. box magazine; 22″ barrel; action is modification of Model 1917 Enfield; checkered pistol-grip stock; bead front sight on ramp, open rear; made only in 1941, as factory facilities were converted to wartime pro-

duction. Used value, $225 to $247.50.

Model 720R is the same as standard 720A, except for 20″ barrel. Used value, $195 to $208.

Model 720S is same as Model 720A, except for 24″ barrel. Used value, $232.50 to $247.50.

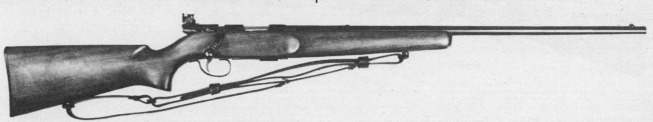

REMINGTON Model 521TL: called the Junior Target Model, this is a takedown bolt-action repeater; .22 LR only; 6-rd. detachable box magazine; 25″ barrel; unchecked tar-

get stock; came with sling, swivels; blade front sight, Lyman 57RS rear peep type. Introduced in 1947; dropped, 1969. Used value, $92 to $98.

Model 514 Standard

REMINGTON Model 514: bolt-action single-shot; .22 short, long, LR; 24″ barrel; unchecked pistol-grip stock; black plastic butt plate; bead front sight, open rear. Intro-

duced in 1948; dropped, 1971. Used value, $34.50 to $40.50.

Model 514P is the same as standard 514, except for ramp front sight, peep type in rear. Used value, $37.50 to $43.50.

Model 721A H&H Magnum

REMINGTON Model 721A: standard grade bolt-action; .30/06, .270 Win.; 24″ barrel, 4-rd. box magazine; bead front sight on ramp, open rear; unchecked walnut sporter

stock. Introduced in 1948; dropped, 1962. Used value, $180 to $202.50.

Model 721ADL differs from standard grade 721A in that

the wood has deluxe checkering on stock and forearm. Used value, $202.50 to $217.50.

Model 721BDL is the same as the Model 721ADL, except that the checkered stock is from more select wood. Used value, $217.50 to $232.50.

The Model 721 Remington was also offered in .300 Holland & Holland, in all variations. In the case of the 721A Magnum, the changes were a heavy 26" barrel, 3-shot magazine and addition of a recoil pad. Used value, $214 to $229. The Model 721ADL H&H Magnum boasted checkering on walnut stock. Used value, $240 to $258. The .300 H&H Model 721BDL, with select walnut, has a used value of $255 to $270.

Model 722A

REMINGTON Model 722A: same as Model 721 series, except for shorter action; .257 Roberts, .300 Savage, .308 Win. Introduced in 1948; dropped, 1962. Used value, $162.50 to $172.50.

Model 722ADL, so-called deluxe grade, is same as standard model, except for checkered stock. Used value, $188.50 to $201.50.

Model 722BDL, termed the deluxe special grade, has same checkering as ADL, but has better wood. Used value, $195 to $208.

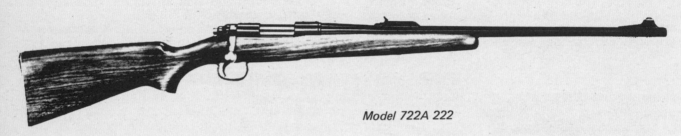

Model 722A 222

REMINGTON Model 722A 222: this series of rifles differs from standard 722A primarily in the fact that it is in .222 Rem.; has 5-shot magazine and 26" barrel. Introduced in 1950; dropped, 1962. Used value, $201.50 to $211.50.

Model 722ADL 222 is the same as 722A 222, except for deluxe checkering on walnut stock. Used value, $211.50 to $221.

Model 722BDL 222 differs from ADL configuration only in that walnut stock is of better grade. Used value, $227.50 to $240.50.

REMINGTON Model 722A 244: has same specs as Model 722A 222, except it is .244 Rem. only and magazine capacity is 4 rds. Introduced in 1955; dropped, 1962. Used value, $201.50 to $211.50.

Model 722ADL 244 differs from standard model only in checkering on pistol grip, forearm. Used value, $217.50 to $227.50.

Model 722BDL 244 is the same as the ADL configuration except for better grade walnut. Used value, $220 to $235.

Model 760 Standard

REMINGTON Model 760: hammerless slide-action repeater; made originally in .223 Rem., 6mm Rem., .243 Win., .257 Roberts, .270 Win., .30/06, .300 Savage, .308 Win., .35 Rem. Since dropped are .223, .257 Roberts, .300 Savage, .35 Rem. Models from mid-60s to early 70s had impressed checkering; others are hand checkered on pistol grip, slide handle; early versions had no checkering on stock, had grooved slide handle; 4-shot magazine; 22" barrel; bead front sight on ramp, open rear. Introduced in 1952; still in production. Used value, $149.50 to $161.

Model 760 carbine; same as standard Model 760, except in .308 Win., .30/06 only; 18½" barrel. Used value, $149.50 to $161.

Model 760 ADL is same as standard Model 760, except

for deluxe checkered stock, grip cap, sling swivels, choice of standard or high comb. Used value, $161 to $169.50.

Model 760 BDL is same as standard model, except for basket-weave checkering on pistol grip, forearm; black forearm tip; early versions available in right or left-hand styles;

.308 Win., .30/06, .270 Win.; Monte Carlo cheekpiece. Used value, $169.60 to $178; 760BDL(D), with fine checkering, engraving, $545 to $605; 760BDL(F), with fine checkering, top grade wood, engraving, $1150 to $1325; 760BDL(F) with gold inlays, $2240 to $2425.

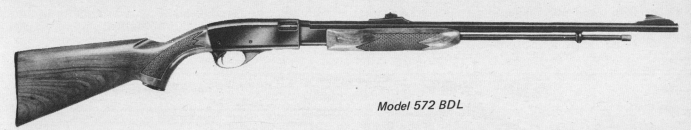

Model 572 BDL

REMINGTON Model 572: slide-action; .22 rimfire; tube magazine holding 20 short, 17 long, 14 LR cartridges; 24" round tapered barrel; walnut pistol-grip stock, grooved slide handle; step adjustable rear sight, bead post front; crossbolt safety; receiver grooved for tip-off scope mount. Introduced in 1955; still in production. Used value, $80 to $85.

Model 572 BDL deluxe is same as Model 572, except for pistol-grip cap, RKW wood finish, checkered grip, slide handle; adjustable rear sight, ramp front. Used value, $85 to $90.

Model 572 SB is same as Model 572, except has smoothbore barrel choked for .22 LR shot cartridge. Used value, $87.50 to $92.50.

Model 740A

REMINGTON Model 740A: gas-operated autoloader; .308 Win., .30/06; 4-rd. detachable box magazine; 22" barrel, uncheckered pistol-grip stock; grooved semi-beavertail forearm; ramp front sight, open rear. Introduced in 1955; dropped, 1960. Used value, $172.50 to $187.

Model 740ADL is same as standard model, except for deluxe checkered stock, grip cap, sling swivels, standard or high comb. Used value, $195.50 to $204.

Model 740BDL is same as ADL model, except for selected walnut stock. Used value, $207 to $218.50.

Model 40X Heavy Barrel

REMINGTON Model 40X: .22 LR single-shot bolt-action target rifle; action is similar to Model 722; adjustable trigger; 28" heavy barrel; Redfield Olympic sights optional; scope bases; target stock; bedding device; adjustable swivel; rubber butt plate. Introduced in 1955; dropped, 1964.

Used value, with sights, $184 to $195.50; sans sights, $161 to $169.50.

Model 40X standard, with lighter barrel, is same as heavyweight model listed above. Used value, with sights, $172.50 to $190; sans sights, $155.50 to $164.

REMINGTON Model 40-XB Rangemaster: rimfire bolt-action single-shot, replacing rimfire Model 40X; .22 LR; 28" barrel, standard or heavyweight; target stock; adjust-

able swivel block on guide rail; rubber butt plate; furnished without sights. Introduced in 1964; dropped, 1974. Used value, $213 to $227.

REMINGTON Model 40X Center-fire: basic specs are same as for 40X rimfire heavy barrel target rifle; standard calibers: .30/06; 7.62 NATO; .222 Rem. magnum, .222 Rem., with other calibers on special request at additional cost. Introduced in 1961; dropped, 1964. Used value, sans sights, $240.50 to $257; with sights, $257 to $279.50.

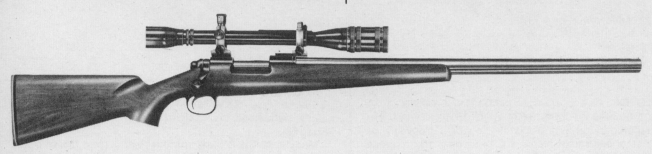

REMINGTON Model 40-XB Center-fire: bolt-action single-shot to replace Model 40X center-fire; .308 Win., .30/06, .223 Rem., .222 Rem. magnum, .222 Rem.; 27¼" barrel, standard or heavyweight; target stock; adjustable swivel block on guide rail, rubber butt plate; furnished without sights. Introduced in 1964; still in production. Used value, $273 to $292.50.

REMINGTON Model 572A Fieldmaster: hammerless slide-action repeater; .22 short, long, LR; tube magazine holds 20 shorts, 17 longs, 15 LR; 25" barrel; ramp front sight; open rear; uncheckered hardwood pistol-grip stock, grooved forearm. Introduced in 1955; still in production. Used value, $78 to $86.50.

REMINGTON Model 725ADL: bolt action; in .243, .270, .280, .30/06; rifle has 22" barrel, 4-rd. box magazine; in .222, has 24" barrel, 5-rd. magazine; Monte Carlo comb, walnut stock; hand-checkered pistol grip, forearm; swivels; hooded ramp front sight, open rear. Introduced in 1958; dropped, 1961. Used value, $240 to $255.

Model 552A

REMINGTON Model 552A Speedmaster: standard model autoloader handles .22 short, long, LR cartridges interchangeably; tube magazine holds 20 shorts, 17 longs, 15 LR; 25" barrel, bead front sight, open rear; uncheckered walnut pistol-grip stock, semi-beavertail forearm. Introduced in 1958; still in production. Used value, $69 to $77.50.

Model 552C carbine is the same as standard Model 552A, except for 21" barrel. Used value, $75 to $80.50.

Model 552GS Gallery Special has same specs as standard model, except for being chambered in .22 short only. Used value, $75 to $80.50.

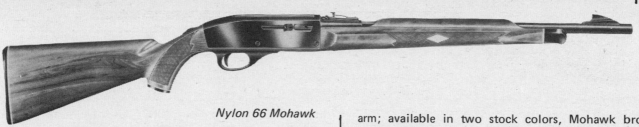

Nylon 66 Mohawk

REMINGTON Nylon 66: autoloader; .22 LR only; tube magazine in butt stock holds 14 rds.; 19½″ barrel; blade front sight, open rear; receiver grooved for tip-off mounts; stock is of moulded nylon, with checkered pistol grip, forearm; available in two stock colors, Mohawk brown and Apache black; latter has chrome-plated receiver. Introduced in 1959; still in production. Used value either color/style, $58 to $60.50.

Nylon 66GS is the same as Nylon 66 Mohawk brown style, except chambered only for .22 shorts. Used value, $66 to $69.

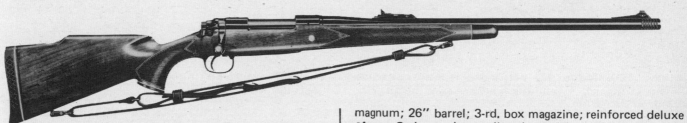

Model 742 Standard

REMINGTON Model 742: gas-operated semi-auto; 6mm Rem., .243 Win., .280 Rem., .308 Win., .30/06; 4-rd. box magazine; 22″ barrel; bead front sight on ramp, open rear; versions of 1960s had impressed checkering on stock, forearm; later versions, cut checkering. Introduced in 1960; still in production. Used value, $172.50 to $181.

Model 742 carbine is same as standard model, except has 18½″ barrel; .308 Win., .30/06 only. Used value, $172.50 to $178.

Model 742BDL is same as standard 742, except in .308 Win., .30/06 only; available in right, left-hand models; Monte Carlo cheekpiece; black tip on forearm; basket-weave checkering. Used value, $190 to $201.50.

REMINGTON Model 725 Kodiak Magnum: built on the same basic action as 725ADL; .375 H&H magnum, .458 Win. magnum; 26″ barrel; 3-rd. box magazine; reinforced deluxe Monte Carlo stock; recoil pad; special recoil reduction device built into barrel; black forearm tip; sling, swivels; made only in 1961. Used value, $520 to $539.50.

REMINGTON International Match Free Rifle: bolt-action single-shot special order calibers were available, but standard chamberings are .22 LR, .222 Rem., .222 Rem. magnum, .30/06, 7.62mm NATO; used same action as earlier Model 40X; 28″ barrel, 2-oz. adjustable trigger; free-style hand-finished stock, with thumbhole; interchangeable, adjustable rubber butt plate and hook-type butt plate; adjustable palm rest; adjustable sling swivel; furnished without sights. Introduced in 1961; dropped, 1964. Used value, $322 to $351.

REMINGTON Nylon 76: .22 LR only; same as standard Mohawk brown 66, except has short-throw lever-action. Introduced in 1962; dropped, 1964. Used value, $58 to $60.50.

REMINGTON Nylon 11: bolt-action repeater; .22 short, long, LR; 6, 10-rd. clip-type magazines; 19-5/8" barrel; blade front sight, open rear; Mohawk brown nylon stock; checkered pistol grip, forearm. Introduced in 1962; dropped, 1964. Used value, $44 to $47.

REMINGTON Nylon 10: bolt-action single-shot; same as Nylon 11, except single-shot. Introduced in 1962; dropped, 1964. Used value, $30 to $33.

REMINGTON Nylon 12: bolt-action repeater; same as Nylon 11 model, except for tube magazine holding 22 shorts, 17 long, 15 LR. Introduced in 1962; dropped, 1964. Used value, $44 to $47.

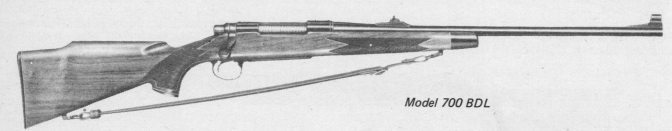

Model 700 BDL

REMINGTON Model 700: this is another of those guns that verges on being an empire. Introduced in 1962, the Model 700 has been Remington's most recent continuing success and is still a top seller, in spite of price increases each year.

Model 700 ADL is bolt-action, .222, .22-250, .243, 6mm Rem., .270, 7mm Rem. magnum, .308, .30/06; 22 and 24" round tapered barrel; walnut Monte Carlo stock, with pistol grip; originally introduced with hand-checkered pistol grip, forearm, was made for several years with RKW finish, impressed checkering; more recent models have computerized cut checkering; removable, adjustable rear sight with windage screw; gold bead ramp front; tapped for scope mounts. Used value, $156 to $169; except for 7mm Rem. mag, $188.50 to $205.

Model 700 BDL is same as 700 ADL, except for black forearm tip, pistol grip cap, fleur-de-lis checkering; matted receiver top; quick release floor plate; quick-detachable swivels, sling; hooded ramp front sight; additional calibers,

.17 Rem., 6.5mm Rem. magnum, .350 Rem. magnum, .264 Win. magnum, .300 Win. magnum. Used value, $208 to $240.50; Peerless grade, with better wood, checkering, custom work, $780 to $838.50; Premier grade, with inlays, engraving, $1625 to $1690.

Model 700 BDL left-hand is the same as 700 BDL, except for left-hand action, stock; available only in .270 Win., .30/06, 7mm Rem. magnum in current production. Used value, $230 to $247, for .270, .30/06; $247 to $266.50 for 7mm Rem. magnum.

Model 700 Safari is same as Model 700 BDL, except in .458 Win. magnum, .375 Holland & Holland; recoil pad, oil-finished, hand-checkered stock. Used value, $403 to $442.

Model 700 C custom rifle is same as Model 700 BDL, except for choice of 20", 22", 24" barrel; with or without sights, hinged floor plate; select walnut, hand-checkered stock; rosewood forearm tip, grip cap; hand-lapped barrel. Used value, in standard calibers, $442 to $461.50; magnum calibers, $461.50 to $481; with optional recoil pad, add $10.

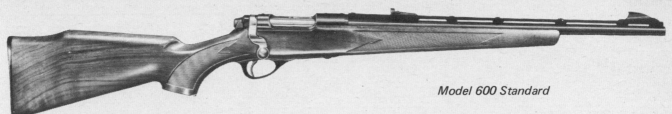

Model 600 Standard

REMINGTON Model 600: bolt-action carbine; 5-rd. box magazine for 6mm Rem., .243 Win., .308 Win., .35 Rem.; 6-rd. magazine for .222 Rem.; 18½″ round barrel, with vent. nylon rib; checkered walnut Monte Carlo pistol-grip stock; blade ramp front sight, open rear; drilled, tapped for scope mounts. Introduced in 1964; dropped, 1967. Used value,

$161 to $172.50.

Model 600 magnum is the same as Model 600, but with 4-rd. box magazine for 6.5mm Rem. magnum, .350 Rem. magnum; heavy magnum type barrel, with bracket for scope backup; stock of laminated walnut/beech; recoil pad; swivels; sling. Introduced in 1965; dropped, 1967. Used value, $215.50 to $230.

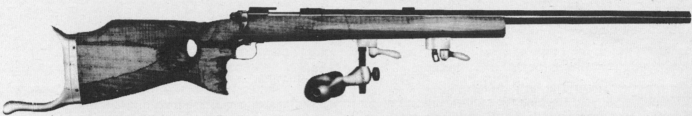

REMINGTON International Free Rifle: in both rimfire, center-fire; has same action as Model 40-XB; .22 LR; .222 Rem., .222 Rem. magnum, .223 Rem., 7.62 NATO, .30/06;

2-oz. adjustable trigger; no sights; hand-finished stock; adjustable butt plate and hook; moveable front sling swivel; adjustable palm rest. Introduced in 1964; dropped, 1974. Used value, $356.50 to $374.

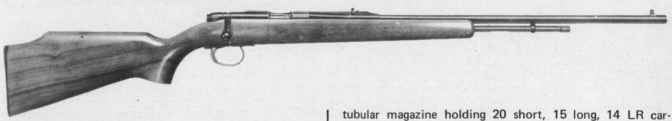

REMINGTON Model 582: same as Model 581, except for

tubular magazine holding 20 short, 15 long, 14 LR cartridges. Used value, $63 to $66.

REMINGTON Model 581: bolt-action, .22 short, long, LR; 5-rd. clip magazine; 24″ round barrel; uncheckered hardwood Monte Carlo pistol-grip stock; screw-adjustable open

rear sight, bead post front; side safety; wide trigger; receiver grooved for tip-off mounts. Introduced in 1967; still in production. Used value, $49.50 to $52.50; left-hand action, stock, $55 to $60.50.

REMINGTON Model 788: bolt-action; .222, .22-250, 6mm Rem., .243, .308; .222 has 5-rd. magazine, others 4-rd.; 24″ tapered barrel for .222, .22-250, 22″ for other calibers; walnut-finished hardwood pistol-grip stock; uncheckered,

with Monte Carlo roll; open rear sight adjustable for windage, elevation, blade ramp front; thumb safety; detachable box magazine; receiver tapped for scope mounts. Introduced in 1967, still in production. Used value, $86.50 to $95; left-hand model, $92 to $100.50.

REMINGTON Model 580: single-shot, bolt action; .22 short, long, LR; 24" tapered barrel; hardwood stock with Monte Carlo comb, pistol grip; black composition butt plate; screw-lock adjustable rear sight, bead post front; side safety; integral loading platform; receiver grooved for tip-off mounts. Introduced in 1957; dropped, 1976. Used value, $52.50 to $58.50.

Model 580 SB is same as standard Model 580, except for smoothbore barrel for shot cartridges. Used value, $57.50 to $60.50.

REMINGTON Model 660: bolt-action carbine, replacing Model 600; 5-rd. box magazine for 6mm Rem., .243 Win., .308 Win.; 6-rd. magazine for .222 Rem.; 20" barrel; bead front sight on ramp, open rear; checkered Monte Carlo stock; black pistol-grip cap, forearm tip. Introduced in 1968; dropped, 1971. Used value, $172.50 to $184.

Model 660 magnum is same as 660 standard, except in 6.5mm Rem. magnum, .350 Rem. magnum; 4-rd. magazine; recoil pad; laminated walnut/beech stock for added strength; quick-detachable sling swivels, sling. Introduced in 1968; dropped, 1971. Used value, $218.50 to $230.

REMINGTON Model 591: bolt-action; 5mm Rem. rimfire; 4-rd. clip magazine; 24" barrel; uncheckered hardwood stock, with Monte Carlo comb; black composition pistol-grip cap, butt plate; screw adjustable open rear sight, bead post front; side safety, wide trigger; receiver grooved for tip-off scope mounts. Introduced in 1970; dropped, 1975. Used value, $67 to $69.50.

REMINGTON Model 592: same as Model 591, except for tube magazine; holds ten 5mm Rem. rimfire rds. Introduced in 1970; dropped, 1974. Used value, $69 to $71.50.

REMINGTON Model 541-S: bolt-action; .22 long, LR; 24" barrel; walnut stock, with checkered pistol grip, forearm; no sights; drilled, tapped for scope mounts, receiver sights; 10-rd. clip; thumb safety; engraved receiver, trigger guard. Introduced in 1972; still in production. Used value, $153 to $159.50.

RIGBY

Best Quality

Second Quality

RIGBY Best Quality: hammerless ejector double rifle; .275 magnum, .350 magnum, .470 Nitro Express; sidelock action; 24" to 28" barrels; hand-checkered walnut stock; pistol grip, forearm; folding leaf rear sight, bead front; engraved receiver. Discontinued prior to World War II. Used value, $4725 to $4800.

Rigby Second Quality has the same general specifications as the Best Quality model, but features box-lock action. Used value, $3525 to $3565.

Rigby Third Quality has the same specifications as the Best Quality rifle, except for lower grade wood, not as well finished. Used value, $2215 to $2290.

RIGBY 350 Magnum: Mauser-type action; .350 magnum only; 24" barrel; 5-rd. box magazine; high quality walnut stock with checkered full pistol grip, forearm; folding leaf rear sight, bead front. Still in production. Used value, $1010 to $1040.

RIGBY 416 Magnum: Mauser-type action; .416 Big Game only; 24" barrel; 4-rd. box magazine; walnut sporting stock with checkered pistol grip, forearm; folding leaf rear sight, bead front. Still in production. Used value, $1200 to $1260.

Rigby 275

RIGBY 275: Mauser-type action; .275 High Velocity, 7x57mm; 25" barrel; 5-rd. box magazine; walnut sporting stock with hand-checkered half-pistol grip, forearm; folding leaf rear sight, bead front. Still in production. Used value, $1010 to $1035.

Rigby 275 Lightweight has same specifications as the standard model, except for 21" barrel. Still in production. Used value, $975 to $1025.

RUGER

Standard Model 44

RUGER Model 44: autoloading carbine; .44 magnum only; 18½" barrel; 4-rd. tube magazine; magazine release button incorporated in 1967; uncheckered walnut pistol-grip carbine stock; barrel band; receiver tapped for scope mount; folding leaf rear sight, gold bead front. Introduced in 1961; still in production. Used value, $129.50 to $135.

Model 44RS carbine is the same as the standard Model 44, except for sling swivels, built-in peep sight. Used value.

$132.50 to $141.

Model 44 Sporter is the same as the standard Model 44, except for sling swivels, Monte Carlo sporter stock, grooved forearm, grip cap, flat butt plate. Dropped, 1971. Used value, $149.50 to $155.

Model 44 International is the same as standard Model 44, except for full-length Mannlicher-type walnut stock, sling swivels. Dropped, 1971. Used value, $164 to $172.50.

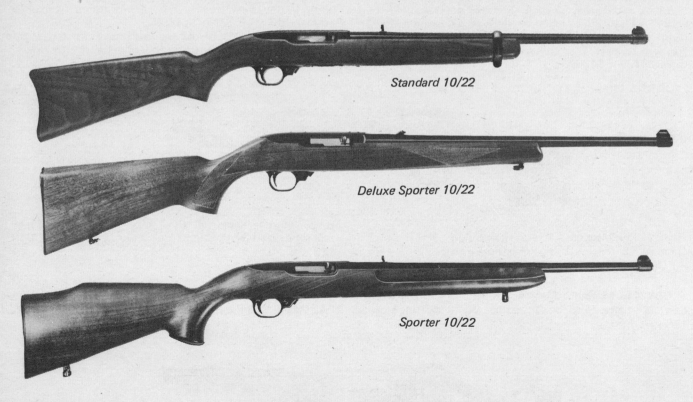

Standard 10/22

Deluxe Sporter 10/22

Sporter 10/22

RUGER Model 10/22: autoloading carbine; .22 LR only; 18½" barrel; detachable 10-rd. rotary magazine; uncheckered walnut carbine stock; barrel band; receiver tapped, grooved for scope blocks or tip-off mount; adjustable folding leaf rear sight, gold bead front. Introduced in 1964; still in production. Used value, $60.50 to $67.

Model 10/22 Sporter is the same as Model 10/22, except for Monte Carlo stock with grooved forearm, grip cap, sling

swivels. Dropped in 1971, but reintroduced in 1973, with hand-checkered pistol-grip stock. Still in production. Used value, $66 to $75.

Ruger Model 10/22 International has the same specifications as standard model, except for full-length Mannlicher-type stock, sling swivels. Dropped, 1971. Used value, $86.50 to $95.

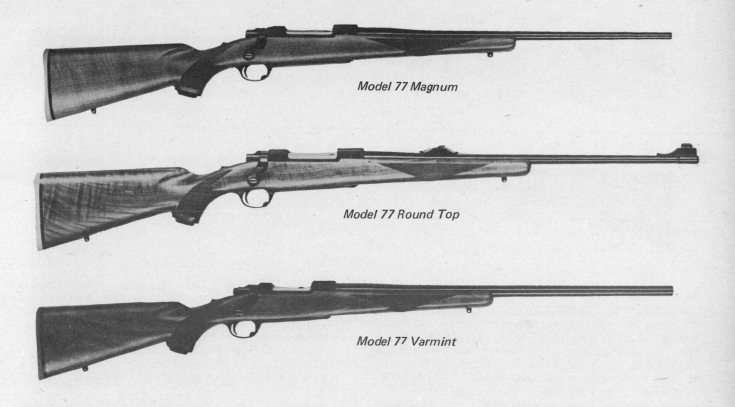

Model 77 Magnum

Model 77 Round Top

Model 77 Varmint

RUGER Model 77 Standard: bolt-action; .22-250; .243 Win., .25/06, .257 Roberts, .250-3000, 6mm, .270 Win., 7x57mm, 7mm Rem. mag., .30/06; 22'' tapered barrel, 3 or 5-rd. capacity, depending upon caliber; hinged floor plate; adjustable trigger; hand-checkered American walnut stock; pistol-grip cap; sling swivel studs; recoil pad; integral scope mount base; optional folding leaf adjustable rear sight, gold bead ramp front. Introduced in 1968; still in production. Used value, $190 to $198.50; with sights, $201.50 to $213.

Model 77 Magnum has same basic design of standard Model 77, except for magnum-size action. Made in .25/06, .270 Win., .30/06, 7x57, 7mm Rem. magnum, .300 Win. magnum, .338 Win. magnum, .458 Win. magnum; magazine capacity, 3 or 5 rds., depending upon caliber; .270, .30/06 have 22'' barrels, all others, 24''. Used value, $213 to $259, depending upon caliber.

Model 77 Round Top Magnum has round top action; drilled, tapped for standard scope mounts, open sights; .25/06, .270 Win., 7mm Rem. mag., .30/06, .300 Win. mag., .338 Win. mag.; other specifications generally the same as Model 77 Standard. Introduced in 1971; still in production. Used value, $201.50 to $213.

Model 77 Varmint is made in .22-250, .220 Swift, .243 Win., 6mm, .25/06 and .308; 24'' heavy straight tapered barrel, 26'' in .220 Swift; drilled tapped for target scope mounts; integral scope mount bases on receiver; checkered American walnut stock. Introduced in 1970; still in production. Used value, $184 to $195.50.

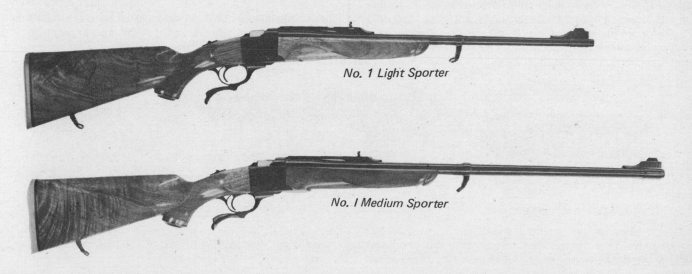

No. 1 Light Sporter

No. I Medium Sporter

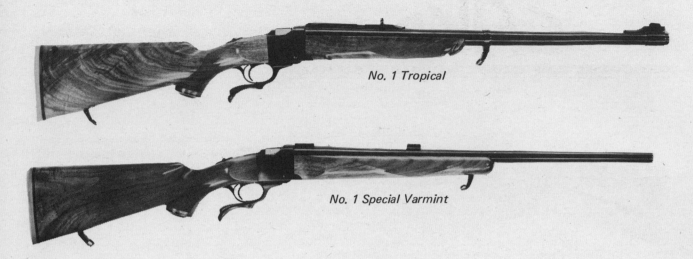

No. 1 Tropical

No. 1 Special Varmint

RUGER No. 1 Standard: under-lever single-shot; .22-250, .243, 6mm Rem., .25/06, .270, .30/06; 7mm Rem. magnum, .300 Win.; 22", 24", 26" barrels, with quarter rib; American walnut, two-piece stock; hand-checkered pistol grip, forearm; open sights or integral scope mounts; hammerless falling block design; automatic ejector; top tang safety. Introduced in 1967; still in production. Used value, $224.50 to $247.50.

Number 1 Light Sporter has the same general specifications as standard model, except for 22" barrel, Alex Henry-style forearm, iron sights; .243 Win., .270 Win., .30/06. Introduced in 1968; still in production. Used value, $224.50 to $247.50.

Number 1 Medium Sporter has the same specifications as the Light Sporter model, except is chambered in 7mm Rem. mag., .300 Win. mag., .45-70; 26" barrel, except .45-70, with 22" barrel. Introduced in 1968; still in production. Used value, $224.50 to $247.50.

Number 1 Tropical Model is chambered for .375 H&H mag., .458 Win. mag.; has 24" heavy barrel; open sights. Introduced in 1968; still in production. Used value, $224.50 to $247.50.

Number 1 Special Varminter has 24" heavy barrel, chambered for .22-250, .25/06, 7mm Rem. mag., .300 Win. mag.; supplied with target scope bases. Introduced in 1970; still in production. Used value, $224.50 to $247.50.

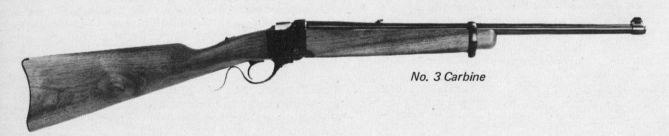

No. 3 Carbine

RUGER No. 3: under-lever single-shot carbine; .22 Hornet, .30-40 Krag, .45-70; 22" barrel; same action as Ruger No. 1, except for different lever; uncheckered American walnut, two-piece carbine-type stock; folding leaf rear sight, gold bead front; adjustable trigger; barrel band on forearm; automatic ejector. Introduced in 1969; still in production. Used value, $144 to $152.50.

Mini-14

RUGER Mini-14: gas-operated, fixed piston carbine; .223 Rem. only; 18½" barrel; 5-rd. detachable box magazine; uncheckered, reinforced American walnut carbine-type stock; positive primary extraction; fully adjustable rear sight, gold bead front. Introduced in 1973; still in production. Used value, $160 to $167.50.

SAKO

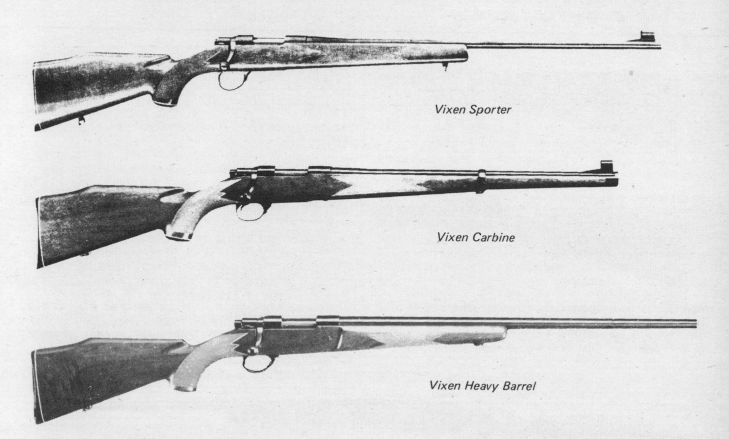

Vixen Sporter

Vixen Carbine

Vixen Heavy Barrel

SAKO Vixen Sporter: bolt-action; .218 Bee, .22 Hornet, .222 Rem., .222 Rem. magnum, .223; built on L461 short Mauser-type action; 23½" barrel; checkered European walnut, Monte Carlo, pistol-grip stock; cheekpiece; no rear sight; drilled, tapped for scope mounts; hooded ramp front; sling swivels. Introduced in 1946; dropped, 1976. Used value, $230 to $241.50.

Vixen Carbine has same specifications as the Vixen Sporter, except for Mannlicher-type stock, 20" barrel. Used value, $250 to $259.

Vixen heavy barrel model has same specifications as sporter, except in .222 Rem., .222 Rem. magnum, .223 only; target-style stock, beavertail forearm; heavy barrel. Used value, $236 to $248.

SAKO Mauser: bolt-action sporter; .270, .30/06; 24" barrel; built on FN Mauser action; 5-rd. magazine; hand-checkered European walnut, Monte Carlo cheekpiece stock; open leaf rear sight, patridge front; sling swivel studs. Introduced in 1946; dropped, 1961. Used value, $325 to $338.

Magnum Mauser has same general specifications as standard Sako Mauser; .300 Holland & Holland magnum, .375 Holland & Holland magnum only; recoil pad. Dropped, 1961. Used value, $364 to $370.50.

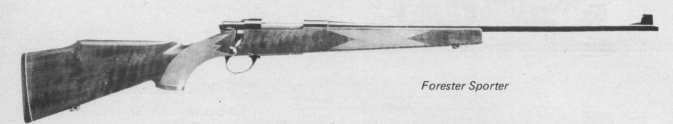

Forester Sporter

SAKO Forester Sporter: bolt-action; .22-250, .243 Win., .308 Win.; 23" barrel; built on L579 medium Mauser-type action; 5-rd. magazine; hand-checkered walnut Monte Carlo pistol-grip stock; no rear sight, hooded ramp front; drilled, tapped for scope mounts; sling swivel studs. Introduced in 1957; dropped, 1971. Used value, $370.50 to $380.

Forester Carbine has same specifications as Forester Sporter, except for Mannlicher-type stock, 20" barrel. Used value, $383.50 to $409.50.

Forester heavy barrel model has same specifications as standard model, except for 24" heavy barrel. Used value, $377 to $390.

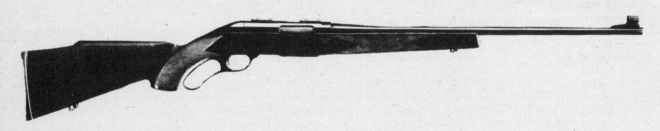

SAKO Finnbear Sporter: bolt-action; .25/06, .264 Win. magnum, .270, .30/06, .300 Win. magnum, .338 magnum, 7mm Rem. magnum, .375 Holland & Holland magnum; 24" barrel; built on L61 long Mauser-type action; magazine holds 5 standard rds., 4 magnums; hand-checkered European walnut, Monte Carlo, pistol-grip stock; recoil pad; sling swivels; no rear sight, hooded ramp front; drilled, tapped for scope mounts. Introduced in 1961; dropped, 1971. Used value, $370.50 to $383.50.

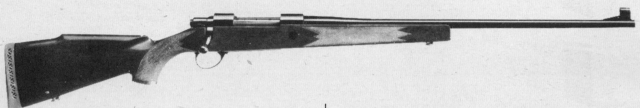

SAKO Finnwolf: hammerless lever-action; .243 Win., .308 Win. only. 23" barrel; no rear sight, hooded ramp front; drilled, tapped for scope mounts; hand-checkered European walnut Monte Carlo stock in left or right-hand styling; sling swivels. Introduced in 1964; dropped, 1972. Used value, $264.50 to $273.

SAKO Model 72: bolt-action; .222 Rem., .223 Rem., .22-250, .243 Win., .25/06, .270 Win., .30/06, 7mm Rem. magnum, .300 Win. magnum, .338 Win. magnum, .375 Holland & Holland magnum; 23" or 24" barrel; adjustable trigger; hinged floor plate; short action in .222, .223, long action on all other calibers; adjustable rear sight, hooded front; hand-checkered European walnut stock. Introduced in 1973; dropped, 1976. Used value, standard calibers, $149.50 to $161; magnums, $167 to $178.50.

Savage

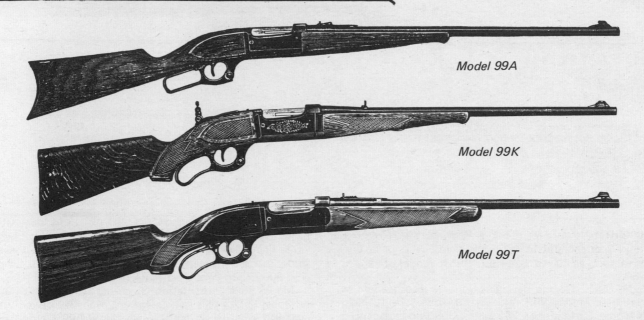

Model 99A

Model 99K

Model 99T

SAVAGE Model 99A: lever-action repeater. Every gun company of major proportions seems to have one or two models that have become legend and upon which much of the company's reputation has been built. This is true of the Model 99 — and it's many variations — for the Savage Arms Corporation. The original Model 99 was introduced in 1899 and replaced in 1922 by the Model 99A. The Model 99A is in .30/30, .300 Savage, .303 Savage; hammerless, solid frame; 24" barrel, 5-rd. rotary magazine; unchecked straight-grip American walnut stock, tapered forearm; open rear sight, bead front on ramp. Introduced in 1922; still in production. Used value, $144 to $149.50.

Model 99B is the same as Model 99A, except has takedown design. Dropped, 1937. Used value, $181 to $190.

Model 99E, in pre-World War II model had solid frame and was chambered for .22 Hi-Power, .250/3000, .30-30, .300 Savage, .303 Savage; 24" barrel for .300 Savage, 22" for all others; other specifications are the same as Model 99A. Model was dropped in 1940, reintroduced in 1961 and still is in production. The current model is chambered in .243 Win., .300 Savage, .308 Win.; 20" barrel; checkered pistol-grip stock. Used values, pre-WWII, $178.50 to $181.50; current model, $129.50 to $135.

Model 99H is solid frame model, with same general specifications as Model 99A, except for carbine stock with barrel band; .250-3000, .30-30, .308 Savage. Used value, $175.50 to $178.50.

Model 99F Featherweight model was discontinued in 1940, reintroduced in 1955; dropped, 1973. Pre-WWII model was takedown style, with same specifications as pre-war Model 99E, except for lighter weight. The 1955 version had solid frame, 22" barrel; .243 Win., .300 Savage, .308 Win.; checkered walnut pistol-grip stock. Used value, pre-WWII model, $210 to $213; 1955 model, $175.50 to $178.50.

Model 99G has the same specifications as pre-WWII Model 99E, except for takedown feature; hand-checkered pistol grip, forearm. Dropped, 1940. Used value, $146.50 to $152.50.

Model 99K is a deluxe version of Model 99G. Has engraved receiver, barrel, Lyman peep rear sight, folding middle sight; fancy grade walnut stock; other specifications identical. Dropped, 1940. Used value, $604 to $621.

Model EG has same specifications as Model G except for uncheckered stock in pre-WWII styling. Dropped in 1940, reintroduced in 1955; dropped, 1961. The 1955 version is in .250 Savage, .243 Win., .300 Savage, .308 Win., .358 Win. Used value, pre-WWII, $110 to $115; 1955 model, $121 to $129.50.

Model 99T Featherweight has same general specifications as standard Model 99s; solid frame design; .22 High-Power, .30-30, .303 Savage, .300 Savage; 22" barrel on .300 Savage, 20" for other calibers; hand-checkered walnut pistol-grip stock, beavertail forearm; weighs approximately 1½ lbs. less than standard. Dropped, 1940. Used value, $218.50 to $230.

Model 99R pre-WWII was solid-frame design; .250-3000, .300 Savage; 22" barrel for .250-3000, 24" for .300 Savage; oversize pistol-grip stock, forearm; hand-checkered American walnut. Dropped, 1940; reintroduced, 1951; dropped, 1961. The 1951 version has same specifications as pre-WWII version, except for 24" barrel; sling swivel studs; .243 Win., .250 Savage, .300 Savage, .308 Win., .358 Win. Used value, pre-WWII model, $218.50 to $230; 1951 model, $175.50 to $181.

Model 99RS was made prior to WWII, dropped in 1940, then reintroduced in 1955, finally being discontinued in 1961. The pre-war model is the same as the pre-war Model 99R, except that it is equipped with quick-detachable sling swivels and sling, a Lyman rear peep sight and a folding middle sight. The pre-war version differs from the 1955

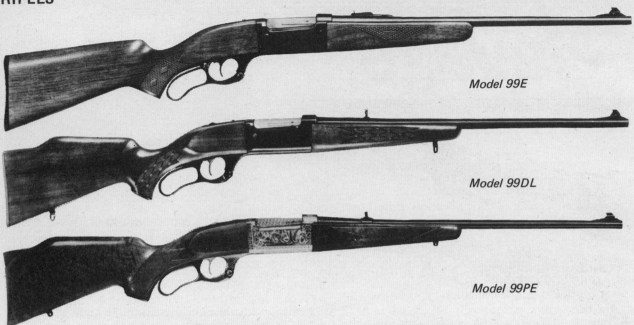

Model 99E

Model 99DL

Model 99PE

Model 99R only in that it has a Redfield 70LH receiver sight and a milled slot for a middle sight. Used value, pre-WWII model, $230 to $244.50; 1951 model, $190 to $195.50.

Model 99DL Deluxe has same general specifications as discontinued Model 99F, except for sling swivels, high-comb Monte Carlo stock; .243 Win., .308 Win. Introduced in 1960; dropped, 1974. Used value, $158 to $167.

Model 99C has same specifications as Model 99F, except clip magazine replaces rotary type; .243 Win., .284 Win., .308 Win., (.284 dropped in 1974); 4-rd. detachable magazine, 3-rds. for .284. Introduced in 1965; still in production. Used value, $167 to $172.50.

Model 99CD is same as Model 99C, except for removable bead ramp front sight, removable adjustable rear sight, white line recoil pad, pistol-grip cap, hand-checkered pistol grip, grooved forearm, quick-detachable swivels, sling; .250-3000, .308 Win. Used value, $187 to $195.50.

Model 99PE Presentation Grade has same specifications as Model 99DL, plus game scene engraved on receiver sides, engraved tang, lever; fancy American walnut Monte Carlo stock, forearm; hand checkering; quick-detachable swivels; .243 Win., .284 Win., .308 Win. Introduced in 1968; dropped, 1970. Used value, $359.50 to $374.

Model 99DE Citation Grade is same as Model 99PE, but engraving is less elaborate. Introduced in 1968; dropped, 1970. Used value, $273 to $287.50.

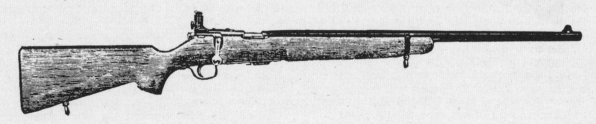

SAVAGE NRA Model 19: bolt-action match rifle; .22 LR only; 25" barrel; 5-rd. detachable box magazine; American walnut military-type full stock, pistol grip, uncheckered; adjustable rear peep sight, blade front. Introduced in 1919; dropped, 1933. Used value, $103.50 to $109.50.

SAVAGE Model 19: bolt-action target rifle, replacing NRA Model 19; .22 LR only; 25" barrel; 5-rd. detachable box magazine; target-type uncheckered walnut stock, full pistol grip, beavertail forearm. Early versions have adjustable rear peep sight, blade front; later models have hooded front sight, extension rear. Introduced in 1933; dropped, 1946. Used value, $115 to $121.

Model 19H is same as 1933 Model 19, except chambered for .22 Hornet only. Used value, $178.50 to $184.

Model 19L has same specifications as 1933 Model 19, except for Lyman 48Y receiver sight, No. 17A front. Used value, $121 to $126.50.

Model 19M has same specifications as 1933 Model 19, except for heavy 28" barrel, with scope bases. Used value, $121 to $126.50.

SAVAGE Model 1920: bolt-action, short Mauser action; .250-3000, .300 Savage; 22" barrel in .250-3000, 24" in .300 Savage; 5-rd. box magazine; hand-checkered American walnut pistol-grip stock, slender schnabel forearm; open rear sight, bead front. Introduced in 1920; dropped, 1926. Used value, $178.50 to $184.

SAVAGE Model 20-1926: bolt-action; has same specifications as Model 1920, except for redesigned stock, 24"

barrel, Lyman No. 54 rear peep sight. Introduced in 1926; dropped, 1929. Used value, $184 to $190.

Model 23AA

SAVAGE Model 23A: bolt-action; .22 LR only; 23" barrel; 5-rd. detachable box magazine; unchecked American walnut pistol-grip stock, thin forearm, schnabel tip; open rear sight, blade or bead front. Introduced in 1923; dropped, 1933. Used value, $100.50 to $109.50.

Model 23AA has the same general specifications as Model 23A, with exception of checkered stock, swivel studs, speed lock. Introduced in 1933; dropped, 1942. Used value, $115 to $121.

SAVAGE Model 25: slide-action hammerless takedown repeater; .22 LR, long, short; 24" octagon barrel; tube magazine holds 15 LR, 17 long, 20 short cartridges; unchecked

Model 23B has same specifications as Model 23A, but is chambered for .25-20 cartridge; no schnabel; 25" barrel; swivel studs. Dropped, 1942. Used value, $103.50 to $109.50.

Model 23C has the same specifications as the Model 23B, except it is chambered for .32-20. Dropped, 1942. Used value, $98 to $106.50.

Model 23D has the same specifications as the Model 23B, except it is chambered for .22 Hornet. Dropped, 1947. Used value, $178.50 to $190.

American walnut pistol-grip stock; grooved slide handle; open rear sight, blade front. Introduced in 1925; dropped, 1929. Used value, $92 to $95.

SAVAGE Model 40: bolt-action sporter; .250-3000, .30-30, .300 Savage, .30/06; 24" barrel in .300 Savage, .30/06; 22" in other calibers; unchecked American walnut pistol-grip

stock, tapered forearm, schnabel tip; open rear sight, bead front on ramp; detachable box magazine; release button on right side of stock. Introduced in 1928; dropped, 1940. Used value, $172.50 to $184.

SAVAGE Model 45: termed Super Sporter, it has same specifications, as Model 40, except for chamberings, hand-

checkered pistol grip, forearm. Introduced in 1928; dropped, 1940. Used value, $207 to $215.50.

Pre-WWII Model 29

SAVAGE Model 29: slide-action hammerless takedown repeater; .22 LR, long, short; 24" barrel; tube magazine holds 15 LR, 17 long, 20 short cartridges; open rear sight, bead

front. Pre-WWII version had octagon barrel, hand-checkered walnut pistol-grip stock, slide-handle; post-war model had round barrel, unchecked wood. Introduced in 1929; dropped, 1967. Used values, pre-WWII, $106.50 to $115; post-war, $98 to $103.50.

Model 3

SAVAGE Model 3: bolt-action takedown single-shot; .22 LR, long, short; pre-WWII version has 26″ barrel, later models, 24″; uncheckered American walnut pistol-grip stock; checkered hard rubber butt plate; open rear sight, bead front. Introduced in 1933; dropped, 1952. Used value,

$26 to $29.

Model 3S has same specifications as Model 3, except for substitution of rear peep sight, hooded front sight. Used value, $29 to $34.50.

Model 3ST has the same specifications as the Model 3S, but was sold with swivels, sling. Dropped, 1941. Used value, $31.50 to $40.50.

Model 4

SAVAGE Model 4: bolt-action takedown repeater; .22 LR, long, short; 24″ barrel, 5-rd. detachable box magazine; pre-WWII version has checkered pistol-grip American walnut stock, grooved forearm; post-war model has uncheckered stock; open rear sight, bead front. Introduced in 1933; dropped, 1965. Used values, pre-WWII, $40 to $46; post-war, $32.50 to $40.

Model 4S has the same specifications as Model 4, except for substitution of rear peep sight, hooded front. Used value, pre-WWII, $46 to $52; post-war, $34.50 to $40.50.

Model 4M has same specifications as post-war Model 4, except it is chambered for .22 rimfire magnum cartridge. Introduced in 1961; dropped, 1965. Used value, $54.50 to $63.50.

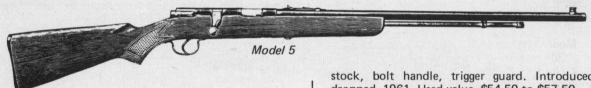

Model 5

SAVAGE Model 5: bolt-action takedown repeater; has the specifications of Model 4, except for tube magazine with capacity of 15 LR, 17 long, 21 short cartridges; redesigned

stock, bolt handle, trigger guard. Introduced in 1936; dropped, 1961. Used value, $54.50 to $57.50.

Model 5S has the same specifications as the Model 5, except for substitution of peep rear sight, hooded front. Used value, $57.50 to $60.50.

Model 219

SAVAGE Model 219: hammerless, takedown single-shot; 25″ barrel; .22 Hornet, .25-20, .30-30, .32-20; shotgun-type action with top lever; uncheckered walnut pistol-grip stock, forearm; open rear sight, bead front on ramp. Introduced in

1938; dropped, 1965. Used value, $47 to $49.50.

Savage Model 219L has same specifications as Model 219, except action is opened with side lever. Introduced in 1965; dropped, 1967. Used value, $47 to $49.50.

SAVAGE Model 221: termed a utility gun, it has the same specifications as the Model 219, except for chambering in

.30-30 only, with interchangeable 30″ 12-ga. shotgun barrel. Introduced in 1939; discontinued, 1960. Used value, $66 to $71.50.

SAVAGE Model 222: has the same specifications as Model

221, except shotgun barrel is 16-ga., 28″. Used value, $55 to $57.50.

SAVAGE Model 223: has the same specifications as the

Model 221, except that shotgun barrel is 20-ga., 28″. Used value, $69 to $71.50.

SAVAGE Model 227: has the same specifications as the

Model 221, except that shotgun barrel is 12-ga., 30″; rifle barrel chambered for .22 Hornet. Used value, $69 to $71.50.

SAVAGE Model 228: has same specifications as the Model 221, except shotgun barrel is 16-ga., 28"; rifle barrel is chambered for .22 Hornet. Used value, $55 to $57.50.

SAVAGE Model 229: has same specifications as Model 221, except shotgun barrel is 20-ga., 28"; rifle barrel is chambered for .22 Hornet. Used value, $66 to $74.50.

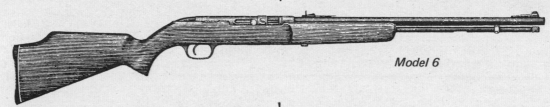

Model 6

SAVAGE Model 6: takedown autoloader; .22 LR, long, short; 24" barrel; tube magazine has capacity of 15 LR, 17 long, 21 short cartridges; pre-WWII version had checkered pistol-grip stock; post-war style has uncheckered walnut stock; open rear sight, bead front. Introduced in 1938; dropped, 1968. Used value, $58 to $60.50.

Model 6S has identical specifications to Model 6, except for substitution of peep rear sight. Used value, $63.50 to $66.

SAVAGE Model 7: autoloader; takedown; same specifications as Model 6, except for 5-rd. detachable box magazine. Introduced in 1939; dropped, 1951. Used value, $47 to $49.50.

Model 7S has same specifications as Model 7, except for substitution of peep rear sight, hooded front. Used value, $49.50 to $52.50.

Model 340

SAVAGE Model 340: bolt-action repeater; .22 Hornet, .222 Rem., .30-30; 24" barrel in .22 Hornet, .222 Rem., 22" in .22 Hornet, .30-30, 20" in .30-30; uncheckered American walnut pistol-grip stock; open rear sight, ramp front. Introduced in 1950; .30-30, .222 Rem. still in production; latter was introduced in 1964; .22 Hornet dropped, 1964. Used values, .30-30, $72 to $75; .222 Rem., $80.50 to $89; .22 Hornet, $80.50 to $89.

Model 340C carbine has identical specifications to standard Model 340, except for 18½" barrel, in .30-30 only. Introduced in 1962; dropped, 1964. Used value, $89 to $95.

Model 340S Deluxe has same specifications as Model 340, except for peep rear sight, hooded front; hand-checkered stock, swivel studs. Dropped, 1958. Used value, $98 to $103.50.

SAVAGE Model 342: bolt-action repeater; .22 Hornet only; has same specifications as Model 340 and, after 1953 was incorporated in manufacturer's line as Model 340. Introduced in 1950; dropped, 1953 as model. Used value, $86.50 to $89.50.

Model 342S has same specifications as Model 340S, but is in .22 Hornet only. Incorporated into Model 340 line in 1953. Used value, $92 to $98.

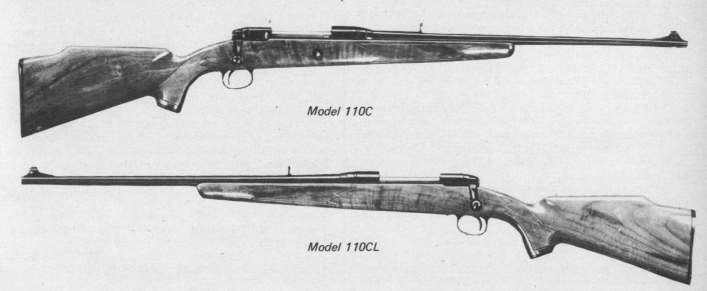

Model 110C

Model 110CL

Model 110D

Model 110DL

Model 110DL Magnum

Model 110EL

SAVAGE Model 110: bolt-action repeater; .243 Win., .270 Win., .308 Win., .30/06; 22" barrel, 4-rd. box magazine; hand-checkered American walnut pistol-grip stock; open rear sight, ramp front. Introduced in 1958; dropped, 1963. This is another of those corporate successes that goes on and on in one variation or another. Used value, $106.50 to $115.

Model 110MC has same specifications as Model 110, except for 24" barrel, Monte Carlo stock; in .22-250, .243 Win., .270 Win., .308 Win., .30/06. Introduced in 1959; dropped, 1969. Used value, $109.50 to $121.

Model 110MCL has the same specifications as Model 110MC, except it is built on left-hand action. Introduced in 1959; dropped, 1969. Used value, $109.50 to $121.

Model 110M magnum has specifications of Model 110MC, except has recoil pad; in .264, .300, .338 Win., 7mm Rem. magnum. Introduced in 1963; dropped, 1969. Used value, $115 to $126.50.

Model 110ML magnum has same specifications as Model 110M, except for being built on a left-hand action. Used value, $126.50 to $132.50.

Model 110E has the same general specifications as earlier versions of Model 110; .243 Win., .30/06, 7mm Rem. magnum; 24" stainless steel barrel for magnum, 20" ordnance steel for other calibers; 3-rd. box magazine for magnum, 4-rd. for others; uncheckered Monte Carlo stock on early versions; current models have checkered pistol grip, forearm; 7mm magnum has recoil pad; open rear sight, ramp front. Introduced in 1963; still in production. Used values, 7mm Rem. magnum, $123.50 to $132.50; other calibers, $109.50 to $115.

Model 110EL has the same specifications as Model 110E, except in 7mm Rem. magnum, .30/06 only; left-hand action. Used values, 7mm magnum, $126.50 to $135; .30/06, $112 to $121.

Model 110P Premier Grade comes in .243 Win., .30/06, 7mm Rem. magnum; 24" barrel of stainless steel for 7mm magnum, 22" for other calibers; 3-shot box magazine for magnum, 4-shot for others; skip-checkered Monte Carlo

French walnut stock, rosewood pistol-grip cap, forearm tip; magnum version has recoil pad; open rear sight, ramp front. Introduced in 1964; dropped, 1970. Used values, 7mm magnum, $299 to $316.50; other calibers, $289.50 to $299.

Savage Model 110PL Premier Grade has the same specifications as Model 110P, except for left-hand action. Used values; 7mm magnum, $299 to $310.50; other calibers, $276 to $289.50.

Savage Model 110PE Presentation Grade has same specifications as Model 110P, except for engraved receiver, trigger guard, floor plate; stock is of choice French walnut. Introduced in 1958; dropped, 1970. Used values, 7mm magnum, $415 to $425; other calibers, $460 to $471.50.

Savage Model 110EL Presentation Grade has same specifications as Model 110PE, except it is built on a left-hand action. Used values, 7mm magnum, $477.50 to $489; other calibers, $448.50 to $466.

Savage Model 110C was introduced in 1966; still in production; .22-250, .243 Win., .25/06, .270 Win., .30/06, .308 Win., 7mm Rem. magnum, .300 Win. magnum. Magnum calibers have 3-shot detachable box magazine; other calibers, 4-rd. magazine; magnum calibers, .22-250 have 24" barrel, others, 22"; hand-checkered Monte Carlo American walnut pistol-grip stock; magnum has recoil pad; open folding leaf rear sight, ramp front. Offered currently in .243, .270, .30/06, 7mm Rem. magnum. Used values, magnum calibers, $154.50 to $160.50; standard calibers, $144.50 to $150.50.

Savage Model 110B (right-hand bolt) and 110BL (left-hand bolt) were introduced in 1977 and are same as Model 110E except chambered for .30/06, .270 Win., and .243 Win. and have internal magazines. Used value, Model 110B, $137.50 to $143.50; Model 110 BL, $142.50 to $148.50.

Model 65M

SAVAGE Model 65: bolt-action; .22 LR, long, short; 20" free-floating barrel; 5-rd. detachable box magazine; sliding safety; double extractors; American walnut Monte Carlo stock; checkered pistol grip, forearm; step adjustable open

rear sight, gold bead ramp front. Introduced in 1965; dropped, 1974. Used value, $52.50 to $56.50.

Model 65M has same specifications as Model 65, but is chambered for .22 rimfire magnum cartridge. Introduced in 1966; still in production. Used value, $52 to $54.50.

SAVAGE/ANSCHUTZ Model 153: bolt-action; .222 Rem. only; 24" barrel; manufactured to Savage specs by J.G. Anschutz, West Germany; skip-checkered French walnut

stock; cheekpiece; rosewood grip cap, forearm tip; sling swivels; folding leaf open rear sight, hooded ramp front. Introduced in 1964; dropped, 1967. Used value, $264.50 to $270.

Model 164M

SAVAGE/ANSCHUTZ Model 164: bolt-action; .22 LR only; 24" barrel; 5-rd. detachable clip magazine; fully adjustable single-stage trigger; receiver grooved for tip-off mount; European walnut stock, hand-checkered pistol grip, forearm; Monte Carlo comb, cheekpiece, schnabel forearm.

Introduced in 1966; still in production. Used value, $161 to $172.50.

Model 164M has same specifications as Model 164, except magazine holds 4 rds.; chambered for .22 rimfire magnum cartridge. Used value, $161 to $172.50.

Model 54

SAVAGE/ANSCHUTZ Model 54: bolt-action; .22 LR only; 23" barrel; 5-rd. clip magazine; adjustable single stage trigger; wing safety; receiver grooved fro tip-off mount, tapped for scope blocks; French walnut stock, with Monte Carlo roll-over comb, schnabel forearm tip. Hand-checkered pistol

grip, forearm; folding leaf sight, hooded ramp gold bead front. Introduced in 1966; still in production. Used value, $276 to $293.50.

Model 54M has same specifications as Model 54, except chambered for .22 rimfire magnum. Introduced in 1973; still in production. Used value, $276 to $293.50.

SAVAGE/ANSCHUTZ Model 184: bolt-action; .22 LR only, 21½" barrel; 5-rd. detachable clip magazine; factory-set trigger; receiver grooved for scope mounts; European walnut

stock with Monte Carlo comb, schnabel forearm; hand-checkered pistol grip, forearm; folding leaf rear sight, hooded ramp front. Introduced in 1966; dropped, 1974. Used value, $89 to $92.50.

STEVENS

STEVENS Ideal No. 44: single-shot, lever-action, rolling block; takedown; .22 LR, .25 rimfire, .32 rimfire, .25-20, .32-20, .32-40, .38-40, .38-55, .44-40; 24" or 26" barrel, round, full octagon, half octagon; uncheckered straight-grip walnut stock, forearm; open rear sight, Rocky Mountain front. Introduced in 1894; dropped, 1932. Primarily of collector interest. Used value, $230 to $241.50.

STEVENS Favorite No. 17: single-shot, lever-action, take-down; .22 LR; .25 rimfire, .32 rimfire; 24" barrel, with other lengths available on special order; uncheckered walnut straight-grip stock, tapered forearm; open rear sight, Rocky Mountain front. Introduced in 1894; dropped, 1935. Used value, $80.50 to $86.50.

STEVENS Favorite No. 18: has the same specifications as the No. 17, except for substitution of vernier peep rear sight, Beach combination front, addition of leaf middle sight. Introduced in 1894; dropped, 1935. Used value, $86.50 to $92.

STEVENS Favorite No. 19: has same specifications as No. 17, except for substitution of Lyman combination rear sight, Lyman front, addition of leaf middle sight. Introduced in 1895; dropped, 1935. Used value, $86.50 to $92.

STEVENS Favorite No. 20: has same specifications as No. 17, except for smoothbore barrel for .22 rimfire, .32 rimfire shot cartridges only. Introduced in 1895; dropped, 1935. Used value, $80.50 to $83.50.

STEVENS Favorite No. 27: has the same specifications as No. 17, except for substitution of octagon barrel. Introduced in 1896; dropped, 1935. Used value, $89 to $95.

STEVENS Favorite No. 28: has same specifications as No. 18, except for substitution of octagon barrel. Introduced in 1896; dropped, 1935. Used value, $98 to $103.50.

STEVENS Favorite No. 29: has same specifications as No. 19, except for substitution of octagon barrel. Introduced in 1896; dropped, 1935. Used value, $98 to $103.50.

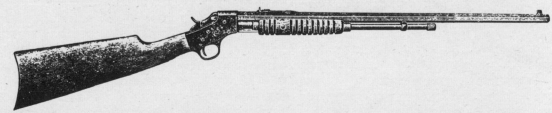

STEVENS No. 70: slide-action repeater; exposed hammer; .22 LR, long, short; 22" barrel; tube magazine holds 11 LR, 13 long, 15 short cartridges; uncheckered straight-grip stock, grooved slide handle; open rear sight, bead front. Introduced in 1907; dropped, 1934. Used value, $92 to $100.50.

STEVENS No. 414: single-shot, lever-action, rolling block; uses same action as Model 44; 26" barrel; .22 LR only or .22 short only; uncheckered straight-grip walnut stock, military-styled forearm, sling swivels; Lyman receiver peep sight, blade front. Introduced in 1912; dropped, 1932. Known as Armory Model, has some collector value affecting price. Used value, $218.50 to $230.

STEVENS Crack Shot No. 26: single-shot, takedown, lever-action; .22 LR, .32 rimfire; 18", 22" barrel; uncheckered straight-grip walnut stock, tapered forearm; open rear sight, blade front. Introduced in 1913; dropped, 1939. Used value, $89 to $95.

STEVENS No. 26½: has the same specifications as No. 26, except for smoothbore barrel for .22, .32 rimfire shot cartridges. Introduced in 1914; dropped, 1939. Used value, $77.50 to $83.50.

STEVENS No. 66: bolt-action takedown repeater; .22 LR, long, short; 24" barrel; tube magazine holds 13 LR, 15 long, 19 short cartridges; uncheckered walnut pistol-grip stock, grooved forearm; open rear sight, bead front. Introduced in 1931; dropped, 1935. Used value, $45 to $49.

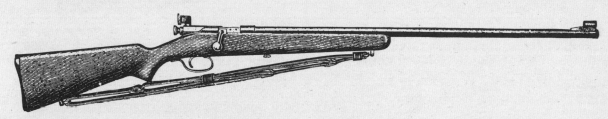

STEVENS No. 419: bolt-action, takedown single-shot; termed the Junior Target Model; .22 LR only; 26" barrel; uncheckered walnut junior target stock; pistol grip; sling, swivels; Lyman No. 55 peep rear sight, blade front. Introduced in 1932; dropped, 1936. Used value, $55.50 to $58.50.

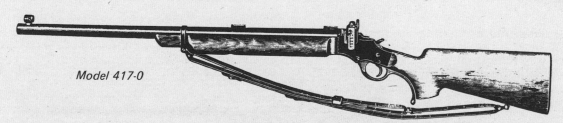

Model 417-0

STEVENS Walnut Hill No. 417-0: single-shot lever-action; .22 Hornet, .22 LR only; .22 short only; 28" heavy barrel or 29" extra-heavy; uncheckered walnut target stock; full pistol grip, beavertail forearm; sling swivels, barrel band, sling; Lyman No. 52L extension rear sight, No. 17A front. Introduced in 1932; dropped, 1947. Value largely based upon collector appeal. Used value, $330 to $345.

No. 417-1 Walnut Hill has the same specifications as the No. 417-0, except for substitution of Lyman No. 48L receiver sight. Dropped, 1947. Used value, $330 to $345.

No. 41-2 Walnut Hill model has same specifications as No. 417-0, except for substitution of Lyman No. 1441 tang sight. Dropped, 1947. Used value, $330 to $345.

No. 417-3 Walnut Hill has the same specifications as No. 417-0, except that it was sold without sights. Dropped, 1947. Used value, $315 to $330.

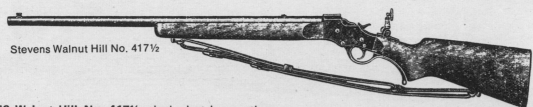

Stevens Walnut Hill No. 417½

STEVENS Walnut Hill No. 417½: single-shot lever-action; same general specifications as 417-0; .22 Hornet, .25 rimfire, .22 WRF, .22 LR; 28" barrel; uncheckered walnut sporting-style stock; pistol grip, semi-beavertail forearm; swivels, sling; Lyman No. 144 tang peep sight, folding middle sight, bead front. Introduced in 1932; dropped, 1940. Used value, $345 to $362.

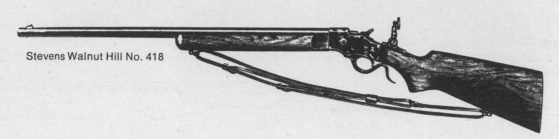

Stevens Walnut Hill No. 418

STEVENS Walnut Hill No. 418: single-shot, takedown lever-action; .22 LR only, .22 short only; 26" barrel; uncheckered walnut stock; pistol grip, semi-beavertail fore-arm; sling swivels, sling; Lyman No. 144 tang peep sight, blade front. Introduced in 1932; dropped, 1940. Used value, $184 to $196.

Stevens Walnut Hill No. 418½

STEVENS Walnut Hill No. 418½: has the same general specifications as No. 418, except for availability in .25 Stevens rimfire, .22 WRF also; substitution of Lyman No. 2A tang peep sight, bead front. Introduced in 1932; dropped, 1940. Used value, $178 to $190.

Model 053

STEVENS Buckhorn Model 053: bolt-action, takedown single-shot; .25 Stevens rimfire, .22 WRF, .22 LR, long, short; 24" barrel; uncheckered walnut stock; pistol grip, black forearm tip; receiver peep sight, open middle sight, hooded front. Introduced in 1935; dropped, 1948. Used value, $34.50 to $37.50.

Model 53 has the same specifications as Model 053, except for open rear sight, plain bead front. Used value, $31.50 to $34.50.

Model 056

STEVENS Buckhorn Model 056: bolt-action, takedown repeater; .22 LR, long, short; 24" barrel, 5-rd. detachable box magazine; uncheckered walnut sporter-type stock; pistol grip, black forearm tip; receiver peep sight, open middle sight, hooded front. Introduced in 1935; dropped,

1948. Used value, $43 to $46.

Model 56 has same specifications as Model 056, except

for open rear sight, plain bead front. Used value, $37.50 to $40.

Model 066

STEVENS Buckhorn Model 066: bolt-action, takedown repeater; .22 LR, long, short; 24" barrel; tube magazine holds 15 LR, 17 long, 21 short cartridges; uncheckered walnut sporting stock; pistol grip, black forearm tip;

receiver peep sight, open middle sight, hooded front. Introduced in 1935; dropped, 1948. Used value, $40 to $46.

Model 66 has the same specifications as Model 066, except for open rear sight, plain bead front. Used value, $34.50 to $37.50.

STEVENS Springfield Model 82: bolt-action, takedown single-shot. Springfield was used as a brand name from 1935 until 1948, with the designation being dropped at that time. It should not be confused in any way with the Springfield Armory, although the name probably was

registered with such mistaken identity in mind. After the Springfield brand name was dropped, rifles were known strictly by Stevens name. In .22 LR, long, short; 22" barrel; uncheckered walnut pistol-grip stock, grooved forearm; open rear sight, bead front. Introduced in 1935; dropped, 1939. Used value, $31.50 to $34.50.

STEVENS Springfield Model 83: bolt-action, takedown single-shot; same basic action as Model 82, but chambered for .25 Stevens, .22 WRF, .22 LR, long, short; 24" barrel;

other specifications are identical to those of Model 82. Introduced in 1935; dropped, 1939. Used value, $31.50 to $34.50.

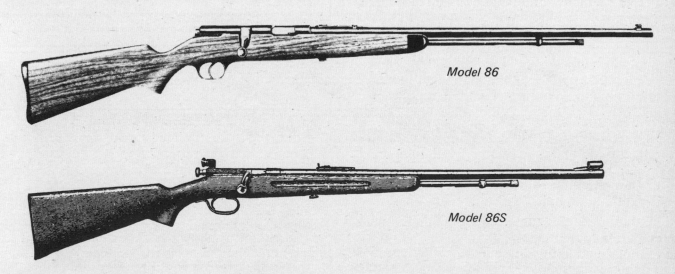

Model 86

Model 86S

STEVENS-Springfield Model 86: bolt-action, takedown repeater; .22 LR, long, short; 24" barrel; plated bolt, trigger; tube magazine holds 15 LR, 17 long, 21 short cartridges; uncheckered military walnut stock; pistol grip, black forearm tip. Introduced in 1935, and produced until 1948 under Springfield brand name; produced from 1948 to 1965 under Stevens name when dropped. Used value, $40 to $46.

Model 086 has the same specifications as Model 86, except for substitution of peep rear sight, hooded front. Marketed under Springfield brand name from 1935 to 1948. Used value, $40 to $46.

Model 85-S is exactly the same as Model 086, but designation was changed when Springfield name was dropped in 1948; marketed as Stevens thereafter, until dropped, 1952. Used value, $40 to $46.

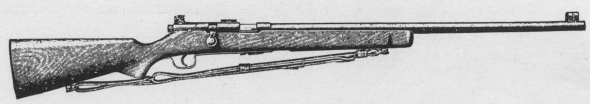

STEVENS Model 416: bolt-action, target model; .22 LR only; 26" heavy barrel; 5-rd. detachable box magazine; uncheckered walnut target-type stock; sling swivels, sling; receiver peep sight, hooded front. Introduced in 1937; dropped, 1949. Used value, $121 to $129.50.

Model 15Y

STEVENS-Springfield Model 15: bolt-action, takedown single-shot; .22 LR, long, short; 22" barrel; uncheckered pistol-grip stock; open rear sight, bead front. Introduced in 1937; dropped, 1948. Used value, $23 to $26.

Stevens Model 15 has identical specifications to Stevens-Springfield Model 15, except for substitution of 24" barrel, redesigned stock, including black forearm tip. Introduced in 1948; dropped, 1965. Used value, $29 to $31.50.

Model 15Y, the so-called Youth Model, has same specifications as standard Stevens Model 15, except for 21" barrel, shorter buttstock. Introduced in 1958; dropped, 1965. Used value, $29 to $31.50.

STEVENS Buckhorn No. 76: takedown autoloader; .22 LR only; 24" barrel; 15-rd. tube magazine; uncheckered sporter-style stock, black forearm tip; open rear sight, plain bead front. Introduced in 1938; dropped, 1948. Used value, $34.50 to $37.50.

No. 076 has same specifications as No. 76, except for peep receiver sight, open middle sight, hooded front. Introduced in 1938; dropped, 1948. Used value, $37.50 to $40.

Model 87

STEVENS Model 87: takedown autoloader; .22 LR only; 24" barrel until late 60s, current production has 20" barrel; uncheckered pistol-grip stock, black forearm tip; open rear sight; bead front. Marketed as Springfield Model 87 from 1938 to 1948, until trade name dropped. Dropped, 1976. Used value, $43 to $49.

Model 087, Springfield designation, has same specs as Model 87, except for peep rear sight, hooded front. Introduced in 1938; redesignated, 1948. Used value, $40 to $46.

Model 87-S is Stevens designation for 087, as of 1948. Dropped, 1953. Used value, $40 to $46.

STEVENS Buckhorn No. 57: takedown autoloader; has the same specifications as No. 76, except for 5-rd. detachable box magazine. Introduced in 1939; dropped, 1948. Used value, $34.50 to $37.50.

No. 057 has the same specifications as the No. 57. Also introduced in 1939; dropped, 1948. Used value, $34.50 to $37.50.

Model 85

STEVENS-Springfield Model 85: has the same specifications as Model 87, except for 5-rd. detachable box magazine. From introduction in 1939 until 1948, was designated as Springfield Model 85. Has been Stevens Model 85 since 1948; dropped, 1976. Used value, $43 to $52.

Model 085 is same as Model 85, except for peep rear sight, hooded front. This designation was used on Springfield brand rifles from 1939 until 1948. Used value, $43 to $47.

Model 85-S is exactly the same as Model 085, but carries Stevens name since 1948; dropped, 1976. Used value, $43 to $47.

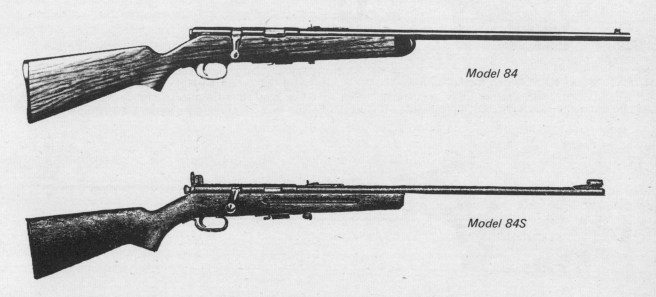

Model 84

Model 84S

STEVENS-Springfield Model 84: bolt-action, takedown repeater; has the same specifications as the Model 86, except for 5-rd. detachable box magazine. Introduced in 1940 as Springfield Model 84; when trade name was dropped in 1948, it was redesignated as Stevens Model 84 and continued until dropped, 1965. Used value, $40 to $46.

Model 084 has the same specifications as Springfield Model 84, except for substitution of rear peep sight, hooded front. Introduced in 1940; when trade name was dropped in 1948, it was redesignated. Used value, $40 to $46.

Model 84-S is exactly the same as Model 084, but designation was changed when Springfield name was dropped. Marketed as Stevens Model 84-S from 1948 until dropped, 1952. Used value, $40 to $46.

STEVENS Model 322: bolt-action carbine; .22 Hornet only; 21'' barrel; 4-rd. detachable box magazine; unchecked walnut pistol-grip stock; open rear sight, ramp front. Introduced in 1947; dropped, 1950. Used value, $86.50 to $89.

Model 322-S has the same specifications as the Model 322, except for substitution of a peep rear sight. Introduced in 1947; dropped, 1950. Used value, $86.50 to $92.

STEVENS Model 325: bolt-action carbine; .30-30 only; 21'' barrel; 3-rd. detachable box magazine; unchecked pistol-grip stock; open rear sight, bead front. Introduced in 1947; dropped, 1950. Used value, $86.50 to $89.

Model 325-S has same specifications as Model 325, except for substitution of peep rear sight. Introduced in 1947; dropped, 1950. Used value, $86.50 to $92.

WALTHER

WALTHER Model KKJ: bolt-action; .22 LR, .22 magnum, .22 Hornet; 24" medium-heavy target barrel; 5-rd. clip magazine; adjustable open rear sight, hooded ramp front; cross-bolt safety; receiver grooved for scope; hand-checkered European walnut pistol-grip stock, forearm; high, tapered comb; sling swivels. Imported originally by Interarms. Introduced in 1957; .22 Hornet still in production. Used value, $286 to $312.

WALTHER Model KKM Match Model: bolt-action; single-shot; .22 LR only; 28" barrel; fully adjustable match trigger; micrometer rear sight, Olympic front with post, aperture inserts; European walnut stock with adjustable hook butt plate, hand shelf, ball-type offset yoke palm rest. Imported from Germany by Interarms. Introduced in 1957; still in production. Used value, $487.50 to $552.50.

WALTHER U.I.T. Match Model: bolt action; single-shot; .22 LR only; 25½" barrel; conforms to NRA, UIT rules; fully adjustable trigger; micrometer rear sight; interchangeable post or aperture front; European walnut stock adjustable for length, drop; forearm guide rail for sling or palm rest. Imported from Germany by Interarms. Introduced in 1966; still in production. Used value, $370.50 to $403.

WALTHER Moving Target Model: bolt-action; single shot; .22 LR only; 23.6" barrel; micrometer rear sight, globe front; especially designed for running boar competition; receiver grooved for dovetail scope mounts; European walnut thumb-hole stock; stippled forearm, pistol grip; adjustable cheekpiece, buttplate. Imported from Germany by Interarms. Introduced in 1972; still in production. Used value, $357.50 to $390.

WALTHER Prone 400 Model: bolt action; single-shot; .22 LR only; has the same general specifications as U.I.T. Match Model except for scope blocks, split stock for cheek-piece adjustment; especially designed for prone shooting. Introduced in 1972; still in production. Used value, $390 to $422.50.

Weatherby

WEATHERBY Deluxe Magnum: Roy Weatherby's first rifle; bolt-action in .220 Rocket, .257 Weatherby magnum, .270 Weatherby magnum, 7mm Weatherby magnum, .300 Weatherby magnum and .375 Weatherby magnum. Mauser actions were built to Weatherby's specs by FN; barrel length was 24 " on all but .375WM, which had 26" barrel; Monte Carlo stock with cheekpiece; hand-checkered pistol grip, forearm; black grip cap, forearm tip; quick-detachable sling swivels. Introduced in 1948; dropped, 1955. Used value, $266.50 to $279.50.

WEATHERBY Deluxe .378 Magnum: has same specs as Deluxe Magnum, except in .378 Weatherby magnum only; 26" barrel. Action is Schultz & Larsen to Weatherby specs. Dropped, 1955. Used value, $279.50 to $292.50.

WEATHERBY Deluxe: same specs as Deluxe Magnum, except chambered for .270 Winchester, .30/06. Dropped, 1955. Used value, $266.50 to $279.50.

WEATHERBY Mark V Deluxe: bolt-action in .22/250, .30/06, .222 Weatherby Varmintmaster and Weatherby magnum chamberings of .240, .257, .270, 7mm, .300, .340, .378 and .460. Mark V action available in right or left-hand model; some actions made by Sauer in Germany to Weatherby specs; depending on caliber, box magazine holds 2 to 5 rds.; 24" barrels; no sights; drilled, tapped for scope mounts; Monte Carlo stock, cheekpiece; skip checkering on pistol grip, forearm; forearm tip, pistol grip cap, recoil pad; quick-detachable sling swivels. Introduced in 1955; still in production. Left-hand action worth $10 more than right-hand. Used values, for right-hand models, .460 Weatherby magnum, $515 to $545; .378 Weatherby magnum, $455 to $475; other calibers, $325 to $370.50.

WEATHERBY Mark XXII Deluxe: .22 LR; semi-automatic 24" barrel, 5, 10-shot clip magazines; Monte Carlo stock, cheekpiece; skip checkering on pistol grip, forearm; forearm tip, grip cap, quick-detachable sling swivels; folding leaf open rear sight, ramp front. Introduced in 1964; still in production. Used value, $115 to $129.50.

WEATHERBY Vanguard: bolt-action; .25/06, .243, .270, .30/06, .308, .264, 7mm, .300 Win. magnum; 3 or 5-rd. magazines, depending on caliber; 24" barrel, adjustable trigger; no sights; receiver drilled, tapped for scope mounts; hinged floor plate; American walnut stock; pistol-grip cap; forearm tip; hand-checkered forearm, pistol-grip. Introduced in 1970; still in production. Used value, $225 to $235.

WINCHESTER

WINCHESTER Model 1886: lever-action repeating rifle; it is more a collector's item than practical rifle; of 10 black powder calibers in which it was made, all are obsolete but .45/70; has 8-shot tube magazine or 4-shot half magazine; 26'' barrel, round, half-octagonal, octagonal; open rear sight; bead or blade front sight; plain straight stock, forearm. Introduced in 1886; discontinued, 1935. Price when discontinued, $53.75; used value, $520 to $550.

Model 1886 carbine is same as rifle, but with 22'' barrel. Used value, $690 to $720.

WINCHESTER Model 90: slide-action repeater, with visible hammer; tubular magazine holds 15 .22 rimfire shorts, 12 longs, 11 LR rds; also chambered for .22 WRF; magazine holds 12 of these. 24'' octagonal barrel; plain, straight stock, grooved slide handle; open rear, bead front sight; originally solid frame design, after serial No. 15,499, all were takedowns. Introduced in 1890; discontinued, 1932. Retail when discontinued, $22.85; used value, $190 to $210.

WINCHESTER Model 92: lever-action repeater; 24'' barrel, round; half-octagonal, octagonal; 13-shot tube magazine, 7-shot half-magazine, 10-shot two-thirds magazine; available in .25-20, .32-40, .38-40, .44-40; plain, straight stock, forearm; open rear, bead front sight. Introduced in 1892; dropped, 1941. Price when discontinued, $22.80; used value, $330 to $375.

Model 92 carbine had 20'' barrel, 11 or 5-shot magazine; used value, $415 to $460.

Model 92 was redesignated as Model 53 in 1924, with modifications, including 6-shot tube half magazine in solid frame, 7-shot in takedown. Barrel was 22'' nickel steel; open rear sight, bead front; straight stock; pistol grip stock optional; forearm was redesigned. Introduced in 1924; dropped, 1932. Used value, $345 to $360.

Model 94 Antique

Standard Model 94

Classic Model 94 Carbine

Classic Model 94 Rifle

WINCHESTER Model 94: Carbine, center-fire lever-action. Originally available in .30-30, .32 Special, .25-35 Winchester, .32-40, .38-55 .44 magnum added in 1967. Originally introduced in rifle length, but discontinued in 1936. Currently made only in .30-30. Rifles had 22", 26" barrels; carbine, 20" barrel; carbine has full-length tube magazine with 6-rnd capacity, half-length magazine with 4-rnd capacity; plain, uncheckered American walnut stock; open rear sight; blade front on early versions; ramp front sight introduced in 1931. Production of receiver mechanism revised from 1964 to 1971. Post-'71 version has redesigned steel carrier with sturdier block design, redesigned lever camming slot, improved loading port; barrel band on forearm; saddle ring. Introduced in 1894; still in production. Used values, pre-1964 version, $200 to $225; pre-1971

version, $80 to $95; post-1971 version, $92 to $109.50.

Model 94 Magnum carbine has same general specifications as the standard Model 94, except that magazine holds 10 .44 magnum cartridges. Introduced in 1968; dropped, 1972. Used value, $103.50 to $115.

Model 94 Classic has same general specifications as standard Model 94, except for octagonal barrel in 20", 26" lengths; steel butt plate, semi-fancy American walnut stock, forearm; scroll work on receiver; .30-30 only. Introduced in 1967; dropped, 1970. Used values: carbine, $115 to $126.50; rifle length, $121 to $129.50.

Model 94 Antique has same general specifications as standard Model 94, except for case-hardened receiver. Introduced in 1968; dropped, 1974. Used value, $109.50 to $115.

WINCHESTER Model 1907: takedown, self-loading rifle; .351 Win; 5 or 10-shot detachable box magazine; 20" barrel. Stock, forearm are plain walnut; pistol grip; open rear sight, bead front. Introduced in 1907; dropped, 1957. Retail, when discontinued, $174.95; used value, $250 to $280.

Model 52 Sporter

WINCHESTER Model 52: bolt-action rifle. Like taxes, this rifle just goes on, some models being dropped to be replaced by updates; there have been no less than 14 variations, one — Model 52-D — still in production. Model 52 target rifle was introduced in 1919; dropped in 1937. Had standard barrel, 28"; .22 LR, 5-shot box magazine; folding leaf peep rear sight, blade front sight, with options available; scope bases; originally had semi-military stock; pistol grip; grooves on forearm; later versions had higher comb, semi-beavertail forearm; slow lock model was replaced in 1929 by speed lock; last arms of model bore serial number followed by letter "A." Used value, slow lock style, $172.50 to $190; speed lock, $195.50 to $213.

Model 52 heavy barrel model had speed lock; same general specs as standard model, except for heavy barrel; a Lyman 17G front sight. Dropped, 1939. Used value, $207 to $230.

Model 52 sporting rifle; same as standard model, except for 24" lightweight barrel; deluxe sporting stock, checkered, with black forend tip; cheekpiece; has Lyman No. 48 receiver sight, gold bead on hooded ramp in front. Dropped, 1958. Used value, $545 to $585.

Model 52-B target rifle, introduced in 1935; dropped, 1947, has 28" barrel, redesigned action; choice of target stock or Marksman stock, with high comb, full pistol grip, beavertail forearm; wide variety of sights was available at added cost. Used value, sans sight, $184 to $207.

Model 52-B heavy barrel has same specs as standard 52-B, except for heavier barrel. Used value, $207 to $230.

Model 52-B bull gun has extra-heavy barrel, Marksman stock; other specs are same as standard Model 52-B. Used value, $230 to $247.50.

Model 52-B sporting rifle is same as first type Model 52 sporting rifle, except that it utilizes Model 52-B action. Dropped, 1961. Used value, $550 to $585.

Model 52-C target rifle — and others in "C" series — introduced in 1947; dropped, 1961. Target rifle has improved action, trigger mechanism, with new Marksman stock, heavy barrel; various sight combs available at added cost; other specs are same as original model. Used value, sans sights, $218.50 to $241.50.

Model 52-C standard model has same specs as the original Model 52 heavy barrel, but with the standard barrel. Used value, $184 to $201.50.

Model 52-C bull gun has same general specs as Model 52 heavy barrel model, but has extra-heavy bull barrel, giving gun weight of 12 lbs. Used value, $230 to $253.

Model 52-D target rifle was introduced in 1961; continues in production. Action has been redesigned as single-shot only for .22 LR; has 28" free-floating standard or heavy barrel; blocks for standard target scopes; redesigned Marksman stock; rubber butt plate; accessory channel in stock with forend stop. Used value, sans sights, $234.50 to $262.50.

Model 52 International Match Rifle, introduced in 1976, features laminated international-style stock with aluminum forend assembly, adjustable palm rest. Used values, sans sights: with ISU trigger, $380 to $410; with Kenyon trigger, $460 to $490.

Model 52 International Prone Rifle, introduced in 1976, has same features as International Match model, except for oil finished stock with removable roll-over cheekpiece for easy bore cleaning. Used value, sans sights, $310 to $335.

Model 54 Improved Sporter

WINCHESTER Model 54: bolt-action center-fire. This is another of those models that verged on being an empire. There were numerous models and styles, in spite of the fact that it had a relatively short life. What the manufacturer calls the "first type" was made from 1925 to 1930; the improved type, from 1930 to 1936.

The early type sporting rifle had a 24" barrel, 5-shot box magazine and was in .270 Win. 7x57mm, .30-30, .30/06, 7.65mmx53mm, 9x57mm; two-piece firing pin; open rear sight, bead front. Stock was checkered, pistol grip design; scored steel butt plate, checkered from 1930 on; forearm tapered. Retail, when dropped 1936, $59.75; used value, $260 to $292.50.

Model 54 carbine — first type — was added in 1927; it had plain stock, grasping grooves on forearm, 20'' barrel. Used value, $292.50 to $338.

Model 54 super grade was same as the early sporter, except for deluxe stock with pistol grip cap, cheekpiece, black forend tip. Came with quick-detachable sling swivels one-inch leather sling. Used value, $338 to $370.50.

Model 54 sniper's rifle has heavy 26'' barrel, Lyman No. 48 rear peep sight, blade front sight; semi-military type stock; only in .30/06. Used value, $357.50 to $390.

Model 54 sniper's match rifle sort of gilds the lily; it is the same as the early sniper model, but with Marksman target stock, scope bases and the same variety of calibers as standard model. Used value, $415 to $455.

Model 54 National Match rifle differs from standard

model only in that it has Lyman sights, Marksman target stock, scope bases. Used value, $338 to $370.50.

Model 54 target rifle is same as standard model, but has 24'' medium-weight barrel, 26'' in .220 Swift; has Marksman target stock, Lyman sights, scope bases. Used value, $370.50 to $422.50.

Model 54 improved sporter has speed lock, one-piece firing pin; NRA-type stock; checkered pistol grip, forearm; 5-shot box magazine; in .22 Hornet, .220 Swift, .250-3000, .257 Roberts, .270 Win, 7x57mm, .30/06; has 24'' barrel, except for 26'' for .220 Swift. Used value, $285 to $325.

Model 54 carbine, improved carbine is same as improved sporter, but has 20'' barrel; stock may be NRA type or lightweight stock used on original version. Used value, $338 to $377.

WINCHESTER Model 56: bolt-action .22 rimfire, choice of .22 shorts, or LRs; 5, 10-shot magazines; 22'' barrel; unchecked pistol grip stock, schnabel-type forearm; open

rear sight, bead front. Introduced in 1926; dropped, 1929. Retail when discontinued, $21; used value, $63.50 to $77.50.

WINCHESTER Model 57: bolt-action target rifle; same as Model 56, but with semi-military-type target stock, swivels, web sling; Lyman peep sight, blade front; .22 LR, but avail-

able until 1930 for .22 short. Introduced in 1926; dropped, 1936. Retail, when discontinued, $25; used value, $98 to $112.

WINCHESTER Model 59: bolt-action, single-shot; .22 long, short, LR; 23'' barrel; pistol grip, unchecked one-piece stock; open rear sight, blade front; takedown configuration.

Produced only in 1930. Retail price, $8.45; used value, $52 to $60.50.

WINCHESTER Model 60: bolt-action, single-shot redesigned Model 59; .22 short, long, LR; introduced in 1931; discontinued, 1934. 23'' barrel, until 1933; 27'' thereafter;

plain, pistol grip stock; open rear sight, blade-type front. Retail, when discontinued, $5.50; used value, $40.50 to $49.

WINCHESTER Model 60A: same as Model 60, except for Lyman rear peep sight, square-top front; has semi-military target stock, web sling; introduced in 1933; discontinued, 1939. Retail price, when discontinued, $8; used value, $49 to $57.50.

Model 61

WINCHESTER Model 61: hammerless slide-action, take-down repeater; .22 short, long, LR; tubular magazine holds 20 shorts, 16 longs, 14 LRs; 24" barrel, open rear sight, bead front; uncheckered pistol grip stock, grooved semi-beavertail slide handle. Also available with 24" octagonal barrel, chambered for .22 shorts only, .22 LR only, .22 WRF only, .22 LR shot cartridge. Introduced in 1932; dropped, 1963. Retail when discontinued, $70; used value, $110 to $140.

The Model 61 magnum, introduced in 1960; dropped, 1963, differs from the standard model only in that it is chambered for .22 rimfire magnum; magazine holds 12 rds. Used value, $200 to $225.

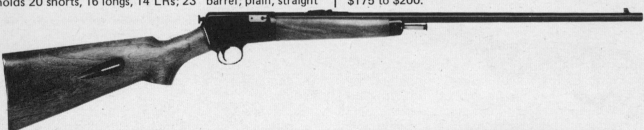

WINCHESTER Model 62: slide-action, visible hammer repeater; chambered for .22 short, long, LR; tube magazine holds 20 shorts, 16 longs, 14 LRs; 23" barrel; plain, straight grip stock; grooved semi-beavertail slide handle; also available in gallery model in .22 short only. Introduced in 1932; dropped, 1959. Retail when discontinued, $53; used value, $175 to $200.

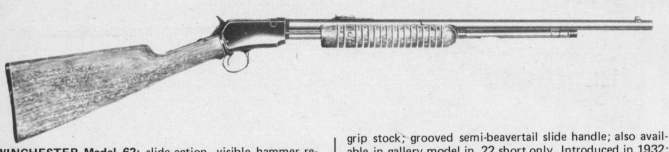

WINCHESTER Model 63: takedown, self-loading rifle; .22 LR Super Speed ammo only; 23" barrel; 10-shot tube magazine in butt stock; open rear sight, bead front; plain pistol grip stock, forearm; available in early series in 20" barrel. Introduced in 1933; discontinued, 1958. Retail when discontinued, $85; used value, $210 to $241.50.

WINCHESTER Model 64: this lever-action rifle has had double life; introduced originally in 1933, discontinued, 1957; reintroduced in 1972, discontinued, 1974. In original model, it was made in various barrel lengths from 20" to 24"; original calibers were .25-35, .30/30, .32 Win Special; .219 Zipper added in 1938, discontinued, 1941. Tubular magazine holds 5 rds; Sporting model had unchecked walnut stock, checkered steel butt plate, pistol grip; Deer model was checkered with hard rubber pistol-grip cap; sling swivels; army-type leather sling; action is same as Model 94. 1972 version was .30/30 only, 24" barrel, no checkering. Both versions have hooded ramp, bead post front sight, adjustable semi-buckhorn rear; '72 version has blued steel

forearm cap, quick detachable sling mounts. Retail when discontinued, $138.45; used value, original version, $253 to $287.50; .219 Zipper version, $414 to $431.50; 1972 version, $138 to $167.

WINCHESTER Model 65: improvement on the Model 53, it's a lever-action solid frame repeater, in .25-20, .32-20; has 22" barrel, 7-shot tube half magazine; open rear sight, bead front on ramp base. Plain pistol grip stock, forearm. Introduced in 1933; dropped, 1947. Price when discontinued,

$70; used value, $325 to $375.

Model 65 .218 Bee introduced in 1938; dropped, 1947. It is same as standard model, except for 24" barrel, peep rear sight. Used value, $520 to $550.

Model 67 Standard

WINCHESTER Model 67: bolt-action, takedown, single-shot; in .22 short, long, LR, .22 WRF; also made with smoothbore for shot; 27" barrel; open rear sight, bead front; unchecked pistol grip stock; early models had grooved forearm. Introduced in 1934; dropped, 1963.

Retail price, when discontinued, $22; used value, $43 to $46.

Model 67 boy's rifle is the same as standard model, but has shorter stock, 20" barrel. Used value, $37.50 to $43.

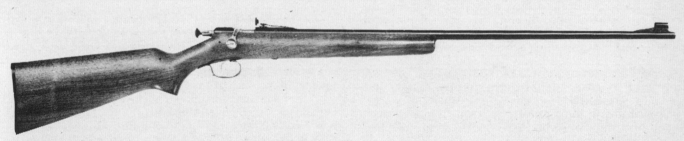

WINCHESTER Model 68: bolt-action, single-shot takedown; the same as the Model 67, except for being equipped with rear peep sight. Introduced in 1934; discontinued,

1946. Retail price, when discontinued, $6.95; used value, $57.50 to $66.

Model 69 Standard

WINCHESTER Model 69: bolt-action, takedown repeater; .22 short, long, LR, detachable 5, 10-rd. box magazine; 25" barrel. Peep or open rear sight; bead ramp front; unchecked pistol grip stock. Introduced in 1935; discontinued, 1963. Retail price, when discontinued, $36; used value, $69 to $72.

Model 69 target rifle is same as standard Model 69, except for rear peep sight, blade front sight, sling swivels. Used value, $69 to $77.50.

Model 69 match rifle differs from the target model only in that it has Lyman No. 57EW receiver sight. Used value, $69 to $77.50.

Model 70 pre-1964 Super Grade

WINCHESTER Model 70: this bolt-action center-fire repeating rifle is a versatile longarm, having been produced in more variations and configurations than any other of the manufacturer's firearms. The rifle is divided into roughly three historical categories, the original variations having been made from 1936 to 1963; at that time the rifle was redesigned to a degree, actually downgraded in an effort to meet rising costs, but to hold the retail price. This series of variations was produced from 1964 until 1972, at which time the rifle was upgraded and the retail price increased.

Model 70 standard grade (1936-1963); available in .375 H&H magnum, 8x57mm, .300 H&H magnum, .308 Win., .30/06, 7x57mm, .270 Win., .257 Roberts, .250-3000, .243 Win., .220 Swift, .22 Hornet (other rare calibers exist, including 9x57mm, .35 Rem., and .300 Savage). 4-shot box magazine in magnum calibers, 5-shot for others; for a short period, a 20" barrel was available; standard was 24", with 26" for .300 magnum, .220 Swift; 25" for .375 H&H magnum; hooded ramp front sight, open rear; hand-checkered walnut stock; later production had Monte Carlo comb as standard. Retail price when introduced, $62; used value, $250 to $450 in standard calibers; $800 to $1500 in rare calibers.

Model 70 standard grade (1964-1971); available in .30/06, .308 Win., .270, .243, .225, .22-250, .222 Rem.; 24" barrel, 5-shot box magazine; hooded ramp front sight, open rear, Monte Carlo cheekpiece, impressed checkering; sling swivels. Used value, $130 to $150.

Model 70 standard grade (1971 to present); available in .30/06, .308, .270, .243, .25/06, .222, .22-250; 22" swaged, floating barrel; walnut Monte Carlo stock; cut checkering on pistol grip, forearm; has removable hooded ramp bead front sight, open rear; receiver tapped for scope mounts; steel grip cap; sling swivels. Used value, $165 to $175.

Model 70 target model (1937-1963); same as standard model of period, except for scope bases, 24" medium-weight barrel, Marksman stock; when introduced, it was available in same calibers as standard model; when discontinued, only in .30/06, .243 Win. Used value, $350 to $750, depending upon caliber.

Model 70 target model (1964-1971); .30/06, .308 Win.; 24" barrel, 5-shot box magazine; target scope blocks, no sights; high-comb Marksman stock; aluminum handstop; swivels. Used value, $190 to $215.

Model 70 target model (1972 to present); same as current standard model, except had 24" heavy barrel; contoured aluminum handstop for either left or right-handed shooter; high-comb target stock; clip slot in receiver; tapped for micrometer sights. Used value, $225 to $250.

Model 70 Super grade (1937-1960); same as standard model of early production period, except for deluxe stock, cheekpiece, black forearm tip, sling, quick-detachable sling swivels; grip cap. Used value, $400 to $750 in standard calibers.

Model 70 Super grade (current production); .300 Win. magnum; .30/06, .270, .243; .300 magnum has recoil pad; same as standard model, except for semi-fancy, presentation-checkered walnut stock; ebony forearm tip with white spacer, pistol grip; nonslip rubber butt plate, knurled bolt handle. Used value, $340 to $365.

Model 70 National Match; same as early standard model, except for Marksman target stock; scope bases; .30/06 only; discontinued, 1960. Used value, $375 to $450.

Model 70 Featherweight Sporter; introduced in 1952; dropped, 1963; same as standard model of period, but has redesigned stock, aluminum trigger guard, butt plate, floor plate; 22" barrel; .358 Win., .30/06, .308 Win., .270 Win., .264 Win. magnum, .243 Win. Used value, $225 to $240.

Model 70 Featherweight Super grade; same as Featherweight Sporter, but with deluxe stock, cheekpiece, sling, quick-detachable swivels, black pistol grip cap, forearm tip; discontinued, 1960. Used value, $500 to $600.

Model 70 Varmint (1956-1963); same as early standard model, except with 26" heavy barrel; varminter stock; scope bases; .243 Win., .220 Swift. Used value, $320 to $350.

Model 70 Varmint (1974 to present); same as earlier version, but in .243, .22-250, .222 only. Used value, $180 to $195.

Model 70 bull gun; same as early model, except for 28" extra heavy barrel, scope bases; Marksman stock, .30/06, .300 H&H magnum; discontinued, 1963. Used value, $385 to $420.

Model 70 African (1956-1963); same as super grade of the era, but with 24" barrel, 3-shot magazine; recoil pad, Monte Carlo stock; .458 Win. magnum only. Used value, $500 to $575.

Model 70 African (1964-1971); same as original version, except for special sights, 22" barrel; hand-checkered stock; twin stock-reinforcing bolts, Monte Carlo stock, ebony forearm tip; recoil pad; quick-detachable swivels. Used value, $260 to $285.

Model 70 African (1971 to present); same as earlier version, except for floating heavy barrel. Used value, $340 to $375.

Model 70 Alaskan (1960-1963); same as early standard model, except for 25" barrel, recoil pad; 3-shot magazine in .338 Win., 4-shot in .375 H&H magnum. Used value, $300 to $325.

Model 70 Westerner (1960-1963); same as standard model of era, except for 26" barrel in .264 Win. magnum, 24" barrel in .300 Win. magnum. Used value, $295 to $320.

Model 70 Deluxe (1964-1971); in .243, .270 Win., .30/06, .300 Win. magnum; 3-shot box magazine, 24" barrel in magnum caliber, 5-shot magazine, 22" barrel in others; hooded ramp front sight, open rear; recoil pad on magnum, hand-checkered forearm, pistol grip, Monte Carlo walnut stock, ebony forearm tip. Used value, $250 to $275.

Model 70 magnum (1964-1971); in .375 H&H magnum, .338, .300, .264 Win. magnum, 7mm Rem. magnum; 24" barrel, 3-shot magazine; twin stock-reinforcing bolts, recoil pad, swivels, checkered Monte Carlo stock; hooded ramp front sight, open rear. Used value, .375 H&H magnum, $165 to $175; other calibers, $150 to $160.

Model 70 Mannlicher (1969-1971); Mannlicher-type stock with Monte Carlo comb, cheekpiece, quick-detachable swivels, checkered wood, steel forearm cap, hooded ramp front sight, open rear; in .30/06, .308 Win., .270, .243; 19" barrel; 5-shot box magazine. Used value, $285 to $320.

Model 70 International Army Match; produced in 1971 only; .308 Win.; 5-shot box magazine, 24" heavy barrel; externally adjustable trigger; International Shooting Union stock; forearm rail for accessories; adjustable butt plate; optional sights. Used value, sans sights, $290 to $320.

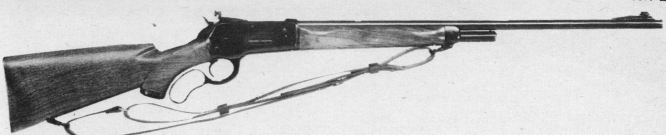

WINCHESTER Model 71: solid frame lever-action repeating rifle; 20", 24" barrel; .348 Win; 4-rd. tubular magazine; open rear sight, bead front on ramp with hood; plain walnut stock, forearm. Introduced in 1936; dropped, 1957.

Retail when discontinued, $138; used value, $374 to $414.

Model 71 Special is same as standard grade, but has checkered stock, forearm; grip cap, quick-detachable sling swivels, leather sling. Used value, $460 to $494.50.

WINCHESTER Model 77: semi-auto, solid-frame, clip type; .22 LR only; 8-shot clip magazine; 22" barrel; bead front sight, open rear; plain, one-piece hardwood stock; pistol grip. Introduced, 1955; dropped, 1963. Retail when dropped, $40; used value, $69 to $86.50.

Model 77, tubular magazine type; same as clip-type Model 77, except for 15-rd. tube magazine. Retail when dropped, $40. Used value, $69 to $80.50.

WINCHESTER Model 677: similar to standard Model 67, except for no sights; scope mounts were mounted on barrel; fired .22 shorts, longs, LRs interchangeably. Enjoyed little success due to poor scope mounting system. Introduced in 1937; dropped, 1939. Enjoys some value as a collectors item, as only 2239 were produced. Retail price, when dropped, $5.95. Used value, $52 to $69.

WINCHESTER Model 697: similar to standard Model 69, except that there were no sight cuts in barrel; scope bases were attached to barrel; no sights; rifle fired .22 short, long, LR cartridges interchangeably; came equipped with choice of 2¾ or 5X scope; 25" round barrel. Introduced, 1937; dropped, 1941. Retail, when dropped, $12.50. Used value, $34.50 to $40.50.

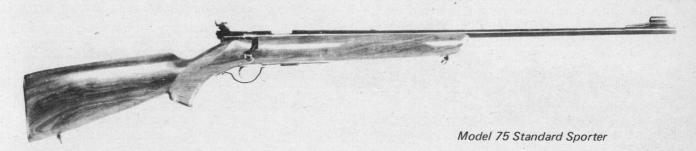

Model 75 Standard Sporter

WINCHESTER Model 75: solid-frame sporting model fires .22 LR ammo; 5-rd. box magazine; 24" barrel; bolt-action repeater, cocked with opening movement of bolt; checkered select walnut stock, pistol grip; hard rubber grip cap; swivels; checkered steel butt plate. Introduced in 1939; dropped, 1958. Retail, when dropped, $70.95; used value, $125 to $175.

Model 75 target model; same as sporting model, but equipped with target scope or variety of sights; predated sporting model. Introduced in 1938; dropped, 1958; uncheckered walnut stock, semi-beavertail forearm; pistol grip, checkered steel butt plate; came with 1" army-type leather sling. Retail price, when dropped, $80.55. Used value, $90 to $125.

RIFLES

WINCHESTER Model 72: bolt-action takedown repeater; tubular magazine holds 22 shorts, 16 longs, 15 LRs; 25" barrel; peep or open rear sight, bead front; uncheckered pistol grip stock. Introduced in 1938; dropped, 1959. Price when discontinued, $38.45. Used value, $60 to $67.50.

WINCHESTER Model 74: self-loading takedown; chambered for .22 short only or .22 LR only; tube magazine in butt stock holds 20 shorts, 14 LR rds. 24" barrel; open rear sight, bead front; uncheckered one-piece pistol grip stock. Introduced in 1939; discontinued, 1955. Price when dropped, $39.20. Used value, $66 to $74.50.

Model 43 Standard

WINCHESTER Model 43: bolt-action sporting rifle; .218 Bee, .22 Hornet; .25-20, .32-20; last two dropped, 1950. 24" barrel; 3-shot detachable box magazine; open rear sight, bead front on hooded ramp; uncheckered pistol grip stock with swivels. Introduced in 1949; dropped, 1957. Retail when dropped, $75. Used value, $198.50 to $208.

Model 43 Special grade; same as standard Model 43, except for grip cap, checkered pistol grip, forearm; open rear sight or Lyman 59A Micrometer. Used value, $234 to $240.50.

WINCHESTER Model 47: bolt-action single-shot; .22 short, long, LR; 25" barrel; uncheckered pistol grip stock; peep or open rear sight; bead front. Introduced in 1949; dropped, 1954. Price when discontinued, $24.25. Used value, $37.50 to $46.

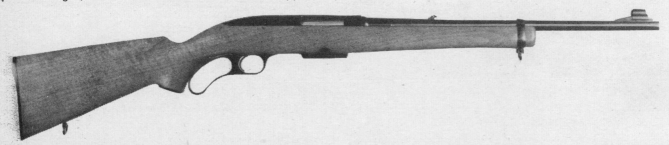

WINCHESTER Model 88: lever-action rifle; available in .243 Winchester, .284 Winchester, .308 Winchester, .358 Winchester; barrel length, 22"; weighs 6½ lbs.; measures 39½" overall; fitted with hooded bead front sight, folding leaf rear sight. Stock is one-piece walnut with steel-capped pistol grip, fluted comb, carbine barrel band, sling swivels. Has four-shot detachable magazine of staggered, box-type, held with double latches. Hammerless action, with three-lug bolt, cross-bolt safety; side ejection. Introduced in 1955; dropped, 1974. Latest retail price, $169.95. Used value, $138 to $152.50.

WINCHESTER Model 55: automatic single-shot; .22 shorts, longs, LRs; 22" barrel; open rear sight, bead front; one-piece uncheckered walnut stock. Introduced in 1957; dropped, 1961. Retail price when discontinued, $16. Used value, $47.50 to $55.

WINCHESTER Model 100: semi-auto, gas-operated carbine; available in .243 Winchester, .284 Winchester, .308 Winchester. Barrel is 22"; weight, 7½ lbs.; measures 42½" overall. In 1967, barrel length was reduced to 19". Stock is one-piece walnut with checkered pistol grip and forearm, sling swivels. Magazine holds 4 rds., except .284, which holds 3 rds.; tapped for receiver sights or scope mounts; equipped with hooded bead front sight, folding leaf rear. Introduced in 1960; dropped in 1974. Last retail price, $179.95. Used value, $138 to $155.50.

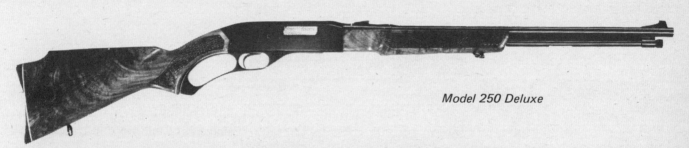

Model 250 Deluxe

WINCHESTER Model 250: .22 rimfire lever-action rifle; standard and deluxe models; 20½" barrel; tubular magazine, with capacity of 21 shorts, 17 longs, 15 LR cartridges, chambered to handle these interchangeably. Stock is walnut-finished hardwood; receiver of aluminum alloy, grooved for tip-off scope mounts; sights include a front square post on a streamlined ramp; square notch sight in rear, adjustable for windage and elevation; cross lock safety is located on front of the trigger guard; weight, 5 lbs. Deluxe model included select walnut stock, fluted comb, cheek piece, basket weave checkering, white spacers between butt plate and stock, sling swivels. Introduced in 1963; discontinued, 1974. Used value, $68.50 to $78.50.

The Model 250 Deluxe differs from the standard only in that it has a fancy walnut Monte Carlo stock, forearm and has sling swivels. It was manufactured from 1965 to 1971. Used value, $78.50 to $88.50.

WINCHESTER Model 255: lever-action rifle; same as Model 250, except chambered for .22 magnum WMR cartridge. Introduced in 1963, discontinued in 1974. Retail price on standard model $74.95. Used value, $57 to $63.

WINCHESTER Model 270: slide-action rifle; .22 rimfire; available in standard and deluxe models; 20½" barrel; tubular magazine with capacity of 21 shorts, 17 longs, 15 LRs; chambered to handle all three interchangeably; stock is walnut-finished hardwood; one version, discontinued in 1965, offered forearm of cycolac; had square post front sight on streamlined ramp; rear sight was square notch type, adjustable for windage, elevation; receiver was of aluminum alloy, grooved for tip-off scope mounts; cross-bolt safety; weight about 5 lbs. Deluxe style featured high-gloss Monte Carlo stock of walnut with fluted comb, basketweave checkering, cheekpiece. Introduced in 1963, dropped in 1974. Last retail price for standard version, $72.95. Used value for standard, $55 to $60.50.

WINCHESTER Model 275: slide-action rifle; same as Model 270, but chambered for .22 rimfire magnum cartridge. Introduced in 1964, dropped in 1974. Last retail price for standard model, $77.95. Used value for standard $58.50 to $63.50.

Model 121 Standard

WINCHESTER Model 121: single-shot; .22 rimfire; fires shorts, longs, LRs; barrel length is 20½"; weighs 5 lbs.; one-piece stock is of American hardwood with modified Monte Carlo profile; sights are standard ramped post bead, adjustable V at rear. Receiver is steel, with front locking bolt; grooved to accommodate tip-off mounts for scope sight. Introduced in 1967; discontinued, 1973. Available in three versions, a Youth model with short buttstock and Standard model, both at $23.95; a Deluxe version with Monte Carlo, fluted comb and sling swivels at $27.95. Used value for Youth model, $17.50 to $22.50; Standard model, $19.50 to $21.50; Deluxe, $21.50 to $26.50.

WINCHESTER Model 131: bolt-action, clip loading .22 rimfire; 20" barrel, overall weight about 5 lbs.; stock is one-piece American hardwood with fluted comb, modified Monte Carlo profile; ramped bead post front, adjustable rear sight; clip-type magazine holds 7 rds., short, long, LR; steel receiver is grooved for telescopic sight mounts; barrel has 1-in-16" twist ratio; front locking bolt; red safety and red cocking indicator. Introduced in 1967; dropped, 1973; last retail price $38.45. Used value, $29 to $37.50.

WINCHESTER Model 135: same as Model 131, except .22 magnum. Introduced in 1967; dropped, 1973; last retail price, $41.45. Used value, $37 to $39.50.

WINCHESTER Model 141: bolt-action; .22 rimfire; hidden tubular magazine holds 19 shorts, 15 longs, 13 LR cartridges interchangeably; barrel is 20½"; weight, 5 lbs.; stock is American hardwood with fluted comb, modified Monte Carlo; front locking bolt, ramped bead post front and adjustable rear sight; red cocking indicator and red-marked safety. Introduced in 1967; dropped in 1973. Last retail price, $41.95; used value, $34.50 to $38.50.

WINCHESTER Model 150: lever-action carbine; .22 rimfire; has 20½" barrel, weighs 5 lbs; stock is walnut-finished American hardwood; forearm has frontier-style barrel band; straight grip; no checkering; tube magazine holds 21 shorts, 17 longs, 15 LR cartridges; receiver is aluminum alloy, grooved for scope sight. Introduced in 1967; dropped, 1974. Retail price $53.95; used value, $43.50 to $50.

WINCHESTER Model 770: bolt-action; available in .222 Remington, .22-250, .243 Winchester, .270 Winchester, .308 Winchester, .30/06; also in .264 Winchester magnum, 7mm Remington magnum, .300 Winchester magnum. Available with 22" barrel for standard calibers, 24" for magnums; weighs 7½ lbs. Stock is walnut with high comb Monte Carlo, undercut cheekpiece; has front sight ramp and hood with adjustable rear sight. Magazine capacities vary, depending upon caliber. Standard models have composition butt plates, magnums, rubber recoil pads. There is a red cocking indicator, serrated trigger. Pistol grip is capped, and grip and forearm checkered. This rifle was designed as a lower echelon Model 70, but failed to meet acceptance, thus was dropped after only four years in the line, being replaced by Model 70A. Introduced, 1969; dropped, 1973; retailed at $139.95 for standard models, $154.95 for magnums. Used value for standards, $121 to $141; magnums, $138 to $178.50.

WINCHESTER Model 310: bolt-action; single-shot; .22 rimfire, 22" barrel; weighs 5-5/8 lbs.; 39" overall in length; 13½" length of pull; stock is American walnut with Monte Carlo, fluted comb; checkered pistol grip, forearm. Has ramped bead post front sight, adjustable rear sight; receiver is grooved for scope sight; also drilled, tapped for micrometer rear sight. Is equipped with sling swivels, serrated trigger, positive safety lever. Introduced in March 1971; dropped, 1974. Last retail price, $44.95; used value, $37.50 to $43.

WINCHESTER Model 320: bolt action; .22 rimfire; 22" barrel; weighs 5-5/8 lbs.; measures 39½" overall; stock is American walnut, with Monte Carlo, fluted comb; checkered pistol grip and forearm; ramped bead post front sight, adjustable rear; grooved for scope mounts; drilled, tapped for micrometer rear sight; magazine holds 5 rds. of .22 short, long, LR. Is equipped with sling swivels, serrated trigger, positive safety. Introduced in March 1971; dropped, 1974. Last retail price, $57.50; used value, $50 to $56.

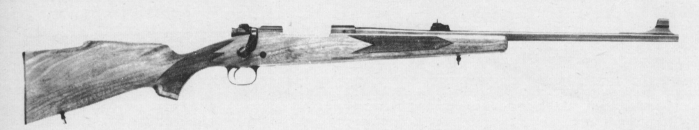

WINCHESTER Model 70A: bolt-action rifle; available in .222 Remington; .22-250; .243 Winchester; .270 Winchester, .30/06, .308 Winchester with 22" barrels, 24" barrels in .264 Winchester magnum, 7mm Remington magnum and .300 Winchester magnum. Incorporates features of Model 70 rifle; action is of chrome molybdenum steel; three-position safety; serrated trigger; engine-turned bolt; rear sight is adjustable leaf with white diamond for quick sighting; front sight is hooded ramp type; stock is dark American walnut with high comb Monte Carlo, undercut cheekpiece. Introduced in 1972, as replacement for Model 770, more closely following style of Model 70. Current retail, standard model, $245.95; magnum model, $261.95. Used value, $167 to $178.50; magnum used value, $170 to $185.

WINCHESTER Model 670: bolt-action; available in carbine style with 19" barrel, sporting rifle, with 22", magnum version with 24" barrel; sporting rifle, carbine held 4 rds. in magazine; magnum, 3 rds.; carbine chambered for .243 Winchester, .270 Winchester, .30/06; sporting rifle, .225, .243, .270, .308 Winchester, .30/06; magnum version, .264 Winchester magnum, .300 Winchester magnum. Has non-detachable box magazine; front sight is bead on ramp, rear, open, adjustable type; both sights easily detached for scope mounting; stock is hardwood with walnut finish, high comb Monte Carlo style; redesigned in 1972, with only 22" version being produced in .243 and .30/06. Dropped in 1974. Last retail price, $134.95; used value, $109.50 to $121.

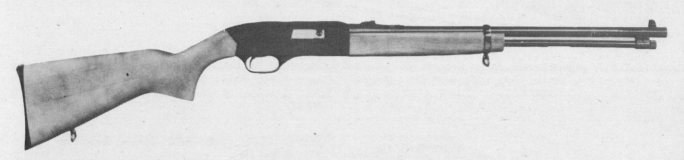

Model 9422 Standard

WINCHESTER Model 9422: lever-action; duplicates appearance of Model 94; in .22 short, long, long rifle and magnum. Has 20½" barrel; weighs 6½ lbs.; stock, forearm are of American walnut, with steel barrel band around latter; front sight is ramp, dovetail bead and hood, with adjustable semi-buckhorn at rear. Standard model holds 21 shorts, 17 longs, 15 LRs, interchangeable. Magnum model holds 11 .22 rimfire cartridges. Receiver is of forged steel, with all-steel action. Both styles are grooved for scope mounts. Both styles were introduced in 1972. Current retail prices are $184.95, standard; $190.95, magnum; used value, $112.50 to $126.50 for standard; $121 to $132.50 for magnum.

WINCHESTER Model 190: semi-auto carbine; .22 rimfire; 20½" barrel with 1-in-16" twist. American hardwood stock, with plain, uncapped pistol grip; forearm encircled with barrel band; tube magazine with capacity of 21 shorts, 15 LRs; sights include bead post front, adjustable V at rear; aluminum alloy receiver is grooved for scope mounts. Weight is approximately 5 lbs, overall length, 39"; sling swivels included. Introduced in 1974. Current retail price, $78.95. Used value, $34.50 to $37.50.

MISCELLANEOUS RIFLES

ARMALITE AR-7 Explorer: survival rifle originally designed for use by U.S. Air Force; .22 LR, semi-automatic; takedown; 8-rd. box magazine; 16" cast aluminum barrel, with steel liner; moulded plastic stock; hollow for storing action, barrel, magazine; designed to float; peep rear sight; blade front. Introduced in 1959; still in production, but manufactured since 1973 by Charter Arms Corporation. Used value, $54.50 to $60.50.

ARMALITE Custom AR-7: same specs as AR-7 Explorer, except with walnut stock; pistol grip, cheekpiece; not designed to float. Introduced in 1964; dropped, 1970. Used value, $80.50 to $86.50.

BUFFALO NEWTON Sporter: bolt-action; .256, .30/06, .35 Newton; 5-rd. box magazine; 24" barrel; reversed set trigger; hand-checkered pistol grip. Introduced in 1922; dropped, 1932. Manufactured by Newton Arms Co., Buffalo, New York. Used value, primarily as collector item, $356.50 to $379.50.

CLERKE Hi-wall: single-shot; .223, .22-250, .243, 6mm Rem., .250 Savage, .257 Roberts, .25/06, .264 Win., .270, 7mm Rem. Magnum, .30-30, .30/06, .300 Win., .375 H&H, .458 Win., .45-70; barrel, 26" medium-weight; walnut pistol-grip stock, forearm; no checkering; black butt plate; no sights; drilled, tapped for scope mounts; exposed hammer; schnabel forearm, curved finger lever. Introduced in 1970; dropped, 1975. Used value, $190 to $195.50.

Deluxe Hi-Wall: same specs as standard model, except for half-octagon barrel, adjustable trigger, checkered pistol grip, forearm, cheekpiece; plain or double set trigger. Used value, single trigger, $218.50 to $230; double set trigger, $247.50 to $253.

CHARLES DALY Hornet: originally made by Franz Jaeger Co. of Germany; miniaturized Mauser action; .22 Hornet only; 24" barrel, double set triggers; walnut stock; hand-checkered pistol grip, forearm; leaf rear sight, ramp front; 5-rd. box magazine attached to hinged floor plate. Introduced 1931; importation discontinued, 1939. Imported by Charles Daly. (Note: Same model was imported by A.F. Stoeger and sold as Herold rifle.) Used value, $678.50 to $718.50.

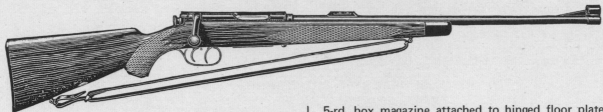

GEVARM Model A2: autoloader; blowback action; takedown; .22 LR only; 21½" barrel; 8-rd. clip magazine; no firing pin (as such) or extractor; fires from open bolt; ridge on bolt face offers twin ignition; tangent rear sight, hooded globe front; uncheckered walnut stock, schnabel forearm. Imported by Tradewinds, Inc., beginning in 1958; dropped, 1963. Used value, $34.50 to $40.50.

HAMMERLI Model Olympia: bolt-action, single-shot designed for 300-meter event; chambered in Europe for 7.5mm, marketed in U.S. in .30/06, .300 H&H magnum; other calibers on special order; 29½" heavy barrel, double-pull or double set trigger; micrometer peep rear sight, hooded front; free-type rifle stock with full pistol grip, thumbhole; cheekpiece, palm rest, beavertail forearm; swivels, Swiss-type butt plate. Introduced in 1949; dropped, 1959. Used value, $592 to $604.

HAMMERLI Model 45: bolt-action, single-shot match type; .22 LR; 27½" barrel; free-rifle stock with full pistol grip, thumbhole, cheekpiece; palm rest, beavertail forearm; Swiss-type butt plate, sling swivels; micrometer peep rear sight, blade front; pistol-grip hardwood stock; knob forearm Used value, $477 to $489.

HOLLAND & HOLLAND Royal: hammerless sidelock double rifle; actually a special-order rifle in the realm of semi-production, with original buyer's options available; .240 Apex, 7mm Holland and Holland magnum, .300 Holland and Holland magnum, .375 Holland and Holland magnum, .458 Win., .465 Holland and Holland; 24", 26", 28" barrels; two-piece choice European stock; hand-checkered pistol grip, forearm; folding leaf rear sight, ramp front; swivels; custom-engraved receiver. Still in production. Used values, pre-WWII model, $6000 to $6300; post-war, $5625 to $6000.

No. 2 Model has the same specifications as H&H Royal, except for less ornate engraving, less figure in stock. Still in production. Used value, pre-WWII, $4425 to $4800; post-war, $4200 to $4500.

Model Deluxe has the same specifications as Royal Model, except for more ornate engraving, better grade European walnut in stock; better fitting. Still in production. Used value, pre-WWII, $7500 to $7875; post-war, $7200 to $7425.

HOLLAND & HOLLAND Best Quality: bolt-action; built on Mauser or Enfield action; .240 Apex, .300 Holland and Holland magnum, .375 Holland and Holland magnum; 24" barrel; 4-rd. box magazine; cheekpiece stock of European walnut; hand-checkered pistol grip, forearm; folding leaf rear sight, hooded ramp front; sling swivels, recoil pad. Still in production. Used value, pre-WWII, $1200 to $1240; post-war, $1170 to $1200.

INTERARMS Mark X: bolt-action; .22-250, .243 Win., .270 Win., .308 Win., .25/06, .30/06, 7mm Rem. mag., .300 Win. mag.; 24" barrel; sliding safety; hinged floor plate; adjustable trigger at added cost; adjustable folding-leaf rear sight, ramp front with removable hood; hand-checkered European walnut Monte Carlo stock, forearm; white spacers on grip cap, butt plate, forearm tip. Imported from Czechoslovakia. Introduced in 1972; still in production. Four additional variations have appeared since 1974. Used values, standard model, $172.50 to $184; with adjustable trigger, $184 to $195.50.

IVER JOHNSON Model X: bolt-action, single-shot; take-down; .22 LR, .22 long, .22 short; 22" barrel; open rear sight, blade front; hardwood pistol-grip stock; knob forearm tip; uncheckered. Introduced in 1928; dropped, 1932. Used value, $29 to $31.50.

IVER JOHNSON Model 2X: same general specs as Model X, but has larger stock, without forearm knob; heavier 24" barrel. Introduced in 1932; dropped, 1955. Used value, $40 to $46.

MUSKETEER Mauser: FN Mauser, bolt-action sporter; .243, .270, .25/06, .264 Magnum, .308, .30/06, 7mm Magnums, .300 Winchester Magnum; magazine capacity, 3 rds., magnum, 5, standard calibers; 24″ barrel; sling swivels; checkered pistol grip, forearm, Monte Carlo stock. Introduced in 1963; dropped, 1972. Imported by Firearms International. Used value, $221 to $237.50.

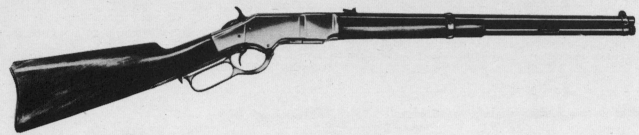

NAVY ARMS Model 66: lever-action; reproduction of Winchester Model 1866; .22 short, long, LR; polished brass frame, butt plate, other parts blued; full-length tube magazine; walnut straight-grip stock, forearm; barrel band; open leaf rear sight, blade front. Introduced in 1966; still in production. Used value, $149.50 to $157.50.

NAVY ARMS Model 1873: lever-action; .357 magnum, .44-40; barrels, 24″ octagon, 20″ round carbine, 16½″ trapped style; walnut stock, forearm; step adjustable rear sight, blade front; designed after the Winchester '73 model; finish is blue, case hardened or nickel, last in .44-40 only; sliding dust cover, lever latch. Manufactured in Italy; imported by Navy Arms. Introduced in 1973; still in production. Used value, $176.50 to $187.50.

NORRAHAMMAR Model N-900: bolt-action; Husqvarna action; .243 Win., .270 Win., .308 Win., .30/06; 20¼″ barrel; single-stage trigger; ebony grip cap, butt plate; side safety; hinged floor plate; hand-checkered European walnut pistol-grip stock, forearm; hooded front sight, adjustable rear; sling swivels. Manufactured in Sweden. Originally imported by Tradewinds, Inc., in 1957; importation dropped, 1967. Used value, $143 to $149.50.

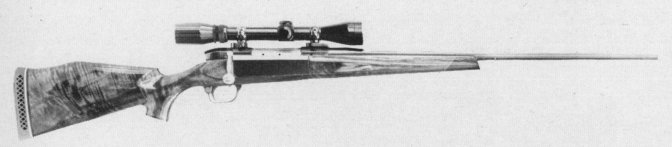

OMEGA III: bolt-action; .25/06, .270, .30/06, 7mm Rem. magnum, .300 Win. magnum, .338 Win. magnum, .358 Norma magnum; barrels, 22″, 24″; choice of Monte Carlo, Classic or thumbhole varminter; claro walnut English laminated or laminated walnut/maple; no sights; right or left-hand action; octagonal bolt; square locking system, enclosed bolt face; rotary magazine holds 5 standard or 4 belted cartridges; fully adjustable trigger. Introduced in 1973; still in production by new maker. Used value, $345 to $362.50.

Standard Carbine

Military Sporter

Deluxe Sporter

PLAINFIELD M-1 Carbine: same as U.S. military carbine, except available in 5.7mm, as well as standard .30 M-1; early models had standard military fittings, some from surplus parts; current model has ventilated metal hand guard, not bayonet lug. Introduced in 1960; dropped, 1976. Used value, $101.50 to $107.50.

M-1 Military Sporter carbine is same as M-1 Carbine, but with unslotted butt stock for sling; has wood hand guard. Used value, $101.50 to $104.50.

M-1 carbine, Commando Model is same as M-1, except with telescoping wire stock, pistol grips front and rear. Used value, $110 to $120.

Deluxe Sporter is same as M-1, except for Monte Carlo sporting stock. Introduced in 1960; dropped, 1973. Used value, $129.50 to $135.

PEDERSEN 3000: bolt-action, Mossberg Model 800 action; .270, .30/06, 7mm Rem. magnum, .338 Win. magnum; 3-rd. magazine; barrels 22″ in .270, .30/06; 24″, all other calibers; American walnut stock, roll-over cheekpiece; hand-checkered pistol grip, forearm; no sights; drilled, tapped for scope mount; adjustable trigger; sling swivels. Grades differ in amount of engraving and quality of stock wood. Introduced in 1972; dropped, 1975. Used values, Grade I, $610 to $650; Grade II, $415 to $440; Grade III, $370 to $390.

PEDERSEN 3500: bolt-action; .270 Win., .30/06, 7mm Rem. mag.; 22″ barrel in standard calibers, 24″ for 7mm mag.; 3-rd. magazine; drilled, tapped for scope mounts; hinged steel floor plate; damascened bolt; adjustable trigger; hand-checkered black walnut stock, forearm; rosewood pistol-grip cap, forearm tip. Introduced in 1973; dropped, 1975. Used value, $275 to $290.

ROSSI Bronco: single-shot; swing-out chamber; .22 LR, long, short; 16½″ barrel; skeletonized crackle-finished alloy stock; cross-bolt safety; instant takedown; adjustable rear sight; blade front. Introduced in 1970; still in production. Used value, $29 to $31.50.

ROSSI Gallery Model: slide action; takedown; .22 LR, long, short, .22 magnum; 22½″ barrel; tube magazine; 14 LR, 16 long, 20 short cartridge capacity; adjustable rear sight, fixed front; uncheckered straight-grip walnut stock, grooved slide handle. Imported from Brazil by Garcia. Introduced in 1973; still in production. Used values, standard model, $98 to $101.50; magnum model, $103.50 to $109.50.

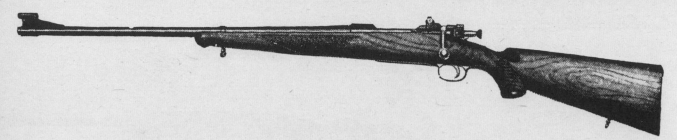

SEDGLEY Springfield Sporter: built on Springfield 1903 bolt-action; .218 Bee, .22-3000, .220 Swift, .22-4000, .22 Hornet, .22-35, .250-3000, .257 Roberts, .270 Win., .30/06, 7mm; 24" barrel; hand-checkered walnut stock; sling swivels, grip cap; Lyman No. 48 rear sight, bead front on matted ramp. Introduced in 1928; discontinued, 1941; Used values, $365 to $385; left-hand model, $338 to $358; Mannlicher stock, 20" barrel, $358 to $377.

SMITH & WESSON Model 125: bolt-action; .270 Win., .30/06; 5-rd. magazine; 24" barrel; step adjustable rear sight, hooded ramp front; action drilled, tapped for scope mounts; thumb safety. Standard grade has hand-checkered stock of European walnut; deluxe grade adds rosewood forearm tip, pistol grip cap. Introduced in 1973; dropped, 1973. Used value, standard grade, $144 to $149.50; deluxe grade, $152.50 to $161.

Standard Carbine

Deluxe Carbine

UNIVERSAL .30 Carbine: same as .30 M-1 military carbine, but sans bayonet lug; 5-rd. clip magazine; made for short period in mid-1960s with Teflon-coated barrel, action; matted finish on metal. Introduced in 1964; still in production. Used value, $100 to $105.

Deluxe .30 Carbine is same as standard model, except for choice of gold-finished, nickel or blued metal parts; Monte Carlo stock; dropped, 1973. Used value, gold-finish, $170 to $180; nickel, $140 to $150; blue, $110 to $115.

Ferret Semi-auto rifle is the same as Universal deluxe .30 Carbine, except for blued finish only, .256 caliber only, no iron sights, equipped with 4X Universal scope. Dropped, 1973. Used value, $135 to $142.50.

In 1974, models were revised and redesignated by model numbers.

Universal 1000 is same as military issue, except for better walnut stock, receiver tapped for scope mounts; dropped, 1977. Used value, $110 to $120.

Model 1002 is the same as Model 1000, except it has blued metal military type perforated hand guard; dropped, 1977. Used value, $115 to $125.

WESTLEY RICHARDS Magazine Model: built on Mauser or magnum Mauser action; .30/06, 7mm High Velocity, .318 Accelerated Express, .375 magnum, .404 Nitro Express, .425 magnum; barrels, 22" for 7mm, 25" for .425, 24" for all other calibers; leaf rear sight, hooded front; sporting stock of French walnut; hand-checkered pistol grip, forearm; cheekpiece; horn forearm tip; sling swivels. Used value, $942.50 to $975.

WESTLEY RICHARDS Double: double rifle favored for African big game; box-lock action; hammerless, ejectors; hand-detachable locks; .30/06, .318 Accelerated Express, .375 magnum, .425 Magnum Express, .465 Nitro Express, .470 Nitro Express; 25" barrels; leaf rear sight, hooded front; French walnut stock; hand-checkered pistol grip, forearm; cheekpiece; horn forearm tip; sling swivels. Used value, $1200 to $1235.

WINSLOW Bolt-Action: chambered in all standard and magnum center-fire calibers; 24" barrel, 26" for magnums; choice of 3 stock styles; hand-rubbed black walnut, hand-checkered pistol grip, forearm; 4-rd. blind magazine; no sights, receiver tapped for scope mounts; recoil pad; quick detachable sling mounts, ebony forearm tip, pistol-grip cap. Introduced, 1963; still in production. Used value, $345 to $370; varmint model in .17/ 222, .17/223, $390 to $420; left-hand models, add $50.

RIFLE NOTES

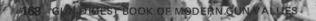

SHOTGUNS

Here Are The Nuts And Bolts Of Buying A Used Shotgun!

HOW MUCH IS an XYZ 12-gauge shotgun worth? This question pops up constantly to anyone associated with firearms. The only really true answer is the price the owner is willing to take and the buyer is willing to pay for the gun, according to Ralph T. Walker, one of the nation's most knowledgeable scattergun buffs.

"A lot of factors are involved in any transaction. This section is intended to serve only as a basic guide, a close guide but still only the basic starting point in determining how many dollars actually change hands in the transaction. There is always a minimum and a maximum price bracket above and below the basic guide. For example, if you are on the paying end, you want to buy the shotgun at the lowest possible price. If you own the gun, it is only natural to try for the highest price. The basic guide price plus additional knowledge of technical points, current market changes, the section of the country and even the time of year will narrow the price bracket to a realistic value and a sale," Walker says.

"To achieve this result, it is first necessary to separate shotguns into two fundamental types or classes. One consists of those in current production and available to the general public. The other involves all shotguns no longer being produced. There is a type consisting of currently manufactured models in high demand but low supply. The price is affected only by a bonus added to the current price and normally the bonus will disappear as the supply increases. You might term this a temporary class."

Concerning current production models, one would think that all the information necessary would be the published retail price of the shotgun. Not so. While the retail price is important, it will not furnish all the facts for arriving at the true value and actual sale price of the shotgun. It is important that the current retail price be known, for inflation often changes that figure during the production year.

"Let's assume that the gun is new and still in the box or has been fired only a few times and is just like the day it left the factory. If it is not in a dealer's stock, it is still considered a used gun. The first factor is the difference between the retail and the wholesale price, usually twenty to twenty-five percent. Even if all other factors are correct and the shotgun is exactly what the buyer wants, chances are that the price paid will be somewhere between the retail and wholesale value. One point that plays an important part is the time of the year. The highest price period is just before or in the early stages of the hunting season. The value starts dropping just after Christmas, reaching the bottom around June. The reason for this is that the dealer is marking the price down from current price to decrease his inventory during the slow sales period. With the exception of skeet and trap shotguns, price of shotguns is more closely tied to the hunting season than that of rifles or handguns. This forces the dealer to carefully calculate his profit margin in relation to the interest on loans or his available operating capital," says Walker.

The section of the country, the game hunted and the hunting conditions will also affect the value. Close hunting range means a higher demand for shorter barrels and more open chokes. Long ranges place more emphasis on tighter chokes and usually longer barrels. This also holds true in the choice of the gauge. For example, the 16 gauge is a white elephant in many sections of the country but has always had a strong following in the southeastern states. Move up into prime goose country and there is a large demand for the 12-gauge, 3-inch magnum with long barrel and tight choke as well as the big 10-gauge, 3½-inch magnum guns.

"These are not hard and fast rules but what might be termed preference percentages with the higher percent translating to a quick sale at a higher price. There are exceptions, of course, but these factors will influence the plus or minus margin surrounding the basic guide price. It all boils down to the right gun type in the right area at the right time for maximum value," according to Walker.

Before we leave the new gun, let's consider extras and accessories. The demand for ventilated ribs has increased to the point that some models offer it as standard equipment even in field grade shotguns. Automatic ejectors and single selective triggers in the side-by-side or over-and-under shotgun also are increasing in popularity. Giant head safeties or the safety on top at the rear of the receiver in pumps and semiautomatics are in great demand. With few exceptions, a recoil pad increases the appeal. These extras almost invariably enhance the sales appeal of any shotgun.

Accessories or alterations to the original gun will increase or decrease the value based primarily on the preference of the buyer more than any standard rule. Generally speaking, an unaltered shotgun will have the widest appeal, but if the right buyer is involved, alterations can increase the gun's value. There has been a slow but steady increase in the overall market toward more choke selection in a single-barrel gun than in the past. The wide acceptance of the built-in Winchester Win-Choke has proved that the change is taking place. Shotguns whose chokes have been hand regulated for a specific range or load will usually increase rather than decrease the value provided the reason and results are known.

As you leave the new gun category, value will naturally decrease. The condition will be the determining factor but this must be subdivided into cosmetic loss and mechanical loss from new gun standards.

Cosmetic depreciation concerns the overall finish, both metal and wood. Normal loss from use distracts less than that from neglect or abuse. Mechanical loss is self-explanatory. Again, if the loss is from normal wear with apparent proper maintenance during use, the drop in value will be less than if it is due to misuse or neglect.

"You simply cannot hide abuse and neglect, for it stands out like a sore thumb. A 10-year-old model showing normal wear — cosmetic and mechanical — will bring a higher price than a similar one-year-old model that looks like it has been tossed in the back of a pick-up truck and ten dogs put on top! The buyer knows that the older gun has received good care over the years and can be reblued and restored with minor mechanical repair. The one-year-old gun showing abuse and neglect can also be restored but it will be a gamble that major mechanical repair will be necessary which means a higher bill from the gunsmith.

"The 10-year-old gun generally will have a bright bore, while the latter gun's bore will be pitted. The usual method to hide the pits is a heavily oiled bore. In some cases, common toothpaste is used to fill deep pits with a coat of oil on top. A couple of dry patches pushed through the bore will bring out the true condition. Touch-up blue is often used in an attempt to hid a defect that has been corrected sloppily. You can generally detect touch-up blue by smelling the surface.

"If you smell copper, chances are the surface has been covered with touch-up blue. Some solutions will not have the smell, but strong light and a close examination of the blue shades will show its use. Check the barrel length with a three-foot tape and note the choke. If the barrel length ends in fractions, it may mean that the muzzle has been cut off and the sight reinstalled. If two inches have been removed, so has the choke. Cylinder and improved cylinder choke barrels are normally twenty-six inches; modified choke barrels are generally twenty-eight inches. A full choke barrel is the one to watch, for it can be twenty-eight, thirty, thirty-two inches, or more. The only exception to the odd-length barrels are those guns made on the metric scale rather than the inch, but these will be imported models rather than those manufactured in the United States. If the gun has a rib or is a double barrel, press down on the rib about every inch over the full length. If it is loose, it will move under your finger. A loose rib means a trip to the gunsmith.

"Check the wood where it joins the metal. If it is solid but oil soaked, this can be corrected. Watch for tiny cracks or oversized wood at this point. Both are indications of a water-soaked stock that has swollen or, in the case of cracks only, an attempt made to dry the stock over heat. Chances are that the stock will have to be replaced. This same thing applies where the butt plate joins the stock," Walker warns.

The locking system of the abused gun is normally battered and burred resulting in hard operation to hand cycle the action. An attempt to hide the defect will be visible from the surface of the locking mechanism appearing dished out. Sharp dents and nicks in the metal surface indicate that the gun has been tossed around and received little if any protection. Any gun that is used will have a few dents in both the wood and metal but the gun that has gotten only normal use will have more rounded-edge dents rather than sharp edges.

These are only a few things that spell out the history of the gun's use. Needless to say, any gun with an action filled with dirt, caked grease and powder residue has been treated the same way since it left the original packing box. You do not have to be an expert to decide whether it has been abused. All that is necessary is a close examination and good common sense, for the signs are there to see.

The question always arises as to the correct value of a refinished gun. This depends on the quality of craftsmanship in the restoration. Look at the metal first. If the edges are rounded, original lines washed out or changed, stamping buffed off or the bluing off shade with a reddish tinge, then back away. The value would have been greater in the original worn (or used) condition, for the gun now looks like it was polished with a number two grit brick and tossed in a home-brew bluing tank for a few seconds. If the same gunsmith also did the stock work, the wood will show sanding marks across the grain, the edge where the wood joins the receiver will be rounded, and the finish will be poorly applied. Reverting to common slang, the gun is a "klunker" with odds heavily in favor of equally poor internal repair.

In the hands of a true craftsman, a shotgun with normal wear, but properly maintained, can be restored to the point that only an expert can detect the restoration. In some cases the restoration will actually produce results superior to the factory standards. Such guns will not have been decreased but actually increased in value by restoration. If the outside shows excellent work, almost one hundred percent of the gun will have been completely disassembled and all internal corrections made with equal care.

Buying and selling used shotguns of current production is like old-fashioned horse trading. The seller tries for a quick sale at the highest dollar, often with his first price purposely set too high. This allows the buyer to talk him down to a lower price and feel the satisfaction of a good deal. The wise buyer never rushes into any transaction. He listens, asks questions and even suggestions from others, takes time to carefully examine the gun from butt plate to muzzle, and most important, gathers as much information as possible on the current market value before making his decision.

In evaluating discontinued models, knowledge is more important here than in current production models. The same general rules will apply but with additional factors involved to narrow the price bracket plus or minus from the basic guide. There are three main categories: guns intended only for shooting purposes, guns for collector purposes, and the classic shotguns that have a foot in each of the two foregoing camps.

The shooting gun will have little if any collector value and its primary interest is simply as a good functioning shotgun. The main difference between it and the similar gun in current production is the availability of spare parts. After production of a model stops, there is a five-year period during which most manufacturers can supply any part required. After this, they simply start exhausting the available supply. As a rule of thumb, after seven to ten years, the shotgun is placed on the no-parts-available list by the manufacturer and any remaing spares are sold to companies that specialize in hard-to-find parts.

You can generally find the parts needed through one of these companies or a qualified gunsmith can make it. The point is that after five years of being out of production, any necessary parts replacement and service will be expensive. This will affect the gun's value. The exception is when a model undergoes production changes to accommodate modern production methods but the basic design remains virtually unchanged. In these cases, the new model's parts can quite often be altered with little difficulty to work in the older model. Again, model knowledge and history can be of vital importance to either the buyer or seller of this type gun.

Some models are widely accepted by the public and even though they are out of production and there is a spare parts problem, their price will remain stable. Others, although technically correct, never enjoy wide acceptance and will drop rapidly in value. If the buyer is willing to make concessions as to choice, he can often buy such a gun at a fraction of its original value. Otherwise, it is a matter of popularity and demand versus available supply that determines the value of guns of this type.

"The classic shotgun is both a shooting gun and a collector item with the dual role putting it in the highest used out-of-production shotgun bracket. The value will increase invariably over the years rather than decline. Models of this type sell for an equal if not higher price than a similar gun of current production," Walker contends.

What makes a classic? There are numerous factors involved but a major one is the quality of workmanship during the original manufacturing process. In buying such guns, place your emphasis on one that has received proper care over the years or one that has been restored by a true craftsman. If you choose to shoot the gun, give it the proper maintenance and avoid the short magnum loads, for the guns were not built to withstand the constant pounding such loads deliver to the mechanism. With such care you can enjoy shooting the piece and at the same time see the value increase as the available supply diminishes and the demand increases.

"Shotgun collectors are increasing steadily in number. The main attraction is that even the collector of modest income can build an interesting collection without spending a small fortune. The other primary reason is that practically every shotgun model was made in a wide variety of gauges, barrel lengths, chokes, grades and custom features, even in the lower field grade. There is virtually no end, even with one model and one manufacturer. A complete collection of every variation is almost impossible.

"For those interested in collecting for profit or pleasure, the shotgun offers the best current challenge and potential. Information and production data is difficult to find but is steadily being accumulated for publication. It is an established fact that once such data becomes available, prices skyrocket. The only suggestion now is to select a make or model that was a quality product. Use the price guide as the foundation for your information file; then gather every scrap of information you can find to add to that file. Knowledge is a powerful asset. One seemingly insignificant piece of information about your choice will often result in a bargain purchase and a valuable addition to your collection," according to Walker.

Trade brand name shotguns involve one of the most confusing aspects of buying and selling used shotguns. Trade brand names or private labels are those stamped on a shotgun and marketed through a large jobber, wholesaler and, in some cases, a large retail outlet. The main question of interest is who actually made the shotgun.

As there is no complete reference manual available, these shotguns must be divided into two general classes. The one of most interest is the shotgun of current manufacture or one manufactured in recent years by an established firm with the only difference being the name stamped on the gun. With other guns, the changes are primarily cosmetic such as a birch stock instead of walnut, different sights, minor changes in the receiver or other external parts and components. The key is not to look at just the name but the overall appearance of the gun. In many cases, one can identify the gun easily and turn an oddball shotgun with a low price into one equal to the same model with the actual manufacturer's name on it. If the outward appearance does not serve for adequate identification, check the internal parts, as these are almost without exception identical to the well-known model.

The other category involves imported guns generally of poor quality and corresponding value. The main method of identification is to look for proof marks under the barrel, in the chamber area or inside the receiver. Not all imports with trade brand names are cheap in quality, however. Many are the equal or superior to similar U.S. models. Look closely for quality of manufacture, for quality always goes hand-in hand with value.

There are two methods for learning how to buy and sell used shotguns. One is through study and accumulated information such as this pricing guide. The other is through trial and error, plus your wallet!

AGUIRRE & ARANZABAL

Matador II

AYA Matador: side-by-side, hammerless double-barrel; 10, 12, 16, 20, 20-ga. magnum; barrels, 26″, 28″, 30″, 32″; any standard choke combo; European walnut stock, forearm; checkered pistol grip, beavertail forearm; Anson & Deeley box-lock; single selective trigger; selective automatic ejectors. Imported as Model 400E by Firearms International. Introduced in 1955; dropped 1963. Used value, $204 to $213.

Matador II has the same general specifications as stan-

dard Matador, except for vent rib barrels. Introduced in 1964; still in production. Used value, $247 to $253.

AYA Bolero: side-by-side, hammerless double-barrel; has the same general specifications as standard Matador, except for nonselective ejectors, trigger; 12, 16, 20, 28-ga., .410.

Imported as Model 400 by Firearms International. Introduced in 1955; dropped, 1963. Used value, $167 to $172.

AYA Model 37 Super: sidelock over/under; 12, 16, 20, 28, .410 gauges; 26″, 28″, 30″ barrels; any standard choke combo; vent rib; single selective trigger; automatic ejectors;

hand-checkered stock, forearm; choice of pistol-grip or straight stock; heavily engraved. Introduced in 1963; still in production. Used value, $1150 to $1322.50.

AYA Model 56: sidelock, triple-bolting side-by-side; 12, 20 gauges; barrel length, chokes to customer's specs; European walnut stock to customer's specs; semi-custom manufacture. Matted rib; automatic safety, ejectors; cocking indi-

cators; gas escape valves; folding front trigger; engraved receiver. Introduced in 1972; still in production. Was imported by JBL Arms. Used value, $834 to $862.

AYA Model 53E: has the same general specifications as Model 56, except for concave rib, hand-detachable locks.

Still in production. Was imported by JBL Arms. Used value, $747 to $776.

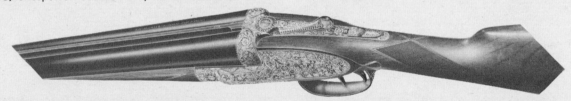

AYA XXV/SL: has the same general specifications as Model 56, except is in 12-ga. only; 25″ barrels; narrow top rib.

Still in production. Was imported by JBL Arms. Used value, $707 to $719.

AYA No. 1: has the same general specifications as Model 56, except for concave rib, double bolting, lightweight

frame. Still in production. Was imported by JBL Arms. Used value, $1006 to $1052.

No. 2

AYA No. 2: has the same general specifications as AYA No. 1, except does not have folding trigger, cocking indicators. Still in production. Was imported by JBL Arms. Used value, $552 to $575.

BERETTA

BERETTA Model 409PB: hammerless box-lock double; 12, 16, 20, 28 gauges; 27½", 28½", 30" barrels; engraved action; double triggers; plain extractors; improved/ modified, modified/full chokes; hand-checkered European walnut straight or pistol-grip stock, beavertail forearm. Introduced in 1934; dropped, 1964. Used value, $374 to $403.

BERETTA Model 410E: hammerless box-lock double; has the same specifications as Model 409PB except for better wood, finer engraving, automatic ejectors. Introduced in 1934; dropped, 1964. Used value, $471.50 to $495.

BERETTA Model 410: hammerless box-lock double; 10-ga. magnum only; 27½", 28½", 30" barrels; improved/ modified, modified/full chokes; hand-checkered European walnut straight stock; recoil pad; plain extractors; double triggers. Introduced in 1934; dropped, 1963. Used value, $471.50 to $489.

BERETTA Model 411E: hammerless box-lock double; 12, 16, 20, 28 gauges; has the same general specifications as Model 409PB, except for automatic ejectors, side plates and better wood, finer engraving. Introduced in 1934; dropped, 1964. Used value, $679 to $719.

BERETTA Model Asel: over/under box-lock; 12, 20 gauges; 25", 28", 30" barrels; single nonselective trigger; selective automatic ejectors; improved/modified, modified/full chokes; hand-checkered pistol-grip stock, forearm. Introduced in 1947; dropped, 1964. Used value, $719 to $747.

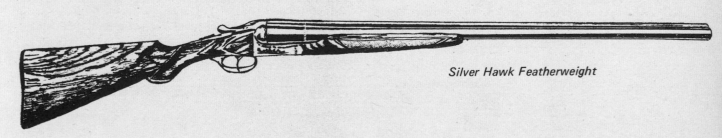

Silver Hawk Featherweight

BERETTA Silver Hawk Featherweight: hammerless box-lock double; 12, 16, 20, 28 gauges; 26" to 32" barrels; plain extractors, double or nonselective single trigger; all standard choke combos; matted rib; hand-checkered European walnut stock, beavertail forearm. Introduced in 1954; dropped, 1967. Used values, single trigger, $345 to $368; double triggers, $282 to $299.

Silver Hawk Magnum has the same general specifications as Silver Hawk Featherweight, except for recoil pad, 12-ga. only; 3" and 3½" chambers; chrome-plated bores; raised rib; has 30", 32" barrels. Introduced in 1954; dropped, 1967. Used value, single trigger, $374 to $385.50; double triggers, $305 to $316.50.

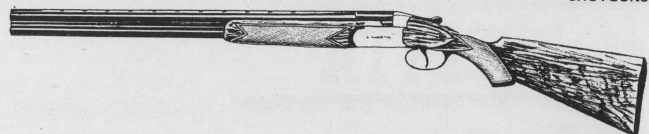

BERETTA Silver Snipe: over/under box-lock; 12, 20 gauges, standard or magnum; 26″, 28″, 30″ barrels; nickel steel receiver; plain or vent rib; improved/modified, modified/ full, full/full chokes; selective, nonselective trigger; hand-checkered European walnut pistol-grip stock, forearm. Introduced in 1955; dropped, 1967. Used values, nonselective trigger, $299 to $328; selective trigger, $328 to $362.

BERETTA Golden Snipe: over/under box-lock; 12, 20 gauges standard or magnum; has same general specifications as the Silver Snipe model except for ventilated rib as standard feature; automatic ejectors. Introduced in 1955; dropped, 1975. Used values, selective trigger, $414 to $443; nonselective trigger, $391 to $408.50.

Golden Snipe Deluxe has the same specifications as standard Golden Snipe, except for finer engraving, better walnut; available in skeet, trap models. Introduced in 1955; dropped, 1975. Used value, $477.50 to $489.

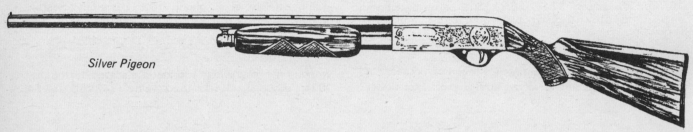

Silver Pigeon

BERETTA Silver Pigeon: slide-action; 12-ga. only; 26″, 30″, 32″ barrels; standard chokes; hand-checkered walnut pistol-grip stock, matching beavertail forearm; hand-polished, engine-turned bolt; 5-rd. magazine; chromed trigger, light engraving; inlaid silver pigeon. Introduced in 1959; dropped, 1966. Used value, $87 to $98.

Gold Pigeon has the same general specifications as Silver Pigeon with vent rib, gold trigger, deluxe engraving, inlaid gold pigeon. Used value, $138 to $144.

Ruby Pigeon has the same specifications as Silver Pigeon, with exception of vent rib, extra deluxe engraving, inlaid gold pigeon with ruby eye. Used value, $224 to $241.

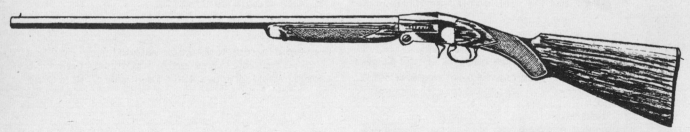

BERETTA FS-1: advertised as the Companion; single-barrel, single-shot; folds to length of barrel; hammerless, under-lever; 12, 16, 20, 28, .410 gauges; 30″ barrel in 12 ga., 28″ in 16, 20 gauges, 26″ in 28, .410 gauges; all full choke; hand-checkered pistol-grip stock, forearm; barrel release ahead of trigger guard. Introduced in 1959; still in production. Used value, $75 to $87.

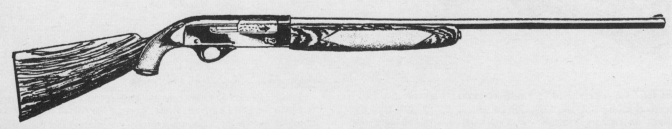

BERETTA Silver Lark: autoloader; gas-operated, takedown; 12-ga. only; 26″, 28″, 30″, 32″ barrels; improved cylinder, modified, full choke; hand-checkered European walnut pistol-grip stock, beavertail forearm; push-button safety in trigger guard; all parts hand-polished. Introduced in 1960; dropped, 1967. Used value, $127 to $138.

SHOTGUNS

Gold Lark has the same specifications as Silver Lark, except for fine engraving on receiver, ventilated rib. Used value, $155.25 to $166.75.

Ruby Lark has the same specifications as Silver Lark with the exception of a floating rib, stainless steel barrel, profuse engraving. Used value, $224.25 to $241.50.

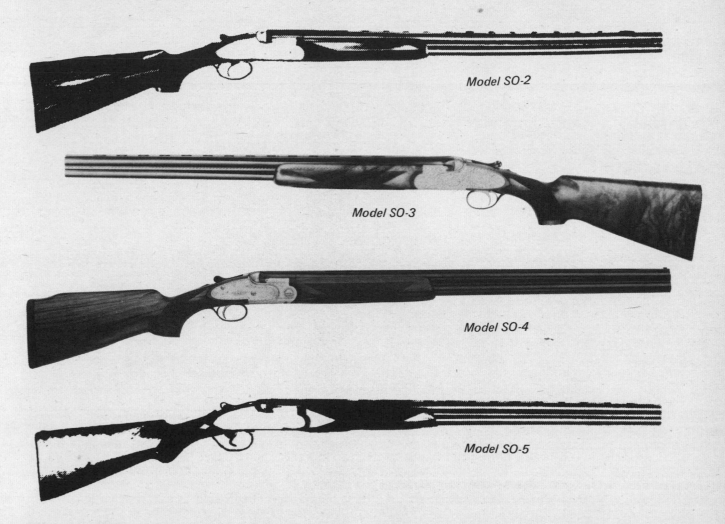

Model SO-2

Model SO-3

Model SO-4

Model SO-5

BERETTA S02 Presentation: sidelock over/under; listed earlier as 502 Presentation series; 12-ga. only; 26" improved/modified, 28" modified/full barrels standard; skeet, trap models also made; vent rib; straight or pistol-grip stock of hand-checkered European walnut; chrome-nickel receiver; Boehler anti-rust barrels; all interior parts chromed; trigger, safety, top lever checkered; scroll engraving; silver pigeon inlaid in top lever. Introduced in 1965; still in production. Used value, $1380 to $1437.50.

Model SO3 has the same specifications as Model SO2, except for fancy selected walnut stock, profuse scroll and relief engraving. Still in production. Used value, $1581.50 to $1639.

Model SO4 has the same specifications as SO2 model, except that sidelocks are hand-detachable; full-grain walnut stock, forearm; more elaborate engraving. Still in production. Used value, $1785 to $1840.

Model SO5 has the same basic specifications as other SO models, but is virtually handmade, built to customer's specifications. Has Crown grade symbol inlaid in gold in top lever. Still in production on special order basis. Used value, $2300 to $2530.

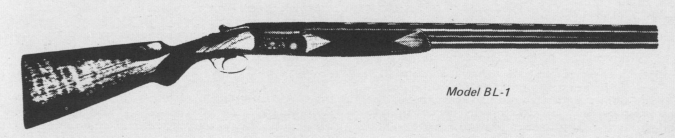

Model BL-1

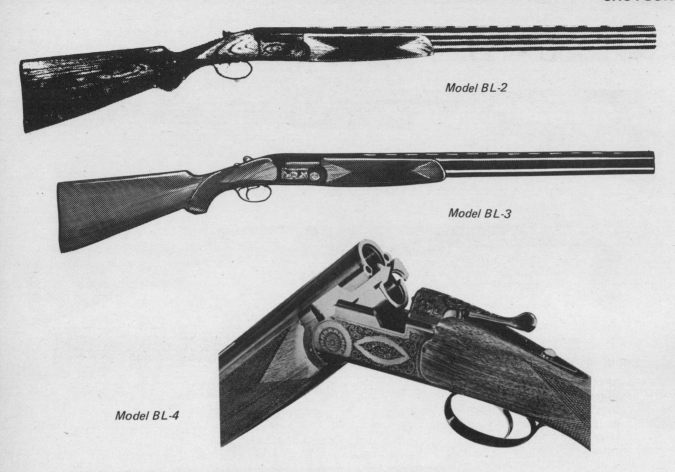

Model BL-2

Model BL-3

Model BL-4

BERETTA BL-1: box-lock over/under; 12-ga. only; 26", 28", 30" barrels; improved/modified, modified/full chokes; Monoblock design; chrome-moly steel barrels; double triggers; no ejectors; ramp front sight with fluorescent inserts; 2¾" chambers; automatic safety; hand-checkered European walnut pistol-grip stock, forearm. Introduced in 1969; dropped, 1972. Used value, $276 to $293.50.

BL-2 has the same basic specifications as BL-1, except for single selective trigger. Dropped in 1972. Used value, $305 to $322.

BL-3 Deluxe model has selective single trigger, plain extractors, vent rib, engraved action. Built in 12-ga. (2¾" or 3"), 20 gauges; trap and skeet versions available; automatic safety on standard models, nonautomatic on competition styles. Still in production. Used values, standard barrels, $403 to $431.50; trap, skeet grades, $480 to $500.

Model BL-4 has the same general specifications as BL-3, but with extensive receiver engraving, deluxe hand checkering, selective automatic ejectors. Still in production. Used values, standard barrels, $483 to $506; trap, skeet models, $604 to $632.50.

Model AL-2

BERETTA Model AL-2: autoloader; gas-operated; 12-ga. (2¾" or 3") 20 gauges; 26", 28", 30" barrels; full, modified, improved cylinder, skeet chokes; interchangeable barrels; vent rib; medium front bead sight; 3-rd. magazine; European walnut stock, forearm; diamond-point hand checkering on pistol grip, forearm. Introduced in 1969; still in production. Used values, standard, $195.50 to $207; trap/skeet, $218.50 to $230; magnum, $213 to $244.50.

Model AL-3 has the same general specifications as AL-2, but with improved wood, hand-engraved receiver; Monte Carlo pistol-grip stock on trap models. Still in production. Used values, standard barrels, $253 to $264.50; skeet/trap, $328 to $333.50; 3" magnum, $287.50 to $299.

BERNARDELLI

Roma 3

Roma 4

Roma 6

BERNARDELLI Roma: side-by-side; hammerless; Anson & Deeley action; sideplates; 12-ga. only in Roma 3 Model, 12, 16, 20 gauges in others; nonejector standard model; double triggers; 27½", 29½" barrels; modified/full chokes; hand-checkered European walnut stock, forearm; straight or pistol-grip style. Differences in grades are type of engraving, quality of wood, checkering, overall finish. Introduced in 1946; Roma No. 6 still in production; imported by Sloans. Others dropped or not imported. Used values, Roma 3, nonejector, $253 to $264; with ejectors, $316 to $333; Roma 4, nonejector, $316 to $333; with ejectors, $374 to $391; Roma 6, nonejector, $368 to $403; with ejectors, $420 to $460.

BERNARDELLI St. Uberto: side-by-side; hammerless; box-lock action; 12, 16 gauges; 26" to 32" barrels; double triggers; all standard choke combos; hand-checkered European walnut stock, forearm; straight or pistol-grip style. Introduced in 1946; dropped, 1972. Used value, $287.50 to $305.

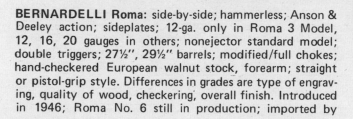

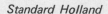

Standard Holland

BERNARDELLI Holland: side-by-side; Holland & Holland-design sidelock action; 12-ga. only; 26" to 32" barrels; all standard choke combos; double triggers; automatic ejectors; hand-checkered European walnut stock, forearm; straight or pistol-grip style. Introduced in 1946; dropped, 1971. Used value, $575 to $661.50.

BERNARDELLI Game Cock: side-by-side; hammerless; box-lock action; 12, 20 gauges; 25" improved/modified or 28" modified/full barrels; straight hand-checkered European walnut stock; double triggers on Standard model. Introduced in 1970; still in production. Imported by Sloans. Used value, $287.50 to $310.50.

Deluxe Holland model has the same specs as standard Bernardelli Holland, except has beavertail forearm, hunting scene engraved on action. Introduced in 1946; still in production on special order only. Imported by Sloans. Used value, $690 to $805.

Deluxe Game Cock model has same specifications as standard, except for light scroll engraving. Used value, $414 to $431.50.

Premier Game Cock model has same specifications as Standard model, except has single selective trigger, extensive engraving. Used value, $460 to $494.50.

Browning

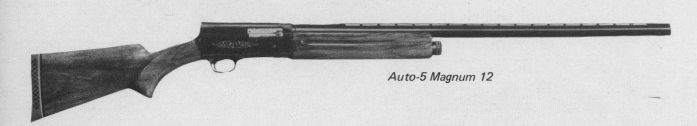

Auto-5 Magnum 12

BROWNING Auto-5: autoloader; takedown, recoil-operated; has been made in a wide variety of configurations, grades and gauges. Browning Special or Standard model was introduced in 1900; redesignated as Grade I in 1940. Available in 12, 16 gauges; 26'' to 32'' barrels; 4-rd. magazine; pre-WWII guns were available with 3-rd. magazine also; hand-checkered pistol-grip stock, forearm of European walnut; plain barrel, vent or raised matted rib. Variations still are being manufactured. Used values, with plain barrel, $300 to $320; with raised matted rib, $325 to $335; with vent rib, $330 to $345.

Auto-5 Grade III has the same general specifications as the Grade I or Standard model, except for better wood, checkering and more engraving. Discontinued, 1940. Used values, plain barrel, $450 to $500; with raised matted rib, $475 to $525; with vent rib, $500 to $550.

Auto-5 Grade IV — sometimes called Midas Grade — has

the same general specifications as Grade III, except for profuse inlays of green, yellow gold. Discontinued, 1940. Used values, plain barrel, $650 to $700; with raised matted rib, $675 to $725; with vent rib, $700 to $750.

Auto-5 Trap model, in 12-ga. only, has the same specifications as the Grade I, except for 30'' vent rib barrel, full choke only, trap stock. Used value, $300 to $325.

Auto-5 Magnum 12 has the same general specifications as Grade I, but is chambered for 3'' magnum shell; has recoil pad, plain or vent rib barrel; 28'' barrel is modified or full, 30'' and 32'' are full choke. Introduced in 1958; still in production. Used values, plain barrel, $300 to $325; vent rib, $320 to $350.

Auto-5 Magnum 20 has the same general specifications as the Magnum 12, except is chambered for 20-gauge magnum shell; 26'' barrel is full, modified or improved; 28'' is full or modified; vent rib. Used value, $320 to $350.

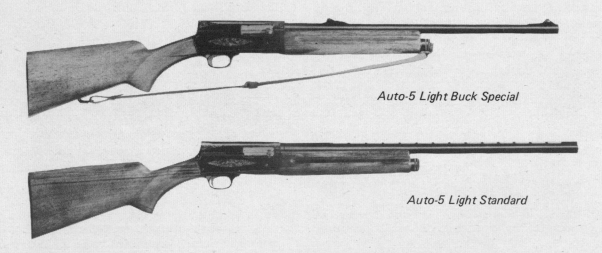

Auto-5 Light Buck Special

Auto-5 Light Standard

BROWNING Auto-5 Light: autoloader; takedown; recoil operated; 12, 16, 20 gauges; same general specifications as Standard Auto-5; 5-rd. magazine, with 3-rd. plug furnished; 2¾'' chamber; 26'', 28'', 30'' barrels, with standard choke choices; receiver is hand engraved; double extractors; barrels are interchangeable; made with vent rib only on current models. Introduced in 1948; still in production. Used value, $310 to $325.

Auto-5 Light Skeet model has the same specifications as

the Light Standard model except for skeet boring; available only in 12, 20 gauges; 28'' barrel, with full or modified choke; 26'' with full, modified or improved cylinder; plain barrel or vent rib; vent rib only on current model. Used value, $310 to $325.

Auto-5 Light Buck Special has the same specifications as Standard model, except for 24'' barrel; choked for slugs; adjustable rear sight, gold bead front on contoured ramp; detachable swivels, sling optional on current model. Used value, $300 to $310; with sling, swivels, $310 to $320.

Twelvette

Twentyweight

BROWNING Double Auto: autoloader; takedown; short recoil system; 2-shot; 12-ga. only; 26″, 28″, 30″ barrels; any standard choke; hand-checkered pistol-grip stock, forearm of European walnut; steel receiver; plain or recessed rib barrel; conservative engraving; weight, about 7¾ lbs. Introduced in 1955; dropped, 1961. Used values, with plain barrel, $181 to $187; recessed rib, $192 to $203.

Twelvette Double Auto model is same as the standard Double Auto, except for aluminum receiver, barrel with plain matted top or vent rib; receiver is black anodized with gold-wiped engraving; some receivers are anodized in brown, gray or green with silver-wiped engraving; weighs about a pound less than standard model. Introduced in 1955; dropped, 1971. Used values, matted barrel, $231 to $247.50; vent rib, $247.50 to $253.

Twentyweight Double Auto model has the same specifications as Twelvette model, but weighs 12 oz. less, largely due to thinner stock; 26½″ barrel only. Introduced in 1956; dropped, 1971. Used values, matted barrel, $242 to $258.50; vent rib, $258.50 to $264.

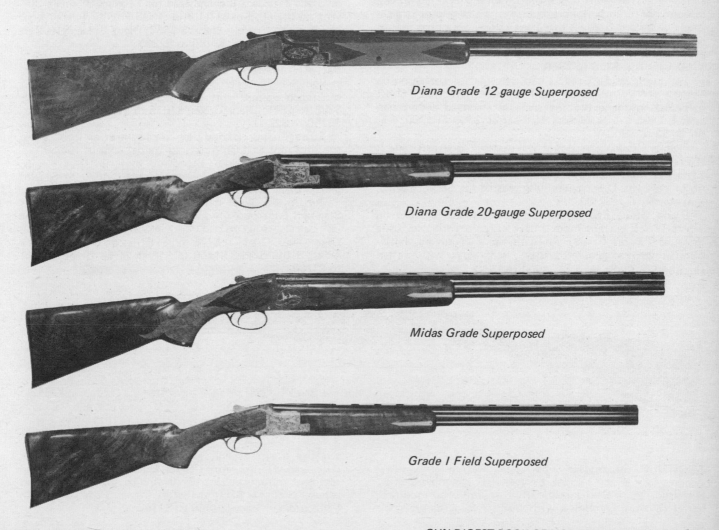

Diana Grade 12 gauge Superposed

Diana Grade 20-gauge Superposed

Midas Grade Superposed

Grade I Field Superposed

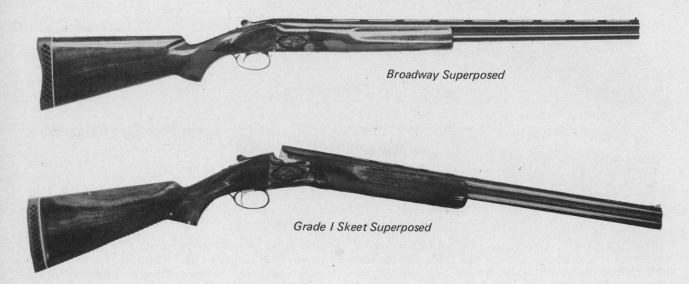

Broadway Superposed

Grade I Skeet Superposed

BROWNING Superposed: over/under; Browning-designed action; 12, 20, 28, .410 gauges; 26½″, 28″, 30″ or 32″ barrels; 32″ not made since WWII; gun is made in a wide spectrum of variations, grades, choke combinations; early models and pre-WWII had double triggers, twin single triggers or nonselective single trigger. Pre-WWII production ended when Belgium was invaded; hand-checkered stocks, forearms of French walnut; choice of pistol-grip or straight stock. Standard Grade is listed as Grade I, has raised matted rib or vent rib. Introduced in 1928; variations still in production. Used values, with raised matted rib, $700 to $750; vent rib, $750 to $800.

Lightning Model Grade I had only matted barrel, no rib before WWII; post-war models have vent rib. Other specifications generally the same as standard Superposed model. Used values, with matted barrel, $700 to $750; vent rib, $750 to $800.

Pigeon Grade Superposed was redesignated as Grade II after WWII. Had better wood, finer checkering, more engraving than Standard Superposed model; raised matted rib or vent rib. Used values, with matted rib, $800 to $850; vent rib, $850 to $900.

Diana Grade had either raised matted rib or vent rib before WWII; current models have only vent rib. Has same specs as Pigeon Grade, but with more engraving, better wood, improved general quality. Used values, with matted rib, $850 to $900; vent rib, $900 to $950.

Midas Grade in pre-war versions has raised matted rib or vent rib; current versions have only wide vent rib. Has same general specifications as standard Superposed, but is heavily engraved, gold inlaid. Used values, raised matted rib, $1200 to $1300; vent rib, $1350 to $1500.

Superposed Magnum model has the same specifications as Grade I, except is chambered for 12-gauge 3″ shells; 30″ vent rib barrel, choked full/full or full/modified; recoil pad. Used values, Grade I, $800 to $850; Diana Grade, $1600 to $1650; Midas Grade, $2100 to $2200.

Superposed Lightning Trap model is 12-ga. only; has 30″ barrels; full/full, full/improved, full/modified chokes; straight hand-checkered stock and semi-beavertail forearm of French walnut; ivory bead sights. Used values, Grade I, $825 to $875; Diana Grade, $1625 to $1675; Midas Grade, $2150 to $2250.

Superposed Broadway Trap model has same specifications as Lightning trap model, except has 30″ or 32″ barrels; 5/8″-wide Broadway vent rib. Used values, Grade I, $875 to $925; Diana Grade, $1675 to $1725; Midas Grade, $2200 to $2300.

Superposed Skeet model has the same specifications as Standard Superposed model, except for choice of 26½″ or 28″ barrels, choked skeet/skeet; made in 12, 20, 28, .410. Used values, Grade I, $775 to $825; Pigeon Grade, $800 to $850; Diana Grade, $1450 to $1500; Midas Grade, $2150 to $2200.

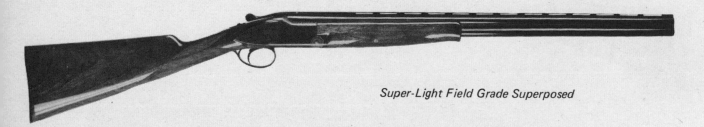

Super-Light Field Grade Superposed

BROWNING Superposed Super-Light: over/under; box-lock action; top lever; 12, 20 gauges; 2¾″ chambers; 26½″ barrels only; choked modified/full or improved/modified; barrel selector combined with manual tang safety; single selective trigger; straight grip stock of select walnut; hand-checkered grip, forearm; slender tapered solid rib; engraved receiver. Introduced in 1970; still in production. Used values, Grade I, $750 to $800; Diana Grade, $1575 to $1625; Midas Grade, $2000 to $2100.

Churchill

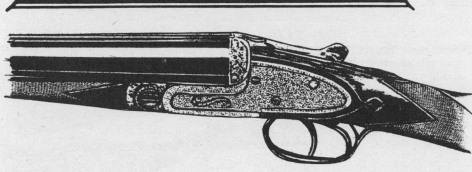

CHURCHILL Premier Quality: side-by-side; hammerless; sidelock; 12, 16, 20, 28 gauges; 25", 28", 30", 32" barrels; any desired choke combo; automatic ejectors; double triggers or single selective trigger; English engraving; hand- checkered European walnut stock, forearm; pistol-grip or straight English style. Introduced in 1900; still marketed. Used values, double triggers, $3220 to $3333.50; single selective trigger, $3672.50 to $3785.50.

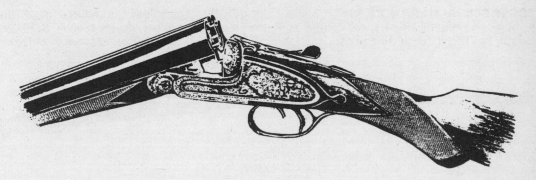

CHURCHILL Field Model: side-by-side; hammerless; sidelock; 12, 16, 20, 28 gauges; has the same general design specifications as Premier Model but has lower grade of wood, less engraving, lower overall quality. Introduced in 1900; still marketed. Used values, double triggers, $2203.50 to $2316.50; single selective trigger, $2599 to $2655.50.

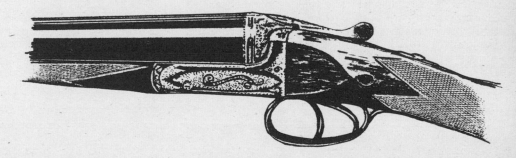

CHURCHILL Utility Model: side-by-side; hammerless; sidelock; 12, 16, 20, 28, .410 gauges; 25", 28", 30", 32" barrels; double triggers or single selective trigger; any desired choke combo; hand-checkered European walnut stock, forearm; pistol-grip or straight English style. Introduced in 1900; still marketed. Used values, double triggers, $1356 to $1412; single selective trigger, $1751 to $1808.

CHURCHILL Premier Over/Under: hammerless; sidelock; 12, 16, 20, 28 gauges; 25", 28", 30", 32" barrels; automatic ejectors; double triggers or single selective trigger; English engraving; hand-checkered European walnut stock, forearm; pistol-grip or straight English style. Introduced in 1925; dropped, 1955. Used values, double triggers, $4972 to $5085; single selective trigger, $5367.50 to $5480.50. Add $450 for raised vent rib.

Cogswell & Harrison

COGSWELL & HARRISON Primac Model: side-by-side; hammerless; hand-detachable sidelocks; 12, 16, 20 gauges; 25", 26", 27½", 30" barrels; any choke combo; automatic ejectors; double triggers, single or single selective triggers; English-style engraving; hand-checkered European walnut straight-grip stock, forearm. Introduced in 1920s; still in production. Used values, double triggers, $2090.50 to $2260; single trigger, $2316.50 to $2486; single selective trigger, $2373 to $2542.50.

COGSWELL & HARRISON Victor Model: side-by-side; hammerless; has the same specifications as Primac model except for better finish, finer wood, checkering, engraving patterns. Introduced in 1920s; still in production. Used values, double triggers, $3107 to $3277; single trigger, $3333 to $3503; single selective trigger, $3390 to $3559.

COGSWELL & HARRISON Konor Avant Tout: side-by-side; hammerless; box-lock action; 12, 16, 20 gauges; 25", 27½", 30" barrels; any desired choke combo; side plates; double, single or single selective triggers; hand-checkered European walnut straight-grip stock, forearm; pistol-grip stock available on special order; fine checkering, engraving. Introduced in 1920s; still in production. Used values, double triggers, $1356 to $1412.50; single trigger, $1582 to $1638.50; single selective trigger, $1695 to $1751.50.

Avant Tout Sandhurst model has the same specifications as Konor model except for less intricate engraving, checkering, lower grade of wood, overall workmanship. Still in production. Used values, double triggers, $1243 to $1299.50; single trigger, $1469 to $1525.50; single selective trigger, $1582 to $1638.50.

Avant Tout Rex model has the same specifications as Sandhurst model except has no side plates, lower grade wood, checkering, engraving, overall finish. Still in production. Used values, double triggers, $960.50 to $1017; single trigger, $1073.50 to $1130; single selective trigger, $1130 to $1186.50.

COGSWELL & HARRISON Huntic Model: side-by-side; hammerless; sidelock action; 12, 16, 20 gauges; 25", 27½", 30" barrels; any desired choke combo; automatic ejectors; double, single or single selective triggers; hand-checkered European walnut straight-grip stock, forearm; pistol-grip stock on special order. Introduced in late 1920s; still in production. Used values, double triggers, $1638.50 to $1695; single trigger, $1864.50 to $1921; single selective trigger, $1949.50 to $2006.

COGSWELL & HARRISON Markor Model: side-by-side; hammerless; box-lock action; 12, 16, 20 gauges; 27½", 30" barrels; any standard choke combo; double triggers; ejector or nonejector; hand-checkered European walnut straight-grip stock, forearm. Introduced in late 1920s; still in production. Used values, ejector model, $960.50 to $1017; nonejector, $847.50 to $904.

COLT

COLT Custom Double Barrel: hammerless; box-lock action; 12 (2¾" and 3"), 16 gauges; barrels are 26" improved/ modified, 28" modified/full, 30" full/full; European walnut stock; hand-checkered pistol grip, beavertail forearm. Made only in 1961. Used value, $250 to $275.

Standard Pump

COLT Coltsman Pump Model: slide-action; takedown; 12, 16, 20 gauges; barrels are 26" improved, 28" modified or 30" full choke; magazine holds 4 rds.; European walnut stock; uncheckered pistol grip, forearm. Manufactured for Colt by Manufrance. Introduced in 1961; dropped, 1965.

Used value, $103.50 to $107.50.

Coltsman Custom pump has the same specifications as standard model, same manufacturer, except has hand-checkered pistol grip, forearm, vent rib. Introduced in 1961; dropped, 1963. Used value, $144 to $149.50.

COLT Ultra Light Auto: autoloader; takedown; alloy receiver; 12, 20 gauges; chrome-lined barrels are 26" improved or modified, 28" modified or full, 30" full only, 32" full only; 4-rd. magazine; plain barrel, solid or vent rib; European walnut stock; hand-checkered pistol grip, forearm. Manufactured for Colt by Franchi. Introduced in 1964; dropped, 1966. Used values, plain barrel, $149.50 to

$155.50; solid rib, $161 to $167; vent rib, $172.50 to $178.50.

Ultra Light Custom Auto is the same as the standard model, except for select walnut stock, forearm; engraved receiver; vent rib only. Introduced in 1964; dropped, 1966. Used values, solid rib, $184 to $190; vent rib, $201.50 to $213.

COLT Magnum Auto: autoloader; takedown; 12, 20 gauges; chambered for 3" magnum shell; other specifications generally the same as those for Ultra Light standard auto. In 12 magnum, barrels are 30" or 32"; 28" in 20 magnum. Produced for Colt by Franchi. Introduced in 1964; dropped, 1966. Used values, plain barrel, $166.75 to $173;

solid rib, $178 to $184; vent rib, $190 to $195.

Custom Magnum Auto has same specifications as standard magnum auto, except for select walnut stock, forearm; engraved receiver; vent rib only. Introduced in 1964; dropped, 1966. Used values, solid rib, $190 to $195.50; vent rib, $201.25 to $207.

COLT Sauer Drilling: box-lock action; top lever; crossbolt; .30/06 or .243 Winchester under side-by-side 12-gauge barrels; 25" barrels; set rifle trigger; side safety; shotgun barrels choked modified/full; folding leaf rear sight, blade front with brass bead; cocking indicators; tang barrel selector; automatic sight positioner; oil-finished American walnut stock; hand-checkered pistol grip, forearm; black pistol grip cap; recoil pad. Made for Colt by Sauer in West Germany. Used value, $1500 to $1800.

Charles Daly

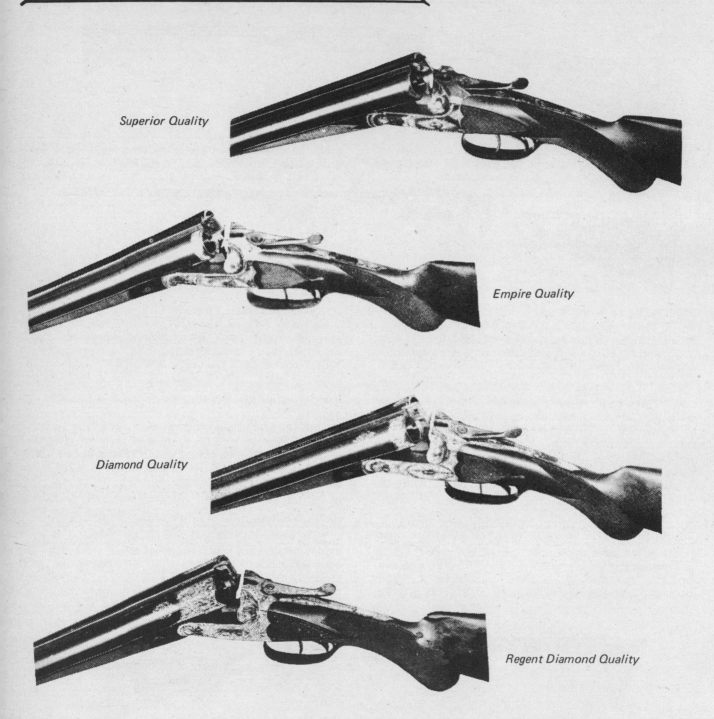

Superior Quality

Empire Quality

Diamond Quality

Regent Diamond Quality

CHARLES DALY Hammerless Double Barrel: Anson & Deeley-type box-lock action; 10, 12, 16, 20, 28, .410 gauges; 26" to 28" barrels with any choke combo; walnut stock; checkered pistol grip, forearm; made in four grades; all have automatic ejectors, except Superior Quality; grades differ in grade of wood, checkering, amount of engraving, general overall quality. Made in Suhl, Germany, for Daly. Introduced about 1920; dropped. 1933. Used values, Regent Diamond Quality, $1610 to $1667.50; Diamond Quality, $1092.50 to $1150; Empire Quality, $690 to $747.50; Superior Quality, $345 to $402.50.

Diamond

CHARLES DALY Empire Quality Over/Under: Anson & Deeley-type box-lock action; 12, 16, 20 gauges; 26" to 30" barrels; any standard choke combo; European walnut stock; hand-checkered pistol grip, forearm; double triggers; automatic ejectors. Made in Suhl, Germany, for Daly. Introduced about 1920; dropped, 1933. Used value, $1035 to $1092.50.

Diamond Quality over/under has the same specifications as Empire Quality, except has more extensive engraving, better wood and improved general overall quality. Used value, $1437.50 to $1495.

CHARLES DALY Empire Quality Trap: single-barrel; Anson & Deeley-type box-lock action; 12-ga. only; 30", 32", 34" vent rib barrel; automatic ejector; European walnut stock; hand-checkered pistol grip, forearm. Made in Suhl, Germany, for Daly in one model only. Introduced about 1920; dropped, 1933. Used value, $1265 to $1351.

CHARLES DALY Sextuple Trap: single-barrel; Anson & Deeley-type box-lock action; 12-ga. only; 30", 32", 34" vent rib barrel; six locking bolts; automatic ejector; European walnut stock; hand-checkered pistol grip, forearm. Made in two grades in Suhl, Germany, for Daly; grades differ only in checkering, amount of engraving, grade of wood, improved overall quality. Introduced about 1920; dropped, 1933. Used values, Empire Quality, $1035 to $1092.50; Regent Diamond Quality, $1610 to $1725.

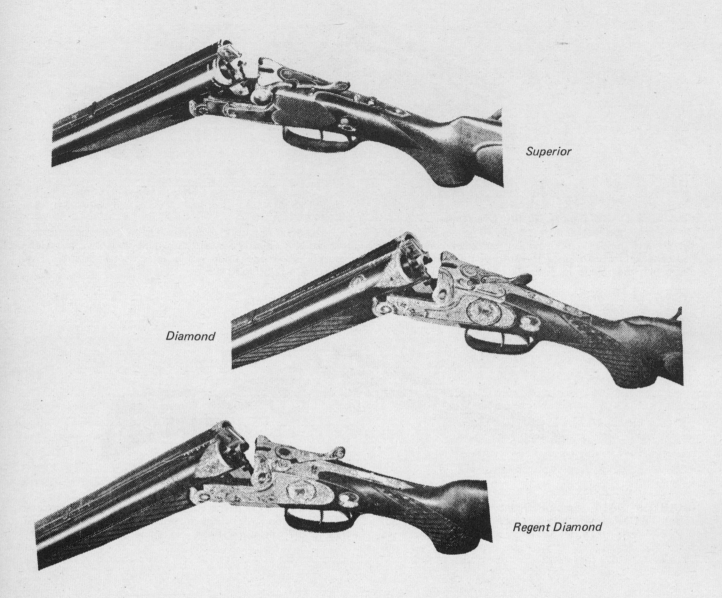

Superior

Diamond

Regent Diamond

CHARLES DALY Hammerless Drilling: Anson & Deeley-type box-lock action; 12, 16, 20 gauges; rifle barrel chambered for .25-20, .25-35, or .30-30 cartridges; plain extractors; automatic rear sight operated by selector for rifle barrel; European walnut stock; hand-checkered pistol grip, forearm. Made in three grades in Suhl, Germany, for Daly; grades differ only in checkering, amount of engraving, wood, overall quality. Introduced about 1921; dropped, 1933. Used values, Superior Quality, $690 to $747.50; Diamond Quality, $1265 to $1380; Regent Diamond Quality, $1897.50 to $2012.50.

Model 100

CHARLES DALY Model 100 Commander: over/under; Anson & Deeley-type box-lock action; 12, 16, 20, 28, .410 gauges; 26″, 28″, 30″ barrels; automatic ejectors; double triggers or Miller single selective trigger; improved/modified,

modified/full chokes; European walnut straight or pistol-grip stock; hand-checkered grip, forearm; engraved receiver. Made in Liege, Belgium, for Daly. Introduced about 1933; dropped at beginning of WWII. Used values, double trigger,

$259 to $287.50; Miller single trigger, $287.50 to $345.

Model 200 Commander has the same specifications as Model 100, except for better wood, more engraving, improved general overall finish. Used values, double trigger, $287 to $316; single trigger, $316 to $374.

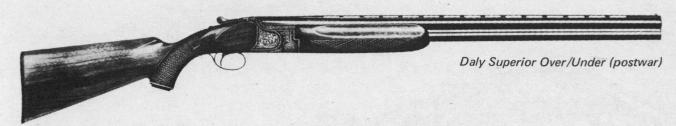

Daly Superior Over/Under (postwar)

CHARLES DALY Field Grade: over/under; box-lock action; 12 (2¾″ or 3″), 20 (2¾″ or 3″), 28, .410 gauges; 26″, 28″ 30″ barrels; choked skeet/skeet, improved/modified, modified/full, full/full; vent rib; engraved receiver; selective single trigger; automatic selective ejectors; safety/barrel selector; walnut stock; hand-checkered pistol grip, fluted forearm; recoil pad on 12-ga. magnum version. This, like other Daly shotguns made following WWII, were manu-

factured in Japan. The 12 and 20-ga. standard and magnum guns were introduced in 1963; 28, .410 gauges in 1965. Used value, $357.50 to $385.

Superior Grade over/under has the same general specifications as Field Grade, but is not chambered for magnum shells; other differences include beavertail forearm; selector device to select auto ejection or extraction only. Imported from Japan. Used values, $385 to $440; Superior skeet, $412.50 to $462; Superior trap, $440 to $478.50.

CHARLES DALY Diamond Grade: over/under; has the same general specifications as the Superior Grade, but is stocked with French walnut, more extensively checkered, engraved receiver, trigger guard. Introduced in 1967; dropped, 1973. Imported from Japan. Used value, $495 to $550.

Diamond-Regent Grade over/under has same specifications as Diamond Grade, except for highly figured French walnut stock, profuse engraving, hunting scenes inlaid in gold, silver; firing pins removable through breech face. Introduced in 1967; dropped, 1973. Imported from Japan. Used value, $797.50 to $852.50.

CHARLES DALY Venture Grade: over/under; box-lock action; 12, 20 gauges; barrels are 26″ skeet/skeet or improved/modified, 28″ modified/full, 30″ improved/full; checkered walnut pistol-grip stock, forearm; vent rib;

manual safety; automatic ejectors; single selective trigger. Imported from Japan. Introduced in 1973. Made in 3 variations. Used values, standard model, $330 to $341; Monte Carlo trap, $357.50 to $374; skeet, $352 to $363.

CHARLES DALY Auto: semi-auto; recoil-operated; 12-ga. only; barrels are 26″ improved, 28″ modified or full, 30″ full; vent rib; walnut stock; hand-checkered pistol grip,

forearm; 5-rd. magazine, 3-shot plug furnished; button safety; copy of early Browning patents. Imported from Japan. Introduced in 1973; dropped, 1975. Used value, $187 to $198.

FOX

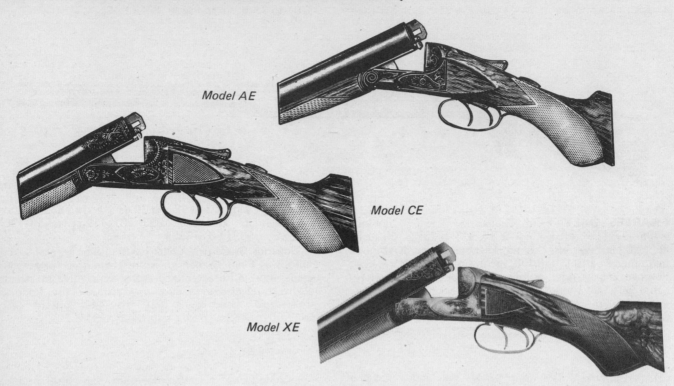

Model AE

Model CE

Model XE

FOX A.H. Fox Model: hammerless side-by-side; box-lock action; originally made in 12-ga. only with Damascus barrels with 2-5/8" chambers; steel later changed to Chromex fluid steel and chambers extended to 2¾" for smokeless powder loads. Guns were made by Fox until firm was absorbed by Savage about 1930. Difference in grades depends upon workmanship, amount of engraving, quality of wood; 12-ga. introduced in 1906; dropped, 1942. With exception of Grade A, all have automatic ejectors. Fox-Kautzky single selective trigger, vent rib were optional at extra cost. Used values, Grade A, $170 to $222; with Kautzky trigger, $252 to $270; with vent rib, $275 to $288; with Kautzky trigger and vent rib, $324 to $342. Grade AE, $234 to $252; with Kautzky trigger, $282 to $300; with vent rib, $306 to $324; with Kautzky trigger and vent rib, $348 to $360. Grade CE, $390 to $420; with Kautzky trigger, $432 to $456; with vent rib, $480 to $520; with Kautzky trigger and vent rib, $510 to $540. Grade XE, $840 to $900; with Kautzky trigger, $900 to $960; with vent rib, $918 to $978; with Kautzky trigger and vent rib, $990 to $1050.

A.H. Fox 16-ga. has the same specifications as 12-ga., except for chambering. Introduced in 1912; dropped, 1941. Used values are generally the same as for 12-ga., depending upon grade, extras, condition; $204 through $1050.

A.H. Fox 20-ga. is a slightly scaled-down version of the 12-ga., but with same general design. Introduced in 1912; dropped, 1946. Used values generally the same as for other gauges, dependent upon grade, extras, condition; $204 to $1050.

FOX Sterlingworth: side-by-side; hammerless; box-lock action; 12, 16, 20 gauges; 26", 28", 30" barrels; any standard choke combo; double triggers, plain extractors standard; automatic ejectors, single selective trigger extra;

has the same general specifications as earlier A.H. Fox doubles, but these were production line guns without much handwork; American walnut stock; hand-checkered pistol grip, forearm. Introduced in 1910; dropped, 1947. Used values, $228 to $246; with automatic ejectors, $288 to $300; single selective trigger, $300 to $318; with ejectors and selective trigger, $462 to $504.

Sterlingworth Deluxe model has the same general specifications as standard model, except it was also available with 32" barrel; single selective trigger is standard; has Lyman ivory bead sights, recoil pad. Introduced in 1930; dropped, 1946. Used values, $312 to $330; with automatic ejectors, $354 to $372.

FOX Single-Barrel Trap Model: box-lock action; 12-ga. only; 30", 32" barrel; automatic ejector; vent rib; American walnut stock and forearm, except for Grade M, which had Circassian walnut; hand-checkered pistol grip, forearm; recoil pad optional. Originally made by A.H. Fox, but taken over by Savage about 1930. In 1932, the gun was redesigned, with full pistol-grip stock, Monte Carlo stock.

FOX Super Fox: side-by-side; box-lock action; 12-ga. only; chambered for 3" shells on special order; 30", 32" barrels; full choke only; double triggers; engraved action; American

Sterlingworth Skeet model has the same general specifications as standard model, except for skeet bore only, straight grip stock, 26" or 28" barrels; 12-ga. only. Introduced in 1935; dropped, 1946. Used values, $354 to $378; with automatic ejectors, $408 to $432.

Sterlingworth Trap model has the same general specifications as standard Sterlingworth, except for trap stock, 32" barrels only; 12-ga. only. Introduced in 1917; dropped, 1946. Used values, $354 to $378; with automatic ejectors, $408 to $432.

Sterlingworth Waterfowl Grade has the same general specifications as the standard model, except for heavier frame, automatic ejectors; 12-ga. only. Introduced in 1934; dropped, 1939. Used value, $288 to $306.

Of Grade M, only 9 were made, giving it collector value. Difference in grades is based upon quality of wood and amount and quality of engraving on receiver. Introduced in 1919; dropped, 1935. Used values, Grade JE, $420 to $480; Grade KE, $480 to $540; Grade LE, $540 to $600; Grade ME, $1080 to $1200.

walnut stock; hand-checkered pistol grip, forearm; automatic ejectors. Introduced in 1925; dropped, 1942. Used value, $390 to $420.

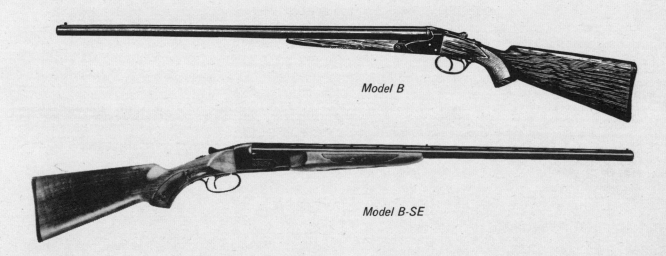

Model B

Model B-SE

FOX Model B: side-by-side; hammerless; box-lock action; 12, 16, 20, .410 gauges; 26", 28", 30" barrels; double triggers; plain extractors; modified/full, improved/modified, full/full chokes; double triggers; American walnut stock, forearm; hand-checkered pistol grip, forearm; case-hardened frame. Introduced in 1940; still in production. Used value, $106.50 to $118.

Model B-ST has the same specifications as standard Model B, except for single selective trigger only. Introduced in 1955; dropped, 1966. Used value, $134.50 to $145.50.

Model B-DL has the same specifications as Model B, except for satin-chrome-finished frame; stock, forearm of select American walnut; side panels; beavertail forearm. Introduced in 1962; dropped, 1965. Used value, $168 to $185.

Model B-DE replaced Model B-DL, with the same general

specifications and improvements, but without side panels. Introduced in 1965; dropped, 1966. Used value, $157 to $174.

Model B-SE has same general specifications as standard Model B, except for white line spacers, automatic ejectors, single nonselective trigger; has white bead front, middle sights. Introduced in 1966; still in production. Used value, $135 to $140.

Model B Lightweight is chambered for 12, 20, .410 gauges; barrels are 24" (12,20 gauges) improved/modified, 26" improved/modified, 28" modified/full, 30" modified/full in 12-ga. only, 26" full/full in .410 only; double triggers; select walnut stock; checkered pistol grip, beavertail forearm; vent rib; color case-hardened frame. Introduced in 1973; still in production. Used value, $140 to $151.50.

FRANCHI

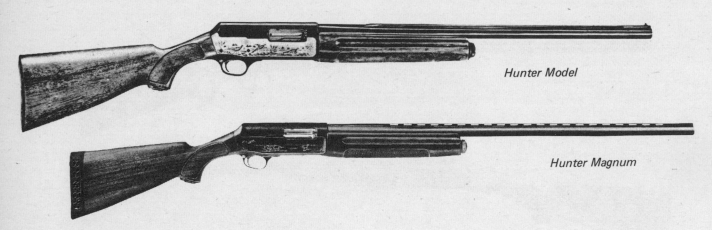

Standard Autoloader

FRANCHI Standard Autoloader: recoil-operated autoloader; 12, 20 gauges; 26", 28", 30" interchangeable barrels; 5-rd. magazine; plain barrel, solid or vent rib; improved, modified, full chokes; alloy receiver; chrome-lined barrels; simplified takedown; European walnut stock, forearm; pistol grip, forearm hand-checkered. Introduced in 1950; still in production. Imported by Stoeger Industries. Used values, plain barrel, $220.50 to $226; solid rib, $236.50 to

$241.50; vent rib, $241.50 to $247.

Standard Magnum Autoloader has the same general specifications as Standard model, except it is chambered for 12 or 20-ga., 3" magnum shotshell; 32" (12-ga.), 28" (20-ga.) plain or vent rib barrel; recoil pad. Introduced in 1952; still in production. Imported by Stoeger Industries. Used values, plain barrel, $252 to $257.50; vent rib, $268 to $273.

Hunter Model

Hunter Magnum

FRANCHI Hunter Model Autoloader: recoil-operated autoloader; 12, 20 gauges; has the same general specifications as Standard model autoloader, except for better wood, engraved receiver; ribbed barrel only. Introduced in 1950; still in production. Imported by Stoeger Industries. Used values, with hollow matted rib, $268 to $273; vent rib, $283.50 to

$289.

Hunter Magnum has same specifications as Hunter model, except is chambered for 12 or 20-ga., 3" magnum shotshell; has 32" (12-ga.), 28" (20-ga.) vent rib, full choke barrel; recoil pad. Introduced in 1955; still in production. Used value, $289 to $294.

FRANCHI Eldorado: recoil-operated autoloader; 12, 20 gauges; has the same general specifications as Standard model autoloader, but with scroll engraving covering 75% of receiver surfaces; gold-plated trigger; chrome-plated

breech bolt; chrome-lined bore; vent rib; select European stock; hand-checkered pistol grip, forearm. Introduced in 1955; still in production. Imported by Stoeger Industries. Used value, $341.50 to $352.

FRANCHI Slug Gun: recoil-operated autoloader; 12, 20 gauges; 22" barrel; alloy receiver; same general specifications as Standard autoloader, except for short cylinder bore barrel; raised gold bead front sight, Lyman folding leaf open rear; 5-rd. magazine; sling swivels. Introduced in 1955; still in production. Imported by Stoeger Industries. Used value, $289 to $299.50.

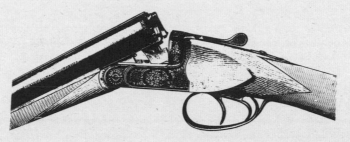

FRANCHI Airon Model: side-by-side; hammerless; Anson & Deeley-type box-lock action; 12-ga. only; all standard barrel lengths, choke combinations; automatic ejectors; straight-grip stock of European walnut; hand-checkered grip and forearm; automatic ejectors; double triggers. Introduced in 1956, special order only; dropped, 1968. Used value, $280 to $308.

Astore S Model

FRANCHI Astore Model: side-by-side; hammerless; Anson & Deeley-type box-lock action; 12-ga. only; all standard barrel lengths, choke combinations; plain extractors; double triggers; straight-grip European walnut stock; hand-checkered stock, forearm. Introduced in 1956; special order only; dropped, 1968. Used value, $314 to $347.50.

Astore S model has the same specifications as standard Astore except for fine engraving on frame. Used value, $358.50 to $392.

Condor Grade

Imperial Monte Carlo Extra

FRANCHI Custom Sidelock Model: side-by-side; hammerless; 12, 16, 20, 28 gauges; barrel lengths, chokes are to individual customer's requirements; automatic ejectors; hand-detachable locks; straight or pistol-grip stock of European walnut; hand-checkered grip section, forearm; self-opening action, single trigger optional. Made in six grades; variations depending upon quality of wood, amount of engraving, checkering, overall workmanship. For self-opening action, add $140; for single trigger, add $101. Introduced in 1956, special order only; dropped, 1968. Used values, Condor Grade, $504 to $532; Imperial Grade, $672 to $700; Imperial S Grade, $672 to $700; Imperial Monte Carlo Grade No. 5, $1001 to $1064; Imperial Monte Carlo Grade No. 11, $1036 to $1092; Imperial Monte Carlo Extra, $1232 to $1288.

FRANCHI Aristocrat Trap Model: over/under; 12-ga. only; 30" barrels; 10mm-wide rib; single selective trigger; automatic ejectors; nonauto safety; selected deluxe grade European walnut stock, beavertail forearm; hand-checkered pistol grip; chrome-lined barrels are improved modified/full; Monte Carlo comb; color case-hardened receiver. Introduced in 1962; dropped, 1968. Used value, $314 to $336.

Aristocrat Skeet Model has the same general specifications as trap version, except for 26" barrels choked skeet/

skeet, grooved beavertail forearm. Introduced in 1962; dropped, 1968. Used value, $336 to $358.50.

Aristocrat Field Model has same general design specs as other Aristocrat models, including vent rib; 12-ga. only; barrels are 24", cylinder/improved cylinder, 26" improved/modified, 28" modified/full; 30" modified/full; selective automatic ejectors; automatic safety; hand-checkered Italian walnut pistol-grip stock, forearm. English scroll engraving on receiver; blue-black finish only. Introduced in 1960; dropped, 1968. Used value, $235.50 to $246.50.

FRANCHI Silver-King Aristocrat: over/under; 12-ga. only; deluxe version of Aristocrat design; has engraved, bright-finish receiver, selected ultra-deluxe walnut stock, forearm, cut from the same blank for match of grain, color, finish;

hand-checkered pistol grip, forearm; vent rib; barrels are 24" cylinder/improved cylinder, 26" improved/modified, 28" modified/full, 30" modified/full; blue-black finish; chrome-lined barrels. Introduced in 1965; dropped, 1968. Used value, $319.50 to $442.50.

FRANCHI Dynamic 12: recoil-operated autoloader; 12-ga. only; has the same general specifications and options as Franchi Standard model, except for heavy steel receiver, chrome-plated breech bolt and lifter; European walnut stock, forearm; chrome-lined barrel; 5-rd. magazine; trigger-

safety-guard-lifter mechanism detachable as single unit; 3-shot plug furnished; plain or vent rib barrel; also skeet, slug-gun configurations; slug gun has 22" barrel, sights. Introduced in 1965; dropped, 1970. Used values, with plain barrel; $168 to $179.50; with vent rib, $202 to $213; slug gun, $212 to $223; skeet model, $246.50 to $258.

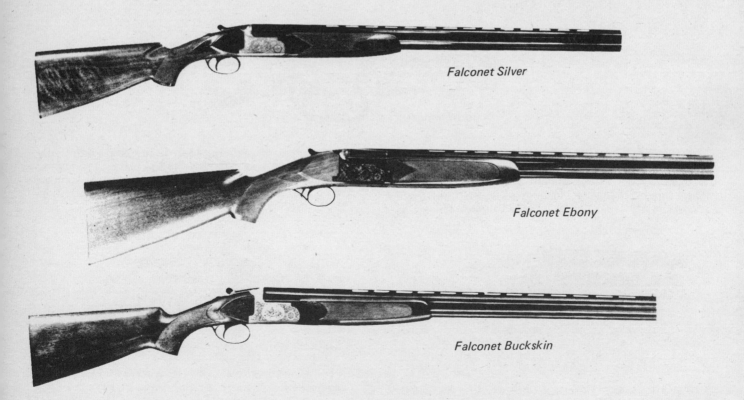

Falconet Silver

Falconet Ebony

Falconet Buckskin

FRANCHI Falconet: originally introduced as Falcon model; over/under; 12, 20 gauges; 12-ga. has 24", 26", 28", 30" barrels, with standard choke combos; 20-ga. has 24", 26", 28" barrels; selective single trigger; barrel selector; automatic safety; selective automatic ejectors; alloy receiver, fully engraved; walnut stock, forearm; checkered pistol grip, forearm; epoxy finish. Introduced in 1969; still in production. Imported by Stoeger Industries. Used value, $420 to $448.

Francotte

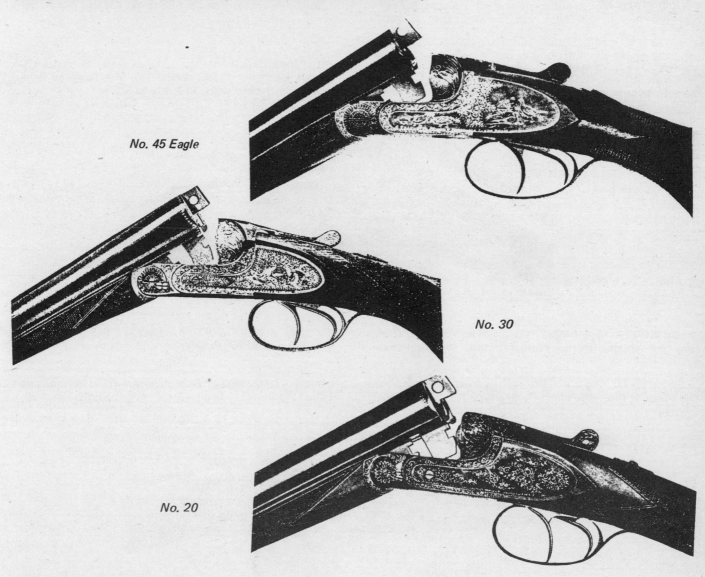

No. 45 Eagle

No. 30

No. 20

FRANCOTTE A&F Series: side-by-side; Anson & Deeley type box-lock action; 12, 16, 20, 28, .410 gauges; in 12-ga., 26″ to 32″ barrels, 26″ to 28″ in other gauges; any desired choke combo; crossbolt; sideplates on all models except Knockabout; double triggers; automatic ejectors; series was made in seven grades for distribution exclusively in this country by Abercrombie & Fitch; grades varied only in overall quality, grade of wood, checkering and engraving. Introduced prior to World War II, dropped in 1960s. Used values, Knockabout Model, $1073.50 to $1186.50; Jubilee Model, $1469 to $1582; No. 14, $1525.50 to $1638.50; No. 18, $1582 to $1695; No. 20, $1751.50 to $1864.50; No. 25, $2090.50 to $2203.50; No. 30, $2260 to $2373; No. 45 Eagle Grade, $2768.50 to $2938.50.

FRANCOTTE Model 6886: side-by-side; Anson & Deeley box-lock action; 12, 16, 20, 28, .410 gauges; all standard barrel lengths, choke combinations available; automatic ejectors; double triggers; hand-checkered European walnut stock, forearm; straight or pistol-grip design. Manufactured before World War II. Used value, $1130 to $1243.

FRANCOTTE Model 8446: side-by-side; Greener crossbolt; side clips; general specifications are the same as Model 6886 except for finish, better construction. Manufactured before World War II. Used value, $1243 to $1356.

FRANCOTTE Model 6930: side-by-side; square crossbolt; Anson & Deeley box-lock action; 12, 16, 20, 28, .410 gauges; all standard barrel lengths, choke combos; auto- matic ejectors; double triggers; hand-checkered European walnut stock, forearm; straight or pistol-grip design. Manu- factured before World War II. Used value, $1243 to $1356.

FRANCOTTE Model 4996: side-by-side; Anson & Deeley box-lock action; side clips; has the same general specifi- cations as Model 8446, except for minor variations in finish, checkering. Manufactured before World War II. Used value, $1243 to $1356.

FRANCOTTE Model 8457: side-by-side, Anson & Deeley box-lock action; 12, 16, 20, 28, .410 gauges; all standard barrel lengths, choke combos; Greener-Scott crossbolt; other specifications are the same as those of Model 4996 except for better finish, checkering. Manufactured before World War II. Used value, $1469 to $1582.

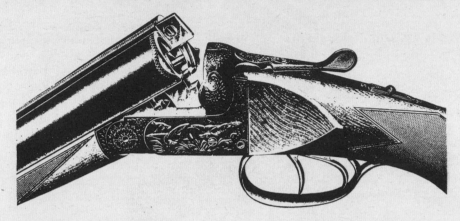

FRANCOTTE Model 9261: side-by-side; Anson & Deeley box-lock action; Greener crossbolt; other specifications are the same as Model 8457. Manufactured before World War II. Used value, $1469 to $1582.

FRANCOTTE Model 11/18E: side-by-side; Anson & Deeley box-lock action; side clips; Purdey-type bolt; other specifi- cations are the same as those of Model 9261. Manufactured before World War II. Used value, $1469 to $1582.

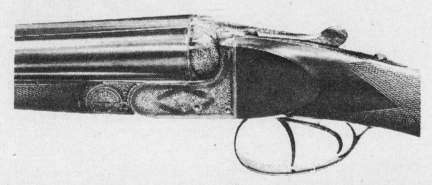

FRANCOTTE Model 10/18E/628: side-by-side; Anson & Deeley box-lock action; side clips; Purdey-type bolt; other specifications are the same as Model 11/18E except overall quality is better, including wood, checkering, engraving, finish. Introduced before World War II; still in production. No current importer. Used value, $2090.50 to $2260.

FRANCOTTE Model 10594: side-by-side; Anson & Deeley box-lock action; sideplates; 12, 16, 20, 28, .410 gauges; all standard barrel lengths, choke combos; reinforced frame, side clips; Purdey-type bolt; automatic ejectors; hand- checkered European walnut stock; straight or pistol-grip de- sign. Introduced about 1950; still in production. Used value, $1582 to $1695.

FRANCOTTE Model 8455: side-by-side; Anson & Deeley box-lock action; has the same specifications as Model 10594 except for style of engraving, Greener crossbolt. In- troduced about 1950; still in production. No current im- porter. Used value, $1582 to $1695.

FRANCOTTE Model 6982: side-by-side; Anson & Deeley box-lock action; has the same specifications as Model 10594, except for style of engraving. Introduced about 1950; still in production. No current importer. Used value, $1582 to $1695.

FRANCOTTE Model 9/40E/38321: side-by-side; Anson & Deeley box-lock action. Has the same general specifications as Model 6982, except for better quality, fine English engraving. Introduced about 1950; still in production. No current importer. Used value, $2090.50 to $2260.

FRANCOTTE Model 120.HE/328: side-by-side; sidelock; automatic ejectors; double triggers; made in all standard gauges, chokes, barrel lengths to customer's order; hand-checkered European walnut stock, forearm; straight or pistol-grip design. Introduced about 1950; still in production. No current importer. Used value $4237 to $4520.

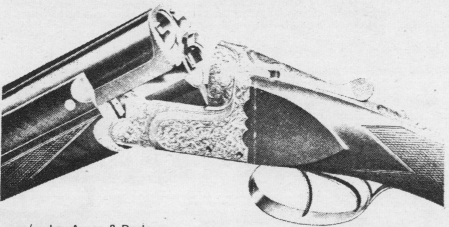

FRANCOTTE Model 9/40.SE: over/under; Anson & Deeley box-lock action; 12, 16, 20, 28, .410 gauges; all standard barrel lengths, choke combos; automatic ejectors; double triggers; hand-checkered European walnut stock, forearm; straight or pistol-grip design; elaborate engraving. Introduced about 1950; still in production. No current importer. Used value, $4237.50 to $4520.

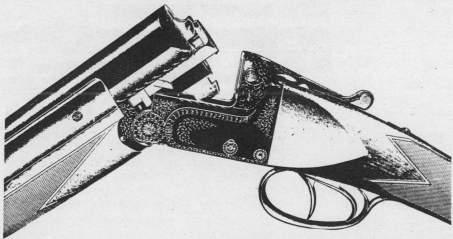

FRANCOTTE Model SOB.E/11082: over/under; Anson & Deeley box-lock action. Same general specifications as Model 9/40SE, but not as profusely engraved. Introduced about 1950; no current importer. Used value, $3107.50 to $3333.50.

GREENER

Greener Sovereign

hand-checkered European walnut straight or pistol-grip stock, forearm; engraved action. Introduced in 1875; dropped, 1965. Used value, $1017 to $1073.50.

Sovereign Model, Grade DH40, has the same specifications as Jubilee model except for better overall quality, better wood, checkering, engraving. Used value, $1130 to $1243.

Crown Model, Grade DH55 has the same specifications as Sovereign Model except for upgraded overall quality, including finer engraving, checkering and better wood. Used value, $1469 to $1582.

Royal Model, Grade DH75 is top of the line for Greener hammerless ejector double style, with same general specifications as others, but with top-quality workmanship, including checkering, engraving and figured walnut in stock, forearm. Used value, $1695 to $1864.50.

Note: On all variations, add $90.50 to $102 for nonselective single trigger; $169.50 to $198 for selective trigger.

GREENER Jubilee Model: Grade DH 35; side-by-side; box-lock action; hammerless; 12, 16, 20 gauges; 26", 28", 30" barrels; any choke combo; double triggers; nonselective or selective single trigger at added cost; automatic ejectors;

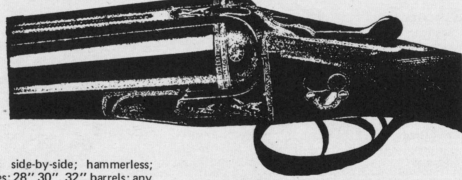

Greener Far-Killer

GREENER Far-Killer Model: side-by-side; hammerless; box-lock action; 12, 10, 8 gauges; 28" 30", 32" barrels; any desired choke combination; nonejectors; automatic ejectors at added cost; hand-checkered European walnut straight or half-pistol grip stock. Introduced about 1895; dropped,

1962. Used values, 12-ga. nonejector model, $1017 to $1073; with ejectors, $1412 to $1525; 8, 10 gauges, nonejector, $1130 to $1186.50; with ejectors, $1582 to $1695.

Greener Empire

GREENER Empire Model: side-by-side; hammerless; box-lock action; 12-ga. only; 28", 30", 32" barrels; any choke combo; hand-checkered European walnut straight or half-pistol grip stock, forearm; nonejector; ejectors at additional cost. Introduced about 1893; dropped, 1962. Used values, nonejector model, $678 to $734.50; ejector model, $819.50 to $847.50.

Empire Deluxe Grade has same general specifications as standard Empire model except has deluxe finish and better craftsmanship. Used values, nonejector model, $751.50 to $785.50; ejector model, $847.50 to $876.

GREENER General Purpose: single-shot; Martini-type action; takedown; 12-ga. only; 26", 30", 32" barrel;

modified, full choke; ejector; hand-checkered European walnut straight grip stock, forearm. Introduced in 1910; dropped, 1964. Used value, $141.50 to $169.50.

GREIFELT

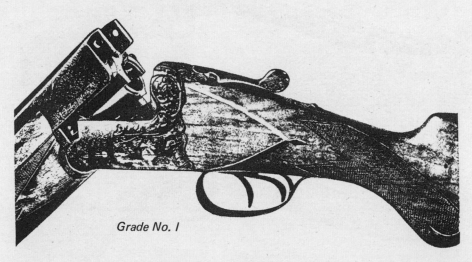

Grade No. I

GREIFELT Grade No. 1: over/under; Anson & Deeley box-lock action; 12, 16, 20, 28, .410 gauges; 26", 28", 30", 32" barrels; automatic ejectors; any desired choke combo; solid matted rib standard; vent rib at added cost; hand-checkered European walnut straight or pistol-grip stock, Purdey-type forearm; double triggers standard; single trigger at added cost; elaborate engraving. Manufactured prior to World War II. Used values, solid matted rib, $2655.50 to $2938; with vent rib, $2825 to $3107. Add $170 to $180 for single trigger.

GREIFELT Grade No. 3: over/under; Anson & Deeley box-lock action; 12, 16, 20, 28, .410 gauges; same general specifications as Grade No. 1 but engraving is less elaborate, wood has less figure. Manufactured prior to World War II. Used values, solid matted rib, $1695 to $1977; vent rib, $1864 to $2147. Add $170 to $180 for single trigger.

GREIFELT Model 22: side-by-side; Anson & Deeley box-lock action; sideplates; 12, 16 gauges; 28", 30" barrels; modified/full choke only; plain extractors; double triggers; hand-checkered stock, forearm; pistol-grip, cheekpiece or straight English style. Introduced about 1950; still in production. No current importer. Used value, $734 to $847.

Model 22E has the same specifications as standard Model 22 except for addition of automatic ejectors. Introduced about 1950; still in production. No current importer. Used value, $904 to $1017.

GREIFELT Model 103: side-by-side; hammerless; Anson & Deeley box-lock action; 12, 16 gauges; 28", 30" barrels, modified/full chokes; plain extractors; double triggers; hand-checkered European walnut stock, forearm; pistol-grip, cheekpiece or straight English style. Introduced about 1950; still in production. No current importer. Used value, $678 to $763.

Model 103E has same specifications as Model 103 except for addition of automatic ejectors. Introduced about 1950; still in production. No current importer. Used value, $847.50 to $904.

GREIFELT Model 143E: over/under; Anson & Deeley box-lock action; 12, 16, 20 gauges; 26", 28", 30" barrels; has the same general design specifications as the Pre-WWII Grade No. 1, but workmanship is of lower quality. Introduced about 1950; still in production. No current importer. Used values, with raised matted rib, double triggers, $1243 to $1356; vent rib, single selective trigger, $1469 to $1582.

Harrington & Richardson

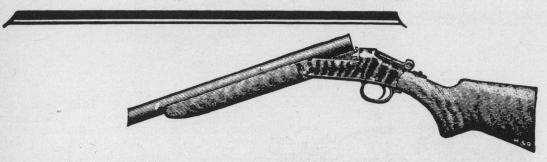

HARRINGTON & RICHARDSON No. 3: single barrel, hammerless; takedown; 12, 16, 20, .410 gauges; 26″, 28″, 30″, 32″ barrels; automatic ejector; no sights; uncheckered American walnut pistol-grip stock, forearm; full choke only; top-lever break-open action. Introduced in 1908; dropped, 1942. Used value, $39.50 to $42.

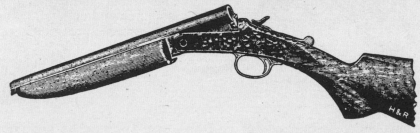

HARRINGTON & RICHARDSON No. 5: single barrel; hammer model; takedown; lightweight configuration; 20, 28, .410 gauges, 26″, 28″ barrels; full choke only; automatic ejector; uncheckered American walnut pistol-grip stock, forearm; top-lever, break-open action; no sights. Introduced in 1908; dropped, 1942. Used value, $39.50 to $42.

HARRINGTON & RICHARDSON No. 6: single barrel; hammer model; takedown; heavy breech; 10, 12, 16, 20 gauges; 28″, 30″, 32″, 34″, 36″ barrels; automatic ejector; uncheckered American walnut pistol-grip stock, forearm; no sights; top-lever, break-open action. Same basic design as No. 5 model except for heavier breech, gauges, barrel lengths. Introduced in 1908; dropped, 1942. Used value, $45 to $48.

HARRINGTON & RICHARDSON No. 8: single barrel; hammer model; takedown; 12, 16, 20, 24, 28, .410 gauges; 26″, 28″, 30″, 32″ barrels; full choke only; automatic ejector; uncheckered American walnut pistol-grip stock, forearm; no sights. Same general design as Model 6 except for different forearm design, gauges, et al. Introduced in 1908; dropped, 1942. Used value, $39.50 to $42.

HARRINGTON & RICHARDSON Bay State No. 7: Also known as Model No. 9; single barrel; hammer model; takedown; 12, 16, 20, .410 gauges; 26", 28", 30", 32" barrels; full choke only; no sights; uncheckered American walnut pistol-grip stock, forearm. Same specifications as No. 8, except for fuller pistol grip, slimmer forearm. Introduced in 1908; dropped, 1942. Used value, $39.50 to $42.

HARRINGTON & RICHARDSON Folding Model: single barrel; hammer model; gun is hinged at front of frame so barrel folds against stock for storage, transport; full choke only; Light Frame version has 22" barrel only, 28, .410 gauges; Heavy Frame is in 12, 16, 20, 28, .410, 26" barrel; bead front sight; uncheckered pistol-grip stock, forearm. Introduced about 1910; dropped, 1942. Used value, $42 to $51.

No. 48 Topper

HARRINGTON & RICHARDSON No. 48 Topper: single barrel; hammer model; takedown; 12, 16, 20, .410 gauges; 26", 28", 30", 32" barrels; modified or full choke; automatic ejector; top-lever, break-open action; specifications similar to those of Model 8. Introduced in 1946; dropped, 1957. Used value, $39.50 to $51.

Model 488 Topper Deluxe has same specifications as No. 48 Topper, except for black lacquered stock, forearm, recoil pad, chrome-plated frame. Introduced in 1946; dropped, 1957. Used value, $34 to $42.

HARRINGTON & RICHARDSON Model 148 Topper: single barrel; hammer model; takedown; improved version of No. 48; 12, 16, 20, .410 gauges; in 12-ga., barrels are 30", 32" or 36"; in 16-ga., barrels are 28" or 30"; in 20, .410 gauges, barrels are 28"; full choke only; side lever; uncheckered American walnut pistol-grip stock, forearm; recoil pad. Introduced in 1958; dropped, 1961. Used value, $39.50 to $51.

Model 188 Deluxe Topper has the same specifications as Model 148, except is .410-ga. only; chrome-plated frame; stock, forearm finished with black, red, yellow, blue, green, pink or purple lacquer. Introduced in 1958; dropped, 1961. Used value, $34 to $39.50.

HARRINGTON & RICHARDSON Model 480 Jr. Topper: single barrel; hammer model; has the same general specifications as No. 48 Topper, except for shorter youth stock; 26" barrel only; .410-ga. only. Introduced in 1958; dropped, 1960. Used value, $35 to $45.

Model 580 Jr. Topper has the same specifications as Model 480, except for variety of colored stock as with Model 188 Topper. Introduced in 1958; dropped, 1961. Used value, $34 to $39.50.

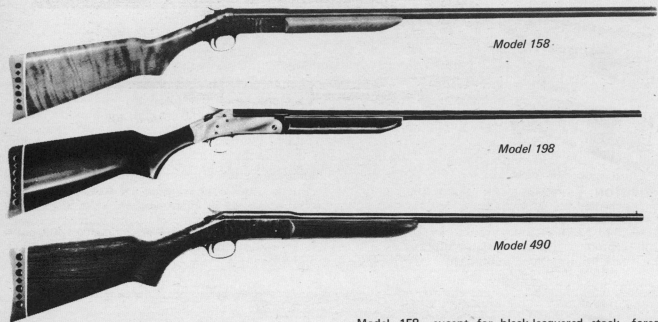

Model 158

Model 198

Model 490

HARRINGTON & RICHARDSON Model 158 Topper: single barrel; hammer model; takedown; side-lever, break-open action; improved version of Model 148 Topper; 12, 16, 20, .410 gauges; in 12-gauge, 30″, 32″, 36″ barrels are all full choke; 28″ is full or modified; 16-ga. has 28″ modified barrel only; 20-ga., 28″ full or modified, .410, 28″ full only; no sights; uncheckered hardwood pistol-grip stock, forearm; recoil pad. Introduced in 1962; still in production. Used value, $39.50 to $45.

Model 198 Topper Deluxe has the same specifications as Model 158, except for black-lacquered stock, forearm; chrome-plated frame; in 20, .410 gauges only. Introduced in 1962; still in production. Used value, $39.50 to $45.

Model 490 Topper has the same specifications as Model 158, except for 26″ barrel only, shorter youth stock; in 20-ga., modified; .410, full choke only. Introduced in 1962; still in production. Used value, $34 to $39.50.

Model 590 Topper has the same specifications as Model 490, except for black-lacquered stock, forearm, chrome-plated frame. Introduced in 1962; dropped, 1963. Used value, $34 to $39.50.

Model 159

HARRINGTON & RICHARDSON Model 159: advertised as the Golden Squire model; single barrel; exposed hammer; 12, 20 gauges; in 12-ga., 30″ barrel, 20-ga., 28″ barrel; full choke only; uncheckered hardwood straight grip stock, forearm with schnabel; no sights. Introduced in 1964; dropped, 1966. Used value, $45 to $51.

Model 459 Golden Squire Jr. has same specifications as Model 459, except for shorter youth stock, 26″ full choke barrel; 20, .410 gauges only. Made only in 1964. Used value, $45 to $50.

HARRINGTON & RICHARDSON Model 348: advertised as Gamemaster model; bolt-action; takedown; 12, 16 gauges; 28″ barrel; full choke only; 2-rd. tube magazine; uncheckered hardwood pistol-grip stock, forearm. Intro-duced in 1949; dropped, 1954. Used value, $34 to $39.50.

Model 349 Gamemaster Deluxe has same specifications as Model 348, except for adjustable choke device, 26″ barrel; recoil pad. Introduced in 1953; dropped, 1955. Used value, $51 to $56.

HARRINGTON & RICHARDSON Model 351: advertised as the Huntsman model; bolt-action; takedown; 12, 16 gauges; 26″ barrel; Harrington & Richardson variable choke; push-button safety; 2-rd. tube magazine; unchecker-ed American hardwood Monte Carlo stock; recoil pad. Introduced in 1956; dropped, 1958. Used value, $51 to $56.

Model 400

Model 402

HARRINGTON & RICHARDSON Model 400: pump action; hammerless; 12, 16, 20 gauges; 28" full choke barrel only; recoil pad on 12, 16-ga. models; uncheckered pistol-grip stock; 5-rd. tube magazine; grooved slide handle. Introduced in 1955; dropped, 1967. Used value, $101 to $112.

Model 401 has the same specifications as Model 400 except for addition of Harrington & Richardson variable choke. Introduced in 1956; dropped, 1963. Used value, $112 to $178.

Model 402 has same general design as Model 400, but is only in .410 gauge. Introduced in 1959; dropped, 1963. Used value, $112 to $178.

Model 403

HARRINGTON & RICHARDSON Model 403: autoloader; takedown; .410 only; 26" barrel; full choke; 4-rd. tube magazine; uncheckered walnut pistol-grip stock, forearm. Made only in 1964. Used value, $146 to $157.

HARRINGTON & RICHARDSON Model 404: double barrel; box-lock action; 12, 20, .410 gauges; in 12-ga., 28" modified/full barrel; 20-ga., 26" modified/improved; .410, 25" full/full; double triggers; plain extractors; checkered hardwood pistol-grip stock, forearm. Made to H&R specifications in Brazil. Introduced in 1968; dropped, 1972. Used value, $168 to $174.

Model 404C has same specifications as Model 404 except for Monte Carlo stock. Used value, $174 to $179.50

Model 442

Model 440

HARRINGTON & RICHARDSON Model 440: pump action; hammerless; 12, 16, 20 gauges; side ejection; 24", 26", 28" barrels; standard chokes; uncheckered American walnut pistol-grip stock, forearm; 4-rd. clip magazine; recoil pad. Introduced in 1972; dropped, 1975. Used value, $101 to $112.

Model 442 has same specifications as Model 440 except for hand-checkered pistol grip, forearm and full length vent rib. Used value, $112 to $123.50.

HARRINGTON & RICHARDSON Harrich No. 1: single barrel; 12-ga. only; 32", 34" barrels; Anson & Deeley-type locking system; Kersten top locks, double under-locking lugs; full length vent rib; hand-engraved sidelocks; select American walnut pistol-grip stock, forearm; hand-checkered; recoil pad. Introduced in 1973; dropped, 1976. Used value, $1512 to $1568.

HIGH STANDARD

Supermatic Field 20

HIGH STANDARD Supermatic Field Model: autoloader; 12-ga. gas-operated; 26" improved, 28" modified or full, 30" full barrels; 4-rd. magazine; uncheckered American walnut pistol-grip stock, forearm. Introduced in 1960; dropped, 1966. Used value, $121 to $126.

Field model 20-ga. has same general design as 12-ga. but chambered for 3" magnum shell; 3-rd. magazine; 26" improved, 28" modified or full barrels; uncheckered pistol-grip stock, forearm. Introduced in 1963; dropped, 1966. Used value, $121 to $126.

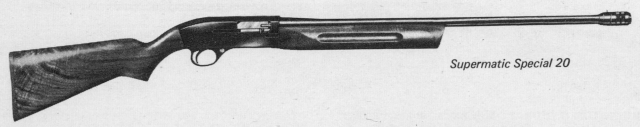

Supermatic Special 20

HIGH STANDARD Supermatic Special: autoloader; 12-ga.; has the same specifications as 12-ga. Field model, except for 27" barrel, adjustable choke. Introduced in 1960; dropped, 1966. Used value, $125 to $130.

Special 20-ga. model has same specifications as 20-ga. Field Grade, except for 27" barrel, adjustable choke. Introduced in 1963; dropped, 1966. Used value, $131 to $136.

Supermatic Deluxe Rib 20

HIGH STANDARD Supermatic Deluxe Rib Model: autoloader; 12-ga.; has same specifications as 12-ga. Field model, except for vent rib; checkered stock, forearm; 28" modified or full barrel, 30" full. Introduced in 1961; dropped, 1966. Used value, $140 to $145.

Deluxe Rib 20-ga. model has same specifications as 20-ga. Field model, except for 28" modified or full barrel; vent rib; checkered pistol-grip stock, forearm. Introduced in 1963; dropped, 1966. Used value, $147 to $152.50.

Supermatic Trophy 20

HIGH STANDARD Supermatic Trophy Model: autoloader; 12-ga.; has same specifications as Deluxe Rib 12-ga. model, except for 27" vent rib barrel, adjustable choke. Introduced in 1961; dropped, 1966. Used value, $157.50 to $163.

Trophy 20-ga. has the same specifications as the Deluxe Rib 20, except for 27" vent rib barrel, adjustable choke. Introduced in 1963; dropped, 1966. Used value, $157.50 to $168.

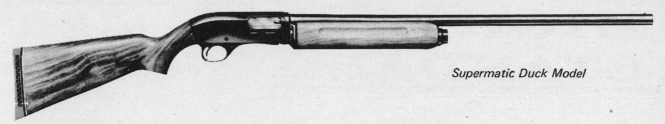

Supermatic Duck Model

HIGH STANDARD Supermatic Duck Model: autoloader; 12-ga. magnum only; has same general specifications as 12-ga. Field model, except for 30" full choke barrel, recoil pad. Introduced in 1961; dropped, 1966. Used value,

$131.50 to $136.50.

Duck Rib 12 magnum has the same specifications as the Duck 12 magnum, except for vent rib, checkered stock and forearm. Introduced in 1961; dropped, 1966. Used value, $147 to $157.50.

HIGH STANDARD Supermatic Skeet: autoloader; 12-ga.; 26" vent rib barrel; skeet choke; other specifications are the same as Deluxe Rib 12 model. Introduced in 1962; drop-

ped, 1966. Used value, $140 to $150.

Skeet 20-ga. has same specifications as Deluxe Rib 20 model, except for skeet choke, 26" vent rib barrel. Introduced in 1964; dropped, 1966. Used value, $147 to $157.

HIGH STANDARD Supermatic Trap: autoloader; 12-ga.; 30" vent rib; full choke only; trap stock; recoil pad. Other

specifications the same as Deluxe Rib 12 model. Introduced in 1962; dropped, 1966. Used value, $147 to $157.50.

Flite-King Field 20

HIGH STANDARD Flite-King Field Model: slide action; 12-ga.; hammerless; 26" improved cylinder, 28" modified or full, 30" full barrel; 5-rd. magazine; uncheckered walnut pistol-grip stock, grooved slide handle. Introduced in 1960; dropped, 1966. Used value, $79 to $84.

Field model 20-ga. is chambered for 3" magnum shell; 4-rd. magazine; other specifications, including barrel lengths, chokes are the same as 12-ga. version. Introduced in 1961; dropped, 1966. Used value, $79 to $84.

Flite-King Special 20

HIGH STANDARD Flite-King Special: slide action; 12-ga.; has the same specifications as Field version, except for 27" barrel, adjustable choke. Introduced in 1960; dropped,

1966. Used value, $94.50 to $100.

Special 20-ga. has same specifications as Field 20, except for 27" barrel, adjustable choke. Introduced in 1961; dropped, 1966. Used value, $94.50 to $100.

Flite-King Deluxe Rib 12

HIGH STANDARD Flight-King Deluxe Rib: slide action; 12-ga.; has the same specifications as Field 12 Flite-King except for 28'' full or modified, 30'' full choke barrel; vent rib; checkered walnut stock, slide handle. Introduced in 1961; dropped, 1966. Used value, $105 to $115.50.

Deluxe Rib 20-ga. has same specifications as Field 20-ga. model, except for 28'' full or modified barrel; vent rib; checkered stock, slide handle. Introduced in 1962; dropped, 1966. Used value, $105 to $115.50.

HIGH STANDARD Flite-King Trophy: slide action; 12-ga.; has the same specifications as Deluxe Rib 12-ga., except for 27'' vent rib barrel, adjustable choke. Introduced in 1960; dropped, 1966. Used value, $126 to $131.50.

Trophy 20-ga. has the same specifications as Field 20-ga., except for vent rib; 28'' modified or full barrel, checkered stock, slide handle. Introduced in 1962; dropped, 1966. Used value, $126 to $131.50.

HIGH STANDARD Flite-King Skeet: slide action, 12-ga.; same specifications as 12-ga. Deluxe Rib except for 26''

skeet-choked barrel, vent rib. Introduced in 1962; dropped, 1966. Used value, $121 to $126.

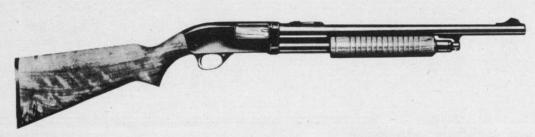

HIGH STANDARD Flite-King Brush Gun: slide action; 12-ga.; has same specifications as Field model except for

18'' or 20'' cylinder bore barrel; rifle sights. Introduced in 1962. dropped, 1964. Used value $100 to $105.

HIGH STANDARD Flite-King Trap: slide action; 12-ga.; has the same specifications as Deluxe Rib 12-ga. except for

30'' barrel; full choke; vent rib; trap stock; recoil pad. Introduced in 1962; dropped, 1966. Used value, $126 to $131.50.

HIGH STANDARD Flite-King 16 Series: slide action; 16-ga.; has same general specifications as various configurations of Flite-King 12-ga., but not available in

Brush, Skeet or Trap models, nor in 30'' barrel lengths. Introduced in 1961; dropped, 1965. Used values, Field, $75 to $84; Special, $100 to $105; Deluxe Rib, $105 to $115.50; Trophy, $121 to $126.

HIGH STANDARD Flite-King 410 Series: slide action; 410-ga.; has same specifications as Flite-King 20-ga., but not available in Special and Trophy grades; 26'' full choke

barrel only. Introduced in 1962; dropped, 1966. Used values, Field, $79 to $84; Deluxe Rib, $105 to $115.50; Brush Gun, $94.50 to $100; Skeet, $115.50 to $126; Trap, $126 to $131.50.

Holland & Holland

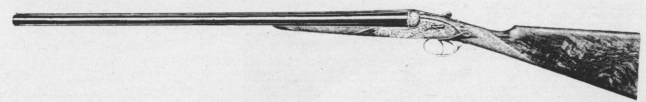

HOLLAND & HOLLAND Royal Model: side-by-side; hammerless; 12, 16, 20, 28 gauges; barrel lengths, chokes to customer's specifications; self-opening action; hand-detachable sidelocks; automatic ejectors; double triggers or single nonselective trigger; made in Game, Pigeon, Wildfowl configurations; hand-checkered straight-grip stock, forearm; English engraving. Introduced in 1885; still in production. Used values, double triggers, $4542.50 to $4657.50; single trigger, $4887.50 to $5002.50.

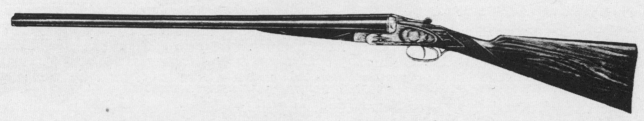

HOLLAND & HOLLAND Badminton Model: side-by-side; hammerless; 12, 16, 20, 28 gauges; has the same specifications as Royal Model side-by-side except action is not self-opening. Introduced in 1890; still in production. Used values, double triggers, $2415 to $2530; single trigger, $2760 to $2875.

HOLLAND & HOLLAND Model Deluxe: side-by-side; hammerless; 12, 16, 20, 28 gauges; barrel lengths and chokes to customer's specifications; self-opening action; hand-detachable sidelocks; has the same general specifications as Royal Model, but with much more ornate engraving. Introduced in 1900; still in production. Used values, double triggers, $4887.50 to $5060; single trigger, $5462.50 to $5635.

HOLLAND & HOLLAND Royal Over/Under: hammerless; hand-detachable sidelocks; 12-ga. only; barrel lengths, chokes to customer's specifications; automatic ejectors; double triggers or single trigger; made in Game, Pigeon, Wildfowl configurations; hand-checkered European walnut straight-grip stock, forearm. Introduced in 1925; dropped, 1950. Used values, double triggers, $6037.50 to $6267.50; single trigger, $6612.50 to $6842.50.

New Royal Model over/under has the same specifications as original model except for narrower, improved action. Introduced in 1951; dropped, 1965. Used values, double triggers, $7762 to $7935; single trigger, $8337 to $8510.

HOLLAND & HOLLAND Dominion Model: side-by-side; hammerless; sidelock; 12, 16, 20 gauges; 25", 28", 30" barrels; choked to customer's specifications; double triggers; automatic ejectors; hand-checkered European walnut straight-grip stock, forearm. Introduced in 1935; dropped, 1965. Used value, $1322.50 to $1437.50.

HOLLAND & HOLLAND Riviera Model: side-by-side; hammerless; designed as pigeon gun; has the same specifications as Badminton Model except for double triggers, two sets of interchangeable barrels. Introduced in 1945; still in production. Used value, $3852.50 to $4025.

ithacagun

Hammerless Double Field Grade

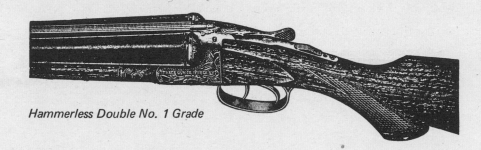

Hammerless Double No. 1 Grade

Hammerless Double No. 2 Grade

Hammerless Double No. 3 Grade

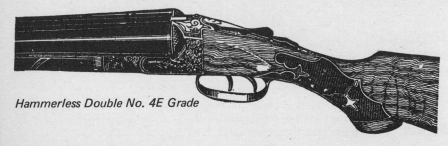

Hammerless Double No. 4E Grade

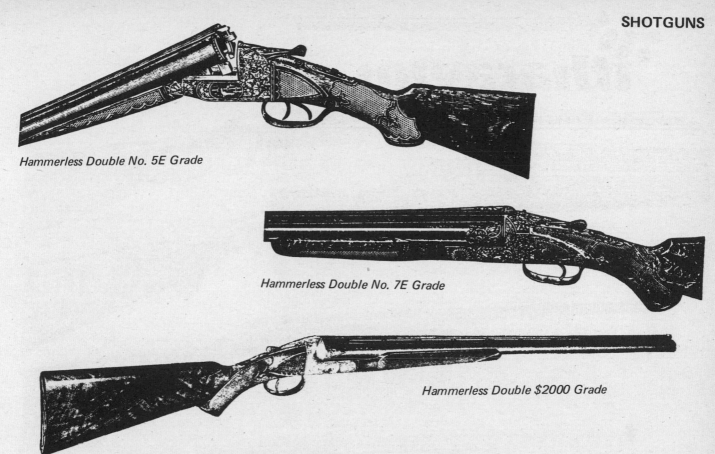

Hammerless Double No. 5E Grade

Hammerless Double No. 7E Grade

Hammerless Double $2000 Grade

ITHACA Hammerless Double Field Grade: side-by-side double barrel; box-lock action; 12, 16, 20, 28, .410 gauges; 26", 28", 30", 32" barrels; any standard choke combination; top-lever breaking; hand-checkered American walnut pistol-grip stock, forearm; pistol-grip cap; various options at additional cost. Introduced with rotary bolt in 1926; dropped, 1948. Used values, standard model, $360 to $384; with automatic ejectors, add $120; with beavertail forearm, add $120; with vent rib, add $180; for 10-ga. magnum, 12-ga. magnum, add $120.

Hammerless Double No. 2 Grade has same general specifications as Field Grade with addition of black walnut stock, forearm, engraving. Various options at added cost. Introduced in 1926; dropped, 1948. Used values, standard version, $420 to $450; with auto ejectors, add $120; with beavertail forearm, add $120; with vent rib, add $180; for 10-ga. magnum, 12-ga. magnum, add $120.

Hammerless Double No. 4 Grade has same basic design as Field Grade, but with many custom facets; double triggers are standard; hand engraved with scroll, line engraving; game scenes on frame, top lever, forearm iron, trigger guard; various options at added cost. Introduced in 1926; dropped, 1948. Used values, standard version, $840 to $900; with single selective trigger, add $120; beavertail forearm, add $120; vent rib, add $180; 10, 12-ga. magnums at no added cost.

Hammerless Double No. 5 Grade has gold nameplate inset in stock; English pheasant inlaid in gold on left side, woodcock on right; American eagle is engraved on bottom; engraved leaf, flower background; has selective single trigger, beavertail forearm; vent rib extra. Introduced in 1926; dropped, 1948. Used values, $1800 to $1860; with vent rib, add $180; no added cost for 10, 12-ga. magnums.

Hammerless Double No. 7 Grade has select walnut stock, hand-fitted action, elaborately checkered wood; beavertail forearm with ebony tip; matted vent rib; profusely engraved receiver with oak leaf, acorn design; inlaid designs in green and yellow gold, silver; gold nameplate inset in stock; single selective trigger is triple gold-plated, hand checkered; automatic ejectors. Introduced in 1926; dropped; 1948. Used value, $3600 to $3780.

Hammerless Double $2000 Grade has same specifications as other grades, but is inlaid with gold in elaborate designs; selective single trigger, vent rib, beavertail forearm. Prior to World War II, was listed as $1000 Grade. Introduced in 1926; dropped, 1948. Used value $5100 to $5400.

One Barrel Trap 4E Grade

ITHACA One Barrel Trap Gun: single-shot, hammerless; box-lock action; 12-ga. only; 30", 32", 34" barrels; vent rib; hand-checkered American walnut pistol-grip stock, forearm; recoil pad; made in four grades, differing only in quality of workmanship, grade of wood, amount of engraving, checkering. $5000 Grade was designated as $1000 model prior to World War II. Introduced in 1922; still in production. Used values, No. 4-E, $2100 to $2220; No. 5-E, $2880 to $3000; No. 7-E, $3480 to $3600; $5000 Grade, $4200 to $4320.

SHOTGUNS

ITHACA Single-Barrel Victory Model: single-shot, hammerless; box-lock action; 12-ga. only; 34" barrel; has same general specifications as other One Barrel models, but less extensive engraving, checkering, lower grade of wood. Introduced in 1922; dropped about 1938. Used value, $784 to $840.

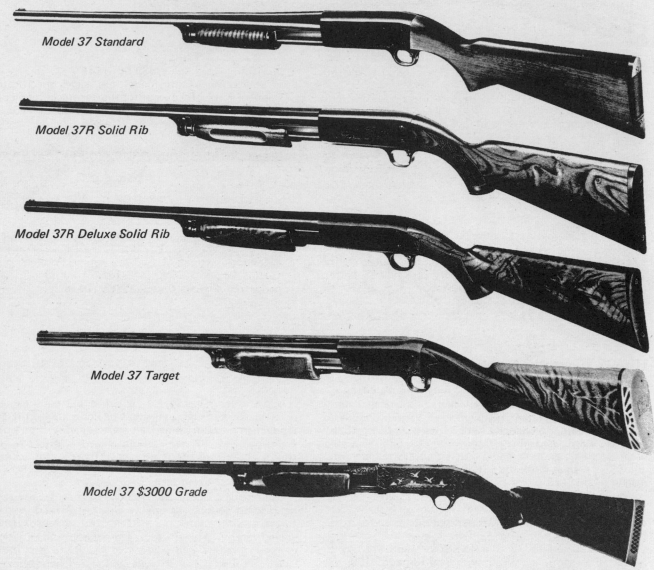

Model 37 Standard

Model 37R Solid Rib

Model 37R Deluxe Solid Rib

Model 37 Target

Model 37 $3000 Grade

ITHACA Model 37: slide-action repeater; hammerless; takedown; 12, 16, 20 gauges; 26", 28", 30" barrels; 4-rd. tube magazine; hand-checkered American walnut pistol-grip stock, slide handle, or uncheckered stock, grooved slide handle. Introduced in 1937; still in production. Used values, with checkered pistol grip, slide handle, $129 to $140; with plain stock, grooved slide handle, $106 to $123.

Model 37R has the same general specifications as standard Model 37 except for raised solid rib. Introduced in 1937; dropped, 1967. Used values, with checkered pistol grip, slide handle, $146 to $157; uncheckered stock, grooved slide handle, $118 to $123.50.

Model 37S Skeet Grade has same general specifications as standard model, except for vent rib, extension slide handle. Introduced in 1937; dropped, 1955. Used value, $252 to $269.

Model 37T Trap Grade has same general specifications as Model 37S except for straight trap stock of selected walnut, recoil pad. Introduced in 1937; dropped, 1955. Used value, $297 to $308.

Model 37T Target Grade replaced Model 37S Skeet Grade and Model 37T Trap Grade. Has same general specifications as standard Model 37 except for hand-checkered stock, slide handle of fancy walnut; choice of skeet or trap stock; vent rib. Introduced in 1955; dropped, 1961. Used value, $280 to $297.

Model 37 $3000 Grade was listed as $1000 Grade prior to World War II. Has same basic design as standard Model 37 but is custom-built, with gold-inlaid engraving; hand-finished parts; hand-checkered pistol-grip stock, slide handle of select figured walnut; recoil pad. Introduced in 1937; dropped, 1967. Used value, $3360 to $3528.

Model 37R Deluxe has same general specifications as standard Model 37R except for hand-checkered fancy walnut stock, slide handle. Introduced in 1955; dropped, 1961. Used value, $174 to $185.

Model 37 Deerslayer has same specifications as standard Model 37 except for 20" or 26" barrel bored for rifled slugs; open rifle-type rear sight, ramp front. Introduced in 1969; still in production. Used value, $146 to $157.

Model 66

ITHACA Model 66 Supersingle: lever-action single-shot; manually cocked hammer; 12, 20, .410 gauges; 30" full choke barrel or 28" full or modified in 12-ga., 28" full or modified in 20-ga., 26" full in .410. Checkered straight stock, uncheckered forearm. Introduced in 1963; still in

production. Used value, $39.50 to $45.

Model 66 Youth Model has same specifications as standard Model 66 except for shorter stock, recoil pad, 25" barrel; 20, .410 gauges only. Introduced in 1965; still in production. Used value, $39.50 to $45.

ITHACA-SKB Model 100: side-by-side, double barrel; box-lock action; 12, 20 gauges; in 12-ga., 30" full/full barrels, 28", full/modified, 26", improved/modified; in 20-ga., 25"

improved/modified only; single selective trigger; plain extractors; automatic safety; hand-checkered pistol-grip stock, forearm. Made in Japan. Introduced in 1967; dropped, 1976. Used value, $258 to $264.

Model 200E Standard

ITHACA-SKB Model 200E: side-by-side, double barrel; box-lock action; has the same general specifications as Model 100 except for automatic selective ejectors, engraved, silver-plated frame, gold-plated nameplate, trigger; beavertail forearm. Introduced in 1967.

Used value, $347.50 to $364.

Model 200E Skeet Grade has the same specifications as standard model except for 25" barrel in 12-ga., 25" in 20-ga.; skeet/skeet; nonautomatic safety; recoil pad. Introduced in 1967; dropped, 1976. Used value, $370 to $381.

Model 500 Standard

ITHACA-SKB Model 500: over/under; hammerless; top lever, box-lock action; 12, 20 gauges; in 12-ga., 25" barrels have improved/modified choke combo, 28", improved/modified or modified/full, 30", modified/full; in 20-ga., 26" barrels have improved/modified, 28", modified/full;

gold-plated single selective trigger; automatic ejectors, nonautomatic safety; chrome-lined barrels, action; Raybar front sight; scroll-engraved border on receiver; hand-checkered walnut pistol-grip stock, forearm; pistol-grip cap; fluted comb. Introduced in 1967; dropped, 1976. Used value, $330 to $342.

Model 500 Magnum has same specifications as standard Model 600 except for magnum chambering. Used value, $336 to $353.

Model 600 Skeet

ITHACA-SKB Model 600 Trap Grade: over/under; hammerless; box-lock action; 12-ga. only; 30", 32" barrels full/full or full/improved; straight or Monte Carlo stock; recoil pad;

other specifications are the same as those of Model 500. Introduced in 1967; dropped, 1976. Used value, $414 to $431.

Model 600 Skeet Grade has the same specifications as Model 500 except for 26", 28" skeet/skeet barrels, recoil pad. Introduced in 1967; dropped, 1976. Used value, $414 to $431.

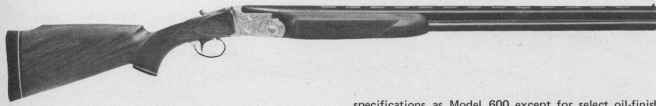

ITHACA-SKB Model 700: over/under; hammerless; box-lock action; in both skeet, trap styles; has the same specifications as Model 600 except for select oil-finished walnut stock, heavily engraved receiver. Introduced in 1967; dropped, 1976. Used value, $504 to $521.

ITHACA MX-8: over/under trap model; box-lock action; 12-ga.; 30″, 32″ barrels bored for international claybird competition; single nonselective trigger; interchangeable trigger/hammer groups; hand-checkered European walnut pistol-grip stock, forearm; oil or lacquer wood finish; vent rib. Introduced in 1968; still in production. Used value, $1792 to $1848.

ITHACA Mirage: over/under; box-lock action; 12-ga.; 32″, 30″, 28″ barrels; extra-full/modified, skeet/skeet boring; interchangeable hammer-trigger groups; single selective trigger; hand-checkered walnut pistol-grip stock, schnabel forearm; recoil pad. Introduced in 1968; still in production. Used value, $1792 to $1848.

Competition 1 Trap

ITHACA Competition I: over/under trap gun; box-lock action; 12-ga; 30″, 32″ barrels; interchangeable hammer/trigger group; single nonselective trigger; improved/modified choke combo; vent rib; standard or Monte Carlo stock design; hand-checkered American walnut pistol-grip stock, forearm. Introduced in 1968; dropped, 1974. Used value, $952 to $980.

Competition I Skeet model has same general specifications as trap gun except for skeet stock, 26¾″ skeet/skeet barrels; leather-faced recoil pad. Introduced in 1968; dropped, 1974. Used value, $952 to $980.

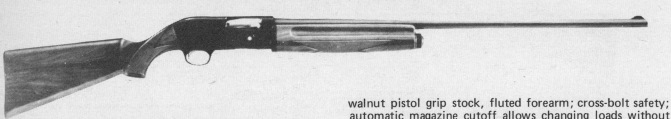

ITHACA Model 300: autoloader; recoil-operated; takedown; 12-ga. only; 30″ full choke barrel, 28″ full or modified, 26″ improved cylinder; checkered American walnut pistol grip stock, fluted forearm; cross-bolt safety; automatic magazine cutoff allows changing loads without unloading magazine; vent rib at additional cost. Introduced in 1969; dropped, 1973. Used values, plain barrel, $129 to $134.50; vent rib, $146 to $151.50.

Model 900 Deluxe Standard

ITHACA Model 900 Deluxe: autoloader; recoil-operated; takedown; 12, 20 gauges; 30″ full choke barrel in 12-ga. only; 28″ full or modified, 25″ improved cylinder; vent rib; hand-checkered American walnut pistol grip stock, forearm; white spacers on grip cap, butt plate; interchangeable barrels; cross-bolt safety; gold-filled engraving on receiver, gold-plated trigger, nameplate inlaid in stock. Introduced in 1969; dropped, 1973. Used value, $179.50 to $190.

Model 900 Deluxe slug gun has same specifications as standard model except for 24″ barrel, rifle sights. Introduced in 1969; dropped, 1973. Used value, $146 to $157.

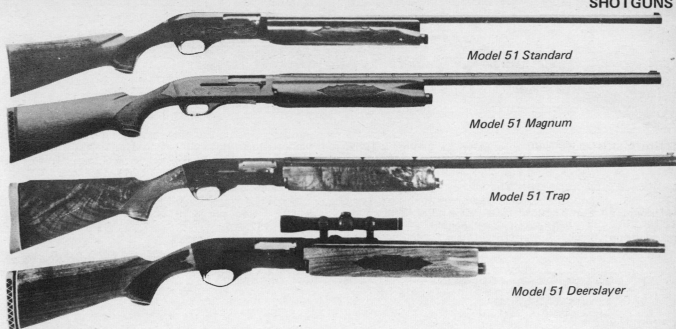

Model 51 Standard

Model 51 Magnum

Model 51 Trap

Model 51 Deerslayer

ITHACA Model 51: autoloader; gas-operated; takedown; 12-ga.; 30″ full choke barrel, 28″ full, modified or skeet, 26″ improved or skeet; Raybar front sight; hand-checkered American walnut pistol-grip stock; white spacer on pistol grip; 3-rd. tube magazine; reversible safety; engraved receiver; vent rib at added cost. Introduced in 1970; still in production. Used values, plain barrel, $207.50 to $218.50; vent rib, $246.50 to $253.50.

Model 51 magnum has same specifications as standard model except for 3″ chambers. Used value, $246 to $258.

Model 51 Trap has same specifications as standard model except for 30″, 32″ barrel, trap stock, trap recoil pad, vent rib. Used value, $291.50 to $302.50.

Model 51 Skeet has same specifications as standard model except for skeet stock, skeet recoil pad, vent rib. Used value, $263.50 to $274.50.

Model 51 Deerslayer is in 12, 20 gauge; 24″ special bore barrel for slugs; has Raybar front sight, open adjustable rear; sight base grooved for scope. Used value, $269 to $280.

Model 51 20-ga. has same general design as standard Model 51; 26″ improved cylinder or skeet barrel; 28″ full or modified; vent rib; magnum chambering at extra cost. Used values, standard model, $207 to $218; with vent rib, $235 to $241; standard magnum, $230 to $235; magnum with vent rib, $246 to $252; skeet version, $252 to $263.

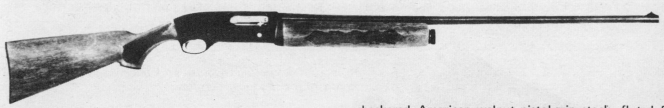

ITHACA Model XL 300: autoloader; gas-operated; 12, 20 gauges; in 12-ga., 30″ full choke barrel, 28″ full or modified, 26″ improved cylinder; in 20-ga., 30″ full or modified, 28″ full or modified, 26″ improved or skeet; checkered American walnut pistol-grip stock, fluted forearm; self-compensating gas system; reversible safety; vent rib at additional cost. Introduced in 1973; dropped, 1976. Used values, plain barrel, $162 to $168; vent rib, $179 to $185.

ITHACA-SKB Model 680 English: over/under; hammerless; box-lock action; 12, 20 gauges; 26″, 28″ barrels, full/modified or modified/improved; single selective trigger; chrome-lined barrels, black chromed exterior surfaces; automatic selective ejectors; Bradley sights; vent rib; straight-grip stock; wraparound checkering. Introduced in 1973; dropped, 1976. Used value, $426 to $442.

Model XL 900 Standard

ITHACA Model XL 900: autoloader; gas-operated; 12, 20 gauges; 5-rd. tube magazine; in 12-ga., barrels are 30" full choke, 28" full or modified, 26" improved cylinder; in 20-ga., 28" full or modified, 26" improved; trap version has 30" full or improved choke; skeet version, 26" skeet; Bradley-type front sight on target grade guns, Raybar front sight on vent rib field grades; uncheckered walnut-finished stock; self-compensating gas system; reversible safety; action release button. Introduced in 1973; still in production. Used values, vent rib, $224 to $235.50; skeet grade, $241 to $252; trap grade (12-ga. only), $241 to $252.

Model XL 900 slug gun has same specifications as standard Model XL 900 except for 24" slug barrel, rifle sights. Introduced in 1973; still in production. Used value, $213 to $218.50.

ITHACA-SKB Model 880 Crown Grade: over/under; box-lock action; side plates; 12, 20 gauges; 32" full/improved barrel, 30" full/improved, 26" skeet/skeet in 12-ga.; 28" skeet/skeet in 20-ga.; Bradley-type front sight; trap or skeet stock; hand-checkered fancy French walnut pistol-grip stock, forearm; hand-honed action; engraved receiver; gold-inlaid crown on bottom of frame. Introduced in 1973; dropped, 1976. Used value, $924 to $980.

ITHACA Light Game Model: over/under; box-lock action; 12-ga.; 27-5/8" barrel; modified/full, improved/full, improved/modified; interchangeable hammer/trigger group; single nonselective trigger; hand-checkered French walnut pistol-grip stock, schnabel forearm; case-hardened frame; hand engraved. Introduced in 1971; dropped, 1974. Used value, $728 to $756.

High quality engraving and inlay work has been an outstanding feature of Ithaca's top-grade guns.

IVER JOHNSON

IVER JOHNSON Champion Grade: single barrel; hammer gun; 12, 16, 20, .410 gauges; 26", 28", 30", 32" barrels; full choke only; top-lever breaking; automatic ejector; uncheckered American walnut pistol-grip stock, forearm; bead front sight. Introduced in 1909; still in production. Used value, $50.50 to $56.

IVER JOHNSON Matted Rib Grade: single barrel; hammer gun; 12, 16, 20, .410 gauges; has the same general specifications as Champion Grade, except for solid matted rib, hand-checkered pistol grip, forearm. Introduced about 1910; dropped, 1948. Used value, $66 to $72.

IVER JOHNSON Special Trap Model: single barrel; hammer gun; 12-ga. only; 32" barrel only; other specifications are the same as those of Matted Rib Grade. Introduced about 1912; dropped, 1949. Used value, $280 to $291.50.

IVER JOHNSON Hercules Grade: double barrel; box-lock action; hammerless; 12, 16, 20, .410 gauges; 26", 28", 30", 32" barrels; full/full modified/full chokes; double triggers; single nonselective or selective trigger at extra cost; automatic ejectors at additional cost; hand-checkered straight or pistol-grip stock, forearm. Introduced about 1920; dropped, 1948. Used values, double trigger, plain extractor model, $196 to $207; double triggers, auto ejectors, $246 to $263; plain extractors, nonselective trigger, $252 to $263; nonselective trigger, auto ejectors, $302 to $319; selective single trigger, plain extractors, $280 to $297; selective single trigger, auto ejectors, $330 to $358.

IVER JOHNSON Skeeter Model: double barrel; box-lock action; hammerless; 12, 16, 20, 28, .410 gauges; 26" or 28" barrels; beavertail forearm. Other specifications the same as Hercules grade, with the same options. Introduced about 1920; dropped, 1949. Used values, double triggers, plain extractors, $364 to $392; double triggers, auto ejectors, $420 to $448; nonselective trigger, auto ejectors, $476 to $504; selective single trigger, plain extractors, $448 to $476; selective trigger, auto ejectors, $504 to $532.

IVER JOHNSON Super Trap Model: double barrel; hammerless; box-lock action; 12-ga. only; 32" barrel, full choke only; vent rib; hand-checkered pistol-grip stock, beavertail forearm; recoil pad. Introduced about 1924; dropped, 1949. Used values, double triggers, $504 to $532; nonselective single trigger, $549 to $582.50; single selective trigger, $616 to $644.

KRIEGHOFF

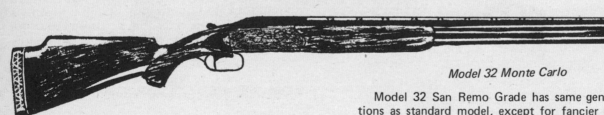

Model 32 Monte Carlo

Model 32 San Remo Grade has same general specifications as standard model, except for fancier walnut, relief engraving. Used value, $1008 to $1120.

Model 32 Monte Carlo Grade carries extra-fancy wood, silver inlays, elaborate engraving, Monte Carlo stock. Basic specifications are same as those of standard Model 32. Used value, $2072 to $2240.

Model 32 Crown Grade has same general specifications as the Monte Carlo except that inlays are of gold. Used value, $3360 to $3584.

KRIEGHOFF Model 32: over/under; near-duplicate of pre-WWII Remington Model 32; box-lock action; 12,20,28,.410 gauges; 28", 30", 32", 34" barrels; any desired choke combo; three-way safety; selective trigger, ejectors; vent rib; hand-checkered walnut pistol-grip stock, beavertail forearm. Manufactured in West Germany. Introduced in 1948; still in production. Used value, $728 to $784.

KRIEGHOFF Single Barrel Trap: single-shot; box-lock action; 12-ga. only; 32" or 34" full choke barrel; thumb safety; vent rib; hand-checkered Monte Carlo pistol-grip stock of European walnut, grooved beavertail forearm. Available in five grades, price depending upon grade of wood, decoration. Manufactured in West Germany. Introduced in 1970; still in production. Used values, standard grade, $1007 to $1064; Sam Remo Grade, $1904 to $1960; Monte Carlo Grade, $4200 to $4368; Crown Grade, $4592 to $4760; Super Crown Grade, $5600 to $5880.

KRIEGHOFF Vandalia Trap: single-barrel or over/under; box-lock action; 12-ga. only; 30", 32", 34" barrels; three-way safety; selective single trigger; ejectors; vent rib; hand-checkered European walnut pistol-grip stock, beavertail forearm. Available at additional cost with silver, gold inlays, relief engraving, fancier wood. Manufactured in West Germany. Introduced in 1973; dropped, 1976. Used value for standard model, $1400 to $1456.

Marlin

MARLIN Model 42A: slide-action repeater; takedown; 12-ga. only; 26" cylinder bore, 28" modified, 30" or 32" full choke; visible hammer; 5-rd. magazine; uncheckered American walnut pistol-grip stock, grooved slide handle; bead front sight. Introduced in 1922; dropped, 1934. Used value, $96 to $102.

Marlin Model 43A

MARLIN Model 43A: slide-action repeater; hammerless; takedown; 12-ga. only; 26" cylinder bore, 28" modified, 30" or 32" full choke; 5-rd. magazine; uncheckered American walnut pistol-grip stock, grooved slide handle. Introduced in 1923; dropped in 1930. Used value, $114 to $120.

MARLIN Model 44A: slide-action repeater; hammerless; takedown; 20-ga. only; 25", 28" barrels, cylinder bore, modified, full choke; 4-rd. magazine; uncheckered American walnut pistol-grip stock, grooved slide handle. Introduced in 1923; dropped, 1935. Used value, $144 to $156.

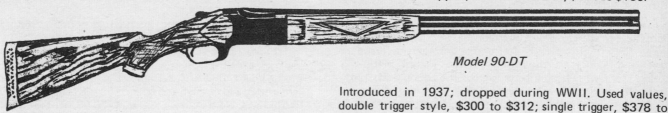

Model 90-DT

MARLIN Model 90: standard over/under; hammerless; box-lock action; 12, 16, 20, .410 gauges; 28", 30" barrels; improved/modified, modified/full choke combos; full-length rib between barrels; double triggers; single nonselective trigger at extra cost; hand-checkered American walnut pistol-grip stock, forearm; recoil pad; bead front sight.

Introduced in 1937; dropped during WWII. Used values, double trigger style, $300 to $312; single trigger, $378 to $390.

Model 90-DT is post-WWII version of Model 90 with double triggers, no rib between barrels, no recoil pad. Introduced in 1949; dropped, 1958. Used value, $300 to $312.

Model 90-ST is post-war single nonselective trigger version; no rib between barrels, no recoil pad. Introduced in 1949; dropped, 1958. Used value, $390 to $402.

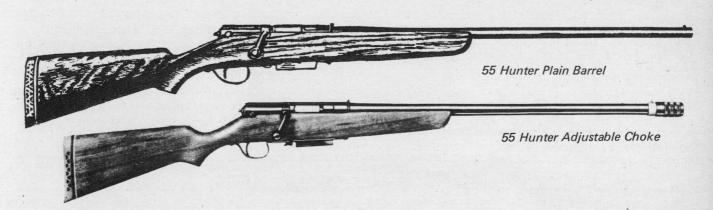

55 Hunter Plain Barrel

55 Hunter Adjustable Choke

MARLIN Model 55 Hunter: bolt-action; takedown; 12, 16, 20 gauges; 28" barrel in 12, 16 gauges, 26" in 20; full choke or with adjustable choke; uncheckered American walnut one-piece pistol-grip stock; 12-ga. has recoil pad. Introduced in 1950; dropped, 1965. Used values, plain barrel, $35 to $37.50; adjustable choke, $40 to $42.50. Model 55-G was marketed as Marlin-Glenfield model.

Has same specifications as Model 55, except for walnut-finished hardwood stock. Used values, plain barrel, $30 to $32.50; with adjustable choke, $35 to $38.

Model 55 Swamp Gun has same specifications as Model 55 Hunter except for 20½" barrel, chambered for 3" 12-ga. magnum shell; adjustable choke; sling swivels. Introduced in 1963; dropped, 1965. Used value, $45 to $50.

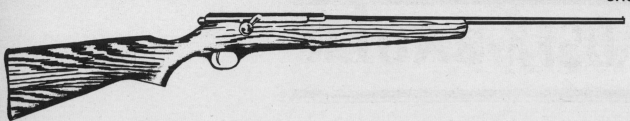

MARLIN Model 59 Olympic: single-shot, bolt-action; take-down; .410 only; 2½" or 3" shells; 24" barrel; full choke only; bead front sight; self-cocking bolt; automatic thumb safety; uncheckered one-piece walnut pistol-grip stock; also available with Junior stock with 12" length of pull. Introduced in 1960; dropped, 1962. Used value, $30 to $32.50.

Model 59, except for walnut-finished hardwood stock. Introduced in 1961; dropped, 1962. Used value, $27.50 to $30.

MARLIN-Glenfield Model 60-G: single-shot, bolt-action; takedown; .410 only; has exactly the same specifications as

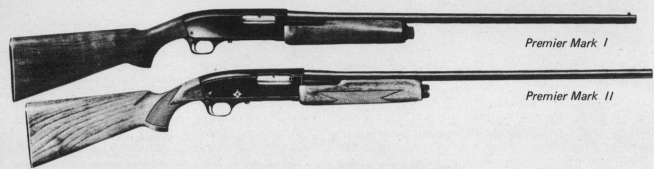

Premier Mark I

Premier Mark II

MARLIN Premier Mark I: slide-action repeater; takedown; hammerless; 12-ga. only; 3-rd. magazine; 26" improved or skeet, 28" modified, 30" full choke barrels; side ejection; cross-bolt safety; uncheckered French walnut pistol-grip stock, forearm; bead front sight. Introduced in 1961; dropped, 1963. Used value, $94.50 to $100.

Premier Mark II has the same specifications as Premier Mark I, except for scroll-engraved receiver, checkered pistol grip, forearm. Introduced in 1961; dropped, 1963. Used value, $115.50 to $126.

Premier Mark IV has the same specifications as Premier Mark II, except for completely engraved receiver, engraved trigger guard, finer checkering, better wood, pistol-grip cap, vent rib at added cost. Introduced in 1961; dropped, 1963. Used values, plain barrel, $168 to $178.50; vent rib, $210 to $220.50.

MARLIN Goose Gun: bolt-action repeater; takedown; 12-ga. only; 36" barrel; full choke only; 2-rd. detachable clip magazine; thumb safety; uncheckered one-piece walnut pistol-grip stock; recoil pad; sling swivels; leather carrying strap; double extractors; tapped for receiver sights. Introduced in 1964; still in production. Used value, $75 to $85.

MARLIN Model 50: bolt-action repeater; takedown; 12, 20 gauges; 28" barrel in 12-ga., 26" in 20-ga.; 12-ga. has recoil pad; other specifications are the same as Goose Gun, except 12-ga. was available with adjustable choke. Introduced in 1967; dropped, 1975. Used values, plain barrel, $65 to $70; with adjustable choke, $75 to $85.

Standard 120 Magnum

MARLIN Model 120 Magnum: slide action; hammerless; 12-ga.; 2¾" or 3" chamber, 26" improved cylinder barrel, 28" modified, 30" full choke; vent rib; checkered walnut pistol-grip stock, semi-beavertail forearm; slide release button; cross-bolt safety; interchangeable barrels; side ejec-tion. Introduced in 1974; still in production. Used value, $120 to $125.

Model 120 Trap has same basic specifications as 120 Magnum, except for hand-checkered Monte Carlo stock, full forearm; 30" full or modified trap choke. Introduced in 1974; still in production. Used value, $185 to $190.

MAUSER-BAUER

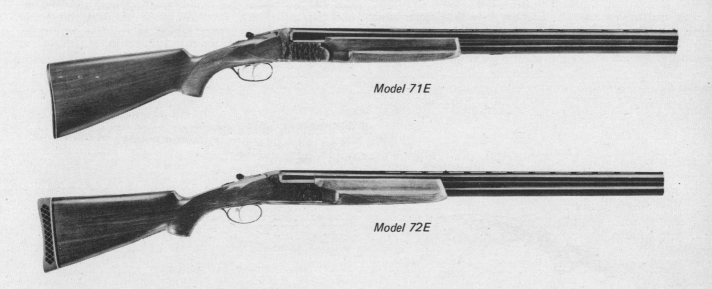

MAUSER-BAUER Model 620: over/under; Greener cross-bolt action; 12 ga.; 28" barrels, modified/full; improved/modified, skeet/skeet, 30", full/modified; single nonselective adjustable triggers; vent rib, automatic ejectors; selective or double triggers available at added cost; hand-checkered European walnut pistol-grip stock, beavertail forearm; recoil pad. Produced in Germany by Mauser. Introduced in 1972; dropped, 1974. Used values, standard model, $600 to $625; single-selective trigger, $675 to $700; double triggers; $675 to $700.

Model 71E

Model 72E

MAUSER-BAUER Model 71E: over/under field model; has the same general specifications as the Model 620 except for double triggers only; no recoil pad; 28" barrels, modified/full or improved/modified. Introduced in 1972; dropped, 1973. Used value, $225 to $240.

Model 72E has the same general specifications as Model 71E, except for wider rib, engraved receiver. Trap version has 30" trap/trap bored barrel; skeet has 28" full/modified. Introduced in 1972; dropped, 1973. Used value, $300 to $325.

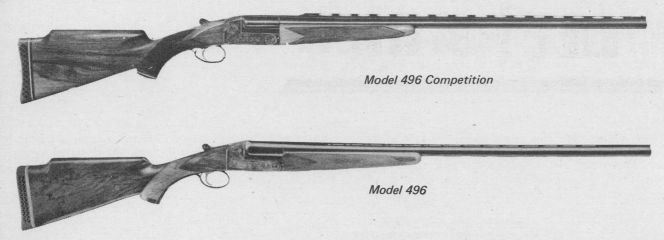

Model 496 Competition

Model 496

MAUSER-BAUER Model 496: single-barrel trap model; single-shot; Greener crossbolt box-lock action; 12 ga; 32″ modified, 34″ full choke barrels; double underlocking blocks; matted vent rib; color case-hardened action; scroll engraving; hand-checkered European walnut Monte Carlo stock, forearm; automatic ejector, auto safety; recoil pad.

Introduced in 1972; dropped, 1974. Used value, $320 to $345.

Model 496 Competition Grade has same general specifications as standard model except for high ramp rib; front, middle sight beads; hand finishing on wood and metal parts. Introduced in 1973; dropped, 1974. Used value, $450 to $475.

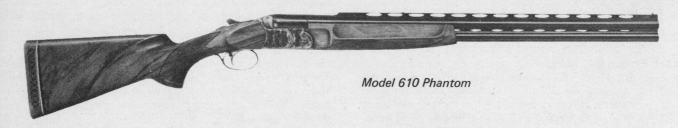

Model 610 Phantom

MAUSER-BAUER Model 610 Phantom: over/under; 12 ga.; 30″, 32″ barrels; standard choke combinations; raised rib; vent rib between barrels for heat reduction; color case-hardened action; coil springs throughout working parts; hand-checkered European walnut stock, forearm; recoil pad. Introduced in 1973; dropped, 1974. Used value, $575 to $600.

Model 610 Skeet version has same general specifications as standard Model 610 except has set of Purbaugh tubes to convert gun for all-gauge competition. Tubes convert to 20, 28, .410 gauges. Introduced in 1973; dropped, 1974. Used value, $800 to $825.

MAUSER-BAUER Model 580: advertised as St. Vincent model; side-by-side; side-lock Holland & Holland action; 12 ga.; 28″, 30″, 32″ barrels; standard choke combos; split sear levers; coil hammer springs; single or double triggers; scroll engraved receiver; hand-checkered European walnut straight stock, forearm. Introduced in 1973; dropped, 1974. Used value, $700 to $725.

MERKEL

MERKEL Model 100: over/under; hammerless; box-lock action; 12, 16, 20 gauges; standard barrel lengths, choke combos; Greener crossbolt safety; double triggers; plain extractors; plain barrel; ribbed barrel at added cost; hand-checkered European walnut stock, forearm; pistol-grip and cheekpiece or straight English type. Manufactured in Germany prior to World War II. Used values, plain barrel, $565 to $593.50; ribbed barrel, $593.50 to $621.50.

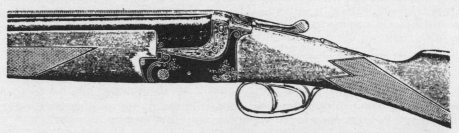

MERKEL Model 101: over/under; hammerless; box-lock action; has the same general specifications as Model 100 except for English engraving motif, standard ribbed barrel, separate extractors. Manufactured in Germany prior to World War II. Used value, $678 to $706.50.

Model 101E has the same specifications as Model 101 except for ejectors. Used value, $706.25 to $734.50.

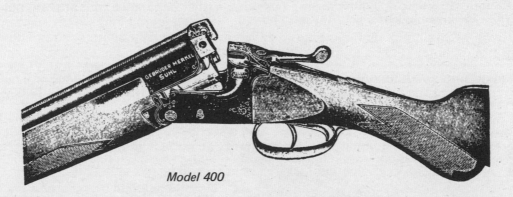

Model 400

MERKEL Model 400: over/under; hammerless; box-lock action; has the same general specifications as Model 101 except for Arabesque engraving on receiver, Kersten double crossbolt, separate extractors. Manufactured in Germany prior to World War II. Used value, $763 to $791.

Model 400E has the same specifications as Model 400 except for ejectors. Used value, $791 to $847.50.

MERKEL Model 401: over/under; hammerless; box-lock action; has the same general specifications as Model 400 except for finer overall workmanship, hunting scene engraving on receiver. Manufactured in Germany prior to World War II. Used value $904 to $932.50.

Model 401E has the same general specifications as Model 400 except for Merkel ejectors. Used value, $960 to $989.

MERKEL Model 200: over/under; hammerless; box-lock action; 12, 16, 20, 24, 28, 32 gauges; Kersten double crossbolt; scalloped frame; Arabesque engraving; separate extractors; double triggers; standard barrel lengths, choke combinations; ribbed barrels; hand-checkered European walnut stock, forearm; pistol-grip and cheekpiece or straight English style. Manufactured in Germany prior to World War II. Used value, $678 to $734.50.

Model 200E has the same general specifications as Model 200 except for ejectors; double, single or single selective trigger. Introduced prior to World War II; still in production; 24, 28, 32 gauges dropped during WW II. Currently imported by Champlin Firearms. Used values, double triggers, $621.50 to $650; single trigger, $650 to $678; single selective trigger, $706.50 to $734.50.

Model 201

MERKEL Model 201: over/under; hammerless; box-lock action; has the same general specifications as Model 200 except for better engraving, wood, checkering, overall quality. Manufactured in Germany prior to World War II. Used value, $847.50 to $876.

MERKEL Model 202: over/under; hammerless; box-lock action; has the same general specifications as Model 201 except for better engraving, dummy side plates, finer wood, checkering. Manufactured in Germany prior to World War

MERKEL Model 203: over/under; hammerless; hand-detachable side locks; 12, 16, 20 gauges; ribbed barrels in standard lengths, choke combos; Kersten double crossbolt; automatic ejectors; Arabesque or hunting scene engraving; hand-checkered European walnut stock, forearm; pistol-

MERKEL Model 204E: over/under; hammerless; 12, 16, 20 gauges; has the same general specifications as Model 203E

Model 201E has the same specifications as Model 201 except for ejectors; double, single or single selective trigger. Still in production. Currently imported by Champlin Firearms. Used values, double triggers, $734 to $763; single trigger, $734 to $763; single selective trigger, $791 to $819.

II. Used value, $960.50 to $1017.
Model 202E has the same specifications as Model 202 except for ejectors. Manufactured prior to World War II. Used value, $1130 to $1243.

grip, cheekpiece or straight English style. Introduced in Germany prior to World War II. Currently imported by Champlin Firearms. Used values, double triggers, $1356 to $1412.50; single trigger, $1356 to $1412.50; single selective trigger, $1525.50 to $1582.

except for fine English-style engraving, double triggers only, Merkel side locks. Manufactured in Germany prior to World War II. Used value, $2090.50 to $2203.50.

Model 300E

MERKEL Model 300: over/under; hammerless; Merkel-Anson box-lock; 12, 16, 20, 24, 28, 32 gauges; standard barrel lengths, choke combos; Kersten double crossbolt; two underlugs; scalloped frame; Arabesque or hunting scene engraving; separate extractors; ribbed barrels; hand-

MERKEL Model 301: over/under; hammerless; Merkel-Anson box-lock action; has the same general specifications as Model 300 except for better engraving, wood, checker-

checkered European walnut pistol-grip, cheekpiece or straight English style stock. Manufactured in Germany prior to World War II. Used value, $1102 to $1186.50.
Model 300E has the same general specifications as Model 300 except for automatic ejectors. Used value, $1186.50 to $1243.

ing. Manufactured in Germany prior to World War II. Used value, $1243 to $1299.50.
Model 301E has the same specifications as Model 301 except for automatic ejectors. Used value, $1356 to $1412.

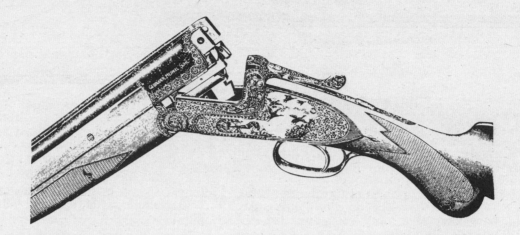

MERKEL Model 302: over/under; hammerless; has the same general specifications as Model 301E except for dummy side plates. Manufactured in Germany prior to World War II. Used value, $1469 to $1525.50.

MERKEL Model 303E: over/under; hammerless; Holland & Holland-type hand-detachable side locks; Kersten crossbolt, double underlugs, automatic ejectors. Has same general design specifications as Model 203E but is of better quality throughout. Introduced prior to World War II; still in production. Currently imported by Champlin Firearms. Used value, $2712 to $2881.50.

MERKEL Model 304E: over/under; hammerless; Holland & Holland-type hand-detachable side locks; has virtually the same specifications as 303E except for better workmanship and quality. Introduced in Germany prior to World War II. Still in production, but not imported at this time. Used value, $4350 to $4520.

MERKEL Model 130: side-by-side; hammerless; box-lock action; 12, 16, 20, 28, .410 gauges; standard barrel lengths, choke combos; Anson & Deeley-type action; side plates; double triggers; automatic ejectors; elaborate Arabesque or hunting scene engraving; hand-checkered European walnut stock, forearm; pistol-grip, cheekpiece or straight English style. Manufactured in Germany prior to World War II. Used value, $2260 to $2429.50.

MERKEL Model 127: side-by-side; hammerless; Holland & Holland-type action; hand-detachable side locks; 12, 16, 20, 28, .410 gauges; standard barrel lengths, choke combos; elaborately engraved with Arabesque or hunting scene; hand-checkered European walnut stock, forearm; pistol-grip, cheekpiece or straight English style. Manufactured in Germany prior to World War II. Used value, $4463.50 to $4689.50.

MERKEL Model 475: side-by-side; hammerless; side locks; 12, 16, 20 gauges; 3'' chamber available; all standard barrel lengths, choke combos; double hook bolting; Greener-type breech; double, single or single selective trigger; cocking indicators; English Arabesque engraving; hand-checkered European walnut stock, forearm; pistol-grip, cheekpiece or straight English style. Introduced prior to World War II; still in production. Currently imported by Champlin Firearms. Used values, double triggers, $621 to $650; single trigger, $621 to $650; single selective trigger, $734 to $763.

MOSSBERG Model 83D: bolt-action; takedown; .410-ga. only; 23" barrel; interchangeable modified, full choke tubes; 2-rd. fixed top loading magazine; unchecked one-piece pistol-grip stock; finger-grooved. Introduced in 1940; replaced in 1947 by Model 183D. Used value, $33 to $38.50.

MOSSBERG Model 85D: bolt-action; takedown; 20-ga. only; 25" barrel, with interchangeable choke tubes for full, modified, improved cylinder; 2-rd. detachable box magazine; unchecked one-piece finger-grooved pistol grip stock, black plastic butt plate. Introduced in 1940; replaced in 1947 by Model 185D. Used value, $33 to $38.

MOSSBERG Model 183D: bolt-action; takedown; .410-ga. only; 24" barrel; all other specifications are the same as Model 83D. Introduced in 1947; dropped, 1971. Used value, $33 to $38.50.

Model 183K has the same specifications as Model 183D, except for C-Lect-Choke instead of interchangeable tubes. Introduced in 1953; still in production. Used value, $47 to $52.50.

MOSSBERG Model 185D: bolt-action; takedown; 20-ga. only; has same specifications as Model 85D, except for 26" barrel, full, improved cylinder choke tubes. Introduced in 1947; dropped, 1971. Used value, $33 to $38.50.

Model 185K has the same specifications as Model 185D except for variable C-Lect-Choke replacing interchangeable tubes. Introduced in 1950; dropped, 1963. Used value, $38.50 to $44.

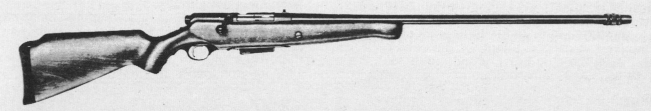

MOSSBERG Model 190D: bolt-action; takedown; 16-ga. only; 26" barrel; other specifications are identical to those of Model 185D, including full, improved cylinder choke tubes. Introduced in 1955; dropped, 1971. Used value, $33 to $38.50.

Model 190K has the same general specifications as Model 185K except for 16-ga. chambering. Introduced in 1956; dropped, 1963. Used value, $38.50 to $44.

MOSSBERG Model 195D: bolt-action; takedown; 12-ga. only; 26" barrel; interchangeable chokes; other specifications are the same as those of Model 185D. Introduced in 1955; dropped, 1971. Used value, $33 to $38.50.

Model 195K has the same general specifications as the Model 185K except is in 12-ga. only; C-Lect-Choke. Introduced in 1956; dropped, 1963. Used value, $38.50 to $44.

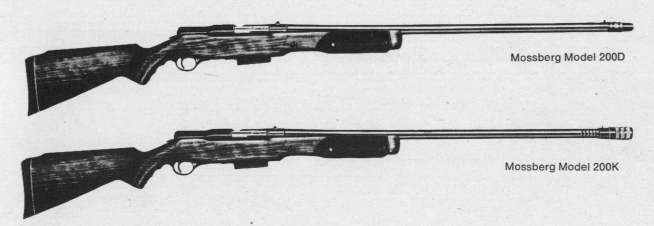

Mossberg Model 200D

Mossberg Model 200K

MOSSBERG Model 200D: slide action; 12-ga. only; 28" barrel; interchangeable choke tubes; 3-rd. detachable box magazine; uncheckered walnut-finish hardwood pistol-grip stock with grooved forearm; black nylon slide handle; recoil pad. Introduced in 1955; dropped, 1959. Used value, $44 to $49.50.

Model 200K has the same specifications as Model 200D except for substitution of C-Lect-Choke. Introduced in 1955; dropped, 1959. Used value, $49.50 to $55.

Mossberg Model 500 Field

Mossberg Model 500 Super

MOSSBERG Model 500 Field Grade: slide action; hammerless; takedown; 12, 16, 20 gauges; 24" Slugster barrel with rifle sights in 12-ga. only, 26" improved or with adjustable C-Lect-Choke; 28" modified/full; 30" full choke in 12-ga. only; 6-rd. tube magazine; 3-shot plug furnished; uncheckered American walnut pistol-grip stock; grooved slide handle; recoil pad. Introduced in 1961; still in production. Used values, standard barrel, $104.50 to $115.50; Slugster barrel, $110 to $121; C-Lect-Choke barrel, $110 to $121; heavy magnum barrel, $110 to $121.

Model 500 Super Grade has the same basic specifications as standard Model 500 except for checkered pistol grip, slide handle; vent rib barrel. Introduced in 1961; still in production. Used values, standard barrel, $126.50 to $132;

C-Lect-Choke, $132 to $137.50; heavy magnum barrel, $132 to $137.50.

Model 500E has the same general specifications as standard Model 500 but is chambered for .410 only; 26" barrel; full, modified, improved chokes; tube magazine holds 6 standard rds., 5 magnum rds.; uncheckered walnut pistol-grip stock, grooved forearm, fluted comb; recoil pad. Used values, standard barrel, $110 to $121; skeet barrel with vent rib, checkering, $165 to $176.

Model 500APR Pigeon Grade trap gun has the same specifications as standard Model 500 except for vent rib 30" barrel; full choke only; checkered walnut Monte Carlo stock, beavertail slide handle; recoil pad. Introduced in 1968; still in production. Used value, $126.50 to $132.

MOSSBERG Model 385K: bolt-action; takedown; 20-ga. only; 26" barrel; C-Lect-Choke; walnut-finished hardwood

Monte Carlo stock; 2-rd. detachable clip magazine; recoil pad. Introduced in 1963; still in production. Used value, $44 to $49.50.

MOSSBERG Model 390K: bolt-action; takedown; 16-ga. only; 28" barrel; other specifications are the same as those

of Model 385K. Introduced in 1963; still in production. Used value, $44 to $49.50.

Mossberg Model 395K

MOSSBERG Model 395K: bolt-action; takedown; 12-ga. only; 28" barrel; other specifications are the same as those

of Model 385K. Introduced in 1963; still in production. Used value, $44 to $49.50.

NEW HAVEN

NEW HAVEN Model 290: bolt-action; takedown; 16-ga.; 28" barrel; detachable full choke tube; other choke tubes available at added cost; 2-rd. detachable clip; thumb safety; oil-finished American walnut Monte Carlo-style pistol-grip stock. Manufactured by Mossberg. Introduced in 1960; dropped, 1965. Used value, $25 to $27.50.

NEW HAVEN Model 295: bolt-action; takedown; 12-ga.; other specifications are the same as those of Model 290. Introduced in 1960; dropped, 1965. Used value, $25 to $27.50.

NEW HAVEN Model 283: bolt-action; takedown; .410-ga.; 25" barrel; 3" chamber. Other specifications are the same as those of Model 290. Introduced in 1960; dropped, 1965. Used value, $22.50 to $25.

NEW HAVEN Model 285: bolt-action; takedown; 20-ga.; has the same specifications as Model 283, except for chambering. Introduced in 1960; dropped, 1965. Used value, $22.50 to $25.

NEW HAVEN Model 273: bolt-action; single-shot; top loading; 24" tapered barrel; full choke only; thumb safety; oil-finished American walnut Monte Carlo-style pistol-grip stock. Introduced in 1960; dropped, 1965. Used value, $17.50 to $20.

NEW HAVEN Model 600: slide action; takedown; 12-ga.; 26" improved cylinder barrel, 28" full or modified, 30" full choke; 6-rd. magazine; choice of standard or 3" magnum barrel; safety on top of receiver; uncheckered walnut pistol-grip stock, extension slide handle. Same general design as Mossberg Model 500. Introduced in 1962; dropped, 1965. Used value, $50 to $52.50.

Model 600K has the same specifications as Model 600, except for C-Lect Choke feature. Used value, $55 to $57.50.

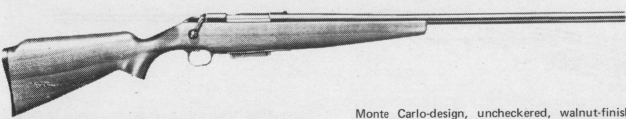

NEW HAVEN Model 495: bolt-action; takedown; 12-ga.; 28" full choke barrel; 2-rd. detachable clip; thumb safety; Monte Carlo-design, uncheckered, walnut-finished hardwood pistol-grip stock. Introduced in 1964; dropped, 1965. Used value, $30 to $32.50.

NOBLE

NOBLE Model 40: slide action; 12-ga. only; 28" barrel; solid frame; 6-rd. magazine; Multi-Choke; recoil pad; un- checkered American walnut pistol-grip stock, grooved fore- arm; push-button safety. Introduced in 1952; dropped, 1956. Used value, $42.50 to $45.

NOBLE Model 50: slide action; 12-ga. only; 28" barrel; solid frame; has the same specifications as Model 40, except without recoil pad and Multi-Choke. Introduced in 1954; dropped, 1956. Used value, $40 to $42.50.

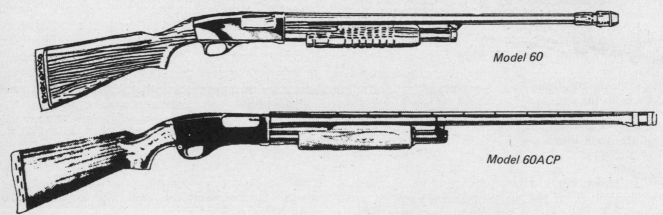

Model 60

Model 60ACP

NOBLE Model 60: slide action; 12, 16 gauges; 28" barrel; solid frame; cross-bolt safety; 5-rd. magazine; uncheckered American walnut pistol-grip stock; grooved slide handle, Vari-Chek choke; recoil pad. Introduced in 1957; dropped, 1969. Used value, $55 to $60.

Model 60AF has the same specifications as Model 60, except for selected steel barrel, damascened bolt, select wal- nut stock with fluted comb. Introduced in 1965; dropped, 1966. Used value, $45 to $50.

Model 60ACP replaced Model 60, Model 60AF; has same general specifications, except receiver is machined from sin- gle block of steel, all lock surfaces are hardened. Introduced in 1967; dropped, 1971. Used value, $65 to $70.

Model 66 RCLP has the same specifications as Model 60ACP, except for checkered pistol grip, slide handle. Introduced in 1967; dropped, 1971. Used value, $75 to $80.

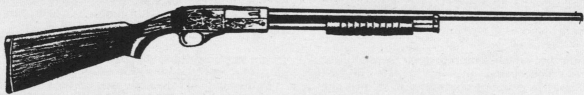

NOBLE Model 65: slide action; 12, 16 gauges, 28" barrel; solid frame; has same specifications as Model 60, except without recoil pad, Vari-Chek choke. Introduced in 1957; dropped, 1969. Used value, $50 to $55.

NOBLE Model 602: slide action; 20-ga. only; solid frame; 28" barrel; adjustable choke; 5-rd. magazine; top safety; side ejection; uncheckered American walnut pistol-grip stock; grooved slide handle; recoil pad. Introduced in 1963; dropped, 1971. Used value, $85 to $90.

NOBLE Model 70: slide action; .410 gauge only 26″ barrel; full choke; solid frame; top safety; uncheckered walnut pistol-grip stock; grooved forearm. Introduced in 1959;

dropped, 1967. Used value, $45 to $50.

Model 70X replaced Model 70; specifications are the same, except has side ejection, damascened bolt. Introduced in 1967; dropped, 1971. Used value, $65 to $70.

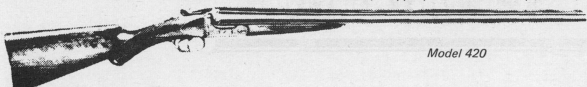

Model 420

NOBLE Model 420: double barrel; hammerless; 12, 16, 20 gauges; 28″ barrels; full/modified only; top lever; double triggers; automatic safety; matted rib; checkered pistol-grip stock, forearm. Introduced in 1959; dropped, 1971. Used value, $80 to $85.

Model 42OEK has the same general specifications as

Model 420, except for demi-block with triple lock; automatic selective ejectors, hand-checkered Circassian walnut pistol-grip stock; beavertail forearm; recoil pad; hand-engraved action; front and middle bead sights; gold inlay on top lever. Made in 1968 only under this designation. Used value, $95 to $105.

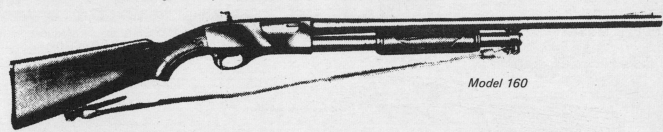

Model 160

NOBLE Model 160 Deergun: slide action; 12, 16 gauges; specifications the same as Model 60, except for 24″ barrel; hard rubber butt plate; sling swivels; detachable carrying strap; Lyman adjustable peep rear sight, ramp post front; tapped for scope. Introduced in 1965; dropped, 1966. Used

value, $55 to $60.

Model 166L Deergun replaced Model 160; general specifications are the same, except for improved workmanship. Introduced in 1967; dropped, 1971. Used value, $70 to $75.

NOBLE Model 80: autoloader; .410-ga. only; recoil operated; 5-rd. magazine; 26″ barrel; full choke only; action release button; push-button safety; uncheckered

American walnut pistol grip stock; grooved forearm; fluted comb. Introduced in 1965; dropped, 1967. Used value, $70 to $75.

NOBLE Model 450E: double barrel; 12, 16, 20 gauges; 28″ barrel; modified/full chokes; demi-block with triple lock;

double triggers; all specifications the same as Model 420EK, which it replaced. Introduced in 1969; dropped, 1971. Used value, $95 to $105.

NOBLE Series 200: slide action; 20-ga. only; 28″ barrel, modified or full choke; solid frame; 5-rd. magazine; tang safety; side ejection; impressed checkering on slide handle;

American walnut stock, slide handle; recoil pad. Made in 1972 only. Used values, standard model, $70 to $75; with Vari-Chek choke; $75 to $80; with vent rib, $80 to $85; Vari Chek and vent rib, $85 to $92.50.

NOBLE Series 300: slide action; 12-ga. only; 28″ barrel; modified or full choke; solid frame; tang safety; side ejection; American walnut stock, slide handle; impressed check-

ering; 6-rd. magazine, 3-shot plug furnished. Made only in 1972. Used values, standard model, $70 to $75; with Vari Chek, $75 to $80; with vent rib, $80 to $85; Vari-Chek and vent rib, $85 to $92.50.

NOBLE Series 400: slide action; .410-ga. only; 25″ barrel; modified or full choke; solid frame, tang safety; side ejection; American walnut stock, slide handle; impressed check-

ering on pistol grip, slide handle; damascened bolt. Made only in 1972. Used values, standard model, $70 to $75; with Vari Chek, $75 to $80; with vent rib, $80 to $85; Vari Chek and vent rib, $85 to $92.50.

NOBLE Model 390 Deergun: slide action; 12-ga. only; 24″ rifled slug barrel; sling swivels; detachable carrying strap; Lyman adjustable peep rear sight, ramp post front; solid

frame; tang safety; American walnut stock, slide handle; impressed checkering. Made only in 1972. Used value, $80 to $85.

NOBLE Model 757: slide action; 20-ga. only; 5-rd. magazine; solid frame; 28″ barrel of aircraft alloy; adjustable choke; barrel, receiver black anodized; decorated receiver;

tang safety; side ejection; American walnut stock; impressed checkering on slide handle, pistol grip. Made only in 1972. Used value, $90 to $95.

The PARKER GUN

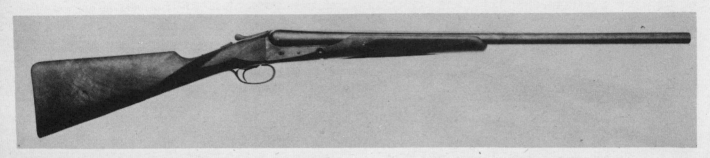

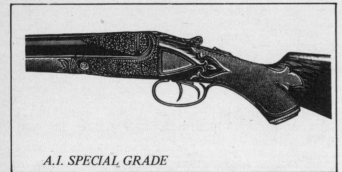

A.I. SPECIAL GRADE

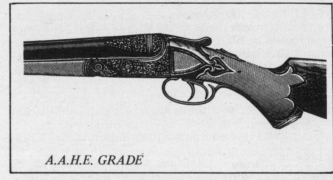

A.A.H.E. GRADE

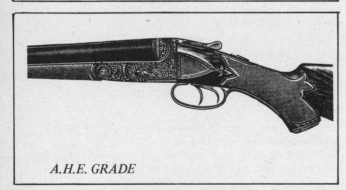

A.H.E. GRADE

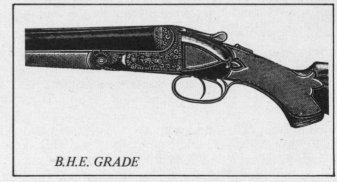

B.H.E. GRADE

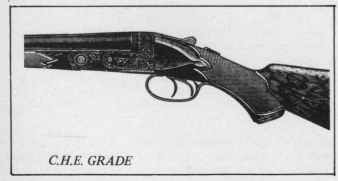

C.H.E. GRADE

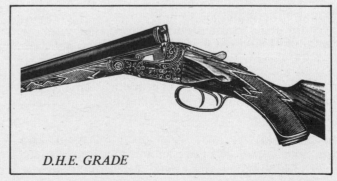

D.H.E. GRADE

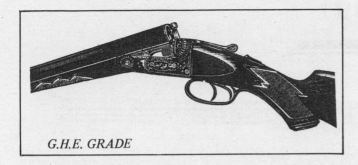

G.H.E. GRADE

V.H.E. GRADE U.H.E.

PARKER Model 920 Hammerless: after Parker Brothers was absorbed by Remington Arms in 1934, shotgun was designated as Remington Parker Model 920; prior to that, it was known simply as Parker Hammerless Double; side-by-side double; 10, 12, 16, 20, 28, .410 gauges; 26″ to 32″ barrels; any standard choke combo; box-lock action; automatic ejectors; choice of straight, half or pistol-grip stock; hand-checkered pistol grip, forearm of select walnut; double or selective single trigger. Because of the wide variations in styles and extras, as well as the number of grades — differing in engraving, checkering and general workmanship — there is a wide range of values. The selective trigger was introduced in 1922, with the raised vent rib; the beavertail forend was introduced in 1923; all add to used value. Prior to 1920, model was built with Damascus barrels, today considered collector items. For all practical purposes, the shootable model was introduced in 1920, dropped in 1940, but some guns were put together from available parts stocks by Remington until 1942. Grades are in descending values, with the A-designated model being worth several times that of the V model. Nonejector models —pre-1934 — are worth about 30% less than values shown for ejector models; if gun has interchangeable barrels, it is worth 30 to 35% more than shown. Those in 20, 28, .410 also have more value. Prices shown are for 12, 16-ga. configurations. Used values, A-1 Special Grade, $7200 to $7440; AAHE, $6120 to $6240; AHE, $4920 to $5040; BHE, $3540 to $3720; CHE, $2520 to $2640; DHE, $2100 to $2220; GHE, $1800 to $1890; VHE, $1170 to $1290.

With single selective trigger, add $180 to $192 to base price shown. For raised vent rib, add $240 to $270. For beavertail forearm addition, in grades VHE, GHE, DHE, CHE, add $120 to $132 to base price; for grades BHE, AHE, AAHE, add $180 to $192 to base; for A-1 Special, add $234 to $258.

PARKER Trojan: hammerless double barrel; 12, 16, 20 gauges; 26″, 28″ barrels, modified/full choke, 30″ full; American walnut stock; hand-checkered pistol grip, forearms; box-lock action; plain extractors; double or single triggers. Introduced in 1915; dropped, 1939. Used values, double trigger, 12, 16 gauges, $600 to $660; 20-ga., $870 to $960; single trigger, 12, 16 gauges, $750 to $780; 20-ga., $1080 to $1148.

PARKER Single-Barrel Trap: after absorption of Parker by Remington, model was listed as Remington Parker Model 930. In 12-ga. only; 30″, 32″, 34″ barrels; any designated choke; vent rib; ejector; hammerless box lock action; straight, half or pistol-grip stock of select American walnut; hand-checkered pistol grip, forearm. Various grades differ with amount of workmanship, checkering, engraving, et al. General specifications are the same for all variations. Introduced in 1917; dropped, 1942. Used values, SA-1 Special, $6000 to $6240; SAA. $3720 to $3810; SA, $2880 to $2940; SB, $2100 to $2190; SC, $1440 to $1500.

Pedersen

Grade I

PEDERSEN 1000 Series Grade I: over/under; box-lock action; 12, 20 gauges; barrel lengths, stock dimensions to customer specifications; hand-checkered American walnut pistol-grip stock, forearm; rubber recoil pad; vent rib; automatic ejectors; single selective trigger; hand-engraved, gold-filled receiver. Introduced in 1973; dropped, 1975. Used value, $700 to $725.

Series 1000 Grade II has the same specifications as Grade I except for standard stock dimensions, no gold filling, less extensive engraving on receiver, less fancy wood in stock, forearm. Introduced in 1973; dropped, 1975. Used value, $460 to $475.

Series 1000 Grade III has the same specifications as Grade II except for no receiver engraving; has gold-plated trigger, forearm release. Introduced in 1973; dropped, 1975. Used value, $375 to $390.

PEDERSEN 1500: over/under; box-lock action; 12-ga. only; 26", 28", 30", 32" barrels; hand-checkered European walnut pistol-grip stock, forearm; rubber recoil pad; field version of Series 1000; automatic selective ejectors; vent rib; choice of sights. Introduced in 1973; dropped, 1975. Used value, $300 to $325.

PEDERSEN Series 2000 Grade I: side-by-side double barrel; box-lock action; 12, 20 gauges; barrel length, stock dimensions to customer's specifications; hand-checkered American walnut pistol-grip stock, forearm; automatic selective ejectors; barrel selector/safety; single selective trigger; automatic safety; gold-filled, hand-engraved receiver. Introduced in 1973; dropped, 1975. Used value, $700 to $725.

Series 2000 Grade II has same specifications as Grade I except for standard stock dimensions, less extensive engraving, less fancy wood. Introduced in 1973; dropped, 1975. Used value, $420 to $440.

PEDERSEN 2500 Grade III: side-by-side double barrel; box-lock action; 12, 20 gauges; has the same specifications as 2000 series but is field version. Hand-checkered pistol grip, beavertail forearm; European walnut stock; standard stock dimensions; no receiver engraving. Introduced in 1973; dropped, 1975. Used value, $175 to $195.

PREMIER Ambassador: double; 12, 16, 20, .410 gauges; triple Greener crossbolt action; barrels, 22", except in .410, 26"; all gauges, modified/full chokes; European walnut stock, hand-checkered pistol grip, forearm; double triggers, cocking indicators; automatic safety. Imported from Europe by Premier Shotguns. Still in production. Used value, $145 to $150.

PREMIER Continental: same as Ambassador model except for outside hammers; not available in .410. Other specs identical. Used value, $140 to $147.50.

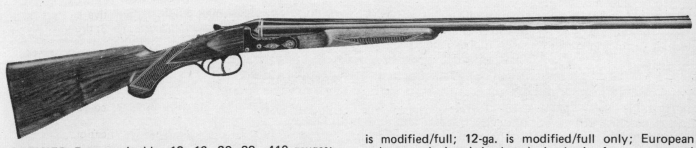

PREMIER Regent: double; 12, 16, 20, 28, .410 gauges; triple Greener crossbolt action; barrels, 26", improved/modified, except in 28, .410, which are modified/full; 28", is modified/full; 12-ga. is modified/full only; European walnut stock, hand-checkered pistol grip, forearm; matted tapered rib; double triggers; automatic safety. Still in production. Used value, $110 to $115.

PREMIER Brush King: double; same as Premier Regent model, except in 12, 20 gauges only; 22" barrels, improved/modified. Still in production. Used value, $105 to $110.

PREMIER Magnum: double; similar to Premier Regent; 10, 12 gauges only; 10 with 32" barrel, 12 has 30"; choked full/full; recoil pad; European walnut stock, hand-checkered pistol grip, forearm; beavertail forearm. Still in production. Used values, 10-ga., $122.50 to $127.50; 12-ga., $117.50 to $120.

Remington

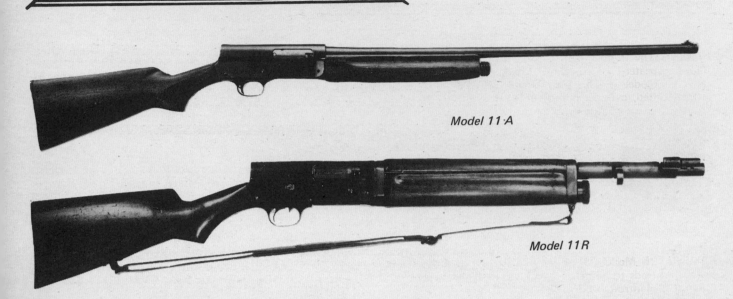

Model 11·A

Model 11R

REMINGTON Model 11A: hammerless, takedown, Browning-type autoloader; 5-rd. capacity; tube magazine; 12, 16, 20 gauges; barrel lengths, 26″, 28″, 30″, 32″; full, modified, improved, cylinder bore, skeet chokes; checkered pistol grip, forearm. Introduced in 1905; dropped, 1949. Was replaced by Model 11-48. Used values with plain barrel, $144 to $152.50; solid rib, $158.50 to $172.50; vent rib, $190 to $201.50.

Model 11R riot gun has same specifications as Model 11A, except that it is 12-ga. only; has sling swivels, 20″ barrel. Introduced in 1921; dropped, 1948. Used value, $126.50 to $144.

Model 11 custom grades, Expert, Special, Tournament and Premier styles, differ from Model 11A only in grade of walnut used in stock, forearm, engraving, checkering. Used values, Special grade (11B), $201.50 to $218.50; Tournament (11D), $443 to $489; Expert (11E), $661.50 to $690; Premier, $891.50 to $920.

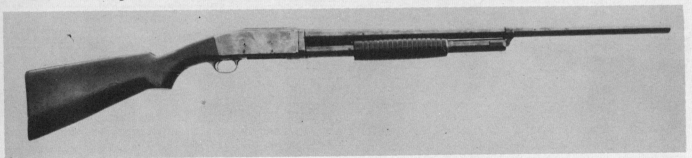

REMINGTON Model 10A: slide-action repeater; hammerless, takedown; barrel lengths, 26″, 28″, 30″, 32″; full, modified, cylinder bore; grooved slide handle; uncheckered pistol-grip stock; 12-ga. only; 6-rd. capacity; tube magazine. Introduced, 1907; dropped, 1929. Used value, $172.50 to $190.

REMINGTON Model 17A: slide-action repeater; hammerless, takedown; 5-rd. capacity; 20-ga. only; tube magazine; barrel lengths, 26″, 28″, 30″, 32″; modified, full, cylinder bore choke choice, grooved slide handle, uncheckered stock, with pistol grip; Browning design. Introduced in 1921; dropped, 1933. Used value, $230 to $247.50.

REMINGTON Model 29: hammerless, takedown slide-action repeater; 12-ga. only; tubular magazine, 5-shot capacity; Model 29A has plain barrel, 26″, 28″, 30″, 32″; full, modified, cylinder bore; hand-checkered slide handle,

Model 31

pistol-grip stock; made from 1929 to 1933. Used value, $195.50 to $213.50.

Model 29T target grade differs from Model 29A only in ventilated rib, longer slide handle, straight grip on trap stock. Used value, $287.50 to $305.

REMINGTON Model 31: this model is one of those successes that leads to numerous versions. In all, there are ten variations, all introduced in 1931, dropped in 1949.

Model 31A, the standard grade slide-action repeater, is a hammerless, takedown model, with either 3 or 5-shot capacity; early models had checkered pistol-grip stock, slide handle; later styles had plain stock, grooved slide handle. Barrels, with choice of plain surface, solid rib or vent rib, were in 26″, 28″, 30″, 32″ lengths, choked full, modified, improved, cylinder bore, skeet. Made in 12, 16, 20 gauges. Used value, with plain barrel, $172.50 to $190; solid rib, $195.50 to $213; vent rib, $230 to $247.50.

Model 31 custom grades are Special, Tournament, Expert and Premier, differing from Model 31A only in the grade of wood, amount and fineness of checkering and the amount

and quality of engraving. Other specifications remain the same. Used values, Special grade (31B), $259 to $276; Tournament (31D), $546.50 to $604; Expert (31E), $862.50 to $897; Premier (31F), $1035 to $1092.50.

Model 31TC Trap grade is same as standard model, but in 12-ga. only, with 30″, 32″ vent rib barrel, full choke, trap stock, pistol grip, recoil pad; extension beavertail forend; stock, forend are checkered. Used value, $414 to $443.

Model 31S Trap Special has same specs as Model 31TC, except half-pistol grip stock, forend of standard walnut, solid rib barrel. Used value, $414 to $431.50.

Model 31H Hunter's Special differs from Model 31S only in that it has a sporting stock with more drop and shorter length. Used value, $368 to $385.50.

Model 31R Riot gun is same as Model 31A, but in 12-ga. only, with 20″ barrel. Used value, $144 to $155.25.

Model 32 Standard

REMINGTON Model 32: this hammerless, takedown over/under is another of those on which the manufacturer built a lengthy reputation, making the model in its various configurations for a decade. Introduced in 1932; dropped, 1942. However, the nostalgia and demand resulted in the basic model which, with modern manufacturing techniques, was reintroduced in 1972 as the Model 3200.

The standard grade Model 32A has automatic ejectors and the earlier model had double triggers; later, it was available only with a single selective trigger; in 12-ga. only, barrels are 26″, 28″, 30″, 32″; standard chokes are full, modified, but options were offered for full, modified, improved, cylinder bore, skeet; choice of plain barrel, raised matted solid rib, vent rib; stock was walnut with checkered pistol grip, forend. Used value, with double triggers, $655 to $673; single trigger, $862 to $897; with vent rib, add $109 to

$126; with raised solid rib, $52 to $63.

Model 32 Skeet grade has same specs as Model 32A, except for choice of 26″, 28″ barrel, skeet boring; selective trigger only, beavertail forend. Used value, with plain barrels, $1064 to $1081; vent rib, $1138.50 to $1184.50; raised solid rib, $1092.50 to $1121.50.

Model 32 custom stylings included Tournament, Expert and Premier grades, differing from standard 32A model only in engraving, fineness of checkering, grade of walnut used. Other specs are the same. Used value, Tournament grade (32D), $1667.50 to $1754; Expert (32E), $2501.50 to $2588; Premier (32F), $2875 to $2932.50.

Model 32TC Trap grade has same specs as Model 32A, except for 30″, 32″ vent rib barrel, trap stock with checkered beavertail forend, pistol grip; either double or single selective triggers; full choke only. Used value, with double triggers, $1064 to $1081; single trigger, $1144 to $1184.

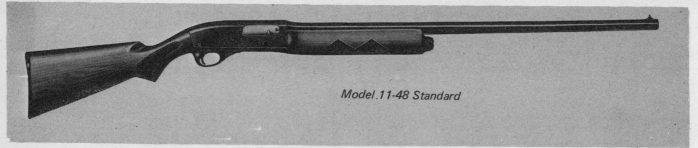

Model 11-48 Standard

REMINGTON Model 11-48A: autoloader; half-pistol grip; hand-checkered stock, forend; 5-shot capacity in 12, 16, 20 gauges; 4-shot in 28, .410; redesigned version of Model 11; introduced in 1949; dropped, 1969; hammerless, takedown; tube magazine; 26" barrel, choked improved cylinder; 28", modified or full; 30", full, in 12-ga. only; plain barrel, matted top surface, ventilated rib choices. Used value, $145 to $170; Special grade (11-48B), Tournament grade (11-48D) and Premier grade (11-48F) had higher grades of wood, more and finer-line checkering, engraving. Used values, Special, $158.50 to $186.50; Tournament, $520 to $565; Premier, $1034 to $1073.

Model 11-48A .410 was introduced in 1954, 28-ga., 1952; both discontinued, 1969. Used value with plain barrel, $147 to $169.50; with matted top surface, $158.50 to $175.50; vent rib, $181 to $198.

Model 11-48SA Skeet model is same as 28-ga. standard model, except for vent rib, skeet choke, 25" barrel; 28-ga. introduced, 1952; 410, 1954. Used value, $203 to $220.

Model 11-48A riot gun is same as standard model, but in 12-ga. only, with 20" plain barrel. Used value, $124.50 to $138.50.

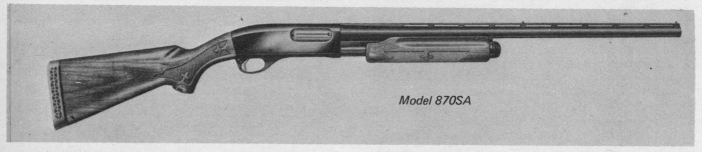

Model 870SA

REMINGTON Model 870: made in 14 styles, this slide-action model has variations even within the styles. This model verged on being an empire, with some still in the line, and the life of even the least popular being extended for the 13 years from 1950 to 1963.

Model 870AP Wingmaster was the standard grade. A hammerless takedown, it had tube magazine, total capacity of 5 rds.; plug furnished with gun; barrels were 25" improved cylinder; 28", modified or full; 30", full, the last in 12-ga. only; choice of plain, matted top surface vent rib; walnut stock, no checkering, grooved slide handle. Introduced in 1950; dropped, 1963. Used values, plain barrel, $96.50 to $104.50; matted surface, $102 to $107.50; vent rib, $115 to $124.50.

Model 870 Wingmaster field gun, still in production, was introduced, 1964. Specs are same as 870AP, except for checkered stock, slide handle. Used value, plain barrel, $126.50 to $132.50; vent rib, $144 to $158.50.

Model 870 Wingmaster custom grades include Tournament, Premier stylings. Only difference from Model 870AP is grade of walnut, amount of engraving, checkering; other specs are the same. Introduced in 1960; still in production. Used values, Tournament (870D), $593 to $610; Premier, $1121 to $1186; Premier gold inlaid, $1695 to $1771.

Model 870ADL Wingmaster is the deluxe grade of the 870AP with the same general specs, except for fine-checkered beavertail forend, pistol-grip stock; choice of matted top surface barrel, vent rib. Introduced in 1950; dropped, 1963. Used values, matted surface, $113 to $124.50; vent rib, $133 to $141.50.

Model 870BDL Wingmaster varies from 870ADL only in selected American walnut for stock, forend. Introduced in 1950; dropped, 1963. Used value, with matted top surface barrel, $127.50 to $133; vent rib, $144 to $152.50.

Model 870SA Wingmaster Skeet gun is same as 870AP, except for 26" barrel, vent rib, skeet boring, ivory bead front sight, metal bead in rear; has extension beavertail slide handle, pistol-grip stock, both fine-checkered. Introduced in 1950; still in production. Used values, Skeet grade (870SA), $144 to $152.50; Skeet Target (870SC), $203.50 to $212; Skeet Tournament (870SD), $593.50 to $610.50; Skeet Premier grade (870SF), $1124 to $1158.

Model 870TB Wingmaster Trap Special has same specs as standard model, except for 28", 30" vent rib barrel, full choke, no rear sight, metal bead front; checkered trap stock, slide handle. Introduced in 1950; still in production. Used value, $158.50 to $167.

Model 870TC Wingmaster Trap grade is same as 870TB, except for both front, rear sights, higher grade of walnut. Introduced in 1950; still in production. Used values, Trap grade (870TC), $220.50 to $248; Trap Tournament (870TD), $593.50 to $605; Trap Premier, $1124.50 to $1158.50.

Model 870 Wingmaster Magnum; same as 870AP, except in 12-ga. 3" magnum only; 30" full choke barrel; recoil pad. Introduced in 1955; discontinued, 1963. Used value, $113 to $124.50.

Model 870 Magnum Deluxe is same as standard 870 Magnum, including lifetime, except for checkered extension beavertail slide handle, stock, matted top surface barrel. Used value, $133 to $141.50.

Model 870 Magnum Duck gun has same specs as 870 field gun, except chambered for 3" 12, 20-ga. magnum shells only; 28", 30" barrel, plain vent rib, modified, full choke recoil pad. Introduced in 1964; still in production. Used values, with plain barrel, $136 to $144; vent rib, $150 to $158.50.

Model 870 Wingmaster field gun has specs of 870AP standard model, except for checkered stock, slide handle. Introduced in 1964; still in production. Used values, with plain barrel, $130 to $136; vent rib, $147 to $155.50.

Model 870R riot gun has same specs as standard 870AC, except in 12-ga. only, with 20" barrel, improved cylinder.

Model 870 deer gun; standard configuration is same as 870 riot model, except for Winchester rifle-type sights. Used value, $110.50 to $113.

Model 870 Brushmaster Deluxe deer gun is same as standard deer gun, but has recoil pad, checkered stock, slide handle; available in 12, 20 gauges. Used value, $144 to $153.

Model 58ADL

REMINGTON Sportsman-58ADL: gas-operated autoloader; 12-ga. only; 3-shot tube magazine; 26", 28", 30" barrels, with plain, vent rib; improved cylinder, modified, full choke, Remington skeet boring, checkered pistol grip, forend. Introduced in 1956; dropped, 1964. Used values, with plain barrel, $167 to $175.50; vent rib, $187 to $198.

Sportsman-58BDL Deluxe Special grade is same as 58ADL, except walnut wood is of select grade; manufactured during same period. Used values, with plain barrel, $195.50 to $201.50; vent rib, $221.50 to $230.

Sportsman-58 Tournament and Premier grades are same as 58ADL, except for vent rib, improved wood, checkering, engraving. Used values, Tournament grade (58D), $552 to $569.50; Premier, $1121.50 to $1144.50.

Sportsman-58SA Skeet gun has same specs as 58-ADL, except for vent rib, special skeet stock, forend. Used value, $193 to $201.50.

Sportsman-58 Skeet Target, Tournament and Premier grades verge on custom guns; with same general specs as Model 58SA, they have better wood, engraving, finer checkering. Used values, Skeet Target grade (58SC), $316.50 to $328; Skeet Tournament (58D), $558 to $604; Premier grade (58SF), $1127 to $1167.50.

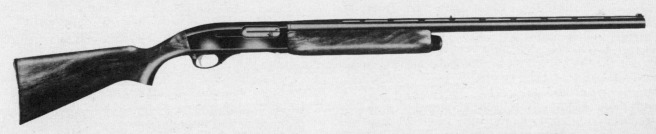

REMINGTON Model 878A Automaster: gas-operated autoloader; 12-ga. only; 3-shot tube magazine; plain or vent rib; uncheckered pistol-grip stock, forend; barrels, 26" improved cylinder; 28" modified, 30" full choke. Introduced in 1959; dropped, 1962. Used value, $101 to $109.

Model 1100 Standard with vent rib

REMINGTON Model 1100: a gas-operated, hammerless takedown, autoloader, this model was introduced in 1963 in several configurations, all of them still in production. In its early days, the stocks had impressed checkering, but this was replaced in 1972 by computerized cut checkering; crossbolt safety; alloy receiver.

The Model 1100 field gun has plain barrel or vent rib, in 12, 16, 20 gauges; barrels 30" full, 28" modified or full, 26" improved cylinder; black plastic butt plate, white spacer. Used value, with plain barrel, $170 to $175.50; vent rib, $181.50 to $189.50.

The Model 1100 Magnum Duck gun is same as field model, except for chambering for 3" 12, 20-ga. magnum shells only; 20-ga. has 28" full or modified barrel; 12-ga., 30" full, modified; recoil pad. Used value, plain barrel, $169.50 to $181; vent rib, $198 to $206.50.

Model 1100SA Skeet model; 12, 20 gauges; same as 1100 field gun, except for 26" barrel, vent rib, skeet choke or

SHOTGUNS

Cutts compensator. Used value, with skeet choke, $198 to $203.50; Cutts compensator, $212 to $223.50.

Model 1100SB skeet gun is the same as 1100SA, except for selected wood and in skeet choke only. Used value, $220.50 to $226.

Model 1100TB trap model; same as 1100 field style, except for trap stock, Monte Carlo or straight comb choice; 30" barrel, full, modified trap choke; vent rib; 12-ga. only; recoil pad. Used value, straight stock, $226 to $237.50;

Monte Carlo stock, $237.50 to $246.

Model 1100 Tournament, Premier grades are same as standard models, except for grade of walnut; amount, fineness of checkering; engraving, gold inlays. Used values, Tournament (1100D), $593 to $610; Premier (1100F), $1138 to $1178; Premier, gold inlaid, $1638 to $1695.

Model 1100 deer gun; same as field gun, but with 22" barrel; 12, 20 gauges; improved cylinder; rifle sights; recoil pad. Used value, $169.50 to $181.

RA Richland

Model 200

RICHLAND Model 200: side-by-side field gun; hammerless; Anson & Deeley type box-lock action; 12, 16, 20, 28, .410 gauges; 26" improved/modified, 28" modified/full; in .410 only; 26" modified/full, 20-ga. only, 22" improved/modified; double triggers; plain extractors; hand-checkered European walnut pistol-grip stock, beavertail forearm; cheekpiece; recoil pad. Imported from Spain. Introduced in

1963; still in production. Used value, $181 to $192.50.

Model 202 has the same specifications as Model 200, but comes with two sets of barrels in same gauge. In 12-ga., barrels are 30" full/full with 3" chambers, 26" improved/modified; in 20-ga., barrels are 26" modified/full, 22" improved/modified with 3" chambers. Introduced in 1963; importation dropped, 1971. Used value, $266 to $282.50.

RICHLAND Model 707 Deluxe: side-by-side field gun; hammerless; box-lock action; 12, 20 gauges; in 12-ga., barrels are 28" modified/full, 26" improved/modified; in 20-ga., barrels are 30" full/full, 28" modified/full; 26" improved/modified; triple bolting system; double triggers; plain extractors; hand-checkered European walnut stock, forearm; recoil pad. Imported from Spain. Introduced in 1963; dropped, 1972. Used value, $271.50 to $282.50.

RICHLAND Model 711 Magnum: advertised as Long Range Waterfowl Magnum; side-by-side; hammerless; Anson & Deeley box-lock-type action; Purdey-type triple lock; 10, 12 gauges; 10-ga. has 3½" chambers, 12-ga., 3"; 32" full/

full barrels in 10-ga., 30" full/full in 12-ga; double triggers; plain extractors; automatic safety; hand-checkered European walnut pistol-grip stock, forearm; recoil pad. Imported from Spain. Introduced in 1963; still in production. Used value, $215 to $226.

RICHLAND Model 808: over/under; box-lock action; 12-ga. only; 30" full/full, 28" modified/full, 26" improved/modified barrels; plain extractors; nonselective

single trigger; hand-checkered European walnut stock, forearm; vent rib. Imported from Italy. Introduced in 1963; importation dropped, 1968. Used value, $294 to $311.

RICHLAND Model 828: over/under; box-lock action; color case-hardened receiver; 28-ga. only; 26" improved/modified, 28" full/modified barrels; sliding crossbolt lock; nonautomatic safety; plain extractors; vent rib; rosette engraving; hand-checkered European walnut stock, quick-detachable forearm. Imported from Italy. Introduced in 1971; available on special order only. Used value. $254.50 to $266.

RICHLAND Model 844: over/under; nickel-chrome steel box-lock action; 12-ga. 12-ga. mag.; 26" improved/modified, 28" modified/full, 30" full/full barrels; plain extractors; nonselective single trigger; hand-checkered European walnut pistol-grip stock, forearm. Imported from Italy. Introduced in 1971; Magnum Model still available. Used vaue, $169.50 to $181.

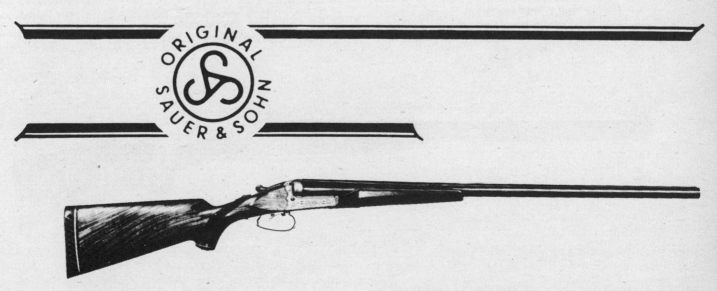

SAUER Royal Model: side-by-side; Anson & Deeley-type box-lock action; 12, 20 gauges; 30" full/full barrels in 12-ga. only, 28" modified/full, 26" improved/modified in 20-ga. only; Greener crossbolt; single selective trigger; automatic ejectors; automatic safety; double underlugs; scalloped frame; Arabesque engraving; hand-checkered European walnut pistol-grip stock, beavertail forearm; recoil pad. Introduced in 1950s; still in production. No current importer. Used value, $508.50 to $537.

Artemis Grade II

SAUER Artemis Model: side-by-side; Holland & Holland-type sidelock action; 12-ga. only; 28" modified/full barrels; Greener-type crossbolt; double underlugs; double sear safeties; automatic ejectors; single selective trigger; hand-checkered European walnut pistol-grip stock, beavertail forearm; recoil pad. Grade I has fine line engraving; Grade II has English Arabesque motif. Introduced in 1950s; still in production. No current importer. Used values, Grade I, $2090.50 to $2260; Grade II, $2655.50 to $2825.

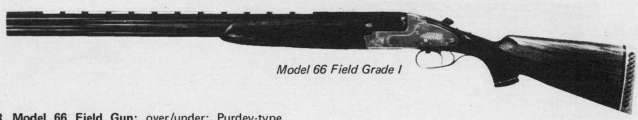

Model 66 Field Grade I

SAUER Model 66 Field Gun: over/under; Purdey-type action; Holland & Holland sideplates; 12-ga. only; 28" modified/full barrels; automatic safety; selective automatic ejectors; single selective trigger; hand-checkered European walnut stock, forearm; recoil pad; three grades of engraving. Introduced in 1950s; still in production. No current importer. Used values, Grade I, $780 to $819.50; Grade II, $904 to $960.50; Grade III, $1412.50 to $1525.50.

Model 66 Trap has same general specifications as field model except for 30" full/full or modified/full barrels; trap stock; wide-vent rib; nonautomatic safety; ventilated beavertail forearm. Introduced in 1960s; still in production. No current importer. Used values, Grade I, $847.50 to $904; Grade II, $960 to $1017; Grade III, $1469 to $1582.

Model 66 Skeet has same general specifications as trap style except for 25" barrels, skeet/skeet chokes. Introduced in 1960s; still in production. No current importer. Used values, Grade I, $847.50 to $904; Grade II, $960.50 to $1017; Grade III, $1469 to $1582.

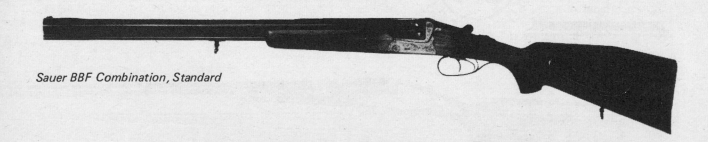

Sauer BBF Combination, Standard

SAUER Model BBF: over/under combo; blitz action; Kersten lock; 16-ga. top barrel; choice of .30-30, .30/06, 7X65R rifle barrel; front set trigger activates rifle barrel; 25" barrels; shotgun barrel full choke only; sliding sear safety; folding leaf rear sight; hand-checkered European walnut pistol-grip stock, forearm; modified Monte Carlo comb, cheekpiece; sling swivels; Arabesque engraving pattern. Introduced in 1950s; still in production. No current importer. Used value, $904 to $960.50.

Model BBF Deluxe has same specifications as standard model, except for hunting scenes engraved on action. Still in production. No current importer. Used value, $1017 to $1073.50.

Savage

SAVAGE Model 28A: slide action; takedown; hammerless; 12-ga. only; 26″, 28″, 30″, 32″ plain barrel; 5-rd. tube magazine; modified, cylinder, full choke; uncheckered American walnut pistol-grip stock, grooved slide handle; black plastic butt plate. Introduced in 1920s; dropped about 1940. Used value, $120 to $130.

Model 28B has the same general specifications as Model 28A except has raised matted rib. Used value, $130 to $140.

Model 28D trap gun has the same specifications as Model 28A except for full-choke barrel, matted rib; hand-checkered pistol-grip, trap stock, checkered slide handle. Used value, $190 to $200.

SAVAGE Model 420: over/under; box-lock action; takedown; hammerless; 12, 16, 20 gauges; 26″, 28″, 30″ barrels, last in 12-ga. only; double triggers; single nonselective trigger at extra cost; automatic safety; choked modified/full or cylinder/improved; uncheckered American walnut pistol-grip stock, forearm. Introduced in early 1930s; dropped, 1942. Used values, double triggers, $240 to $258; single trigger, $288 to $312.

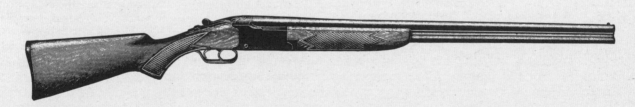

SAVAGE Model 430: over/under; box-lock action; takedown; hammerless; has the same specifications as Model 420 except for hand-checkered American walnut stock, forearm; recoil pad; matted top barrel. Introduced in early 1930s; dropped, 1942. Used values, double triggers, $264 to $288; single trigger, $312 to $336.

SAVAGE Model 720: autoloader; Browning design; takedown; 12, 16 gauges; 26″, 28″, 30″, 32″ barrels, last in 12-ga. only; 4-rd. tube magazine; cylinder, modified, full chokes; hand-checkered American walnut pistol-grip stock, forearm; black plastic butt plate. Introduced in 1930; dropped, 1949. Used value, $136 to $147.

SAVAGE Model 726: autoloader; takedown; 12, 16 gauges; has the same specifications as Model 720 except tube

magazine has 2-rd. capacity. Introduced in 1930; dropped, 1949. Used value, $130 to $141.50.

SAVAGE Model 740C: autoloader; skeet gun; takedown; 12, 16 gauges; has the same specifications as Model 726,

except for skeet stock, beavertail forearm, Cutts Compensator; 24½" barrel. Introduced in late 1930s; dropped, 1949. Used value, $164 to $175.50.

SAVAGE Model 745: autoloader; takedown; 12-ga. only; 28" barrel; has the same general specifications as Model 720

except for alloy receiver; 3-rd. or 5-rd. tube magazine. Introduced in 1946; dropped, 1949. Used value, $141.50 to $153.

Model 220 Standard

SAVAGE Model 220: single-barrel; single-shot; takedown; hammerless; 12, 16, 20, .410 gauges; 28" to 36" barrels in 12-ga.; 28" to 32" in 16-ga.; 26" to 32" in 20-ga., 28" in .410; full choke only; automatic ejector; uncheckered American walnut pistol-grip stock, forearm. Introduced about 1947; dropped, 1965. Used value, $65 to $75.

Model 220AC has the same specifications as standard Model 220 except for Savage adjustable choke. Used value, $65 to $75.

Model 220P has the same specifications as standard Model 220 except for Poly Choke; 12-ga. has 30" barrel only, 16 and 20 gauges have 28" barrel; not made in .410; recoil pad. Used value, $65 to $75.

SAVAGE Model 755: autoloader; takedown; 12, 16 gauges; 26" improved cylinder, barrel; 28" full or modified, 30" full in 12-ga. only; hand-checkered American walnut pistol-grip stock, forearm; 2 or 4-rd. tube magazine. Introduced in

1949; dropped, 1958. Used value, $141.50 to $153.

Model 755-SC has same general specifications as standard Model 755 except for 25" barrel, adjustable Savage Super Choke. Used value, $153 to $164.

Model 24 Standard

SAVAGE Model 24: over/under combo; top barrel, .22 LR, long, short; lower barrel, .410 3" shotshell; full choke bottom barrel; 24" barrels; open rear sight, ramp front rifle sight; uncheckered walnut pistol-grip stock; sliding button selector; single trigger. Introduced in 1950; dropped, 1965. Used value, $56.50 to $73.50.

Model 24-M has the same specifications as Model 24 except that top barrel is chambered for .22 rimfire magnum

cartridge. Used value, $68 to $73.50.

Model 24-DL has same specifications as standard Model 24 except checkered stock has Monte Carlo comb, beavertail forearm; in 20, .410-ga. lower barrel; satin chrome-finished receiver, trigger guard. Used value, $85 to $96.

Model 24-MDL has same specifications as Model 24-DL except upper barrel is chambered for .22 rimfire magnum cartridge. Used value, $85 to $96.

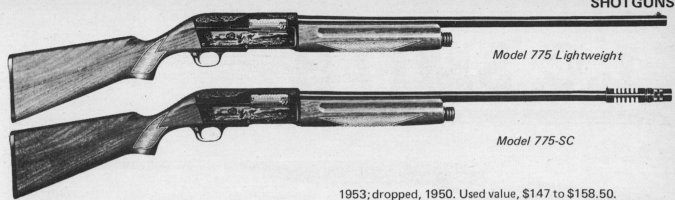

Model 775 Lightweight

Model 775-SC

SAVAGE Model 775 Lightweight: autoloader; takedown; 12, 16 gauges; has the same general specifications as standard Model 755 except for alloy receiver. Introduced in 1953; dropped, 1950. Used value, $147 to $158.50.

Model 775-SC has same specifications as Model 775 Lightweight except for 26" barrel, Savage Super Choke. Used value, $153 to $164.

Model 30-D

Model 30-T

Model 30-AC

SAVAGE Model 30: slide action; hammerless; solid frame; 12, 20, .410 gauges 26", 28", 30" barrels; improved, modified, full chokes; 5-rd. magazine in 12, 20 gauges, 4-rd. in .410; uncheckered American walnut stock, grooved slide handle; hard rubber butt plate. Introduced in 1958; still in production. Used value, $102 to $113.

Model 30-AC has the same specifications as standard Model 30 except for 26" barrel, adjustable choke; 12-ga. only. Introduced in 1959; dropped, 1975. Used value, $113 to $124.50.

Model 30-ACL has same specifications as Model 30-AC but ejection port, safety are on left side. Introduced in 1960; dropped, 1964. Used value, $113 to $124.

Model 30-T has the same specifications as standard model except for 30" full choke barrel only; 12-ga. only; Monte Carlo trap stock, recoil pad. Introduced in 1964; dropped, 1975. Used value, $136 to $147.

Model 30 Slug Gun has the same specifications as standard Model 30 except for 22" slug barrel, rifle sights; 12, 20 gauges. Introduced in 1964; still in production. Used value, $40 to $107.50.

Model 30-D has same specifications as standard model except is chambered for 12, 20, .410 3" magnum shells; checkered pistol-grip, fluted extension slide handle; alloy receiver; etched pattern on receiver; recoil pad. Introduced in 1972; still in production. Used value, $113 to $124.50.

Model 750 Standard

SAVAGE Model 750: autoloader; Browning design; takedown; 12-ga. only; 26" improved, 28" full or modified barrel; 4-rd. tube magazine; checkered American walnut pistol-grip stock, grooved forearm. Introduced in 1960; dropped, 1963. Used value, $147 to $158.50.

Model 750-SC has same specifications as standard Model 750 except for 26" barrel only, Savage Super Choke. Introduced in 1962; dropped, 1963. Used value, $147 to $158.

Model 750-AC has same specifications as Model 750 except for 26" barrel only, adjustable choke. Introduced in 1964; dropped, 1967. Used value, $147 to $158.50.

L.C. SMITH

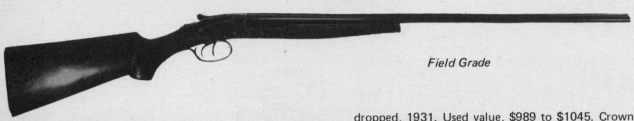

Field Grade

L.C. SMITH Single-Barrel: single-shot; box-lock; hammerless; 12 ga. only; automatic ejector; 32", 34" barrels; vent rib; walnut stock; hand-checkered pistol grip, forearm; recoil pad. Made in 7 grades, original retail depending upon the quality of workmanship, engraving, quality of wood. Specialty Grade, introduced in 1917; dropped, 1948. Used value, $565 to $621. Eagle Grade, introduced in 1919; dropped, 1931. Used value, $989 to $1045. Crown Grade, introduced in 1919; dropped, 1946. Used value, $1130 to $1243. Monogram Grade, introduced in 1919; dropped, 1946. Used value, $1582 to $1695. Olympic Grade, introduced in 1928; dropped, 1951. Used value, $234 to $452. Premier Grade, introduced in 1931; dropped, 1946. Used value, $3390 to $3560. Deluxe Grade, introduced in 1931; dropped, 1946. Used value, $5650 to $5876.

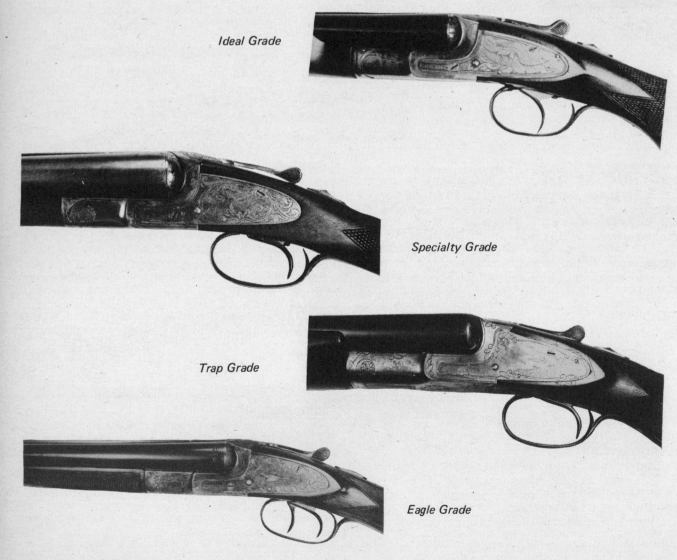

Ideal Grade

Specialty Grade

Trap Grade

Eagle Grade

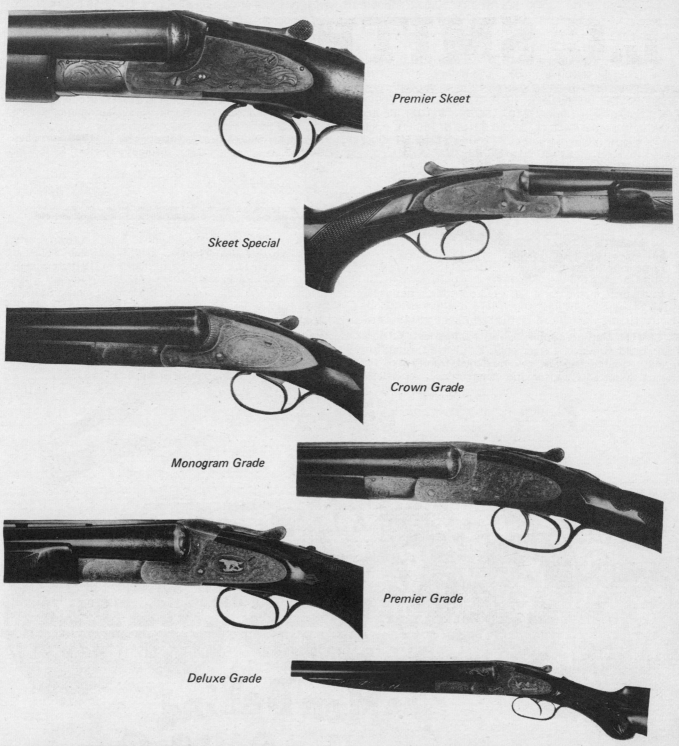

Premier Skeet

Skeet Special

Crown Grade

Monogram Grade

Premier Grade

Deluxe Grade

L.C. SMITH Hammerless: double barrel; sidelock; 12, 16, 20, .410 gauges; 26″ to 32″ barrels; standard choke combos; hand-checkered walnut stock, forearm; choice of straight stock, half or full pistol grip; beavertail or standard forearm; general specifications are the same on all grades, but grades depend upon quality of workmanship, checkering, engraving and wood. Guns were made by Hunter Arms from 1913 until 1945; by L.C. Smith from 1945 to 1951. Values shown are for 12-ga. guns; 16-ga. are worth 5% less than 12s; 20-ga. guns are worth about 20% more than 12s; .410 guns are worth 50 to 75% more than 12-ga. guns; models made by L.C. Smith Gun Company are worth 5% less than Hunter Arms Company guns:

Field Grade, introduced in 1913; dropped, 1951; double triggers, plain extractors. Used value, $282 to $294; with automatic ejectors, $367 to $384; with nonselective single trigger, plain extractors, $339 to $356; single trigger, automatic ejectors, $424 to $441.

Ideal Grade, introduced in 1913; dropped, 1951; double triggers, plain extractors, $396 to $418; double triggers, automatic ejectors, $480 to $503; single nonselective trigger, plain extractors, $452 to $463; single selective trigger, automatic ejectors, $537 to $554.

Specialty Grade, introduced in 1913; dropped, 1951;

double triggers, plain extractors, $593 to $621; double triggers, automatic ejectors, $678 to $706; single selective trigger, plain extractors, $650 to $678; single selective trigger, auto ejectors, $734 to $763.

Trap Grade, introduced in 1913; dropped, 1939; made only with single selective trigger, automatic ejectors. Used value, $734.50 to $763.

Eagle Grade, introduced in 1913; dropped, 1939; double triggers, plain extractors, $1073.50 to $1102; double triggers, automatic ejectors, $1158.50 to $1186.50; single selective trigger, plain extractors, $1130 to $1158.50; single trigger, auto ejectors, $1186.50 to $1243.

Crown Grade, introduced in 1913; dropped, 1945; double triggers, automatic ejectors, $1356 to $1412.50; single selective trigger, auto ejectors, $1412.50 to $1469.

Monogram Grade, introduced in 1913; dropped, 1945; selective single trigger, automatic ejectors, $1582 to $1695.

Premier Grade, introduced in 1913; dropped, 1941; single selective trigger, automatic ejectors, $3390 to $3616.

Deluxe Grade, introduced in 1913; dropped, 1945, $5650 to $5876.

Skeet Special, introduced in 1939; dropped, 1942; selective or nonselective single trigger, automatic ejectors, $547 to $554.

Premier Skeet Grade, introduced in 1949; dropped, 1951; single selective trigger, automatic ejectors, $395.50 to $424.

Marlin Deluxe Grade

L.C. SMITH Marlin: double barrel; hammerless; sidelock action; Field Grade is 12 ga. only; 28" barrels; modified/full only; double triggers; case-hardened frame; vent rib; standard extractors; automatic tang safety; checkered pistol-grip stock of select walnut; pistol-grip cap. Deluxe Grade has same specifications as Field Grade, except for better wood, full beavertail forearm, Simmons floating vent rib. Introduced in 1968; dropped, 1972. Used values, Field Grade, $277 to $294; Deluxe Grade, $333 to $350.

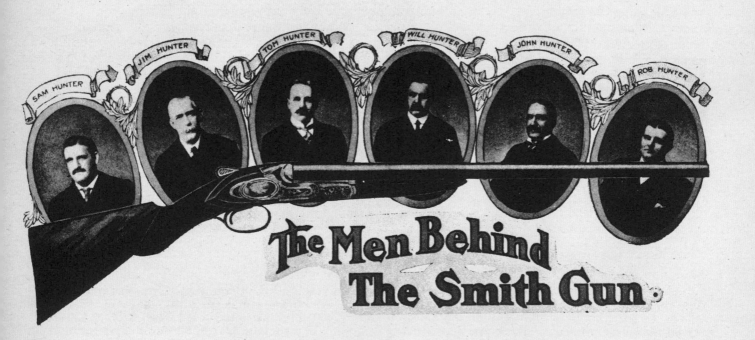

In early days of L.C. Smith manufacture, family members of the Hunter Gun Co. took credit for success in advertisements.

STEVENS

STEVENS Model 620: slide action; hammerless; 12, 16, 20 gauges; 26″, 28″, 30″, 32″ barrels; takedown; 5-rd. tube magazine; cylinder, improved, modified, full chokes; hand-checkered American walnut pistol-grip stock, slide handle; black plastic butt plate. Introduced in 1927; dropped, 1953. Used value, $107.50 to $113.

STEVENS Model 621: slide action; hammerless; 12, 16, 20 gauges; has the same specifications as the Model 620 except for raised solid matted rib. Introduced in 1927; dropped, 1953. Used value, $124.50 to $130.

STEVENS-Springfield Model 311: side-by-side; hammerless; box-lock action; 12, 16, 20, .410 gauges; 26″, 28″, 30″, 32″ barrels; modified/full, cylinder/modified, full/full chokes; early guns had uncheckered American walnut pistol-grip stock, forearm; current production has walnut-finished hardwood stock, fluted comb; double triggers; plastic butt plate. Introduced in 1931; still in production as Savage-Stevens Model 311. Used value, $107.50 to $113.

STEVENS Model 59: bolt-action repeater; takedown; .410-ga. only; 24″ barrel, full choke only; 5-rd. tube magazine; uncheckered one-piece walnut-finished hardwood pistol-grip stock; plastic butt plate. Introduced in 1934; dropped, 1973. Used value, $40 to $45.50.

Model 530ST

STEVENS Model 530: side-by-side; hammerless; box-lock action; 12, 16, 20, .410 gauges; 26″, 28″, 30″, 32″ barrels; modified/full, cylinder/modified, full choke combos; double triggers; early models have recoil pads; hand-checkered American walnut pistol-grip stock, forearm. Introduced in 1936; dropped, 1954. Used value, $113 to $124.50.

Model 530M has the same specifications as Model 530 except stock, forearm are of Tenite plastic. Introduced before World War II; dropped, 1947. Used value, $79.50 to $90.50.

Model 530ST has the same specifications as Model 530 except for single selective trigger. Introduced in 1947; dropped, 1954. Used value, $141.50 to $153.

STEVENS Model 58: bolt-action repeater; takedown; .410-ga. only; 24" barrel; full choke only; 3-rd. detachable box magazine; unchecked one-piece walnut-finished hard- wood pistol-grip stock; plastic butt plate; current model has machine-checkering on grip, forearm. Introduced in 1937; still in production as Savage-Stevens Model 58. Used value, $40 to $45.

STEVENS Model 258: bolt-action repeater; takedown; 20-ga. only; 25" barrel, full choke only; double triggers; unchecked hardwood one-piece pistol-grip stock; black plastic forearm cap, butt plate. Introduced in 1937; dropped, 1965. Used value, $40 to $45.

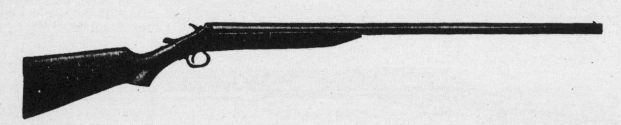

STEVENS Model 107: single-barrel; single-shot; hammer gun; takedown; 12, 16, 20, .410 gauges; 28", 30" barrels in 12, 16 gauges, 28" in 20-ga., 26" in .410; full choke only; automatic ejector; unchecked walnut-finished hardwood pistol-grip stock, forearm. Introduced in 1937; dropped, 1953. Used value $40 to $45.

No. 22-410

STEVENS Model 22-410: over/under combo gun; .22 LR, long, short barrel over .410 shotgun barrel; visible hammer; takedown; 24" barrels; full choke shotgun barrel; single trigger; open rear sight, rifle-type ramp front; original models had unchecked American walnut pistol-grip stock, forearm; later production had Tenite plastic stock, forearm. Introduced in 1938; dropped, 1950. Still in production by Savage Arms as Model 24, with variations. Used values, walnut stock, $68 to $79; plastic stock, $51 to $62.50.

STEVENS Model 240: over/under; hammer gun; takedown; .410-ga. only; 26″ barrels, full choke only; double triggers; early models had uncheckered American walnut pistol-grip stock, forearm; later versions had stock, forearm of Tenite plastic. Introduced in 1939; dropped, 1942. Used values, walnut stock, $200 to $225; plastic stock, $175 to $200.

STEVENS Model 94C: single-barrel; single-shot; hammer gun; 12, 16, 20, .410 gauges; full choke only; 28″, 30″, 32″, 36″ barrels; automatic ejector; top lever breaking; walnut-finished hardwood pistol-grip stock, forearm; machine checkering on current models; color case-hardened frame. Introduced before World War II; still in production as Savage-Stevens Model 94C. Used value, $34 to $40.

STEVENS-Springfield Model 5151: side-by-side; hammerless; box-lock action; 12, 16, 20, .410 gauges; has the same general specifications as Stevens Model 311 except for hand-checkered pistol grip, forearm; recoil pad; two Ivoroid sights. Manufactured prior to World War II. Used value, $113 to $124.50.

Model 5151-ST has the same specifications as Model 5151 except for nonselective single trigger. Used value, $147 to $158.50.

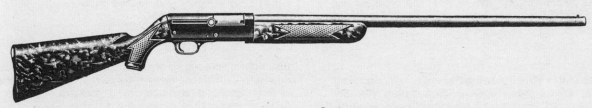

STEVENS Model 124: autoloader; solid frame, hammerless; 12-ga. only; 28″ barrel; improved, modified, full chokes; 2-rd. tube magazine; checkered Tenite plastic stock, forearm. Introduced in 1947; dropped, 1952. Used value, $65 to $75.

Model 77 Standard

STEVENS Model 77: slide action repeater; solid frame; hammerless; 12, 16 gauges; 26″ barrel improved; 28″ modified or full choke; 5-rd. tube magazine; uncheckered walnut-finished hardwood stock, slide handle. Introduced in 1954; dropped, 1971. Used value, $113 to $124.50.

Model 77SC has the same specifications as standard Model 77, except for Savage Super Choke. Used value, $130 to $136.

niversal Firearms

UNIVERSAL Model 101: single-shot, external hammer; takedown; 12-ga. only; 28″, 30″ full-choke barrel; 3″ chamber; top-breaking action; unchecked pistol-grip stock, beavertail forearm. Introduced in 1967; dropped, 1969. Replaced by Single Wing model. Used value, $33 to $38.50.

UNIVERSAL Model 202: side-by-side double barrel; box-lock action; 12, 20 gauges; 26″ improved/modified barrels, 28″ modified/full; 3″ chambers; top breaking; double triggers; hand-checkered European walnut pistol-grip stock, European-style forearm. Introduced in 1967; dropped, 1969. Replaced by Double Wing model. Used value, $93.50 to $99.

Model 203 has the same specifications as Model 202, except is chambered for 3½″ 10-ga. shells; has 32″ full/full barrels. Introduced in 1967; dropped, 1969. Used value, $104.50 to $110.

UNIVERSAL Double Wing: side-by-side; box-lock; top-breaking action; 12, 20 gauges; 26″ improved/modified barrels, 28″ and 30″ modified/full; double triggers; recoil pad; checkered European walnut pistol-grip stock, beavertail forearm. Introduced in 1970; dropped, 1974. Used value, $104.50 to $110.

UNIVERSAL Model 2030: side-by-side; top-breaking box-lock action; has the same general specifications as Double Wing Model except chambered for 3½″ 10-ga. shells; 32″ full/full barrels only. Introduced in 1970; dropped, 1974. Used value, $121 to $126.50.

UNIVERSAL Auto Wing: autoloader; recoil operated; takedown; 12-ga. only; 5-shot magazine, 3-shot plug furnished; 2¾″ chamber; 25″, 28″, 30″ barrel; improved, modified, full chokes; vent rib; ivory bead front, middle sights; cross-bolt safety; interchangeable barrels; checkered European walnut pistol-grip stock, grooved forearm. Introduced in 1970; dropped, 1974. Used value, $100 to $105.

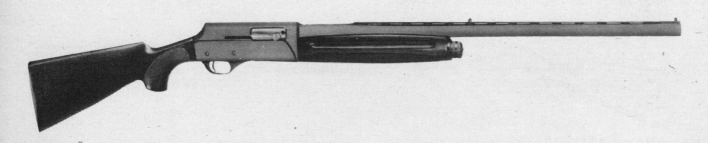

UNIVERSAL Duck Wing: autoloader; recoil operated; takedown; 12-ga. only. Has the same specifications as Auto Wing model except has 28″, 30″ barrel only; full choke only; exposed metal parts coated with olive green Teflon-S. Introduced in 1970; dropped, 1972. Used value, $120 to $125.

UNIVERSAL Over Wing: over/under; hammerless; box-lock; top-breaking action; 12, 20 gauges; 3" chambers; 26" improved/modified, 28" or 30" modified/full barrels; vent rib; front, middle sights; checkered European walnut pistol-grip stock, forearm; recoil pad; double triggers; single trigger model with engraved receiver at added cost. Introduced in 1970; dropped, 1974. Used values, double trigger model, $165 to $170.50; single trigger, $231 to $236.50.

UNIVERSAL Single Wing: single-shot; external hammer; top-breaking action; 12-ga. only; 3" chamber; takedown; 28" full or modified barrel; uncheckered European walnut pistol-grip stock, beavertail forearm; automatic ejector. Introduced in 1970; dropped, 1974. Used value; $33 to $39.50.

UNIVERSAL BAIKAL MC-21: autoloader; takedown; 12-ga. only; 5-rd. magazine; 26" improved, 28" modified, 30" full choke barrels; vent rib; hand-checkered European walnut cheekpiece stock; white spacers at pistol grip, butt plate; hand-rubbed finish; grooved forearm; chrome-lined barrel, chamber; reversible safety; target grade trigger. Manufactured in Russia. Introduced in 1973. Used value, $250 to $260.

UNIVERSAL BAIKAL TOZ-66: side-by-side; exposed hammers; 12-ga. only; 2¾" chambers; 20" improved/modified, 28" modified/full barrels; hand-checkered European hardwood pistol-grip stock, beavertail forearm; chrome-lined barrels, chambers; hand-engraved receiver; extractors. Manufactured in Russia. Introduced in 1973. Used value, $100 to $110.

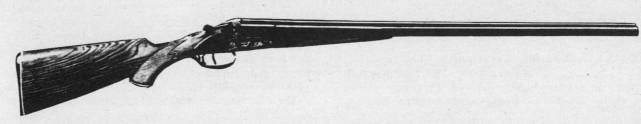

UNIVERSAL BAIKAL IJ-58M: side-by-side; hammerless; 12-ga. only; 2¾" chambers; 26" improved/modified, 28" modified/full barrels; hand-checkered European walnut pistol-grip stock, beavertail forearm; hinged front double trigger; chrome-lined barrels, chambers; hand-engraved receiver; extractors. Manufactured in Russia. Introduced in 1973; Used value, $120 to $130.

UNIVERSAL BAIKAL MC-10: side-by-side; hammerless; 12, 20 gauges; 2¾" chambers; 12-ga. has 28" modified/full barrels, 20-ga., 26" improved/modified; hand-checkered fancy European walnut stock, semi-beavertail forearm; choice of pistol grip or straight stock; chrome-lined barrels, chambers, internal parts; raised solid rib; double triggers; auto safety; extractors or selective ejectors; receiver engraved with animal bird scenes; engraved trigger guard, tang. Manufactured in Russia. Introduced in 1973. Used value, $450 to $475.

SHOTGUNS

UNIVERSAL BAIKAL IJ-25: over/under; 12-ga. only; 2¾″ chambers; 26″ skeet/skeet barrels, 28″ modified/full, 30″ improved/full; hand-checkered European walnut pistol-grip stock, ventilated forearm; white spacers at pistol-grip cap, recoil pad; single nonselective trigger; chrome-lined barrels, chambers, internal parts; vent rib; hand-engraved, silver inlaid receiver, forearm latch, trigger guard. Manufactured in Russia. Introduced in 1973. Used value, $330 to $350.

UNIVERSAL IJ-27: over/under; 12-ga. only; has the same general specifications as IJ-25, except for double triggers, automatic safety, nonselective ejectors. Introduced in 1973; Used value, $215 to $225.

Universal Baikal IJ-27E has same specifications as the IJ-27, except for substitution of selective ejectors. Used value, $225 to $235.

UNIVERSAL BAIKAL MC-5: over/under; 12-ga. only; 2¾″ chambers; 26″ improved/modified, skeet/skeet barrels; fancy hand-checkered European walnut stock; choice of straight or pistol-grip stock, with or without cheekpiece; nonremovable forearm; engraved receiver; double triggers; extractors; hand-fitted solid rib; hammer interceptors; chrome-lined barrels, chambers, internal parts. Manufactured in Russia. Introduced in U.S. in 1973; Used value, $350 to $370.

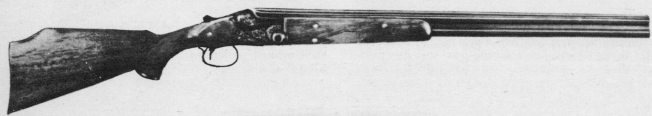

UNIVERSAL BAIKAL MC-6: over/under; 12-ga. only; has the same specifications as MC-5, except is skeet model, with single nonselective trigger, raised rib. Used value, $575 to $600.

UNIVERSAL BAIKAL MC-7: over/under; 12, 20 gauges; 2¾″ chambers; 12-ga., 28″ modified/full, 20-ga., 26″ improved/modified barrels; hand-checkered European walnut straight or pistol-grip stock, beavertail forearm; double triggers; selective ejectors; solid raised rib; chrome-lined barrels, chambers, internal parts; hand-chiseled, engraved reciever. Manufactured in Russia. Introduced in U.S. in 1973; Used value, $1100 to $1175.

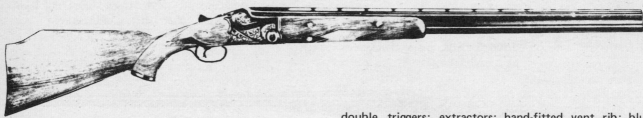

UNIVERSAL BAIKAL MC-8: over/under; 12-ga. only; 2¾″ chambers; 26″ special skeet barrels; 28″ modified/full; two-barrel set; fancy hand-checkered European walnut Monte Carlo pistol-grip stock, nonremovable forearm; double triggers; extractors; hand-fitted vent rib; blued, engraved receiver; chrome-lined barrels, chambers, internal parts; single selective trigger, selective ejectors available at no extra cost. Manufactured in Russia. Introduced in U.S. in 1973; Used value, $450 to $475.

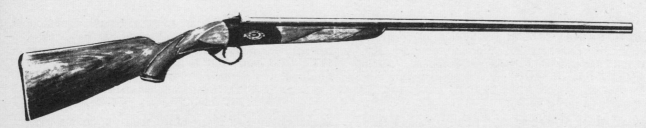

UNIVERSAL BAIKAL IJ-18: single-barrel, single-shot; 12, 20 gauges; 2¾″ chamber; in 12-ga., 28″ modified, 30″ full choke barrel, 20-ga., 26″ modified; hand-checkered European walnut pistol-grip stock, forearm; white spacers at pistol grip, plastic butt plate; cross-bolt safety in trigger guard; cocking indicator; chrome-lined barrel, chamber. Manufactured in Russia. Introduced in U.S. in 1973; Used value, $32.50 to $35.

WESTLEY RICHARDS

WESTLEY RICHARDS Best Quality: side-by-side; double barrel; hammerless; box-lock action; 12, 16, 20 gauges; barrel lengths, chokes to order; hand-detachable locks; hinged lockplate; selective ejectors; hand-checkered walnut stock, forearm; choice of straight, half-pistol grip; double or single selective trigger. Introduced in 1890; dropped, 1965. Used values, double trigger model, $3450 to $3622.50; single selective trigger, $3967.50 to $4140.

Best Quality Pigeon or Wildfowl Model has same specifications as standard model except for stronger action, triple bolting, 12-ga. only, chambered for 2¾", 3" shells; 28", 30" full choke barrels. Introduced in 1900; still in production. Used values, double trigger model, $3967.50 to $4140; single selective trigger, $4600 to $4772.50.

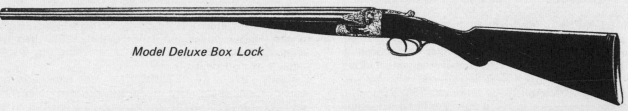

Model Deluxe Box Lock

WESTLEY RICHARDS Model DeLuxe Quality: side-by-side double barrel; hammerless; box-lock action; hand-detachable locks; triple-bite lever work; other specifications are same as Best Quality model, except for better workmanship throughout. Available in Pigeon or Wildfowl Model at same price. Introduced in 1890; still in production. Used values, double trigger model, $5692.50 to $5980; single selective trigger, $6267.50 to $6440.

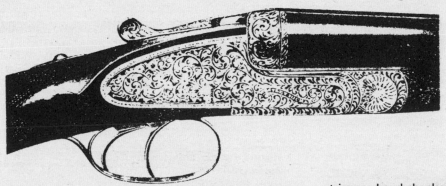

Model Deluxe Sidelock

WESTLEY RICHARDS Sidelock Model DeLuxe Quality: side-by-side double barrel; hammerless; hand-detachable side locks; 12, 16, 20 gauges; barrel lengths, chokes to order; selective ejectors; double triggers, single selective triggers; hand-checkered European stock, forearm; straight or half-pistol grip available in Pigeon or Wildfowl Model at same price. Introduced in 1910; still in production. Used values, double trigger model, $6267.50 to $6440; single selective trigger, $6785 to $7187.50.

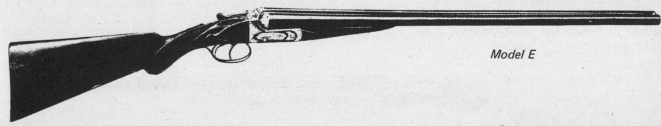

Model E

WESTLEY RICHARDS Model E: side-by-side double barrel; hammerless; Anson & Deeley box-lock action; 12, 16, 20 gauges; barrel lengths, choking to order; selective ejector or nonejector; double triggers; hand-checkered European walnut stock, forearm; straight or half-pistol grip; Pigeon or Wildfowl Model available at same price. Introduced in late 1920s; still in production. Used values, ejector model, $2472 to $2587; nonejector, $2012 to $2127.

WESTLEY RICHARDS Ovundo: over/under; hammerless; box-lock action; 12-ga. only; barrel lengths, chokes to order; hand-detachable locks, dummy side plates; single selective trigger; hand-checkered European walnut stock, forearm; straight or half-pistol grip. Introduced in 1920; dropped, 1945. Used value, $8280 to $8452.50.

WINCHESTER

WINCHESTER Model 97: slide-action shotgun; visible hammer, takedown or solid frame in 12, 16 gauges, 5-shot tube magazine. Barrel lengths: 26″, 28″, 30″, 32″; last in 12-ga. only; choked full, modified, cylinder bore, with intermediate chokes introduced in 1931. Gun, introduced in 1897, was revamp of Model 1893. Numerous variations were introduced, discontinued over the years, with model discontinued, 1957. Standard grade has plain stock and grooved slide handle, side ejection port. Retail price when discontinued, $89.95; used value, $201.50 to $218.50.

Model 97 also was available in higher grade trap, tournament, pigeon grades. Stocks on higher grades were of better walnut, checkered. On these, slide handles also were of better wood, checkered, in standard or semi-beavertail conformation, without the deep wood grooves of standard model. Higher grades were discontinued, 1939. Used value on trap grade, $334 to $375; tournament grade, $414 to $460; pigeon grade, $632.50 to $747.50.

Model 97 also was offered as riot gun with same specifications as standard model, takedown or solid frame. In 12-ga. only, it had 20″ cylinder bore barrel. Trench gun, the same as riot model, was issued with bayonet by U.S. government in 1917-18. Used value on riot model, $207 to $218.50; trench model, $287.50 to $328.

WINCHESTER Model 1911: autoloading shotgun was hammerless, takedown, in 12-ga. only. Barrels were plain in 26″, 28″, 30″, 32″; standard chokes; 4-shell tubular magazine; stock and forearm plain or checkered. Introduced in 1911; discontinued, 1925. Original retail price, $61.50; used value, $213 to $230.

WINCHESTER Model 12: slide-action shotgun; in 12, 16, 20 and 28 gauges, in three standard versions; has blued receiver of chrome-moly steel, engine-turned bolt and carrier, ventilated rib; butt stock and slide handle are walnut with fine-line hand checkering; magazine capacity, 5 rds. Field gun has 26″, 28″, 30″ barrels, with choice of improved cylinder, modified or full, full chokes, respectively. Model 12 trap gun is full choke only with 30″ barrel, choice of standard or Monte Carlo stock, recoil pad; skeet gun is skeet choked, with 26" barrel, fitted stock, recoil pad. Introduced originally in 1912; dropped from line in 1965; reintroduced in 1972; retail price on current models starts at $575, depending upon style. Price in 1965, when dropped was $237.50, for skeet model, for 1972 model, $290 to $360, depending on style; for pre-1965 models, $185. Nostalgia has resulted in older Model 12s often selling for more than original retail price. As an example of supply and demand, in 1965, price for pigeon grade was $372.50. One year later — with Model 12 discontinued and considered a custom gun, price leaped to $825.

Prior to discontinuance in 1965, there were many variations of Model 12 and an even wider variation of used values. Model 12 Featherweight, made from 1959 to 1962, had plain barrel, modified takedown, alloy guard, in 12-ga. only; available in 26", improved cylinder; 28", modified or full; 30", full. Used value, $253 to $276. Standard version with matted rib, discontinued after WWII, has used value of $345 to $374. Standard grade, with vent rib, also discontinued after WWII, was 12-ga. only with 26¾" or 30" barrel. Used value, $385 to $414. Manufactured from 1918 to 1963 was Model 12 riot model, in 12-ga., with 20" cylinder bore barrel. Used value, $230 to $253.

The Model 12 has appeared in several skeet configurations. The standard skeet model, discontinued after WWII, was in 12, 16, 20, 28 gauges, with 5-shot tube magazine, 26" barrel, skeet choke. Featured red or ivory bead front sight, 94B mid-sight. Pistol grip was checkered as was extension slide handle. Used value, $402 to $436. Skeet model with plain barrel, sans sights, was manufactured from 1937 to 1947; used value, $345 to $374. Style featuring Cutts Compensator, with plain barrel, was discontinued, 1954; used value, $402 to $420. Discontinued in 1965, skeet style with ventilated rib was 12, 20 gauges; used value, $454.50 to $483.

Of trap configurations, original was discontinued after WWII. It had specs of standard Model 12, plus extension slide handle, recoil pad, straighter stock, checkered pistol grip, recoil pad, 30" matted rib barrel; 12-ga., full choke only. Used value, $402 to $431. Trap model with ventilated rib was same as standard trap otherwise; used value, $437 to $489. Model 12 trap with Monte Carlo stock and vent rib; used value, $517 to $546.

Model 12 also was produced in two styles for duck hunters. The heavy duck gun, in 12-ga. only, handled 3" shells, had 3-shot magazine, recoil pad, 30" or 32" barrel lengths, full choke only. Discontinued, 1964; used value, $368 to $385. Same style, with matted rib, was discontinued, 1959; used value, $402.50 to $420.

Model 12 pigeon grade guns virtually constitute an empire unto themselves. These were deluxe versions of the standard, field, duck, skeet or trap guns made on special order only. Pigeon grade guns had finer finishes, hand-worked actions, engine-turned bolts, carriers. Stock dimensions were to specs of individual, with top grade walnut, fancy hand-checkering. At added cost from $50 to $250 or more, engraving and carving could be added. This particular grade was discontinued, 1965; prices are based upon variations, sans added engraving and carving. Range of used values is: field gun, plain barrel, $460 to $489; with vent rib, $604 to $632; skeet gun, matted rib, $604 to $632; vent rib, $799 to $834; skeet, Cutts Compensator, $644 to $673; trap gun, matted rib, $684 to $719; with vent rib, $862 to $880.

Used values for Winchester Model 12 Super Pigeon grade can be no more than an approximation, since these are rare as pearls and, like pearls, are worth what the buyer wants to pay. Super Pigeon grade, introduced, 1965, still is produced in conjunction with the Model 12, reintroduced to the trade in 1972. Custom Model 12 has the same general specs as standard models; available in 12-ga. only, with any standard choke and barrel length choice of 26", 28", or 30", with vent rib. Receiver is engraved with a hand-honed and fitted action. Stocks, forearm are fancy walnut and made to individual order. Used value starts at $1150. After that, you're on your own.

WINCHESTER Model 20: single-shot shotgun. Takedown hammer gun, .410 only, for 2½" shell. Only in 26", full choke barrel; checkered pistol grip, forearm. Introduced in 1919; discontinued, 1924. Retail when discontinued, $16.50; used value, $172.50 to $201.50.

WINCHESTER Model 36: single-shot bolt-action takedown shotgun. Cocks by pulling rearward on knurled firing-pin head, the same mechanism used in some Winchester single-shot rifles. Shot 9mm short or long shot or ball cartridges interchangeably. Has one-piece plain wood stock, forearm, special trigger guard that forms the pistol grip, composition butt plate. Round 18" barrel. No guns were serialized. Introduced in 1920; discontinued, 1927. Price at time discontinued, $7.05; used value, $103.50 to $115.

WINCHESTER Model 41: single-shot bolt-action shotgun. Standard takedown style only, with 24" full choke barrel, firing .410-ga., 2½" ammo. Chambering was changed in 1933 for 3" shell. Stock is plain one-piece walnut; pistol grip; hard rubber butt plate. Straight grip was optional at no increase in price; checkered stocks on special order. Model 41s were not numbered serially; increase in value reflects interest as a collector item. Introduced in 1920; discontinued, 1934. Original retail, $9.95; used value, $200 to $225.

Standard Model 21

WINCHESTER Model 21: double barrel hammerless field gun; boxlock; automatic safety. Early models have double triggers, nonselective ejection; post WWII guns have selective single trigger, selective ejection features. Made in 12, 16, 20 gauges, with 26", 28", 30", 32" barrels, last only in 12-ga.; raised matted or ventilated rib. Chokes are full, improved modified, modified, improved cylinder, skeet; choice of straight or pistol grip stock; regular, beavertail forearm; checkered walnut. Introduced in 1931; discontinued, 1959. Retail when discontinued, $425; used value with double triggers, nonselective ejection, $914 to $977; double triggers, selective ejection, $1144 to $1265; selective single trigger, nonselective ejection, $1144 to $1265; selective single trigger, selective ejection, $1380 to $1466.50; with ventilated rib, add $144 to $172.50.

Model 21 skeet gun is same general design as standard model, but has 26", 28" barrels only; skeet chokes; red bead front sight; selective single trigger, selective ejection, nonauto safety, checkered French walnut stock, beavertail forearm; wooden butt is checkered without pad or butt plate; discontinued, 1958. Used value, with matted rib, $1437 to $1524; with ventilated rib, $1610 to $1725.

Model 21 trap model differs from standard with 30" or 32" barrels, full choke, selective trigger, nonauto safety, selective ejection; pistol grip or straight stock, beavertail forearm of checkered walnut. Discontinued, 1958. Used value, with matted rib, $1437.50 to $1524.50; with vent rib, $1610 to $1725.

Model 21 duck gun has same general specs as field gun, but is chambered for 3", 12-ga. shells; has 30", 32" barrels, full choke; selective ejection, selective single trigger, recoil pad, checkered beavertail forearm, pistol grip stock. Discontinued, 1958; used value, with matted rib, $1466.50 to $1552.50; with vent rib, $1639 to $1754.50.

As with the Model 12, the Winchester Model 21 has become a special order gun. Since 1960, it has been offered only in custom, pigeon and Grand American grades. General specs are as for the standard Model 21, but these have full fancy American walnut stocks, forearms, with fancy checkering, hand-honed working parts. Carved woodwork, gold inlays and engraving are available at added cost. The custom trio still is being manufactured. Used value, custom grade, $2587 to $2760; pigeon grade, $3622 to $3910; Grand American, $4660 to $4887.

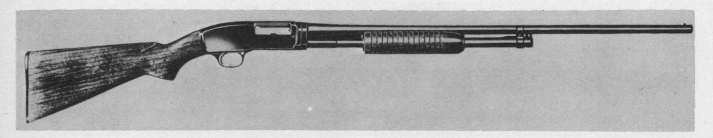

WINCHESTER Model 42: hammerless slide-action shotgun; .410 only; 26" or 28" barrel, full or modified choke; chambered for 3" shells; available with plain walnut stock, no checkering; slide handle grooved; capacity of 6 shells in 2½" length, 5 shells in 3" length; weight, 5-7/8 to 6 lbs. Trap grade had full fancy wood and checkering, until dropped in 1940. Introduced in May, 1933; dropped in 1963; last retail price, $101.95; used value, $300 to $400.

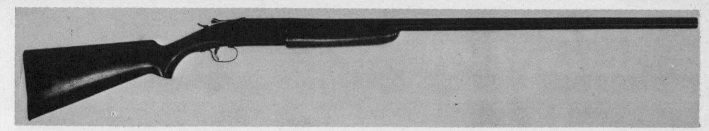

WINCHESTER Model 37: single-shot shotgun; is top lever, breakdown construction with automatic ejector, semi-hammerless action; plain barrel only in 12, 16, 20, .410 gauges; barrel lengths, 28", 30", 32" in all but .410, with choice of 26" or 28"; all full choke. Stock is plain walnut with composition butt plate, pistol grip, semi-beavertail forearm. On special order, at no extra charge, barrels could be modified or cylinder choke. Introduced in 1936, discontinued, 1963. Last retail price was $35; used value, $57.50 to $72.

WINCHESTER Model 24: hammerless double-barrel shotgun in 12, 16, 20 gauges. With 26" barrels, chokes were improved/modified; 28", modified/full and improved/modified; 30" barrels, modified/full, in 12-ga. only. Stock is plain walnut, with pistol grip, semi-beaver-tailed forearm, composition butt plate; straight stocks at no added charge; a breakdown model, it has double triggers, automatic ejectors. Introduced in 1940; discontinued, 1957. Price when discontinued, $96.20; used value, $300 to $350.

WINCHESTER Model 40: autoloading shotgun; 12-ga. only, with streamlined receiver, hammerless action; 4-rd. tube magazine; 28" or 30" barrels; choke, modified or full. Had plain pistol-grip stock, semi-beavertail forearm, ramp bead front sight. Introduced, 1940; discontinued, 1941. Retail, when discontinued, $68.15; used value, $250 to $300.

Model 40 skeet model had 24" barrel, with Cutts compensator; checkering on pistol grip, forearm; grip cap. Original price, $73.50; used value, $270.50 to $305.

Standard Model 50 Field

WINCHESTER Model 50: autoloading shotgun; field grades available in 12 and 20 gauges; skeet, 12; trap, 12; 12-gauge barrels were 30" full choke, 28" full or modified, 28" improved or skeet. There were numerous options, including a ventilated rib and gun was chambered for field or high-velocity loads, without adjustment; stock was of American walnut, hand-checkered with fluted comb, composition butt plate; magazine tube was below barrel, with two-shell capacity, side ejection. Featherweight model was adopted in 1958. Weight for standard was 7¼ lbs. for 12-gauge, 7 lbs. for Featherweight, 5¾ lbs. for 20-gauge. Pigeon grade gun was available with any combination of barrel lengths and chokes. Barrels interchangeable, with bead front sight. Gun worked on short recoil principle. When fired, floating chamber moved rearward to start the action moving to the rear. Bolt continued to rear, extracting and ejecting spent shell, lifting new one into position. Introduced in late 1954; discontinued in 1961. Retailed at $144.95 for standard grade; used value, $260 to $300.

The Model 50 field gun is the same as the standard, except for ventilated rib; used value, $300 to $325. Skeet version has 26" barrel vent rib, skeet stock in selected walnut, skeet choke; used value, $300 to $335. Model 50 trap, 12-ga. only; full choke 30" vent rib barrel; Monte Carlo stock of select walnut; used value, $375 to $400.

WINCHESTER Model 25: slide-action repeating shotgun; solid frame; hammerless; 12-ga. only, with 4-rd. tubular magazine. Made with 28" plain barrel in improved cylinder, modified or full choke; metal bead front sight. Stock, grooved slide handle are walnut, with pistol grip. Introduced, 1950; discontinued, 1954. Used value, $250 to $275.

Model 25 was made in riot model from 1949 to 1955; only change from standard was a 20" cylinder choke barrel. Used value, $155.50 to $172.50.

WINCHESTER Model 59: autoloading shotgun; 12-ga. only. Had checkered stock, forearm. Choices were 26" barrel, improved cylinder; 28", modified or full; 30" full choke. Special order 26" barrel has Versalite choke system of cylinder tubes (introduced in 1961) to allow any choke variation. Introduced in 1959; discontinued, 1965. Retail price when discontinued, $160; used value, $230 to $287.50.

(Winchester also made a Model 59 rimfire rifle in 1930 — don't be confused by the model numbers.)

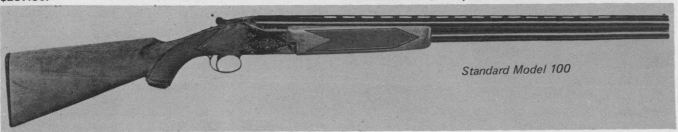

Standard Model 100

WINCHESTER Model 101: field gun with box-lock action, engraved receiver, automatic ejectors, single selective trigger, combo barrel selector, safety; vent ribbed barrels. Model 101 is virtually an empire in itself, being made in various configurations and styles. Handles 2¾" shells in 12, 28 gauges, 3" in 20, .410; 30" barrels on 12 only, choked modified/full; 28", modified/full; 26", 12-ga. only, and 26½", choked improved/modified. Stock, forearm are checkered French walnut. Made in Japan by Olin Kodensha. The 12-ga. was introduced in 1963; other gauges, 1966. Still manufactured, Used value, 12, 20 gauges, $424 to $452; 28, .410, $452 to $480.50.

Model 101 magnum field gun is same as standard field gun, but chambered for 12 and 20-ga., 3" magnum shells.

The 30" barrels are choked full/full, modified/full; has recoil pad. Introduced, 1966, still in production; used value, $429.50 to $452.

Model 101 skeet gun is the same as the field model, except for skeet stock, forearm; barrels for 12-ga. are 26", for 20-ga., 26½"; 28, .410, 28"; all gauges skeet choked. Introduced in 1966, still in production; used value for 12, 20 gauges, $452 to $480; 28, .410, $480 to $508.

Model 101 over/under trap gun has trap stock, Monte Carlo or straight; recoil pad; 12-ga. only; barrels are 30", 32", improved modified/full, full/full. Introduced in 1966, still produced. Used value, straight stock, $508.50 to $537; Monte Carlo, $520 to $537.

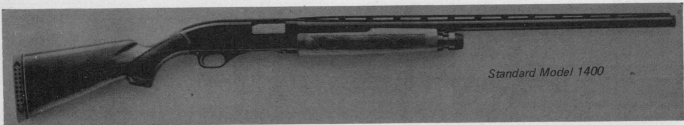

Standard Model 1400

WINCHESTER Model 1400: field gun; gas-operated take-down autoloader; 2-shot magazines; 2¾" chamber for 12, 16, 20 gauges; plain barrel or with vent rib in 26", 28", 30" lengths; improved cylinder; modified, full choke, or with WinChoke; stock, forearm had impressed checkering on walnut; recoil pad was available with recoil reduction system and Cycolac stock. Introduced in 1964; dropped in 1968 to be replaced by Model 1400 Mark II. Original price, $149.95; used value, with plain barrel, $102 to $119; with vent rib, $136 to $141; with WinChoke, add $3.50 to $6; with recoil reduction system add $40 to $56.50.

Model 1400 Mark II, introduced in 1968, has restyled stock, forearm, push-button carrier release; has front-locking, rotating bolt locking into barrel extension. Self-compensating gas system for standard and 2¾" loads; aluminum receiver, engine-turned bolt, push-button action release,

cross-bolt safety. Used value, plain barrel, $124.50 to $136; vent rib, $141.50 to $158.50.

Model 1400 deer gun, made from 1965 to 1968, was same as standard Model 1400, but had 22" barrel rifle sights for slugs or buckshot. Used value, $124 to $136.

Model 1400 skeet gun, is 12, 20 gauges only; has 26" vent rib barrel, skeet choke; stock, forearm are semi-fancy walnut; stock is Cycolac when recoil reduction system is used. Introduced in 1965, discontinued, 1968; used value, $181 to $198; with recoil reduction system, add $39.50 to $56.50.

Model 1400 trap gun, made from 1965 to 1968, 12-ga., 30" vent rib barrel, full choke; has semi-fancy walnut stock or recoil reduction system. Used value, with trap stock, $181 to $198; with Monte Carlo, $198 to $209; with recoil reduction system, add $40 to $56.50.

WINCHESTER Model 1200: slide action takedown shotgun, with front-lock rotary bolt; 4-rd. magazine; in 12, 16, 20 gauges, with 2¾" chambers; plain or vent barrels, 26", 28", 30" in length; improved cylinder, modified, full choke choice, or with interchangeable WinChoke tubes for

cylinder, modified or full. Stock, slide handle are press-checkered; walnut stock; recoil pad. Introduced in 1964. Model with Winchester recoil reduction system, introduced with Cycolac stock, introduced in 1966, discontinued, 1970. Original plain model was priced at $185. Used value, with plain barrel, $102 to $113; with vent rib barrel, $113 to $115; with WinChoke, add $3.50 to $6; with recoil reduction system, add $40 to $56.50.

The Model 1200 magnum field gun was introduced in 1966; same as standard Model 1200 field gun, but chambered for 3" magnum shells in 12, 20 gauges; choice of plain or vent rib; 28", 30" full choke barrels. Used value, with plain barrel, $113 to $130; with vent rib barrel, $141 to $147; for recoil reduction system, add $40 to $56.50.

The Model 1200 appeared as a deer gun from 1965 to 1974. Same as standard model, has rifle-type sights on 22" barrel. It was meant for rifled slugs or buckshot; 12-ga. only, with sling swivels. Used value, $113 to $124.50.

Model 1200 skeet gun, made from 1965 to 1973, was 12, 20 gauges only, with 2-shot magazine, tuned trigger; 26" vent rib barrel; semi-fancy walnut stock, forearm; skeet choke. Used value, $169.50 to $181; with Winchester recoil system, add $40 to $56.50.

Model 1200 trap gun was in 12-ga. only; 2-shot magazine; 30" full choke vent rib barrel; 28" with WinChoke; regular or Monte Carlo trap stock of semi-fancy walnut; made from 1965 to 1973. Used value, with regular trap stock, $169 to $186; Monte Carlo stock, $181 to $198; with Winchester recoil reduction system, add $40 to $56.50; with WinChoke, add $3.50 to $6.

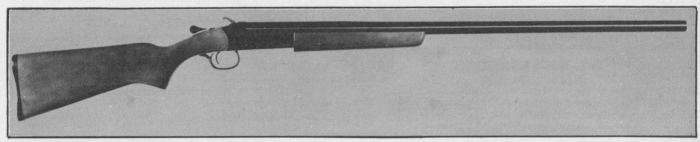

WINCHESTER Model 370: single-barrel shotgun; available in 12-gauge in 36", 32" and 30" barrel lengths; in 16-gauge with 32" and 30"; 20 and 28-gauge, 28" barrels, .410 with 26" barrels. All are chambered for 3" shells, except 16 and 28 gauges, which use 2¾" shells. Weight varies with gauges and barrel length, ranges from 5½ to 6¼ lbs. Break-open type, it has automatic ejection, plain American hardwood stock; uncapped pistol grip and hard rubber butt plate. In full choke only; with bead front sight. Introduced in 1968; discontinued, to be replaced by Model 37A. Last retail price, $35.95; used value, $32 to $36.

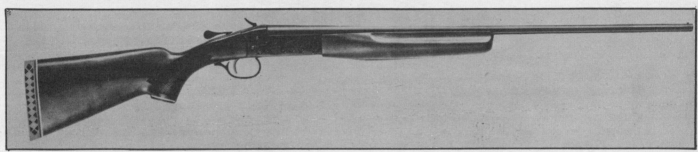

WINCHESTER Model 37A: single-shot shotgun; available in all gauges from 12 through .410, with choice of barrel in 25", 28", 30", 36"; with exception of 16 and 28 gauges, all are chambered for 3" shells; all full chokes. Also available in Youth model with 26" barrel in 20 and .410 gauges in improved-modified and full chokes respectively; stock is of walnut-stained hardwood with checkering on bottom of forearm and sides of capped pistol grip; features top lever opening to right or left, concave hammer spur; white spacer between grip cap and butt plate. Introduced in 1973; retail price, $68.95 for 12-gauge with 36" barrel and Youth model; all others, $62.95; used value, $37 to $41.

MISCELLANEOUS SHOTGUNS

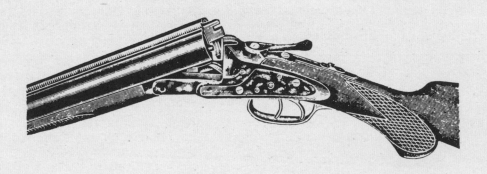

ARMALITE AR-17 Golden Gun: 12-ga. only; 2-shot only; recoil operated, semi-auto; barrel, receiver housing of aluminum alloy; 24" barrel; interchangeable choke tubes for improved, modified; full chokes; polycarbonate stock, forearm; recoil pad; gold-anodized finish; also with black-anodized finish. Introduced, 1964; discontinued, 1965. Some collector value, as only 2000 made. Used value, $328 to $362.

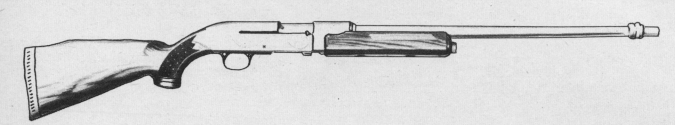

BAKER Batavia Leader: hammerless double; 12, 16, 20 gauges; 26" to 32" barrel, any standard choke combo; sidelock; automatic ejectors or plain extractors; hand-checkered pistol grip, forearm; American walnut stock. Introduced in 1921; discontinued, 1930. Manufactured by Baker Gun Co., Batavia, New York. Used value, with automatic ejectors, $299 to $316.50; plain extractors, $207 to $224.50.

BAKER Black Beauty Special: same specs as Batavia Leader, but with higher quality finish; dropped, 1930. Used value, with auto ejectors, $569.50 to $592.50; plain extractors, $454.50 to $471.50.

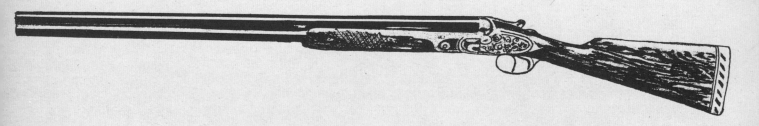

BOSS Over/Under: sidelock action; 12, 16, 20, 28, .410 gauges; 26", 28", 30", 34" barrels; any desired choke combo; automatic ejectors; double or nonselective single trigger; selective single trigger extra; hand-checkered European walnut stock, forearm; recoil pad; matted or vent rib. Introduced about 1952; still in production. Not currently imported. Used values, double triggers, $5750 to $6037.50; nonselective single trigger, $5750 to $6037.50; selective single trigger, $6210 to $6498.

BOSS Double Barrel: side-by-side; sidelock; 12, 16, 20, 28, .410 gauges; 26'', 28'', 30'', 32'' barrels; any desired choke combo; automatic ejectors; double or nonselective single trigger; selective single trigger extra; hand-checkered European walnut stock, forearm; straight or pistol-grip stock. Introduced after WWI; still in production. Not currently imported. Used values, double triggers, $4600 to $4830; nonselective single trigger, $4600 to $4830; selective single trigger, $5060 to $5290.

BREDA Autoloader: takedown autoloader; 12-ga. only; 4-rd. tube magazine; 25½'', 27½'' barrels; chromed bore; plain or with matted rib; hand-checkered European walnut stock, forearm; straight or pistol-grip style; available in three grades with chromed receivers, engraving. Grade, value depends upon amount of engraving, quality of wood. Introduced in 1946; still in production. Used values, Standard, with plain barrel, $149.50 to $172.50; with matted rib, $161 to $185; Grade I, $299 to $316.50; Grade II, $345 to $368; Grade III, $379.50 to $402.50.

Magnum 12 Autoloader model has the same specs as Standard Breda Autoloader, except is chambered for 12-ga. 3'' magnum shell. Introduced in 1950; still in production. Used values, with plain barrel, $161 to $178.50; with matted rib, $172.50 to $190.

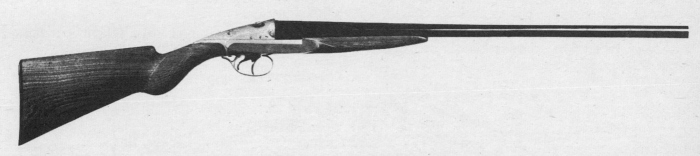

DARNE Bird-Hunter: double, 20, 12 gauges; sliding breach action; double triggers; automatic selective ejection; 25½'' barrels; improved cylinder, modified; raised rib; deluxe walnut stock, hand-checkered forearm; case-hardened receiver. Manufactured in France; imported by Firearms Center, Victoria, Texas. Used value, $356.50 to $368.

Darne Pheasant-Hunter is same as the Bird-Hunter, except for highly engraved receiver, fancy walnut stock, forearm; 12-ga. only, 27½'' barrels, modified and full chokes. Used value, $454.50 to $477.50.

Darne Quail-Hunter Supreme is same as Bird-Hunter model, except for premium grade engraving, extra-fancy wood; 20, 28 gauges only; 25½'' barrels, improved/modified chokes. Used value, $604 to $632.50.

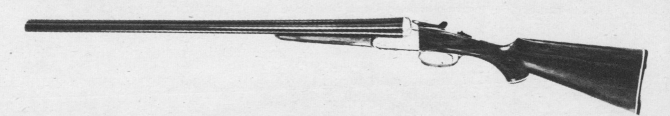

DAVIDSON Model 63B: double barrel; 12, 16, 20, 28, .410 gauges; Anson & Deely box-lock action; plain extractors, automatic safety; engraved, nickel-plated frame; barrel lengths, 25'' in .410, 26'', 28'' and also 30'' in 12-ga. only; chokes are improved cylinder/modified, modified/full, full/full; hand-checkered walnut stock; pistol grip. Manufactured in Spain; imported by Davidson Firearms Co., Greensboro, North Carolina. Introduced in 1963; still in production. Used value, $155.50 to $161.

DAVIDSON Model 63B Magnum: same specs as standard 63B, except chambered for 3'' 12-ga. magnum shells and 3½'' for 10-ga.; 10-ga. has 32'' full/full barrels; still in production. Used value, 10-ga. magnum, $172.50 to $178.50; 12, 20-ga. magnums, $155.50 to $172.50.

SHOTGUNS

DAVIDSON Model 69SL: double; sidelock action, detachable sideplates; 20, 12 gauges; 26" barrels, modified/improved; 28" barrels, modified/full; nickel-plated, engrav-ed action; hand-checkered European walnut stock. Introduced in 1963; still in production. Used value, $138 to $144.

FERLACH Constant Companion: side-by-side double barrel; Anson & Deeley-type action; 12, 16, 20 gauges; 28", 30" barrels; tapered boring; quadruple Greener bolt; auto safety; ejectors; engraved receiver; double triggers; hand-checkered black walnut pistol-grip stock; cheekpiece. Manufactured in Austria. Originally imported by Flaig's. Introduced in 1956; dropped, 1958. Used value, $201 to $213.

GALEF/ZABALA: double; 10, 12, 16, 20, 28, .410 gauges; Anson & Deeley-type box-lock action; barrels, 32", 10, 12 gauges only, full/full; 30", 12-ga. only, modified/full; 28", all except .410, modified/full; 26", 12, 20, 28 gauges, improved/modified; 26", .410 only, modified/full; 22", 12-ga. only, improved/improved; hand-checkered European walnut stock; beavertail forearm; recoil pad; automatic safety, plain extractors. Imported from Spain; still in production. Used value, 10-ga., $149.50 to $158.50; other gauges, $123.50 to $129.50.

GALEF/ZOLI Silver Snipe: over/under; 12, 20 gauges, 3" chambers; Purdey-type double box-lock, cross-bolt action; barrels, 26", improved/modified; 28", modified/full; 30", 12-ga. only, modified/full; 26" skeet, skeet/skeet; 30" trap, full/full; European walnut stock; hand-checkered pistol grip, forearm; automatic safety, except on trap, skeet models; vent rib, single trigger, chrome-lined barrels. Imported from Italy; still in production. Used value, field model, $213 to $224; trap, skeet models, $259 to $273.50.

GALEF/ZOLI Golden Snipe: over/under; same specs as Silver Snipe, except for automatic selective ejectors. Still in production. Used value, field model, $264.50 to $270.50; trap, skeet, $310.50 to $319.50.

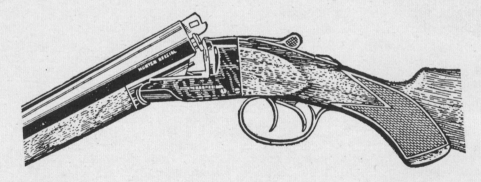

HUNTER Fulton: hammerless, double; box-lock; 12, 16, 20 gauges; 26" to 32" barrels, standard choke combos, double triggers, or nonselective single trigger; walnut stock, hand-checkered pistol grip, forearm. Introduced, 1920; dropped, 1948. Manufactured by Hunter Arms Company, Fulton, New York. Used value, single trigger, $431.50 to $448.50; double triggers, $339.50 to $374.

HUNTER Special: hammerless double; box-lock; plain extractors; 12, 16, 20 gauges; 26 to 30" barrels, standard choke combos; walnut stock, hand-checkered pistol grip, forearm; dropped, 1948. Used value, single trigger, $569.50 to $604; double triggers, $489 to $506.

KESSLER Three-Shot Repeater: bolt-action, takedown; 12, 16, 20 gauges; 28" barrel in 12, 16 gauges, 26" in 20-ga.; 2-rd. detachable box magazine; full choke only; unchecker-ed one-piece pistol-grip stock; recoil pad. Introduced in 1951; dropped, 1953. Made by Kessler Arms Corp., Silver Creek, New York. Used value, $32 to $34.

KESSLER Lever-Matic: lever-action repeater; takedown; 12, 16, 20 gauges; 26", 28", 30" barrels, full choke only; 3-rd. magazine; uncheckered pistol-grip stock; recoil pad; dropped, 1953. Used value, $46 to $51.50.

KLEINGUENTHER Condor: over/under; 12, 20 gauges; Purdey-type double-lock action; barrels, 26" improved/modified or skeet/skeet; 28", full/modified or modified/modified; 30", 12-ga. only, full/modified, full/full; European walnut stock; hand-checkered pistol grip, forearm; single selective trigger; automatic ejectors, vent rib; skeet model has extra-wide rib. Imported from Italy; still in production. Used value, field grade, $283 to $293.50; skeet, $305 to $316.50.

KLEINGUENTHER Condor Trap: has same specs as field grade, except for wide vent rib, Monte Carlo stock; 12-ga. only; barrels, 28", full/modified; 30", 32", modified/full or full/full. Still in production. Used value, $342 to $356.50.

KLEINGUENTHER/BRESCIA: double; 12, 20 gauges; Anson & Deeley-type action; barrels, 28", full/modified or improved/modified, chrome-lined; European walnut stock; hand-checkered pistol grip, forearm; recoil pad; double triggers; engraved action. Still in production. Imported from Italy. Used value, $184 to $194.

LEFEVER Nitro Special: side-by-side double barrel; box-lock action; 12, 16, 20, .410 gauges; 26", 28", 30", 32" barrels; standard choke combos; double triggers; single non-selective trigger at added cost; plain extractors; hand-checkered American walnut pistol-grip stock, forearm. Introduced in 1921; dropped, 1948. Used values, double triggers, $207 to $218.50; single trigger, $264.50 to $276.

LEFEVER Single Barrel Trap: single-shot; box-lock action; hammerless; 12-ga. only; 30", 32" barrels; ejector; full choke only; vent rib; bead front sight; hand-checkered American walnut pistol-grip stock, forearm; recoil pad. Introduced about 1923; dropped, 1942. Used value, $230 to $259.

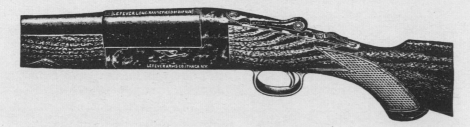

LEFEVER Long Range: single-shot; box-lock action; hammerless; 12, 16, 20 gauges; 26", 28", 30", 32" barrels; standard chokes; bead front sight; no recoil pad; field stock; other specifications similar to those of single-barrel trap model. Introduced about 1923; dropped, 1942. Used value, $103.50 to $115.

PURDEY Hammerless Double Model: side-by-side; sidelock; 12, 16, 20 gauges; 26", 27", 28", 30" barrels, last in 12-ga. only; double triggers or single trigger; any choke combo desired; choice of rib style; automatic ejectors; hand-checkered European walnut straight-grip stock, forearm standard; pistol-grip stock on special order; made in several variations including Game Model, Featherweight Game, Pigeon Gun, with side clips; Two-Inch Model for 2" shells. Prices are identical for all. Introduced in 1880; still in production. Used values, double triggers, $5117.50 to $5290; single trigger, $5635 to $5860.50.

PURDEY Single Barrel Trap Model: single-barrel, single-shot; Purdey action; 12-ga. only; barrel length, choke to customer's specifications; vent rib; engraved receiver; hand-checkered European walnut stock, forearm; straight English style or pistol-grip design. Introduced in 1917; still in production. Used value, $6555 to $6900.

PURDEY Over-and-Under Model: sidelock action; 12, 16, 20 gauges; 26", 27", 28" barrels, last in 12-ga. only; any choke combo; any rib style to customer's preference; Pre-WWII guns are built on Purdey action, post-war versions on Woodward action; engraved receiver; double or single trigger, latter at added cost; hand-checkered European walnut stock, forearm; straight English or pistol-grip style. Introduced in 1925; still in production. Used values, with Purdey action, double triggers, $6670 to $6900; Purdey action with single trigger, $7187.50 to $7475; Woodward action, double triggers, $8912.50 to $9200; Woodward action, single trigger, $9487.50 to $9775.

RIGBY Sidelock Double: side-by-side; in all gauges, barrel lengths, chokes to customer's specifications; automatic ejectors; double triggers; hand-checkered European walnut straight-grip stock, forearm; English engraving; two grades, differing in overall quality, amount of engraving. Introduced in 1885; dropped, 1955. Used values, Sandringham Grade, $2530 to $2760; Regal Grade, $3737.50 to $4025.

RIGBY Box-lock Double: side-by-side; in all gauges, barrel lengths, chokes to customer's desires; automatic ejectors; double triggers; hand-checkered European walnut straight-grip stock, forearm; English engraving; in two grades, differing in amount and nature of engraving, overall quality. Introduced in 1900; dropped, 1955. Used values, Chatsworth Grade, $1500 to $1750; Sackville Grade, $1750 to $2000.

No. 10

SARASQUETA Sidelock Double: side-by-side; hammerless; 12, 16, 20, 28 gauges; barrel lengths, choke combinations to customer's order; double triggers; hand-checkered European walnut straight-grip stock, forearm. Gun is made in 13 grades; except for No. 6 and No. 7, all have automatic ejectors. Grades differ in quality of wood, checkering, and amount and quality of engraving. Used values, No. 4, $218 to $230; No. 4E, $276 to $287; No. 5, $264 to $276; No. 5E, $322 to $333; No. 6, $287 to $299; No. 6E, $345 to $360 No. 7, $322 to $333; No. 7E, $379 to $402; No. 8, $529 to $546; No. 9, $644 to $667; No. 10, $644 to $667; No. 11, $690 to $719; No. 12, $862 to $891.

SARASQUETA No. 2: over/under; hammerless, box-lock action; 12, 16, 20, 28 gauges; manufactured in all standard barrel lengths, choke combinations; plain extractors; double triggers; hand-checkered European walnut straight-grip stock, forearm; Greener crossbolt; engraved. Introduced in mid-1930s; still in production. Used value, $161 to $172.

No. 3 has same specifications as No. 2, but no Greener crossbolt; engraving style is different. Still in production. Used value, $161 to $172.50.

SARASQUETA Super Deluxe: over/under; sidelock action; hammerless; 12-ga. only; barrel lengths, choke combos to customer's order; automatic ejectors; double triggers; hand-checkered European walnut pistol-grip stock, forearm; engraved action. Introduced in 1930s; still in production. Used value, $805 to $977.50.

SMITH & WESSON Model 916: slide action; 12, 16, 20 gauges; 6-shot; barrel lengths, 20″ cylinder choke, 26″ improved cylinder, 28″ modified, full or adjustable choke; 30″ full; vent rib on 26″ and 28″ barrels available; uncheckered walnut stock; fluted comb, grooved slide handle; satin-finished steel receiver, no-glare top. Introduced in 1973; still in production. Used value, plain barrels, sans recoil pad, $83.50 to $86.50; plain barrel, with adjustable choke, $86 to $92; plain barrel, recoil pad, $83 to $86; with vent rib, recoil pad, $89 to $98.

SMITH & WESSON Model 1000: gas-operated autoloader; 12-ga. only, 2¾″ chamber, 4-rds.; barrel lengths, 26″ skeet, improved cylinder, 28″ improved, modified, full; walnut stock, checkered pistol grip, forearm; crossbolt safety; vent rib; front, middle beads; engraved alloy receiver; pressure compensator. Introduced in 1973; still in production. Used value, $178.50 to $187.

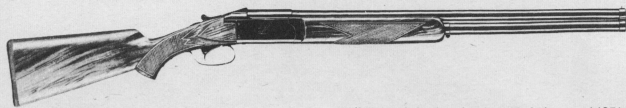

VALMET Over/Under: box-lock action; 12-ga. only; single selective trigger; plain extractors; barrels, 26", improved/modified; 28", modified/full; 30", modified/full or full/full; hand-checkered walnut stock. Imported 1951-1967 by Firearms International, dropped 1967. Since 1968 the similar Model 330 has been imported by Savage. Used value, $293 to $310.

WEATHERBY Patrician: slide-action repeater; 12-ga. only, 2¾" chamber; barrels, 26", modified, improved or skeet; 28", full or modified; 30", full; vent rib; walnut stock; hand-checkered pistol-grip, forearm; recoil pad; hidden magazine cap; cross-bolt safety. Introduced in 1970; still in production. Used value, field or skeet grade, $207 to $216; trap grade, $230 to $241.50.

WEATHERBY Centurion: autoloader; 12-ga. only, 2¾" chamber; barrels, 26", skeet or improved cylinder; 28", improved, modified, full; 30", full; American walnut stock; hand-checkered pistol grip, forearm; vent rib with front, middle bead sights; engraved alloy receiver; pressure compensator. Introduced in 1970; still in production. Used value, $210 to $218.50.

WEATHERBY Regency: over/under; 12, 20 gauges; box-lock action with simulated sidelocks; selective automatic ejectors, single selective trigger; barrels, 28" only, full/modified, modified/improved, skeet/skeet; vent rib, bead front sight; American walnut stock, hand-checkered pistol grip, forearm; fully engraved receiver; recoil pad. Used value, 12, 20-ga. field, skeet, $517 to $546; trap, $604 to $632.

WESTERN ARMS Long Range Hammerless: double, box-lock; double or single trigger; plain extractors; in 12, 16, 20, .410 gauges; barrels, 26" to 32", modified/full chokes; uncheckered walnut stock, forearm. Introduced in 1924; discontinued, 1942. Made by Western Arms Corp., later absorbed by Ithaca Gun Co. Used value, with single trigger, $218.50 to $224.50; double triggers, $172.50 to $184.

SHOTGUN NOTES

COMMEMORATIVES

What Is A Commemorative And What Gives It Value? Here Are Some Answers:

IN THE YEARS since 1961, when the Geneseo, Illinois, 125th Anniversary Deringer became the first commemorative gun, the collecting of commemorative guns has become one of the most important and fastest growing facets of the collecting field. It has grown from what was originally more or less a novelty into a full-fledged separate area of gun collecting. The reason for this can be attributed to several things, according to Robert E. P. Cherry, the nation's leading authority on commemoratives.

"The most important of these is, I believe, the fact that a new collector can enter the commemorative gun field without the vast, solid knowledge that is necessary to the assembly of an antique collection. All of the antique gun collectors of my acquaintance have spent much more time in research than they have in the pursuit of guns for their collections. The serious antique collector must be a voracious reader, and a most perceptive one, if he is to make use of the material which he is able to find.

"One antique gun collector friend of mine, Karl Moldenhauer, the most respected authority on Remington handguns in the world, gives a piece of advice to all beginning collectors – 'When you buy a gun, buy a book.' And a sound piece of advice it is," Cherry says.

The beginning collector who is attracted to commemorative guns does not have that problem, however. The commemorative concept allows him to enter the field without that great storehouse of knowledge. The historical lure is still there, as each model is issued to commemorate some specific person or event of national or international significance. Hundreds of people who are attracted to gun collecting, but are frightened off because of their lack of knowledge of antiques, have become commemorative collectors as an alternative.

The second most important reason for the growth of commemorative collecting is the eye-catching appearance of these guns. Although historical significance is often the prime reason an antique collector wants to own a specific piece, the most frequent motivation is the appearance of the gun. In this area, the commemorative has no peer. The combination of finishes on these guns is extremely attractive, and is probably the greatest inducement to the new collector. A display of only two or three of these guns is an outstanding eye-catcher and provides the new collector with a great sense of pride when showing them to his non-gun-collecting friends.

"This attraction has developed serious gun collectors out of a growing number of people who would not have otherwise entered the field of gun collecting at all. As a matter of fact, I can even name several serious and advanced antique gun collectors who were originally attracted to gun collecting by their original interest in, and purchase of, commemorative guns.

"Unfortunately, another lure of collecting commemoratives is the past history of investment appreciation. I always have tried to discourage a new collector from buying commemoratives as an investment. He should buy them because he likes them and will enjoy owning them. If he gains some appreciation on his original investment, fine, but that should be only an incidental benefit, not a goal," Cherry says.

There are several basic and sound rules in building any kind of gun collection, whether a commemorative, antique or modern collection, and they should be adhered to rigidly!

One of the things that a new collector can be counted upon to do is to want to buy every gun to which he is exposed. The initial excitement affects every new collector the same way. This is the most serious mistake he can make. He first should obtain a complete listing of every commemorative gun produced to date, along with the production figures and a current price listing of all of the guns. He then should attempt to put together some semblance of a plan for his collection. Unfortunately, this particular piece of advice is one which the neophyte almost certainly will ignore, human nature being what it is.

Before he makes any purchase, he should consult his list and study it carefully, noting which guns are the rarer issues of his chosen category or general collection, for that matter. The most common issues, and the ones he will be the most tempted to buy, because they are the most available, should not be sought. Rather, he should make an attempt to locate the scarce key guns, as the common ones will almost always be available, and the appreciation of these will be the least. The key guns, on the other hand, are those which will rise the most in price, so the sooner he can obtain them, the more money he will save.

If you intend to be a serious collector, don't be frightened off by the apparently astronomical price on one of the rare guns. They are higher priced for a reason and, if the unforeseen happens and you are forced to liquidate your collection, these same high-priced guns will be the easiest to move.

As an example, an Abercrombie & Fitch Trailblazer at $1550 is an instant sale for a dealer, as would be a Geneseo, Illinois, Deringer at $400, while an Arkansas Scout or a Nebraska Scout may go begging at $200. If a collector does not have the price of one of the scarcer issues, he should keep putting a little money aside until he does have the price. One rare issue will be a much wiser acquisition than a dozen common pieces. The more low production guns any collection has, the easier it will be to move if that ever becomes necessary.

"I also realize it is an extremely difficult thing for the new collector to do, as he almost certainly will be overcome by the urge to buy something if he really has commemorative fever. My advice would be to go ahead and buy something, but make a sincere effort to put something aside for the later purchase of the key guns. The sooner you can buy them, the less expensive they will be," Cherry advises.

As a graphic example, consider the first year of production, 1961. A Colt 125th Anniversary Model .45 SAA originally sold for $150, but 7390 pieces were produced; a rather large production figure, and not a key gun. This gun currently sells for about $500, just slightly over three times the original price.

On the other hand, the Sheriff's Model .45 SAA, with 478 pieces produced, is a key gun. It originally sold for $129.95, and now retails for $950 up, but try to find one! This is 6½ times the original price! In addition, you can be sure that future appreciation will be much greater on the Sheriff's Model than on the Colt 125th Anniversary. Another first-year issue, the Geneseo, Illinois, 125th Anniversary Model Deringer originally sold for $27.95 and will now bring $400 if you are able to locate one! This is caused by the fact that only 104 pieces were produced, an extremely low production figure.

One of the most important things a new collector can do is to budget himself. He must decide how much money he can spend on his new hobby, then stick to his budget! Many budding collections have gone on the block because the beginner overextended himself. There will be times when the desire for a particular piece which becomes available will be too great and overextension will be unavoidable, but a collector should exercise a great deal of self-discipline, as it is a common pitfall.

We reiterate an earlier statement that a beginner should not be motivated by a desire for profit. Although all of the commemoratives have appreciated in value and some of them substantially, this should not be a siren song for the brand-new collector. He should collect for the resulting enjoyment. If appreciation in value results, it should be regarded as a bonus.

The total value of a complete commemorative collection today will preclude all but a wealthy few from attaining that goal. There are several collections of commemoratives in existence with a value far exceeding $100,000 — each, that is! It would, therefore, behoove the beginner to look for a more realistic goal. Since commemoratives are categorized in several groups, there are a number of choices for a conservative aim. These categories are as follows:

Territorial or Statehood Anniversaries — New Mexico, Arizona, etc.

Historic Personalities — Generals Hood, Lee, Grant, etc.; Lawmen Earp, Masterson, Garrett, etc.; other historical figures, such as Joaquin Murietta.

Historic Organizations — Pony Express, Texas Rangers, etc.

Historic Locations — Geneseo, Illinois, Old Ft. Des Moines, etc.

Historic Events — Battle of Little Big Horn, Battle of Gettysburg, etc.

Of these five groups, by far the largest is the statehood or territorial category, with some thirty-seven issues commemorating various states. It is also probably the most popular of the categorical collections, as many of the statehood commemoratives were issued only in the less expensive .22 caliber, making them one of the most inexpensive ways to begin a collection. The statehood guns also make an outstanding display as the finishes on both rifles and handguns run the entire gamut of combinations.

Some people prefer to collect only those guns with military significance. This is also a fertile field, as many individual military figures have been honored, as have the battles and events of four different wars.

The possibilities are numerous, and can be chosen only by the collector himself. Collecting commemoratives is no different than collecting anything else; a collector buys what he likes and what appeals to him.

Some individuals prefer to collect long guns only. Winchester has produced the greatest number of commemorative long guns, and is the most popular with long gun collectors. They have produced about twenty-five different models in rifles, carbines and muskets. Harrington & Richardson follows closely with Remington, Ithaca, Marlin, Ruger, Savage and Stevens which all produce at least one commemorative rifle. Browning has produced one rifle and one shotgun.

"If you have ever collected anything — stamps, coins, plates or whatever — you will know that the most important factor to be considered when purchasing any piece is condition. Commemorative collecting is no different in that respect, except that condition is even more important. Any commemorative gun one is considering acquiring must be unfired, show absolutely no handling wear, and the display case should be in the same condition. As much of the original factory packaging — boxes, sleeves, brochures, etc. — as possible should be kept with the gun. All of this will add value to your collection if you should someday decide to dispose of it," Cherry suggests.

A factory cardboard box and cardboard sleeve for a Winchester '66 Centennial, for instance, is quite necessary. Without these pieces of paper, the gun is worth about $50 less. Any guns which have gold-plated backstraps and trigger guards should be inspected carefully for evidences of wear on the gold from cowboying with the gun. This gold is extremely fragile and will wear quite quickly.

There are a number of ways for the new collector to find guns to buy as a nucleus. We would recommend first of all that he try his local gun dealers. They may have a few commemoratives in stock. If not, you might be able to interest them in stocking some.

There may be a collector near you. If you can find such a person, he can offer you considerable help in building your collection and may have some duplicates you can buy or trade. Gun shows also can provide an area of acquisition. However, you must insist upon condition! Be extremely critical in your inspection of both the guns and the display cases. You will often find that these guns have been badly mishandled by persons who do not appreciate commemoratives. You also might try some of the national dealers in these fine guns. There are several with excellent reputations who offer a wide variety of inventory. These people are specialists in commemoratives and can offer you much information.

An absolute necessity for any collector of commemoratives is the only book ever published on the subject, R.L. Wilson's "Colt Commemorative Firearms." This book supplies both descriptions and pictures of all of the Colt commemoratives produced to date and is an outstanding source of information. It is 126 pages of background information, production figures, serial-numbering information and color photographs. It is available in paperback at $7.95 and hardbound at $15.95 from the publisher, Cherry's, 1041 S. Oakwood Avenue, Geneseo, Illinois 61254 or from book dealers.

"So the collector may have a better picture and understanding of the commemorative concept, a little history is in order. The first commemorative gun was built for me by Colt's in 1961 in honor of Geneseo, Illinois' 125th Anniversary. It was a single-shot .22 short No. 4 Deringer, made up in an all-gold finish. Only 104 pieces were produced, and they were quickly gobbled up by the local townfolk at $27.95 each. Colt subsequently produced two other issues in 1961, the Colt 125th Anniversary Model and the Kansas Statehood model, both of which were successful," Cherry recalls.

"Colt would, at that time, produce a special barrel length, special finish and special markings for anyone who ordered a minimum of fifty guns of a model. This continued until 1966, with a number of private commemorative issues being brought forth."

However, it soon became apparent that, to preserve the integrity of the commemorative program, some control would have to be exercised over the number of issues produced and the events commemorated. In 1965, Colt established their Commemorative Committee which consisted of three dealers — Herb Glass, Charles Kidwell and Robert E.P. Cherry — and one collector, Wallace Q. Beinfeld. This group met with Colt's management twice each year to study and discuss the proposed commemorative suggestions for the future months. One of the first decisions reached by this committee was the discontinuance of private issues. Another was the institution of a policy barring the issue of city commemoratives due to the profusion of requests. The committee also addressed itself to the selection of just what things would be commemorated, and decided that any event or person proposed must be of national or international significance.

Colt's Commemorative Advisory Committee has, since 1965, had a rotating membership, with many other dealers and collectors serving. The only permanent members of the committee are Beinfeld and Cherry. This group still meets twice a year to determine what commemoratives will actually get into production. After several days of discussion and study, only extremely significant events are eventually selected. Some other commemorative gun manufacturers have also established commemorative advisory boards or informal consultants. These include Harrington & Richardson and High Standard.

"It is my hope that any new collector who reads this article will go back and read it again and again. I have seen too many new collectors rush out with a fistful of money, buy everything in sight and accumulate a disoriented collection of guns, then lose interest. It is those key guns in dormant collections which keep all collectors hanging in there. These are the really exciting guns and the ones which will make a cohesive collection," Cherry insists.

1961

COLT Sheriff's Model: single-action Army revolver; made exclusively for Centennial Arms Corp.; "Colt Sheriff's Model .45" on left side of 3" barrel; .45 Colt only; walnut grips without medallions; 25 made with nickel finish; 478, blued; made only in 1961. Original price, nickel, $139.50; blued, $150. Current values, nickel, $3250 to $3350; blued, $950 to $1050.

COLT 125th Anniversary Model: single-action Army revolver; "125th Anniversary — SAA Model .45 Cal." on left side of 7½" barrel; .45 Colt only; varnished walnut grips; gold-plated Colt medallions; gold-plated hammer, trigger, trigger guard; balanced blued; originally cased in red velvet-lined box; 7390 made in 1961 only. Original retail, $150. Current value, $500 to $525.

COLT Kansas Statehood Centennial: Frontier Scout revolver; "1861 — Kansas Centennial — 1961" on left side of 4¾" barrel; .22 LR only; walnut grips; no medallions; gold-plated in entirety; originally cased in velvet-lined box with Kansas State seal inlaid in lid; 6201 made in 1961 only. Original retail, $75. Current value, $200 to $210.

COLT Geneseo Anniversary: No. 4 Derringer replica; "1836 — Geneseo Anniversary Model — 1961" on left side of 2½" barrel; .22 short only; walnut grips; gold-plated in entirety; originally cased in velvet/satin-lined box; made especially for Cherry's Sporting Goods, Geneseo, Ill.; 104 made in 1961 only. Original retail, $27.50; current value, $400 to $415.

COLT Pony Express Centennial: Frontier Scout revolver; "1860-61 — Russell, Majors and Waddell/Pony Express Centennial Model — 1960-61" on left side of 4¾" barrel; .22 LR only; varnished walnut grips; gold-plated Colt medallions; gold-plated in entirety; originally cased in rosewood box with gold-plated centennial medallion in lid; 1007 made in 1961 only. Original retail, $80. Current value, $400 to $415.

COLT Civil War Centennial: single-shot replica of Colt Model 1860 Army revolver; "Civil War Centennial Model — .22 Caliber Short" on left side of 6" barrel; .22 short only; varnished walnut grips; gold-plated Colt medallions; gold-plated frame, backstrap, trigger guard assembly, balance blued; originally in Leatherette case; 24,114 made in 1961 only. Original retail, $32.50. Current value, $125.

1962

COLT Rock Island Arsenal Centennial: single-shot replica of Colt Model 1860 Army revolver; "1862 — Rock Island Arsenal Centennial Model — 1962" on left side of 6" barrel; .22 short only; varnished walnut grips; blued finish; originally in blue and gray Leatherette case; 550 made in 1962 only. Original retail, $38.50. Current value, $150.

COLT Columbus, Ohio, Sesquicentennial: Frontier Scout revolver; "1812 — Columbus Sesquicentennial — 1962" on left side of 4¾" barrel; .22 LR only; varnished walnut grips with gold-plated medallions; gold-plated in entirety; originally cased in velvet/satin-lined walnut case; 200 made in 1962 only. Original retail, $100. Current value, $425 to $435.

COLT Fort Findlay, Ohio, Sesquicentennial: Frontier Scout revolver; "1812 — Fort Findlay Sesquicentennial — 1962" on left side of 4¾" barrel; .22 LR, .22 magnum; varnished walnut grips; gold plated in entirety; originally cased in red velvet/satin-lined walnut box; 110 made in 1962 only. Original retail, $89.50. Current value, $440 to $460. Cased pair, .22LR, .22 magnum, 20 made in 1962. $2250 to $2295.

COLT New Mexico Golden Anniversary: Frontier Scout revolver; "1912 — New Mexico Golden Anniversary — 1962" wiped in gold on left side of 4¾" barrel; .22 LR only; varnished walnut grips; gold-plated medallions; barrel, frame, base pin screw, ejector rod, rod tube, tube plug and screw, bolt and trigger, hammer screws blued; balance gold plated; originally cased in redwood box with yellow satin/velvet lining; 1000 made in 1962 only. Original retail, $79.95. Current value, $250 to $265.

COLT West Virginia Statehood Centennial: Frontier Scout revolver; "1863 — West Virginia Centennial — 1963" wiped in gold on left side of 4¾" barrel; .22 LR only; pearlite grips, gold-plated medallions; blued, with gold-plated backstrap, trigger guard assembly and screws, stock screw; originally cased in blonde wood box with gold velvet/satin lining; 3452 made in 1962 only. Original retail, $75. Current value, $195 to $210.

West Virginia Statehood Centennial single-action Army revolver has same legend on barrel as .22 version; 5½" barrel; .45 Colt only; same blue/gold finish as Scout version; same type of casing; 600 made in 1963 only. Original retail, $150. Current value, $500 to $525.

1963

COLT Fort McPherson, Nebraska, Centennial: No. 4 Derringer replica; "Fort McPherson/1863 — Centennial — 1963" wiped in gold on left side of 2½" barrel; .22 short only; Ivorylite grips, no medallions; gold plated with blued barrel, bolt, trigger screw, hammer and screw, trigger and stock screw; originally cased in walnut-finished box, with gold velvet/satin lining; 300 made in 1963 only. Original retail, $28.95. Current value, $190 to $200.

COLT Arizona Territorial Centennial: Frontier Scout revolver; "1863 — Arizona Territorial Centennial — 1963" wiped in gold on left side of 4¾" barrel; .22 LR only; Pearlite grips, gold-plated medallions; gold plated, with blue barrel, frame, base pin screw, ejector rod, rod tube, tube plug and screw, bolt and trigger screws, hammer and hammer screw; originally cased in blonde-finished box, with yellow velvet/satin lining; 5355 made in 1963 only. Original retail, $75. Current value, $190 to $200.

Arizona Territorial Centennial single-action Army revolver has same legend on barrel as Scout version; 5½" barrel; .45 Colt only; same blue/gold-plated finish as Scout; same type case; 1280 made in 1963 only. Original retail, $150. Current value, $500 to $525.

COLT Carolina Charter Tercentenary: Frontier Scout revolver; "1663 — Carolina Charter Tercentenary — 1963" wiped in gold on left side of 4¾" barrel; .22 LR only; walnut grips; gold-plated medallions; gold plated, with

barrel, frame, cylinder, base pin screw, ejector rod, rod tube, tube plug, tube screw, bolt, trigger and hammer screws blued; originally cased in blonde-finished box with yellow velvet/satin lining; 300 made in 1963 only. Original retail, $75. Current value, $250 to $260.

Carolina Charter Tercentenary .22/.45 combo set includes Frontier Scout described above, single-action Army revolver, with same legend on 5½" barrel, .45 Colt only; same finish on grips as Frontier version; larger case to fit both guns; 251 sets made in 1963 only. Original retail for set, $240. Current value, $690 to $700.

COLT H. Cook 1 of 100: Frontier Scout/single-action Army revolvers, sold as set; "H. Cook 1 of 100" on left side of barrels; Scout has 4¾" barrel, .22 LR only; SA Army has 7½" barrel, .45 Colt only; Pearlite grips; nickel-plated medallions; both nickel plated with blued frame, base pin, trigger and hammer screws; originally cased in silver-colored box with blue satin/velvet lining; 100 sets made in 1963 only for H. Cook Sporting Goods, Albuquerque, N.M. Original retail for set, $275. Current value, $850 to $875.

COLT Fort Stephenson, Ohio, Sesquicentennial: Frontier Scout revolver; "1813 — Fort Stephenson Sesquicentennial — 1963" wiped in silver on left side of 4¾" barrel; .22 LR only; laminated rosewood grips, nickel-plated medallions; nickel-plated finish, with blued barrel, frame, base pin screw, ejector rod, rod tube, tube plug and screw, bolt and trigger and hammer screws; originally cased in blonde-finished wood, with yellow velvet/satin lining; 200 made only in 1963. Original retail, $75. Current value, $425 to $450.

COLT Battle of Gettysburg Centennial: Frontier Scout revolver; "1863 — Battle of Gettysburg Centennial — 1963" wiped in gold on left side of 4¾" barrel; .22 LR only; walnut grips; gold-plated medallions; gold plated with blued barrel, frame, base pin screw, ejector rod tube, tube plug and screw, and bolt, trigger and hammer screws; originally cased in blonde-finished wood with yellow velvet in bottom, blue satin in lid; 1019 made in 1963 only. Original retail, $89.95. Current value, $190 to $200.

COLT Idaho Territorial Centennial: Frontier Scout revolver; "1863 — Idaho Territorial Centennial — 1963" wiped in silver on left side of 4¾" barrel; .22 LR only; pearlite grips; nickel-plated medallions; nickel plated with blue frame, barrel, base pin screw, ejector rod tube, tube plug and screw, and bolt, trigger and hammer screws; originally cased in blonde-finished wood, with gold velvet/satin lining; 902 made in 1963 only. Original retail, $75. Current value $270 to $285.

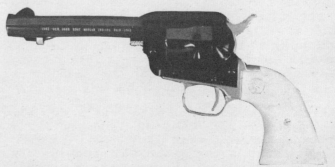

COLT General John Hunt Morgan Indian Raid: Frontier Scout revolver; "1863 — Gen. John Hunt Morgan Indian

Raid — 1963" wiped in gold on left side of 4¾" barrel; .22 LR; Pearlite grips, gold-plated medallions; gold plated with blued frame, barrel, cylinder, base pin screw, ejector rod, rod tube, tube plug and tube screw and bolt and trigger screws; originally cased in blonde-finished wood, with gold velvet/satin lining; 100 made in 1963 only. Original retail, $74.50. Current value, $575 to $600.

1964

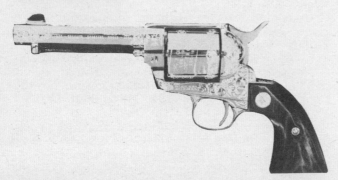

COLT Cherry's Sporting Goods 35th Anniversary: Frontier Scout/single-action Army revolvers, sold as set; "1929 — Cherry's Sporting Goods — 1964" on left side of barrel; Scout has 4¾" barrel, .22 LR only; SA Army has 4¾" barrel, .45 Colt only; both have laminated rosewood grips; gold-plated medallions; gold plated in entirety; originally cased in embossed black Leatherette, with black velvet/satin lining; 100 sets made in 1964 only. Original retail, $275. Current value, $900 to $950.

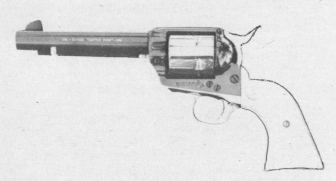

COLT Nevada Statehood Centennial: Frontier Scout revolver; "1864 — Nevada Centennial — 1964" wiped in silver on left side of 4¾" barrel; .22 LR only; Pearlite grips; nickel-plated medallions; nickel-plated finish, with blued barrel, frame, base pin screw, cylinder, ejector rod, rod tube, tube plug and tube screw, hammer, bolt, trigger screws; originally cased in gray-finished wood with blue velvet-lined bottom, silver satin-lined lid; 3984 made in 1964 only. Original retail, $75. Used value, $200 to $210.

Nevada Statehood Centennial single-action Army revolver has same legend on barrel as Frontier Scout; 5½" barrel; .45 Colt only; grips, medallions, finish identical to Scout; same casing motif; 1688 made in 1964 only. Original retail, $150. Current value, $500 to $525.

Nevada State Centennial Frontier Scout/single-action Army set includes the two handguns described above in

oversized case; 189 standard sets were made, plus 577 sets featuring extra engraved cylinders; made in 1964 only. Original retail, standard set, $240; with extra engraved cylinders, $350. Current values, standard set, $700 to $725; with extra engraved cylinders, $800 to $825.

COLT Nevada Battle Born Commemorative: Frontier Scout revolver; "1864 — Nevada 'Battle Born' — 1964" wiped in silver on left side of 4¾" barrel; .22 LR only; Pearlite grips; nickel-plated medallions; nickel plated, with blued frame, barrel, base pin screw, ejector rod, tube, tube plug and screw, bolt, trigger and hammer screws; cased in blue-finished wood box, with blue velvet/satin lining; 981 made in 1964 only. Original retail, $85. Current value, $200 to $210.

Nevada Battle Born Commemorative single-action Army revolver has same legend on barrel as Frontier Scout version; 5½" barrel; .45 Colt only; same grips, finish, casing as Frontier Scout; 80 made in 1964 only. Original retail, $175. Used value, $950 to $1000.

Nevada Battle Born Commemorative Frontier Scout/single-action Army set includes the two handguns previously described in oversize case; 20 sets were made in 1964 only. Original retail, $265. Current value, $1450 to $1500.

COLT Montana Territory Centennial: Frontier Scout revolver; "1864 — Montana Territory Centennial — 1964" on left side of barrel, "1889 — Diamond Jubilee Statehood — 1964" on right side; both markings wiped in gold; 4¾" barrel; .22 LR only; rosewood or Pearlite grips; gold-plated medallions; gold-plated finish, except for blued barrel, frame, base pin screw, cylinder, ejector rod, rod tube, tube plug and tube screw, bolt, and trigger and hammer screws; originally cased in walnut-finished box with red velvet/satin lining; 2300 made in 1964 only. Original retail, $75. Current value, $195 to $210.

Montana Territory Centennial single-action Army revolver has same barrel markings as Frontier Scout version; 7½" barrel, .45 Colt only; same grips, finish, except frame is color case-hardened; same casing as Frontier Scout; 851 made in 1964 only. Original retail, $150. Current value, $550 to $575.

COLT Wyoming Diamond Jubilee: Frontier Scout revolver; "1890 — Wyoming Diamond Jubilee — 1965" on left side of barrel; 4¾" barrel; .22 LR only; rosewood grips, nickel-plated medallions; nickel-plated finish, except for blued barrel, frame, ejector rod, rod tube, tube plug and plug screw. Cased in blonde-finished box, with blue velvet bottom lining, silver satin-lined lid; 2357 made in 1964 only. Original retail, $75. Current value, $200 to $210.

COLT General Hood Centennial: Frontier Scout revolver; "1864 — General Hood's Tennessee Campaign — 1964" on left side of 4¾" barrel; .22 LR only; laminated rosewood grips, gold-plated medallions; gold-plated finish, except for blued trigger, hammer, base pin, ejector rod, rod head and screw and screws for base pin, hammer, trigger, backstrap and trigger guard; originally cased in blonde-finished wood box, with green velvet/satin lining; 1503 made in 1964 only. Original retail, $75. Current value, $200 to $210.

COLT New Jersey Tercentenary: Frontier Scout revolver; "1664 — New Jersey Tercentenary — 1964" on left side of barrel; 4¾" barrel; .22 LR only; laminated rosewood grips; nickel-plated medallions; blued finish, with nickel-plated barrel, frame, ejector rod tube, tube plug and screw; originally cased in blonde-finished box with blue velvet lining in bottom, silver satin in lid; 1001 made in 1964 only. Original retail, $75. Current value, $200 to $210.

New Jersey Tercentenary single-action Army revolver has same legend on barrel; 5½" barrel, .45 Colt only; grips, medallions, finish the same as on Frontier Scout version; same casing; 250 made in 1964 only. Original retail, $150. Current value, $525 to $550.

COLT St. Louis Bicentennial: Frontier Scout revolver; "1764 — St. Louis Bicentennial — 1964" wiped in gold on left side of 4¾" barrel; .22 LR only; laminated rosewood grips; gold-plated medallions; gold plated, except for blued frame, barrel, cylinder, ejector rod, rod tube, tube plug and screw; nonfluted cylinder; originally cased in blonde-finished wood box; yellow velvet/satin lining; 802 made in 1964 only. Original retail, $75. Current value, $200 to $210.

St. Louis Bicentennial single-action Army revolver has same legend on barrel as Frontier Scout version; 5½" barrel, .45 Colt only; same grips, medallions, finish, casing as Scout version; 200 made in 1964 only. Original retail, $150. Current value, $425 to $450.

St. Louis Bicentennial Frontier Scout/single-action Army set includes the two handguns described above in oversize case; 200 sets made in 1964 only. Original retail, $240. Current value, $650 to $700.

COLT California Gold Rush Commemorative: Frontier Scout revolver; "California Gold Rush Model" on left side of 4¾" barrel; .22 LR only; Ivorylite grips; gold-plated medallions; gold plated in entirety; originally cased in blonde wood box; blue velvet lining in bottom, gold in lid; 500 made in 1964 only. Original retail, $79.50. Current value, $220 to $250.

California Gold Rush single-action Army has same barrel legend as Frontier Scout version; 5½" barrel, .45 Colt only; same finish, grips, casing; 130 made in 1966 only. Original retail, $175. Current value, $950 to $975.

COLT Pony Express Presentation: single-action Army revolver; "Russell, Majors and Waddell — Pony Express Presentation Model" on left side of barrel. Various Pony Express stop markings on backstraps; 7½" barrel; .45 Colt; walnut

grips; nickel-plated medallions; nickel plated in entirety; originally cased in walnut-finished wood with transparent Lucite lid; lined with burgundy velvet; 1004 made in 1964 only. Original retail, $250. Current value, $750 to $775.

COLT Chamizal Treaty Commemorative: Frontier Scout revolver; "1867 Chamizal Treaty — 1964" wiped in gold on left side of 4¾" barrel, .22 LR only; Pearlite grips; gold-plated medallions; gold-plated finish; blued frame, barrel, ejector rod, ejector tube, rod plug and screw, base pin and base pin screw and hammer, trigger and bolt screws; originally cased in blonde-finished wood; yellow velvet/satin lining; 450 made in 1964. Original retail, $85. Current value, $225 to $245.

Chamizal Treaty single-action Army revolver has same legend on 5½" barrel; .45 Colt only; same grips, finish as Frontier Scout version; same type of case; 50 made in 1964. Original retail, $170. Current value, $1000 to $1050.

Chamizal Treaty Frontier Scout/single-action Army combo includes the two guns described above in one oversize case; 50 pairs made in 1964. Original retail, $280. Current value, $1550 to $1650.

COLT Col. Sam Colt Sesquicentennial Presentation: single-action Army revolver; "1815 — Col. Saml Colt Sesquicentennial Model — 1964" on left side of 7½" barrel; .45 Colt only; rosewood grips; roll-engraved scene on cylinder; nickel-plated medallions; silver-plated finish, with blued frame, barrel, ejector rod tube and screw, hammer and trigger; originally cased in varnished walnut box, with 12 dummy nickel-plated cartridges in cartridge block; burgundy velvet lining; 4750 made in 1964 only. Original retail, $225. Current value, $525 to $550.

Sam Colt Sesquicentennial Deluxe has the same specifications as standard presentation model, except grips are hand-fitted rosewood with escutcheons rather than medallions; hand-engraved cylinder; case has plate marked "1 of 200"; 200 made in 1964 only. Original retail, $500. Current value, $1550 to $1650.

Custom Deluxe model has same specifications as Deluxe, except for facsimile of Samuel Colt's signature engraved on backstrap, lid of case engraved with "1 of 50", name of purchaser engraved when requested; 50 made in 1965. Original retail, $1000. Used value, $2750 to $2850.

COLT Wyatt Earp Buntline: single-action Army revolver; "Wyatt Earp Buntline Special" on left side of 12" barrel; .45 Colt only; laminated black rosewood grips; gold-plated medallions; gold plated in entirety; originally cased in black-finished wood, lined with green velvet/satin; 150 made only in 1964. Original retail, $250. Used value, $1250 to $1300.

COLT Wichita Commemorative: Frontier Scout revolver; "1864 — Kansas Series — Wichita — 1964" wiped in silver on left side of 4¾" barrel; .22 LR only; Pearlite grips; gold-plated medallions; gold plated in entirety; originally cased in blonde-finished wood; lined with red velvet/satin; 500 made in 1964 only. Original retail, $85. Current value, $225 to $240.

ITHACA Model 49 St. Louis Bicentennial: lever-action single-shot; hand-operated rebounding hammer; .22 LR, long, short; 18" barrel; Western carbine-style straight stock; open rear sight, ramp front. Only 200 manufactured in 1964. Original retail, $34.95. Current value, $125 to $135.

REMINGTON Montana Centennial: Model 600 carbine; bolt action; 6mm Rem. mag. only; deviates from standard Model 600 specifications only in better walnut, commemorative medallion inlaid into the stock; 1005 made in 1964 only. Original retail, $124.95. Current value, $200 to $210.

WINCHESTER Wyoming Diamond Jubilee Commemorative: Model 94 carbine; .30-30 only; 1500 made, distributed exclusively by Billings Hardware Co.; same as standard M94, except for color case-hardened, engraved receiver, commemorative inscription on barrel; brass saddle ring, loading gate; state medallion imbedded in stock; made only in 1964, with retail of $100. Current value, $950 to $1000.

1965

COLT Dodge City Commemorative: Frontier Scout revolver; "1864 – Kansas Series – Dodge City – 1964" wiped in silver on left side of 4¾" barrel; .22 LR only; Ivorylite grips, gold-plated medallions; gold-plated finish, with blued base pin and screw, ejector rod, ejector rod head, bolt and trigger screw, hammer and hammer screw, trigger; originally cased in blonde-finished wood; lined with kelly green velvet/satin; 500 made in 1965 only. Original retail, $85. Current value, $225 to $240.

COLT Colorado Gold Rush Commemorative: Frontier Scout revolver; "1858 – Colorado Gold Rush – 1878" wiped in silver on left side of 4¾" barrel; .22 LR only; laminated rosewood grips; nickel-plated medallions; gold-plated finish, with nickel-plated hammer, base pin and screw, ejector rod head, hammer and trigger screws, trigger, grip screw; originally cased in blonde-finished wood; black velvet/satin lining; 1350 made in 1965 only. Original retail, $85. Current value, $200 to $215.

COLT Oregon Trail Commemorative: Frontier Scout revolver; "Oregon Trail Model," wiped in gold, on left side of 4¾" barrel; .22 LR only; Pearlite grips; gold-plated medallions; blued finish with gold-plated backstrap and trigger guard assembly and screws, hammer, trigger and screws, base pin, base pin screw and ejector rod head; originally cased in blonde-finished wood; lined with blue velvet in bottom, gold satin in lid; 1995 made only in 1965. Original retail, $75. Current value, $200 to $210.

COLT Joaquin Murrieta 1 of 100: Frontier Scout/single-action Army combo; both have "Joaquin Murrietta 1 of 100" on left side of barrels; Scout has 4¾" barrel, .22 LR

only; SAA has 5½" barrel, .45 Colt only; grips on both are Pearlite, with gold-plated medallions; finish for both is gold-plate with blued barrels, frames, ejector rod tubes; originally in one oversize case of walnut-finished wood; blue velvet/satin lining; 100 sets made in 1965 only. Original retail, $350. Current value, $850 to $900.

COLT Forty-Niner Miner: Frontier Scout revolver; "The '49er Miner" wiped in gold on left side of 4¾" barrel, .22 LR only; laminated rosewood grips; gold-plated medallions; gold-plated finish with blued barrel, frame, backstrap and trigger guard assembly, ejector rod, tube and tube plug, ejector tube screw; originally cased in walnut-finished wood; lined with velvet in bottom, blue satin in lid; 500 made only in 1965. Original retail, $85. Current value, $200 to $210.

COLT Old Fort Des Moines Reconstruction Commemorative: Frontier Scout revolver; "Reconstruction of Old Fort Des Moines" wiped in silver on left side of 4¾" barrel; .22 LR only; Pearlite grips; gold-plated medallions; gold-plated in entirety; originally cased in white-finished wood; royal purple velvet lining in bottom, white satin in lid; 700 made in 1965 only. Original retail, $89.95. Current value, $220 to $230.

Old Fort Des Moines Reconstruction single-action Army revolver; has same legend on 5½" barrel; .45 Colt only; grips, finish the same as on Frontier Scout version; same casing; 100 made in 1965 only. Original retail, $169.95. Current value, $500 to $525.

Old Fort Des Moines Frontier Scout/single-action Army combo has the same specifications as those for two guns described above, in one oversize case; 100 sets made in 1965 only. Original retail, $289.95. Current value, $725 to $775.

COLT Appomattox Centennial: Frontier Scout revolver; "1865 – Appomattox Commemorative Model – 1965" wiped in silver on left side of 4¾" barrel; .22 LR only; laminated rosewood grips; nickel-plated medallions; nickel-plated finish, with blued barrel, frame, backstrap and trigger guard screws, ejector rod tube, tube plug and tube screw; originally cased in blonde-finished wood lined with blue velvet in bottom, gray satin in lid; 1001 made in 1965 only. Original retail, $75. Current value, $200 to $215.

Appomattox Centennial single-action Army has same legend on 5½" barrel; .45 Colt only; grips, finish, casing same as for Frontier Scout version; 250 made in 1965. Original retail, $150. Current value, $500 to $525.

Appomattox Centennial Frontier Scout/single-action Army combo consists of two guns described above in one oversize case; 250 sets made in 1965 only. Original retail, $240. Current value, $750 to $800.

COLT General Meade Campaign Commemorative: Frontier Scout revolver; "Gen. Meade Pennsylvania Campaign Model" wiped in gold on left side of 4¾" barrel; .22 LR only; Ivorylite grips, gold-plated medallions; gold-plated finish; blued frame, barrel, cylinder, ejector rod tube, tube plug and screw, hammer and trigger screws; originally cased in walnut-finished wood; blue velvet lining in bottom, gold satin in lid; 1197 made in 1965 only. Original retail, $75. Current value, $225 to $240.

General Meade Campaign single-action Army revolver has same legend on the 5½" barrel; .45 Colt only; same finish, casing as Frontier Scout version; 200 made in 1966 only. Original retail, $165. Current value, $550 to $575.

COMMEMORATIVES

COLT St. Augustine Quadricentennial: Frontier Scout revolver; "1565 — St. Augustine Quadricentennial — 1965" wiped in gold on left side of 4¾" barrel; .22 LR only; Pearlite grips; gold-plated medallions; gold-plated finish, with blued barrel, base pin, ejector rod, tube, tube plug and screw, frame, hammer and trigger screws, backstrap and trigger guard assembly and screws; cased in blonde-finished wood; gold velvet/satin lining; 500 made in 1965 only. Original retail, $85. Current value, $225 to $235.

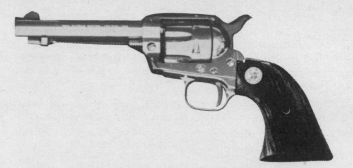

1966

COLT Oklahoma Territory Commemorative: Frontier Scout revolver; "1890 — Oklahoma Diamond Jubilee — 1965" wiped in gold on left side of 4¾" barrel; .22 LR only; laminated rosewood grips; gold-plated medallions; blued finish with gold-plated backstrap and trigger guard assembly and screws, cylinder, ejector rod head, base pin and screw, bolt and trigger cased in blonde-finished wood; red velvet/satin lining; 1343 made only in 1966. Original retail, $85. Current value, $200 to $210.

COLT Dakota Territory Commemorative: Frontier Scout revolver; "1861 — Dakota Territory — 1889" wiped in gold on left side of 4¾" barrel; .22 LR only; laminated rosewood grips; gold-plated medallions; blued finish with gold-plated backstrap and trigger guard assembly and screws, ejector rod and head, base pin, trigger, hammer, stock screw; originally cased in blonde-finished wood; red velvet/satin lining; 1000 made in 1966 only. Original retail, $85. Current value, $200 to $210.

COLT Abercrombie & Fitch Trailblazer: New Frontier single-action Army revolver; "Abercrombie & Fitch Co." wiped in gold on left side of 7½" barrel; .45 Colt only; rosewood grips; gold-plated medallions; gold-plated finish, blued barrel, cylinder, hammer, sights, ejector rod tube, ejector rod screw; case-hardened frame; roll-engraved, non-fluted cylinder; originally cased in varnished American walnut with brass-framed glass cover; bottom lined with crushed blue velvet; 200 made in 1966 with "New York" marked on butt, 100 with "Chicago" butt marking; 200 with "San Francisco" butt marking. Original retail, $275. Current value, $1550 to $1650.

COLT Indiana Sesquicentennial: Frontier Scout revolver; "1816 — Indiana Sesquicentennial — 1966" wiped in gold on left side of 4¾" barrel; .22 LR only; Pearlite grips; gold-plated medallions; blued finish, with gold-plated back-strap and trigger guard assembly, base pin and screw, ejector rod head, cylinder, bolt and trigger screw, hammer and hammer screw, trigger, stock screw; originally cased in blonde-finished wood; bottom lined with gold velvet, lid with blue satin; 1500 made in 1966 only. Original retail, $85. Current value, $200 to $210.

COLT Abilene Commemorative: Frontier Scout revolver; "1866 — Kansas Series — Abilene — 1966" wiped in silver on left side of 4¾" barrel; .22 LR only; laminated rosewood grips; gold-plated medallions; gold plated in entirety; originally cased in blonde-finished wood; blue velvet/satin lining; 500 made in 1966 only. Original retail, $95. Current value, $225 to $235.

REMINGTON 150th Anniversary Model 1100 SA: autoloading skeet shotgun; 12-ga. only; 26" barrel; vent rib; specifications the same as standard Model 1100, except for stamp-engraved legend on left side of receiver: "Remington Arms Company, Inc., 1816-1966, 150th Anniversary" with corporate logo; 1000 made in 1966 only. Original retail, $185. Current value, $250 to $260.

Model 1100 TB 150th Anniversary commemorative has same specifications as skeet version, except for recoil pad, 30" barrel, trap stock; same stamp-engraved legend on receiver; 1000 made in 1966 only. Original retail, $220. Current value, $275 to $290.

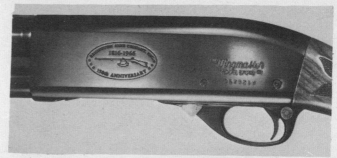

REMINGTON 150th Anniversary Model 870 SA: pump action skeet gun; 12-ga. only; 26" barrel; vent rib; specifications the same as standard Model 870, except for stamp-engraved legend on left side of receiver: "Remington Arms, Company Inc., 1816-1966, 150th Anniversary" with corporate logo; 1000 made in 1966 only. Original retail, $130. Current value, $140 to $150.

Model 870 TB 150th Anniversary commemorative has same specifications as skeet version, except for recoil pad, 30" barrel, trap stock; same stamp-engraved legend on receiver; 1000 made in 1966 only. Original retail, $165. Current value, $175 to $190.

REMINGTON 150th Anniversary Model 742 ADL: autloading rifle; .30/06 only; impressed basket weave checkering; has same specifications as standard 742 ADL, except for stamp-engraved legend on left side of receiver: "Remington Arms Company Inc., 1816-1966, 150th Anniversary" with corporate logo; 1000 made in 1966 only. Original retail, $150. Current value, $200 to $215.

REMINGTON 150th Anniversary Model 760 ADL: pump action rifle; .30/06 only; has the same specifications as standard 760 BDL Deluxe model, except for stamp-engraved legend on left side of receiver: "Remington Arms Company Inc., 1816-1966, 150th Anniversary," with corporate logo; 1000 made in 1966 only. Original retail, $135. Current value, $175 to $190.

REMINGTON 150th Anniversary Model 552A: autoloading rifle; .22 LR, long, short; has same specifications as standard Model 552, except for stamp-engraved legend on left side of receiver: "Remington Arms Company Inc., 1816-1966, 150th Anniversary," with corporate logo; 1000 made in 1966 only. Original retail, $58. Current value, $70 to $80.

REMINGTON 150th Anniversary Model 572A: pump action rifle; .22 LR, long, short; has same specifications as standard Model 572, except for stamp-engraved legend on left side of receiver; "Remington Arms Company Inc., 1816-1966, 150th Anniversary," with corporate logo; 1000 made in 1966 only. Original retail, $60. Current value, $80 to $90.

REMINGTON 150th Anniversary Nylon 66: autoloading rifle; .22 LR; has same specifications as standard Nylon 66 Apache Black model, except for stamp-engraved legend on left side of receiver: "Remington Arms Company Inc., 1816-1966, 150th Anniversary," with corporate logo; 1000 made in 1966 only. Original retail, $50. Current value, $75 to $90.

WINCHESTER Nebraska Centennial Commemorative: Model 94 carbine; .30-30 only; same as standard M94 except for gold-plated loading gate, butt plate, barrel band, hammer; commemorative inscription on barrel, medallion in stock; only 2500 made and distributed only in Nebraska; made only in 1966. Original retail, $100. Current value, $850 to $900.

WINCHESTER Centennial '66 Commemorative: Model 94; rifle and carbine versions commemorate Winchester's 100th anniversary; produced in 1966 only; 100,478 were made; .30-30 only; rifle version has 26" ½-octagon barrel; full-length, 8-rd. magazine; gold-plated forearm cap, receiver; post front sight, open rear; walnut stock, forearm with epoxy finish; saddle ring; brass butt plate; commemorative inscription on barrel and top tang. Retail price, $125; used value, $300 to $325. Carbine differs only in shorter forearm, 20" barrel, 6-rd. magazine. Used value, $300 to $325. Matched set, with consecutive serial numbers. Current value, $650 to $700.

1967

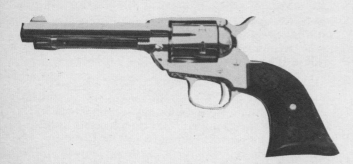

COLT Bat Masterson: Frontier Scout revolver; "Lawman Series — Bat Masterson" on left side of 4¾" barrel; .22 LR only; checkered rubber eagle grips; nickel-plated finish; cased originally in black Leatherette; red velvet/satin lining; 3000 made in 1967 only. Original retail, $90. Current value, $225 to $240.

Bat Masterson single-action Army has same legend on 4¾" barrel, .45 Colt only; grips, finish, casing are the same as for Frontier Scout version; 500 made in 1967 only. Original retail, $180. Current value, $500 to $525.

COLT Alamo Commemorative: Frontier Scout revolver; "Alamo Model," flanked by stars, wiped in gold on left side of 4¾" barrel; .22 LR only; Ivorylite grips, with inlaid gold-plated Texas star below screw on left grip. Gold-plated finish; blued barrel, frame, ejector rod tube, tube plug and screw; originally cased in blonde-finished wood box; blue velvet/satin lining; 4250 made in 1967 only. Original retail, $85. Current value, $200 to $210.

Alamo Commemorative single-action Army has same legend on barrel; same grips, finish, but with blued barrel, frame and ejector rod tube and tube screw; same casing; 750 made in 1967 only. Original retail, $165. Current value, $550 to $575.

Alamo Commemorative Frontier Scout/single-action Army combo. Includes two guns described above in one oversize case; 250 sets made in 1967 only. Original retail, $265. Current value, $800 to $850.

COLT Coffeyville Commemorative: Frontier Scout revolver; "1866 — Kansas Series — Coffeyville — 1966" wiped in silver on left side of 4¾" barrel; .22 LR only; walnut grips; gold-plated medallions; gold-plated finish; blued backstrap and trigger guard assembly screws, base pin and screw, ejector rod, ejector rod head, hammer and hammer screw, trigger; originally cased in blonde-finished wood; black velvet/satin lining; 500 made in 1967 only. Original retail, $95. Current value, $225 to $235.

COLT Chisholm Trail Commemorative: Frontier Scout revolver; "1867 — Kansas Series — Chisholm Trail — 1967" wiped with silver on left side of 4¾" barrel; .22 LR; Pearlite grips; nickel-plated medallions; blued finish, with nickel-plated backstrap and trigger guard assembly and screws, trigger, hammer, base pin, ejector rod head, stock screw; originally cased in blonde-finished wood, gold velvet/satin lining; 500 made in 1967 only. Original retail, $100. Current value, $200 to $210.

COLT Chateau Thierry Commemorative: automatic, Model 1911A1; "1917 World War I Commemorative 1967" on right side of slide; roll-engraved scene on left depicting WWI battle; 5" barrel; .45 auto; checkered walnut grips; inlaid commemorative medallions; left grip inlaid with Chateau Thierry battle bar; blued finish with slide scene, serial number, banner, Colt markings wiped in gold; several features including no trigger finger relief cuts, non-grooved trigger, safety lever, adapted from original Model 1911 design; Standard model cased in olive drab box; Deluxe and Custom models have oiled, waxed teak cases; Deluxe model case inscribed "One of Seventy-Five/Deluxe Engraved/Chateau Thierry Commemoratives"; Custom model case inscribed "One of Twenty-Five/Custom Engraved/Chateau Thierry Commemoratives"; gun bears gold-filled signature of A.A. White engraver; 7400 Standard versions made in 1967-68, 75 Deluxe, 25 Custom. Original retail prices: Standard, $200; Deluxe, $500; Custom, $1000. Current values: Standard, $350 to $375; Deluxe, $1000 to $1100; Custom, $1950 to $2050.

REMINGTON Canadian Centennial: Model 742 rifle; auto-loader; .30/06 only; same as standard model except for impressed checkering on pistol grip. Left side of receiver is engraved with maple leaves, special insignia, "1867-1967 — Canadian Centennial Gun," wiped in white; serial number is preceded by letter C; 1000 made in 1967 only. Original retail, $119.95. Current value, $200 to $215.

WINCHESTER Alaskan Purchase Centennial: Model 94 rifle; sold only in Alaska; receiver is engraved in 19th Century filigree for "antique" appeal; centered in stock is the official Alaskan Purchase centennial medallion with totem pole symbol of the state; barrel is 26", with magazine capacity of 8 rds.; other facets are standard of Model 94. Introduced, 1967. Original price, $125. Current value, $950 to $1000.

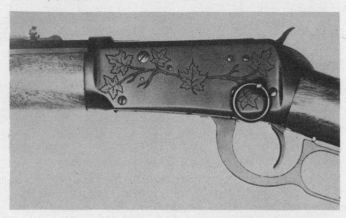

WINCHESTER Canadian Centennial: Model 64; action, obviously, is the Model 94; not to be confused with Winchester's Model 64 boy's rifle, discontinued in 1963. Canadian commemorative is in .30-30 caliber, with octagonal 26" rifle or 20" carbine barrel; black-chromed receiver is engraved with maple leaf motif; forearm tip is black chromed; straight stock is finished with "antique-gloss." Both versions have a dovetail bead-post front sight, buckhorn rear. Carbine is equipped with saddle ring, has 6-shot magazine, the rifle, 8. Gold-filled inscription on barrel reads, "Canadian Centennial 1867-1967." Introduced in 1967. Original price for rifle or carbine, $125; matching set, with consecutive serial numbers, $275. Current value, rifle, $400 to $450; carbine, $400 to $450; matched set, $900 to $1000.

1968

COLT Nebraska Centennial: Frontier Scout revolver; "1867 — Nebraska Centennial — 1967" on left side of 4¾" barrel; .22 LR; Pearlite grips; gold-plated barrel, frame, hammer, trigger, ejector rod head, stock screw; originally cased in blonde-finished wood; lined with blue velvet in bottom, gold satin in lid; 7001 made in 1968 only. Original retail, $100. Current value, $200 to $210.

COLT Gen. Nathan Bedford Forrest: Frontier Scout revolver; "General Nathan Bedford Forrest" on left side of 4¾" barrel; .22 LR only; laminated rosewood grips; gold-plated medallions; gold-plated finish; blued cylinder, backstrap and trigger guard assembly; originally cased in dark brown Leatherette; red velvet/satin lining; 3000 made in 1968-69. Original retail, $110. Current value, $200 to $210.

COLT Pawnee Trail Commemorative: Frontier Scout revolver; "1868 — Kansas Series — Pawnee Trail — 1968" wiped in silver on left side of 4¾" barrel; .22 LR; laminated rosewood grips; nickel-plated medallions; blued finish; nickel-plated backstrap and trigger guard assembly and screws, cylinder, base pin, ejector rod head, trigger, hammer, stock screw; originally cased in blonde-finished wood; lined with blue velvet in bottom, silver satin in lid; 501 made in 1968. Original retail, $110. Current value, $200 to $210.

COLT Pat Garrett Commemorative: Frontier Scout revolver; "Lawman Series — Pat Garrett" on right side of 4¾" barrel; .22 LR only; Pearlite grips; gold-plated medallions; gold-plated finish; nickel-plated barrel, frame, backstrap and trigger guard assembly, ejector rod; loading gate is gold plated; originally cased in black Leatherette with gold velvet/satin lining; 3000 made in 1968 only. Original retail, $110. Current value, $225 to $235.

Pat Garrett single-action Army revolver has same barrel legend; 5½" barrel; .45 Colt only; same grips, finish, casing as Frontier Scout version; 500 made in 1968. Original retail, $220. Current value, $500 to $525.

COLT Santa Fe Trail Commemorative: Frontier Scout revolver; "Kansas Series — Santa Fe Trail — 1968" wiped in silver on left side of 4¾" barrel; .22 LR; Ivorylite grips; nickel-plated medallions; blued finish with nickel-plated backstrap and trigger guard assembly and screws, hammer, trigger, stock screw, base pin, ejector rod head; originally cased in blonde-finished wood; green velvet/satin lining; 501 made in 1968-69. Original retail, $120. Current value, $200 to $210.

COLT Belleau Wood Commemorative: automatic; Model 1911A1; "1917 World War I Commemorative 1917" on right side of slide; roll engraved scene on left side of machine gun battle; 5" barrel; .45 auto only; rosewood grips inlaid with commemorative medallions; left grip inlaid with Belleau Wood battle bar; blued finish; slide scene, serial number, banner, Colt markings wiped in gold on Standard model; Deluxe version has slides, frames hand engraved, serial numbers gold-inlaid; Custom has more elaborate engraving; the same features of 1911 model adapted to Chateau Thierry model are incorporated; cases

are same as Chateau Thierry model, with brass plate for Deluxe engraved "One of Seventy-Five/Deluxe Engraved/Belleau Wood Commemorative"; plate on Custom model reads "One of Twenty-Five/Custom Engraved/Belleau Wood Commemoratives"; production began in 1968, with 7400 Standard types, 75 Deluxe, 25 Custom. Original retail: Standard, $200; Deluxe, $500; Custom, $1000. Current values: Standard, $350 to $365; Deluxe $1000 to $1250; Custom, $2000 to $2100.

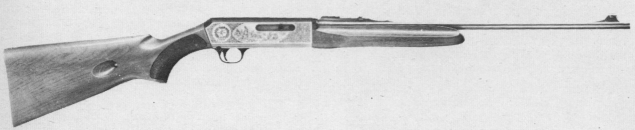

FRANCHI Centennial: semi-automatic takedown rifle; .22 LR only; commemorates 1868-1968 centennial of S.A. Luigi Franchi; centennial seal engraved on receiver; 21" barrel, 11-rd. butt stock magazine; hand-checkered

European walnut stock, forearm; open rear sight, gold bead front on ramp. Deluxe model has better grade wood, fully engraved receiver. Made only in 1968. Original retail: deluxe, $124.95; standard, $86.95. Current values, deluxe model, $150 to $160; standard model, $100 to $110.

WINCHESTER Buffalo Bill Commemorative: Model 94; available with either 20" or 26" barrel, both with bead-post front sights, semi-buckhorn rear sights. Hammer, trigger, loading gate, forearm tip, saddle ring, crescent butt plate are nickel plated. Barrel, tang are inscribed respectively, "Buffalo Bill Commemorative" and "W.F. Cody — Chief of Scouts." Receiver is embellished with scrollwork. American walnut stock has Buffalo Bill Memorial Assn. medallion imbedded; rifle has 8-rd. tubular magazine, carbine, 6 rds. Introduced, 1968. Original price, $129.95. Current value, rifle, $225 to $235; carbine, $225 to $235.

1969

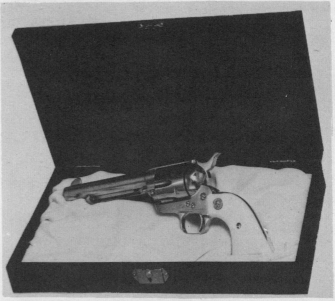

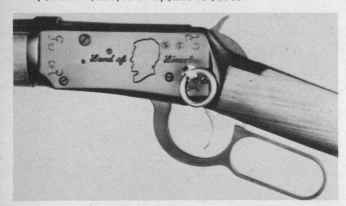

WINCHESTER Illinois Sesquicentennial: Model 94; standard design, except for words, "Land of Lincoln," and a profile of Lincoln engraved on the receiver, with gold-filled inscription on barrel, "Illinois Sesquicentennial, 1818-1968"; gold plated metal butt plate, trigger, loading gate and saddle ring. Official souvenir medallion is imbedded in the walnut stock. This was the first state commemorative to be sold outside the celebrating state by Winchester. Introduced in 1968. Original price, $110. Current value, $275 to $290.

COLT Alabama Sesquicentennial: Frontier Scout revolver; "1819 — Alabama Sesquicentennial — 1969" on left side of 4¾" barrel; .22 LR only; Ivorylite grips; gold-plated medallions; gold-plated finish; nickel-plated loading gate, cylinder, ejector rod, rod head and tube, base pin and screw, bolt and trigger guard assembly screws, hammer and screw, trigger; originally cased in red leatherette-covered wood box; white velvet lining in bottom, red satin in lid; 3001 made in 1969. Original retail, $110. Current value, $225 to $235.

COLT Wild Bill Hickok Commemorative: Frontier Scout revolver; "Lawman Series — Wild Bill Hickok" wiped in silver on right side of 6" barrel; .22 LR only; nonfluted cylinder; Pearlite grips; nickel-plated medallions; nickel-plated finish; blued barrel, frame, ejector tube screw; originally cased in black Leatherette-covered box; bottom lined in blue velvet, lid in silver satin; 3000 made, production began in 1969. Original retail, $116.60. Current value, $225 to $235.

Wild Bill Hickok Commemorative single-action Army has the same legend on 7½" barrel; .45 Colt only; same finish as Frontier Scout version, except for nickel-plated loading gate; same casing; 500 made, production beginning in 1969. Original retail, $220. Current value, $500 to $525.

COLT Golden Spike: Frontier Scout revolver; "1869 — Golden Spike — 1969" on right side of 6" barrel, standard barrel markings on left, both wiped in gold; .22 LR only; sand-blasted walnut-stained fir grips; gold-plated medallions; gold-plated finish; blued barrel, frame, backstrap and trigger guard assembly and ejector tube plug and screw; originally cased in hand-stained, embossed simulated mahogany; 11,000 made in 1969. Original retail, $135. Current value, $200 to $210.

COLT Second Battle of the Marne Commemorative: automatic, Model 1911A1; "1917 World War I Commemorative 1967" on right side of slide; roll-engraved combat scene on left side of slide; 5" barrel, .45 auto; white French holly grips; inlaid commemorative medallions; left grip inlaid with 2nd Battle of the Marne battle bar; blue finish, with slide engraving, serial number on Standard, banner, other markings wiped in gold; Deluxe and Custom models are hand engraved, with serial numbers gold inlaid; work on Custom model is in greater detail; cases are same as others in series, except Deluxe case has brass plate inscribed "One of Seventy-Five/Deluxe Engraved/2nd Battle of the Marne Commemorative"; Custom case has same type of plate inscribed "One of Twenty-five/Custom Engraved/2nd Battle of the Marne Commemorative"; 7400 Standard guns made in 1969, 75 Deluxe, 25 Custom. Original retail, Standard, $220; Deluxe, $500; Custom, $1000. Current values, Standard, $350 to $365; Deluxe, $1000 to $1050; Custom, $2000 to $2100.

COLT Shawnee Trail Commemorative: Frontier Scout revolver; "1869 — Kansas Series — Shawnee Trail — 1969" wiped in silver on left side of 4¾" barrel; .22 LR only; laminated rosewood grips; nickel-plated medallions; blued finish; nickel-plated backstrap and trigger guard assembly and screws, cylinder, base pin, ejector rod head, hammer, trigger and stock screw; originally cased in blonde-finished wood; red velvet/satin lining; 501 made in 1969 only. Original retail, $120. Current value, $200 to $210.

COLT Texas Ranger Commemorative: single-action Army revolver; "Texas Ranger Commemoratives/One Riot-One Ranger" wiped in silver on left side of barrel; "Texas Rangers" roll engraved on backstrap; sterling silver star, wreath on top of backstrap behind hammer; YO Ranch brand stamped on bottom of backstrap; 7½" barrel; .45 Colt only; Standard model has rosewood grips, silver miniature Ranger badge inlaid in left grip; blued finish; case-

hardened frame; nickel-plated trigger guard, base pin and screw, ejector rod and head, ejector tube screw; gold-plated stock screw, stock escutcheons, medallions. First 200 are custom models, with finish, decoration to customer's desires at increasing prices; custom-finished guns had deluxe engraved serial numbers, ivory grips with star inlay; originally cased in special hand-rubbed box with drawers, glass top; red velvet lining; 200 Custom, 800 Standard guns made; production began in 1969. Original values, Custom, varying with customer's desires; Standard, $650. Current value, Standard, $950 to $1000.

COLT Arkansas Territorial Sesquicentennial: Frontier Scout revolver; "1819 — Arkansas Territory Sesquicentennial — 1969" on left side of 4¾" barrel; .22 LR only; laminated rosewood grips; gold-plated medallions; aluminum frame; blued frame, backstrap and trigger guard assembly, ejector rod head; gold-plated stock screw nut; originally cased in blonde-finished baswood; red velvet/satin lining; 3500 made; production began in 1969. Original retail, $110. Current value, $175 to $185.

COLT Meuse Argonne Commemorative: automatic, Model 1911A1; "1917 World War I Commemorative 1967" on right side of slide; left has roll-engraved charge on pillbox on Standard; slides, frames on Deluxe, Custom models are hand engraved, serial numbers inlaid in gold; Custom model is more elaborately engraved, inlaid; 5" barrel, .45 auto only; varnished crotch walnut grips; inlaid commemorative medallions; left grip inlaid with Meuse Argonne battle bar; blued finish; engraving, numbers, et al., gold wiped on Standard model; same case as earlier WWI Commemoratives; brass plate for Deluxe reads "One of Seventy-Five/Deluxe Engraved/Meuse Argonne Commemoratives"; plate on Custom case is inscribed "One of Twenty-Five/Custom

COMMEMORATIVES

Engraved/Meuse Argonne Commemoratives''; production began in 1969; 7400 Standard, 75 Deluxe, 25 Custom. Original retail, Standard, $220; Deluxe, $500; Custom, $1000. Current values, Standard, $350 to $365; Deluxe, $1000 to $1050; Custom, $1950 to $2000.

COLT California Bicentennial: Frontier Scout revolver; ''1769 — California Bicentennial — 1969'' on left side of 6'' barrel; .22 LR only; laminated rosewood grips; gold-plated medallions; gold-plated finish; all screws nickel-plated, except base pin, grip screws; hammer, trigger also nickel plated; originally cased in California redwood; black velvet/satin lining; 5000 made in 1969-70. Original retail, $135. Current value, $200 to $210.

COLT Fort Larned Commemorative: Frontier Scout revolver; ''1869 — Kansas Series — Fort Larned — 1968'' on left side of 4¾'' barrel; .22 LR; Pearlite grips; nickel-plated medallions; nickel-plated finish; blued backstrap and trigger guard assembly, base pin and screw, cylinder, ejector rod head and tube screw, hammer and stock screw, bolt and trigger screw; originally cased in blonde-finished wood; blue velvet lining in bottom, silver satin in lid; 500 made in 1969-70. Original retail, $120. Current value, $200 to $210.

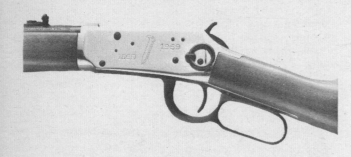

WINCHESTER Golden Spike: Model 94; features 20'' barrel with twin barrel bands plated in yellow gold; yellow gold receiver, engraved with decorative scrolled border on right side, inscribed on other side with railroad spike flanked by dates, 1859 and 1969. Barrel carries ''Golden Spike Commemorative'' inscription; upper tang bears words, ''Oceans United By Rail.'' Butt stock, forearm are straight-line design of satin-finished American walnut, with fluted comb. Inset in stock is centennial medallion of engines of Central Pacific, Union Pacific meeting on May 10, 1969. It has straight brass butt plate, blued saddle ring; chambered for .30-30, weight is 7 lbs. Introduced in 1969. Original retail price, $119.95. Current value, $300 to $325.

WINCHESTER Theodore Roosevelt Commemorative: Model 94 rifle and carbine; made in 1969 only; 49,505 manufactured; .30-30 only; rifle has 26'' octagonal barrel; 6-rd. half-magazine; forearm cap, upper tang, receiver plated with white gold; receiver engraved with American eagle, ''26th President 1901-1909,'' Roosevelt's facsimile signature; contoured lever, half-pistol grip; medallion in stock. Retail price, $125; used value, $250 to $265. Carbine differs from rifle in shorter forearm, full-length 6-rd. tubular magazine; 20'' barrel. Current value, $250 to $265. Matched set with consecutive serial numbers, $575 to $600.

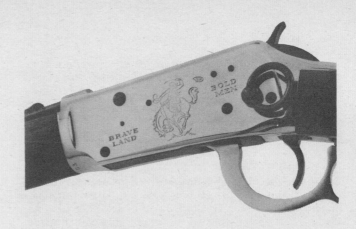

WINCHESTER Cowboy Commemorative: Model 94; receiver, upper and lower tang, lever, barrel bands are nickel plated; butt plate is stainless steel, with tang that extends over top of stock for square comb look; stock is straight grip with extended forearm of American walnut; imbedded in right side of stock is medallion of cowboy roping a steer; etched on left side of receiver, ''Brave Land — Bold Men.'' Opposite side is engraved with coiled lariat, spurs; barrel is 20'', carrying ''Cowboy Commemorative''; upper tang has inscription, ''Winchester Model 1894.'' Has adjustable semi-buckhorn rear sight, blued saddle ring; in .30-30 only. Introduced in 1969; original retail price, $125. Current value, $300 to $315.

1970

COLT World War II/European Theater: automatic, Model 1911A1; slide is marked ''World War II Commemorative/European Theater of Operations'' on left side; right side is roll-engraved with major sites of activity; 5'' barrel; .45 auto only; bird's-eye maple grips; gold-plated medallions; nickel-plated finish in entirety; originally cased in oak box with oak cartridge block; lid removable; 7 dummy cartridges included; infantry blue velvet lining; 11,500 made; production began in 1970. Original retail, $250. Current value, $350 to $365.

COLT World War — Pacific Theater: automatic, Model 1911A1; slide is marked "World War II Commemorative/Pacific Theater of Operations" on right side; left side roll-engraved with names of 10 major battle areas; both sides of slide bordered in roll marked palm leaf design; 5" barrel; .45 auto only; Brazilian rosewood grips; gold-plated medallions; nickel plated in entirety; originally cased in Obichee wood; light green velvet lining; 7 nickel-plated dummy cartridges in cartridge block; 11,500 made; production began in 1970. Original retail, $250. Current value, $350 to $365.

COLT Maine Sesquicentennial: Frontier Scout revolver; "1820 — Maine Sesquicentennial — 1970" on left side of 4¾" barrel; .22 LR only; nonfluted cylinder; Pearlite grips; gold-plated medallions; gold-plated finish; nickel-plated backstrap and trigger guard assembly, cylinder, base pin screw, hammer and hammer screw, ejector rod, ejector rod head, ejector tube screw, bolt and trigger screw; originally cased in natural knotty white pine; lined with royal blue velvet in bottom, light blue satin in lid; 3000 made in 1970. Original retail, $120. Current value, $200 to $210.

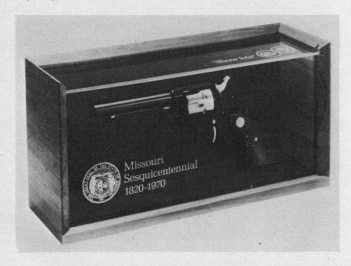

COLT Missouri Territorial Sesquicentennial: Frontier Scout revolver; "1820 — Missouri Sesquicentennial — 1970" wiped in gold on left side of 4¾" barrel; .22 LR only; walnut grips; gold-plated medallions; blued finish; gold-plated cylinder, loading gate, base pin, ejector rod head, ejector tube, tube screw, bolt and trigger screw, hammer, trigger, stock screw, top backstrap screws; originally cased in natural finish willow, lined in red velvet; 3000 made in 1970. Original retail, $125. Current value, $200 to $210.

Missouri Territorial Sesquicentennial single-action Army has same legend on the 5½" barrel, .45 Colt only; grips, medallions, finish and plating are same as Frontier Scout version, except for case-hardened frame, loading gate; same casing; 900 made; production started in 1970. Original retail, $220. Current value, $500 to $525.

COLT Wyatt Earp Commemorative: Frontier Scout revolver; "Lawman Series — Wyatt Earp" on right side of barrel; standard model markings on left side; 12" Buntline barrel; .22 LR only; walnut grips; nickel-plated medallions; blued finish; nickel-plated barrel, cylinder, ejector tube plug, ejector tube screw, rod head, base pin and base pin screw, hammer, trigger and backstrap and trigger guard assembly; originally cased in black Leatherette-covered box; bottom lined with burgundy velvet, lid with red satin; 3000 made; production started in 1970. Original retail, $125. Current value, $250 to $265.

Wyatt Earp single-action Army has same legend on barrel, but wiped in silver; 16-1/8" barrel; .45 Colt only; same grips, medallions as Frontier Scout version; blued finish; case-hardened frame; nickel-plated hammer, trigger, base pin, base pin crosslatch assembly; same casing as Frontier Scout; 500 made; production began in 1970. Original retail, $395. Current value, $1000 to $1050.

COLT Fort Riley Commemorative: Frontier Scout revolver; "1870 — Kansas Series — Fort Riley — 1970" wiped in black on left side of 4¾" barrel; .22 LR only; Ivorylite grips; nickel-plated medallions; nickel-plated finish; blued backstrap and trigger guard assembly, cylinder, base pin and screw, ejector rod head and tube screw, bolt and trigger screw, hammer and screw, trigger, stock screw; originally cased in blonde-finished wood; black velvet/satin lining; 500 made in 1970. Original retail, $130. Current value, $200 to $210.

COLT Fort Hays Commemorative: Frontier Scout revolver; "1870 — Fort Hays — 1970" wiped in silver on left side of 4¾" barrel; .22 LR only; hard rubber grips; nickel-plated finish; blued barrel, backstrap and trigger guard assembly screws, cylinder, base pin screw, ejector tube screw, bolt and trigger screw, hammer screw, trigger; originally cased in blonde-finished wood; bottom lined with blue velvet, gold satin in lid; 500 made in 1970. Original retail, $130. Current value, $200 to $210.

MARLIN Centennial Matched Pair: combines presentation-grade Model 336 centerfire, rimfire Model 39, in luggage-type case; matching serial numbers, for additional collector value. Both rifles have fancy walnut straight-grip stocks, forearms; brass forearm caps, brass butt plates, engraved receivers with inlaid medallions. Model 336 is chambered for .30-30 only, Model 39 for .22 LR, .22 long, .22 short cartridges. Only 1000 sets were manufactured in 1970. Original retail, $750. Current value, $1000 to $1100.

MARLIN Model 39 Century Ltd: marking Marlin Centennial, 1870-1970, specs are same as standard Model 39A, except for square lever, fancy walnut straight grip un-checkered stock, forearm; 20'' octagonal barrel, brass forearm cap; nameplate inset in stock, butt plate. Produced only in 1970. Original retail, $125. Current value, $175 to $190.

SAVAGE Anniversary Model 1895: replica of Savage Model 1895; hammerless lever-action; marks 75th anniversary of Savage Arms Corp. (1895-1970); .308 Win. only; 24'' octagon barrel; 5-rd. rotary magazine; engraved receiver, brass-plated lever; brass butt plate; brass medallion inlaid in stock; uncheckered walnut straight-grip stock, schnabel-type forearm. Made only in 1970; 9,999 produced. Original retail, $195. Current value, $200 to $215.

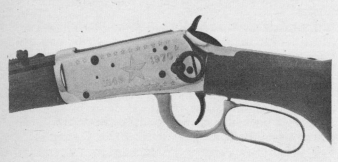

WINCHESTER Lone Star Commemorative: Model 94; produced in rifle version with 26'' barrel and carbine with 20'' length. Receiver, upper and lower tang, lever, forearm cap, magazine tube cap all are gold plated; butt plate is crescent shaped, solid brass. Stocks are American walnut with half-pistol grip, fluted comb; commemorative medal with faces of Sam Houston, Stephen F. Austin, William Travis, Jim Bowie and Davy Crockett is inset in right side of stock. Left side of receiver is engraved with star and dates, 1845, 1970; both sides are bordered with series of stars; barrel carries inscription, "Lone Star Commemorative." Upper tang has "Under Six Flags," referring to banners of Spain, France, Mexico, Texas Republic, Confederacy and United States, which have flown over territory. It has bead-post front sight, semi-buckhorn rear, plus saddle ring. Introduced in 1970; original price, $140 for either rifle or carbine; $305 for matched set with consecutive serial numbers. Current values, carbine, $300 to $315; rifle, $300 to $315; matched set, $650 to $750.

1971

COLT Fort Scott Commemorative: Frontier Scout revolver; "1871 — Kansas Series — Fort Scott — 1971" on left side of 4¾'' barrel; .22 LR only; checkered rubber, eagle-style grips; nickel-plated finish; blued barrel, cylinder, base pin screw, ejector tube screw, bolt and trigger screw, hammer, hammer screw, trigger; originally cased in blonde-finished wood; gold velvet/satin lining; 500 made in 1971. Original retail, $130. Current value, $200 to $210.

COLT NRA Centennial Commemorative: single-action Army; "1871 NRA Centennial 1971" wiped in gold on left side of 4¾'', 5½'', or 7½'' barrels; .357 magnum, .45 Colt;

goncalo alves grips; gold-plated NRA medallion inlays; blued finish; case-hardened frame; nickel-silver grip screw escutcheons; originally cased in walnut, with inlaid NRA plate; gold velvet/satin lining; 2412 .357 magnums, 4131 .45 Colts made; production began in 1971. Original retail, $250. Current value, $400 to $425.

COLT NRA Centennial Commemorative: automatic; Gold Cup National Match model; "1871 NRA Centennial 1971/The First 100 Years of Service/.45 Automatic Caliber" wiped in gold on left side of slide; MK IV barrel; Eliason rear sight; 5" barrel; .45 auto only; checkered walnut grips; gold-plated NRA medallion inlays; blued; has same type of case as NRA commemorative SAA; 2500 made; production began in 1971. Original retail, $250. Current value, $395 to $420.

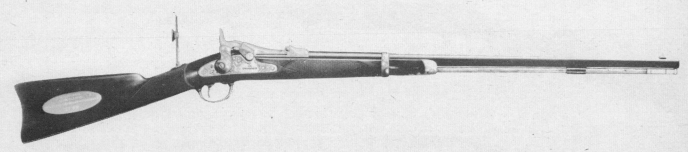

HARRINGTON & RICHARDSON Anniversary Model 1873: replica of Officer's Model 1873 trapdoor Springfield commemorating 100th anniversary of H&R (1871-1971). Single-shot action; .45-70 only; 26" barrel; engraved receiver, breech block, hammer, lock, band, butt plate; hand-checkered walnut stock with inlaid brass commemorative plate; peep rear sight, blade front; ramrod. Made only in 1971. Production limited to 10,000. Current value, $275 to $300.

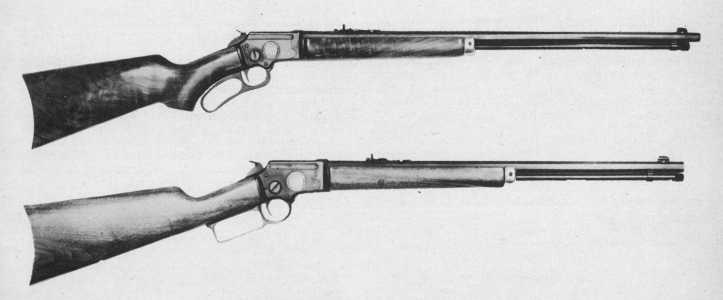

MARLIN 39A Article II: same general specs as Model 39A; commemorates National Rifle Association Centennial, 1871-1971. Medallion with legend "The Right to Bear Arms" set on blued receiver; 24" octagonal barrel; tube magazine holds 19 LR, 21 longs, 25 shorts; fancy un-checkered walnut pistol-grip stock, forearm; brass butt plate, forearm cap. Produced only in 1971. Original retail, $135. Current value, $150 to $165.

Article II carbine is same as Article II rifle, except it has straight-grip stock, square lever, shorter magazine, reduced capacity; 20" octagonal barrel. Produced only in 1971. Original retail, $135. Current value, $152.50 to $165.

GUN DIGEST BOOK OF MODERN GUN VALUES **283**

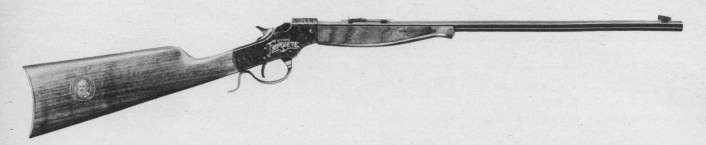

SAVAGE Model 71: single-shot lever-action; replica of Stevens favorite, issued as commemorative to Joshua Stevens, founder of Stevens Arms Co.; .22 LR only; 22" octagon barrel; brass-plated hammer, lever; uncheckered straight-grip stock, schnabel forearm; brass commemorative medallion inlaid in stock; brass butt plate; open rear sight, brass blade front; made in 1971 only; 10,000 produced. Original retail, $75. Current value, $100 to $110.

WINCHESTER National Rifle Association Centennial Model: Introduced in two versions: musket and rifle, both on Model 94 actions; musket resembles Model 1895 NRA musket with military lever to meet requirements for NRA match competition at turn of century; has 26" tapered, round barrel; full length American walnut forearm; black-chromed steel butt plate; rear sight has calibrated folding rear leaf sight, blade front sight; magazine holds 7 rds.

Rifle model resembles Model 64, also made on 94 action. Has half magazine holding 5 rds., 24" tapered round barrel, hooded ramp and bead-post front sight, adjustable semi-buckhorn rear sight, contoured lever, blued steel forearm cap.

Both models are .30-30, have quick detachable sling swivels; receivers are black-chromed steel; NRA seal in silver-colored metal is set in right side of stocks; left side of receivers inscribed appropriately with "NRA Centennial Musket" or "NRA Centennial Rifle." Both were introduced in 1971; retail price on each was $149.95; matched set with consecutive serial numbers, $325. Current values, musket, $225 to $240; rifle, $225 to $240; cased set, $550 to $600.

1972

COLT Florida Territorial Sesquicentennial: Frontier Scout revolver; "1822 — Florida Territory — 1972" on left side of 4¾" barrel; .22 LR only; cypress wood grips; gold-plated medallions; blued finish; case hardened frame, loading gate; gold-plated base pin, base pin screw, ejector rod head and screws, hammer, trigger and trigger screws; originally cased in cypress box; gold velvet/satin lining; 2001 made; production began in 1972. Original retail, $125. Current value, $150 to $160.

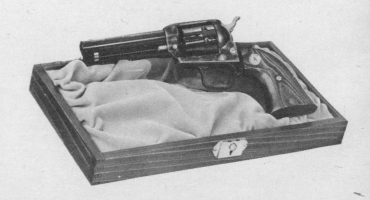

MARLIN Model 336 Zane Grey: same specs as Model 336A, except in .30-30 only; 22" octagonal barrel. Commemorates centennial of Zane Grey's birth, 1872-1972; commemorative medallion attached to receiver; selected un- checkered walnut pistol-grip stock, forearm; brass forearm cap, butt plate; 10,000 produced with special serial numbers, ZG1 through ZG10,000. Produced only in 1972. Original retail, $150. Current value, $165 to $175.

1973

COLT Arizona Ranger Commemorative: Frontier Scout revolver; "Arizona Ranger Commemorative" on left side of 4¾" barrel; .22 LR only; laminated rosewood grips; nickel-plated medallions; blued finish; case-hardened frame; nickel-plated backstrap and trigger guard assembly, hammer, trigger, base pin, base pin assembly, screw for backstrap/trigger guard assembly, grips; originally cased in walnut with glass window lid; replica Arizona Ranger badge included in case; lined with maroon velvet; 3001 made; production began in 1973. Original retail, $135. Current value, $200 to $210.

COLT Peacemaker Centennial: single-action Army revolver, Frontier Six Shooter configuration; "The Frontier Six-Shooter" etched on left side of barrel, "1873 Peacemaker Centennial 1973" roll marked on right side; 7½" barrel; .44-40 only; checkered rubber eagle-style grips; nickel-plated in entirety; originally cased in leather-covered wood box; brown velvet lining; 1500 made; production began in 1973. Original retail, $300. Current value, $425 to $450.

Peacemaker Centennial in .45 Colt Peacemaker configuration has "1873 Peacemaker Centennial 1973" roll marked on left side of 7½" barrel, .45 Colt only; one-piece varnished walnut grip; blued finish; case-hardened frame, hammer; originally cased in oiled walnut with brass-framed glass cover; maroon velvet lining; 1500 made; production began in 1973. Original retail, $300. Current value, $425 to $450.

Peacemaker Centennial .45 Colt/.44-40 combo includes both guns described above in oversize case of walnut-stained willow; lined with dark maroon velvet; matching serial numbers on guns; 500 sets made in 1973. Original retail, $625. Current value, $1100 to $1200.

REMINGTON 1973 Ducks Unlimited Commemorative: Model 1100 autoloading shotgun; 12-ga. only; 30" barrel; full choke; vent rib. Other specifications the same as standard Model 1100, except that serial number is preceded by DU; Ducks Unlimited medallion, surrounded by gilded scrollwork, is attached to left side of receiver; 500 made in 1973 only. Original retail, $230. Current value, $275 to $300.

WINCHESTER Texas Ranger Commemorative: Model 94; features stock, forearm of semi-fancy walnut, with the butt stock having square comb, metal butt plate. Chambered in .30-30, tube magazine holds 6 rds.; a facsimile of Texas Ranger star badge is imbedded in the stock; saddle ring is included. Of standard grade, only 4850 were released in April 1973, all of them in the state of Texas. Another 150 so-called Special Edition guns, at $1000 each, were released, in presentation cases, only to the Texas Ranger Association. These were hand-checkered, with full fancy walnut stocks, barrel and receiver highly polished. Magazine holds only 4 rds.; gun has 16" barrel, weighs 6 lbs; standard model weighs 7 lbs; has 20" barrel. With Special Edition guns, commemorative star is mounted inside the presentation case instead of in the stock. Also introduced April 1973. Original price, standard model, $134.95. Current value, $550 to $575; Special Edition model, original price, $1000. Current value, $2500 to $3000.

FOREIGN ARMS MANUFACTURERS

AUSTRALIA

Slazengers (Australia) Pty., Ltd., Alexandria, N.S.W.

AUSTRIA

Sport und Waffen — Dschulnigg, Griesgasse 8, Salzburg
Johann Fanzoi, Postfach 25, Ferlach, Kaernten
Hirtenberger Patronen, Zundhutchen und Metallwarenfabrik A.G., Hirtenberg
Gottfried Juch, Ferlach, Kaernten
Josef Just, Ferlach, Kaernten
Richard Mahrholdt & Sohn, Postfach 177, Innsbruck
Franz Sarnitz, 10 Osterleitengasse, Vienna 19
Franz Sodia, Gartengasse 6, Ferlach, Kaernten
Johann Springer's Erben, 10 Josefsgasse, Vienna 8
Steyr-Daimler-Puch A.G., Postfach 4, Steyr
Vereinigte Ferlacher Jagdwaffenerzeuger G.m.b.H., Ferlach, Kaernten
Benedikt Winkler, Postagasse 1, Ferlach, Kaernten

BELGIUM

Armaf S.A. — Manufacture Liegeoise, 54 Rue du Vertbois, Liege
A. Jos. Defourny, Herstal
Delcour S.A., 315 Rue des Allies, Nessonvaux, Fraipont
Jean Duchateau, Rue Louis Fraigneux, 8, Liege
Dumoulin & Fils, 16-18 Rue du Tilleul, Milmort, Liege
Dumoulin Frs. & Cie, 2 Rue Thier de la Fontaine, Liege
Fabrique Nationale d'Armes de Guerre, Herstal, Liege
Auguste Francotte & Cie, 61 Rue Mont Saint Martin, Liege
N. Lajot & Cie, Rue aux Chevaux, 33, Liege
Etablissements Georges Laloux, 3, Rue des Urbanistes, Liege
Lebeau-Courally, 386 Rue St. Gilles, Liege
Lecocq & Hoffmann, 31 Rue de L'Ecuyer, Brussels
Ancienne Maison H. Mahillon S.A., 208, Rue Royale, Brussels
Anciens Etablissements Pieper, S.A., Herstal, Liege
Manufacture d'Armes de Chasse "Masquelier", 88 Rue de la Cathedrale, Liege
Neumann & Co., Rue Cheri 39, Liege
Manufacture Generale d'Armes J. Saive, 10, Rue Theodore Schwann, Liege
Maison Fernand Thonon, 51, Rue Monulphe, 51, Liege

BRAZIL

Farma S.A., Rua Antonio de Godoi, Sao Paulo
Forjas Taurus S.A., Caixa Postal 44, Porto Alegre, Rio Grande do Sul
Fundicao E Industria De Armas "Lerap" Ltda., Rua Sao Leopoldo 833, Sao Paulo
Industria Nacional de Armas S.A., Rua Coronel Xavier Toledo 123, 60, cj, 63, Sao Paulo
Lisariturri & Cia., Ltda., Rua Tobias Barreto 621, Sao Paulo
Metalurgica Serrana Ltda., Caixa Postal 464, Erechim, Rio Grande do Sul
Amadeo Rossi & Cia., Caixa Postal 28, Sao Leopoldo, Rio Grande do Sul

CANADA

Canadian Industries, Ltd., P.O. Box 10, Montreal 101, Quebec
Gevelot of Canada Ltd., Saskatoon, Sask.
Ithaca Gun Co. of Canada, 211 Park Ave., Dunnville, Ontario
Remington Arms of Canada, Ltd., 36 Queen Elizabeth Blvd., Toronto, Ontario
Valcartier Industries Inc., P.O. Box 790, Courcelette, Co. Portneuf, P.Q.
Winchester-Western (Canada) Ltd., Coburg, Ontario

CZECHOSLOVAKIA

Povazske Strojarne, Narodni Podnik, Povazska Bystrica (Kovo Ltd., Metal & Engineering Products and Raw Materials Trading Co., P.O. Box 889, Prague)
Sellier & Bellot, Vlasim, Omnipol, Washingtonova 11, Prague
Zbrojovka Brno — Jan Sverma Works, National Corp. (Ominipol, Washingtonova 11, Prague)

DENMARK

Haerens Ammunitionsarsenalet, Copenhagen (Danish Government)
Schultz & Larsen Gevaerfabrik, Otterup
Dansk Industri Syndikat, Compagnie Madsen, Copenhagen

FINLAND

Lapuan Patrunatehdas, Lapua
Oy Sako Ab, Riihimaki
Oy Tikkakoski Ab, Tikkakoski
Valmet Oy, Valmet Building, Punanotkonkatu 2, Helsinki

FRANCE

Verney Carron, St. Etienne, (Loire)
Charlin Cie, 16 a 20 rue Beranger, St. Etienne (Loire)
Etablissements Damon & Cie, 7, rue des Francs-Macons, St. Etienne
Darne, Cours Fauriel, St. Etienne
Gastinne-Renette, 39, Avenue Roosevelt, Paris 8e, (Champs-Elysees)
J. Gaucher Armes, St. Etienne, (Loire)
Gevelot, 50, rue Ampere, Paris
Manufacture d'Armes Automatiques, 35, Allees Marines, Bayonne
Manufacture Nationale d'Armes de Chatellerault, Chatellerault
Manufacture d'Armes des Pyrenees Francaises, Hendaye
Manufrance, St. Etienne, (Loire)
Manufacture d'Armes de Chasse Kerne, 18 rue des Etats Generaux, Versailles
Societe Francaise d'Armes et Cycles de St. Etienne, St. Etienne
Societe Generale de Mecanique, 21 rue Clemont Forissier, St. Etienne, (Loire)
Societe Moderne de Fabrications Mecaniques, 56 rue Tarentaize, St. Etienne, (Loire)

EAST GERMANY

Buhag G.m.b.H., Suhl
PGH Hubertus, Suhl

VEB Fahrzeug und Geratwerk Simson, Suhl
VEB Sprengstoffwerk 1, Schonebeck (Elbe)
VEB Ernst-Thalmann Werk, Suhl (Thur.) (Fortuna; Merkel)
Albert Wilhelm Wolf K.G., Suhl

WEST GERMANY

J.G. Anschutz G.m.b.H., Daimlerstrasse 12, Ulm/Donau
B.S.F. Bayerische-Sportwaffenfabrik, Postfach 121, Erlangen
Wilhelm Brenneke K.G., Berlin-Schoneberg
Gewehrfabrik H. Burgsmuller & Sohne G.m.b.H., Postfach 5, 335 Kreiensen
Deutsche Jagdpatronenfabrik G.m.b.H., Rottweil/Neckar
Dianawerk Mayer & Grammelspacher, Murgtalstrasse 34, Rastatt/Baden
Dynamit Nobel A.G., 5 Koln-Niehl
EM-GE Sportgerate K.G., Gerstenberger & Eberwein, Gussenstadt/Wurtt
Erma Werke B. Geipel G.m.b.H., Johann Ziegler Strasse 13/15, Dachau
Feinwerkbau Westinger & Altenburger G.m.b.H., 7238 Oberndorf/Neckar
Walter Gehmann, Karlstrasse 41-43, Karlsruhe
Heckler & Koch G.m.b.H., Oberndorf/Neckar
Hege Jagd und Sportwaffen G.m.b.H., 717 Schwabisch Hall
Friedrich Wilhelm Heym, 8732 Munnerstadt
Industrie-Werke Karlsruhe A.G., 75 Karlsruhe
Albrecht Kind, Hunstig bei Dieringhausen (Rhld.)
Krico-Kriegeskorte & Co. G.m.b.H., 7 Stuttgart-Hedelfingen
Heinrich Krieghoff, 79 Ulm/Donau
Mauser Werke A.G., 7238 Oberndorf/Neckar
Mayer & Riem G.m.b.H., Neheim-Husten 2, Am Wagenberg
Reck Sportwaffenfabrik, Karl Arndt K.G., Lauf/Pegnitz
Rheinmetall G.m.b.H., Abteilung VA, 4 Dusseldorf 1
Rhoner Sportwaffenfabrik G.m.b.H., Weisbach/Rhon, Kr. Bad Neustadt/Saale
Rohm G.m.b.H., Kreis Heidenheil/Brenz, 7927 Sontheim/Brenz
J.P. Sauer & Sohn A.G., 5 Koln-Niehl
Herbert Schmidt Waffenfabrik, Ostheim/Rhon
Voere G.m.b.H., 7714 Vohrenbach/Schw.
Carl Walther G.m.b.H., 79 Ulm/Donau
Lothar Walther, 7923 Konigsbronn (Wurtt.)
Hermann Weihrauch Sportwaffenfabrik, 8744 Mellrichstadt/Bayern
Winchester G.m.b.H., Grafenberger Allee 66, 4 Dusseldorf

GREAT BRITAIN

Atkin, Grant & Lang Ltd., 7 Bury St., St. Jame's, London, S.W.1
Thomas Bland & Sons Ltd., 4/5 William IV Street, Strand, London W.C. 2
Boss & Co. Guns, 13-14 Cork St., Picadilly, London, W.1
Charles Boswell Ltd., P.O. Box 433, Wrethem Works, Strafford Road, London, W.3
BSA Guns, Ltd., Birmingham 11
E.J. Churchill, Ltd., Orange St., Gun Works, Leicester Square, London, W.C.2
John Dickson & Son, 21 Frederick St., Edinburgh
G.E. Fulton & Son, Ltd., Bisley Camp, Brookwood, Surrey
Stephen Grant & Joseph Lang, Ltd., 7 & 8 Bury Street, St. James's, London, S.W.1
W.W. Greener, Ltd., St. Mary's Row, Birmingham 16
Holland & Holland, Ltd., 13 Bruton St., London, W.1
Imperial Metal Industries (Kynoch) Ltd., Witton, Birmingham 6
W.J. Jeffery & Co. Ltd., 13 Bruton Street, London, W.1
Parker-Hale Ltd., Bisley Works, Golden Hillock Road, Sparbrook, Birmingham 11
William Powell & Son, 35 Carr's Lane, Birmingham 4
James Purdey & Sons, Ltd., 57-58 South Audley St., London, W.1
John Rigby & Co., 43 Sackville St., London, W.1
Webley & Scott, Ltd., Park Lane, Handsworth, Birmingham 21
Westley Richards & Co. Ltd., 13 Bruton St., London, W.1

GREECE

Greek Powder & Cartridge Co., Ltd., Athens

HOLLAND

Nederlandsche Wapen-en Munitiefabriek N.V., De Kruithoorn's-Hertogenbosch

HUNGARY

Artex, Via Hador 31, Budapest

ITALY

Armigas-Comega, Via Valle Inzino 34, Gardone V.T., (Brescia)
Luigi Belleri, Via Convento 27, Gardone V.T., (Brescia)
Andrea Benetti, Via Matteotti, 60, Gardone V.T., (Brescia)
Pietro Beretta S.p.A., Gardone V.T., (Brescia)
L. Santina Bernardelli, Via Zanardelli 9/E, Gardone V.T., (Brescia)
Vincenzo Bernardelli, Gardone V.T., (Brescia)
Angelo & Emilio Boniotti, Gardone V.T., (Brescia)
Breda Meccanica Bresciana, Via Lunga 2, Brescia
Fabbrica Bresciana Armi, Brescia
Bruno Castellani, Via S. Giovanni Bosco 4, Gardone V.T., (Brescia)
Rodolfo Cosmi & Figli, Via Flaminia 307, Torrette, (Ancona)
Libero Daffini, Vicolo Tri Archi 9, Brescia
Fratelli Di Maggio, Vai Leonardo da Vinci 29, Gardone V.T., (Brescia)
Guilio Fiocchi, Lecco
Luigi Franchi S.p.A., Via Calatafimi 17, Brescia
Fratelli Galsei, Via Trento 10/A, Collebeato, (Brescia)
Rigarmi di Rino Galesi, Via Italia 1/3, Brescia
Le Armerie Italiane Dei Fratelli Gamba, Gardone V.T., Brescia
Armotecnica Gardonese, Via C. Battisti 8, Gardone V.T., (Brescia)
Fabbrica Pietro Giacomelli di Giov., Magno di. Gardone V.T., (Brescia)
Giuseppe Gitti & Figli, Via Matteotti, 2 b-c, Gardone V.T., (Brescia)
Pierino Gitti, Via Leonardo da Vinci 2, Gardone V.T., (Brescia)
Umberto Gitti, Gardone V.T., (Brescia)
Armi San Marco di Buffoli Giuseppe, Via A. Canossi, 2, Gardone, V.T., (Brescia)
Gnali Graziano, Via Puccini 4, Gardone V.T., (Brescia)
F.A.V.S.-Fabbrica Armi Valle Susa di Guglielminotti, Via Nazionale 19, Villarfocchiardo (Torino)
Luigi Maffi, Via San Mario 8, Gardone V.T., (Brescia)
Stefano Marocchi & Figli, Gardone V.T., (Brescia)
Davide Pedersoli, Vicolo Bolognini 2, Gardone V.T., Brescia
Pedretti & Ongaro, Via Convento 54, Gardone V.T., (Brescia)
Manifattura Armi Perazzi, Via S. Orsola 98, S. Eufemia, Brescia
Fabbrica Italiana Armi Pietro Perugini, Nuvolera, Brescia
Fratelli Piotti, Via Magno 37, Gardone V.T., (Brescia)
Jager Armi di Armando Piscetta, Via Campazzino 55/b, Torino
Armi San Marco di Ruffoli, Via A. Canossi 2, Brescia
Fabbrica Italiana Armi Sabatti, Via A. Volta 32-A, Gardone V.T., (Brescia)
Fratelli Serena, Brescia
Manifattura Riunite Armi di Enrico Salvinelli, Via 2 Giugno 8, Gardone V.T., (Brescia)
Fabbrica d'Armi Sarezzo, Via Mantova 6, Brescia
Manifattura Bresciana Armi Stocchetta, Brescia
Fratelli Tanfoglio, Via Pratello 8, Gardone V.T., (Brescia)
Fratelli Toschi, Villa San Martino Di Lugo, Ravenna
Aldo Uberti & Figli, Via XX Settembre 7, Gardone V.T., (Brescia)
Pietro Zanoletti "IAPZ", Via Guglielmo, 4, Brescia
Fabio Zanotti, Gardone V.T., (Brescia)
Angelo Zoli & Figli, Via Matteotti 5, Gardone V.T., (Brescia)
Antonio Zoli, Via Zanardelli 9/D, Gardone V.T., (Brescia)

JAPAN

Arakawa Kogyo K.K., 1969, Itsukaichi, Itsukaichi-machi, Nishitama-gun, Tokyo (air rifles)
Asahi Chemical Industry Co., Ltd., Hibiya-Mitsui Building, 12, 1-chome Yuraku-cho, Chiyoda-ku, Tokyo (gunpowder, percussion caps)
Goshi Kaisha Nitto Enkan Seizosho, 20, Fukagawa Tokiwa-cho, Koto-ku, Tokyo (shot)
Hasuike Seisakusho Co., Ltd., 16, 5-chome Oimazato-honmachi, Higashinari-ku, Osaka (air rifle pellets)
Heirinkan Arms Co., Ltd., 10, 3-chome Kanda-Ogawamachi, Chiyoda-ku, Tokyo (rifles, air rifles, shotguns)
Hoshino Shito Kogyo K.K., 80, Shinsakamoto-cho, Daito-ku, Tokyo (sporting rifles)
Howa Machinery Ltd., Sukaguchi, Shinkawa-cho, Nishikasugai-gun, Aichi-ken (sporting rifles)
Kawaguchiya Firearms Co., Ltd., 3, 4-chome Muromachi, Nihonbashi, Chuo-ku, Tokyo (shotguns, shotgun shells)
Keiheisha Honten, Gose-mochi, Gose-shi, Nara-ken (air rifles)
K.K. Jinmeisha, 36, 1-chome Ueshio-machi, Minami-ku, Osaka (shot)
K.K. Kohame Seisakusho, 1, 1-chome Ishihari-machi, Sumida-ku, Tokyo (shot)
Kunii Shokai, 65, Tsutsumishita-machi, Koriyama-shi, Fukushima-ken (air rifle pellets)
K.K. Nihon Ryoju Seiki Seisakusho, 12, Aza Minamigahara Onishi-machi, Okazaki-shi, Aichi-ken (automatic shotguns)
K.K. Sanshin Shojuki Seisakusho, 634, 3-chome Nippori, Arakwa-ku, Tokyo (shotguns)

K.K. Yamamoto Juho Seisakusho, 88, 4-chome Imasato-machi, Higashinari-ku, Osaka (shotguns)

Marusan Seiki Yugen Kaisha, 29, 2-chome Higashiobase Kitano-cho, Higashinari, Osaka (shotguns, air rifles)

Miroku Firearms Mfg., Co., 180, Inari-cho, Kochi-shi, Kochi-ken (shotguns, pistols)

Naniwa Kogyo K.K., 423, Nonogami, Hahikino-shi, Osaka-fu (shotguns, air rifles)

Nihon Juho Kogyosho, Shimogo, Iwama-machi, Nishi Ibaragi-gun, Ibaragi-ken (air rifles, shotguns)

Nikkosha Ryodan Kogyo K.K., 27, 1-chome Miyakojima-hondori, Miyakojima-ku, Osaka (shot)

Nippo Kogyo Co. Ltd., 118, Kami-cho, Idogaya, Minami-ku, Yokohama (shotgun shells)

Nippon Juki Co., Ltd., 22, Ikenouchi-cho, Nishinokyo, Nakayo-ku, Kyoto (shotguns, rifles, air rifles)

Nippon Oils & Fats Co., Ltd., Tokyo Building, 2, 3-chome Marunouchi, Chiyoda-ku, Tokyo (gunpowder)

Olin-Kodensha Co., Ltd., 1225, Sonobe-cho, Tochigi-shi, Tochigi-ken (shotguns)

Sanwa Seisakusho, 1618, Ohhasu, Fuse-shi, Osaka-fu (air rifle pellets)

Sasaki Seiju Kayakuten, 34-18, 1-chome Amanuma, Suginami-ku, Tokyo (shotguns, air rifles)

Sharp Rifle Mfg. Co., Ltd., 8, 2-chome Yotsuya, Shinjuku-ku, Tokyo (rifles, air rifles, rifle scopes)

Shimada Seisakusho, 1396, Ohhasu, Fuse-chi, Osaka-fu (pellets)

Shimaya Seisakusho, 51, 2-chome Nishiimazato-cho, Higashinari-ku, Osaka (air rifles)

Shinbisha Air-Rifle Mfg. Co., 319, 2-chome Komagome, Toshima-ku, Tokyo (rifles, air rifles)

Shin Chuo Kogyo K.K., 18-18, 4-chome Omori-Nishi, Ota-ku, Tokyo (shotguns, pistols)

SKB Arms Co., Sampuku Building, 5, 4-chome Ginza, Chuo-ku, Tokyo (shotguns, air rifles)

Teikoku Kahohin Mfg. Co., Ltd., 18, 2-chome Marunouchi, Chiyoda-ku, Tokyo (percussion caps)

Washino Kinzoku Kogyosho, 11, 3-chome Ajiro, Fuse-chi, Osaka-fu (air rifle pellets)

Watanabe Seisakusho Co., Ltd., 231, Koun-cho, Maebashi-shi, Gunma-ken (shotgun parts)

Yoshizawa Shoten Co., Ltd., 8, Saya-cho, Takasaki-chi, Gunma-ken (shotgun shells)

Yugen Kaisha Shoki Seisakusho, 1146, Higashiura-machi, Utsunomiya-shi, Tochigi-ken (shot)

YSS Fire Arms Co., Ltd., 635, Ohsone-cho, Kohoku-ku, Yokohama (rifles)

MEXICO

Armamex, S.A., Mexico, D.F.
Cartuchos Deportivos de Mexico, S.A., Cuernavaca, Morelos
Fabrica de Armas Llama, S.A., Mexico, D.F.
Fabrica Nacional de Armas, Mexico, D.F. (Government)
La Cazadora, S.A., Mexico, D.F.
Productos Mendoza, S.A., Mexico, D.F.
Sucesor de Angel Adame Laje, Mexico, D.F.

NEW ZEALAND

Colonial Ammunition Co., Ltd., Normandy Road, Mt. Eden C3, Auckland

NORWAY

Kongsberg Vapenfabrikk, Kongsberg
Raufoss Ammunisjonsfabrikker, Raufoss

PHILIPPINES

Squires Bingham Mfg. Co., Inc., Marikina, Rizal

SPAIN

Pedro Arosa Aguirre, Santa Ana 10, Elgoibar
Alkatsuna Fabrica de Armas, Guernica
Hijos de v. Armaberri y Cia, P.O. Box 55, Eibar
Aguirre y Aranzabal, Eibar (Guipuzcoa)
Eusebio Arizaga, 30 Fuenterrabia St., San Sebastian
Echaza Echave Arizmendi y Cia S.A., Ubicha, Eibar
Norberto Arizmendi y Cia., S.R.C., Apartado 68, Eibar (Guipuzcoa)
Union Armeria S.L., Eibar
Astra Unceta y Cia, Guernica (Vizcaya)
Armas Bost, S.L., P.O. Box 47, Eibar
Centro de Estudios Tecnicos de Materiales Especiales, Madrid
Industrias Danok, Barrio San Lorenzo, 38-Vergara, Guipuzcoa
Star Bonifacio Echeverria S.A., Eibar
Egan, Elqueta, Eibar
Armas EGO, Macharia 1, Eibar
Trust Eibarres S.A., Apartado De Correos 32, Eibar (Guipuzcoa)
Armas Erbi, S.C.I., P.O. Box 45, Elgoibar
Gabilondo y Cia, P.O. Box 2, Elgoibar
La Industrial Guipuzcoana, Elgoibar
Crucelegui Hermanos, P.O. Box 13, Eibar
Zabala Hermanos, S.R.C., P.O. Box 97, Eibar
Armas "Jacob," Elgueta, Eibar
Miguel Larranaga, Guipuzcoa
Laurona, Muzatequi, Eibar
Armas Marixa, Eibar
Felix Sarasqueta y Cia, Apartado 233, Eibar
Victor Sarasqueta, S.A., Eibar
Sarriugarte, Elgoibar
I. Ugartechea, Eibar
Jose Uriquen, Urquizu 2, Eibar
Armas de Tiro y Caza, Eibar

SWEDEN

Carl Gustafs Stads Gevarsfaktori, Eskiltsuna (Swedish Government)
Nitro Nobel, A.B., Gyttrop
Norma Projektilfabrik, Amotfors
Vanasverken, Karlsborg (Swedish Government)
Husqvarna Vapenfabriks Aktiebolag, Huskvarna

SWITZERLAND

W. Glaser, 42 Loewenstrasse, Zurich
Hammerli Jagd und sportwaffenfabrik A.G., Lenzburg
Schweizerische Industrie-Gesellschaft, Neuhausen am Rheinfalls
Eidgenossischen Munitionsfabrik Altdorf, Altdorf (Swiss Government)
Eidgenossischen Munitionsfabrik Thun, Thun (Swiss Government)

URUGUAY

Armeria El Cazador, Uruguay 868, Montevideo
Armeria "El Ciervo", Sarandi 683, Montevideo